United
We Stand

United We Stand

The Unprecedented Story of the GM–UAW Quality Partnership

Thomas L. Weekley

Jay C. Wilber

Edited by

Betsy Reid Creedon

McGraw-Hill

New York   San Francisco   Washington, D.C.   Auckland   Bogotá
Caracas   Lisbon   London   Madrid   Mexico City   Milan
Montreal   New Delhi   San Juan   Singapore
Sydney   Tokyo   Toronto

Library of Congress Cataloging-in-Publication Data

Weekley, Thomas L.
    United we stand : the unprecedented story of the GM-UAW quality
partnership / Thomas L. Weekley, Jay C. Wilber.
        p.   cm.
    Includes bibliographical references and index.
    ISBN 0-07-068958-X (acid-free paper)
    1. General Motors Corporation.   2. International Union, United
Automobile, Aerospace, and Agricultural Implement Workers of America.
3. Trade-unions—Automobile industry workers—United States.
4. Automobile industry and trade—United States.—Quality control.
I. Wilber, Jay C. II. Title.
HD9710.U63G46   1996
338.7'6292'0973—dc20   95-42393
                                                            CIP

McGraw-Hill

A Division of The McGraw-Hill Companies

3 4 5 6 7 8 9 10 FGR/FGR 0 5 4 3 2 1

ISBN 0-07-068958-X

*The sponsoring editor for this book was Philip Ruppel, the editing supervisor
was Peggy Lamb, and the production supervisor was Donald F. Schmidt. It
was set in Palatino by Terry Leaden of McGraw-Hill's Professional Book
Group composition unit. Printed and bound by Quebecor/Book Press.*

This book is printed on recycled, acid-free paper containing a
minimum of 50% recycled, de-inked fiber.

We dedicate this book to the memory of Dr. W. Edwards Deming, without whose admonition and guidance the spark of inspiration leading to this work would not have ignited with such a sense of urgency and purpose. His guidance on Tom's Doctoral Committee and his advice to us concerning the urgency of our message provided constant encouragement that what we were doing could truly impact the environment of any organization in a positive and meaningful way.

Contents

12. Continuous Pursuit to Answer the Right Questions   352

Epilogue   362

Preface

Jay Wilber and Tom Weekley are co-directors of General Motors Quality Network, which is the enterprise that encompasses the principles and practices of Total Quality Management for the corporation. Mr. Wilber is Executive Director of Quality Network for General Motors Corporation and Mr. Weekley is Assistant Director of the United Automobile Workers (UAW), GM Department. Total Quality Management at General Motors has been uniquely joint since its inception.

As leaders of this quality effort, Tom and Jay often lecture and teach the philosophy and operational policies and practices of the Quality Network to groups within the corporation as well as those external to General Motors. "The Crowd" is one such group, comprised of GM statisticians and like interested parties. "The Crowd" invited Jay and Tom to lead off a day's symposium on August 25, 1991. The guest teacher for the remainder of the day was to be Dr. W. Edwards Deming. The challenge was to describe General Motors' quality system to Dr. Deming and, incidentally, the one hundred or so other members of this Deming study group. The presentation became known as *Theory of a System*, which was the name of the day's symposium.

Unfortunately, Dr. Deming was unable to attend. William Scherkenbach, chairperson of "The Crowd" and author of several books exploring Dr. Deming's principles, sent Dr. Deming a copy of the presentation. Subsequently, Jay and Tom and Ron Haas, Vice President-NAO Quality and Reliability, had a private meeting with Dr. Deming to talk about what was "going on in quality" at GM. They discussed *Theory of a System*. Dr. Deming turned to Jay and Tom and exhorted them, "... the two of you have the responsibility to communicate to American industry that you have to do this (system management) together."

Both Jay and Tom began their General Motors careers on the plant floor building parts for cars and trucks, one in an engine plant in Flint, Michigan, and one in a sheet metal fabricating plant in Lordstown, Ohio. Over the years they took dramatically different career paths that ultimately led to opposite sides of the negotiating table. Now they are partners charged with helping General Motors make cars and trucks better. They both have a passionate belief in what they are doing together. This book is an attempt to fulfill Dr. Deming's challenge to them and as such is dedicated to him.

The challenge was twofold: to document the GM–UAW jointly designed, developed, and implemented process management system and to capture the essense of being on an emotional roller coaster ride characteristic of an undertaking of this magnitude. Jay and Tom have included personal stories about their experiences to help transform theory to real life happenings, to articulate their personal passion and commitment to quality, General Motors, and the UAW respectively, and the men and women who are part of each organization. Many of these experiences are included to illustrate how barriers and obstacles can be viewed as opportunities for improvement; innovation can often spring from impossible situations.

Tom and Jay liken implementing a common process to manage General Motors, and do it with the UAW, to a white-water raft ride that started seven years ago, and the water is just now beginning to smooth out and become navigable. They are very proud of what GM and the UAW have accomplished together. Although the joint GM–UAW journey in pursuit of total quality will never end, Tom and Jay are convinced a well-executed process management system will certainly improve the scenery along the way.

Acknowledgments

Our life experiences and personal faith in God have taught us that knowledge and insight come from many sources in many guises. Neither of us is foolish enough to believe that we have all the answers; we have come to rely on others who have graced us with their knowledge and have deepened our understanding. We have been the learners. Our mission is to bring together and employ this collective intelligence to further the goals of our respective organizations and the men and women who are reshaping our foundation for the future.

Originally we intended to write a book on total quality management. However, such a wealth of information exists on this topic that our McGraw-Hill editor asked that we start over and write a personal account of our attempt to implement a jointly developed process management system in General Motors Corporation. Therefore, our renewed efforts have been directed toward documenting the contributions of the men and women in the United Auto Workers Union and General Motors Corporation and their pursuit of quality, while providing a safe, secure, and fulfilling work environment. We have found the secret lies in relying on the organizations' greatest strength—the collective wisdom of its people.

Our record of General Motors' and the UAW's quest for quality could not have come to fruition without the help and support of a great number of people whom we wish to acknowledge.

Professional Acknowledgments

Betsy Reid Creedon, the primary editor for this book as well as a great friend.

Our leadership who provided both direction and support: UAW President Steve Yokich, General Motors Chief Executive Officer Jack Smith, and former General Motors Chief Executive Officer Bob Stempel. General Motors President Rick Wagoner and Former General Motors President Lloyd Reuss, General Motors Vice President for Quality and Reliability Ron Haas.

Our support staff and colleagues who were both teachers and benevolent critics: UAW–GM Administrative Secretary Dianne Weekley; GM Administrative Secretary Linda Garrison; consultant John Roach; members and former members of both the UAW and GM Quality Network Staffs and their secretarial assistants; members of the UAW–GM NAO Quality Council; Group, Staffs, and Divisional Quality Network Representatives; Plant Quality Network Representatives; Members of the Divisional and Plant Quality Councils; the Quality Network Implementation Support Team (QNIST); Action Strategy Team members; and the UAW and GM Public Relations Departments.

Finally, to all those friends and associates who have provided us with the support and experiences necessary to be able to contribute, in a small way, to changing General Motors and, in so doing, impact the corporation's many stakeholders.

Tom's Personal Acknowledgments

My wife Dianne, my parents who taught me many of life's principles, long time friend Charles Sarbach, those elected officials I served with in my local union, and especially the men and women in my local union and throughout this country who have supported and believed in me and honor me by considering me a friend.

Jay's Personal Acknowledgments

My wife Henrietta and our son Thomas Jay Wilber; my mother and my six brothers and sisters, their spouses and their children, many of whom work in this industry and were great sources of information and inspiration; my father, grandfather, and great-grandfather who began the tradition and set the standards for all of us to follow; Mike and Sally Tierney for their friendship and support; retired GM Vice-President Blair Thompson who inspired and encouraged me to change my career direction; Ed Czapor, retired Vice President and GM's "people guy," whose vision helped me establish my foundational direction for the Quality Network.

We have benefited from knowing and working with many people who have contributed to our growth in jointness and in quality, and therefore are ultimately responsible for our writing this book. Our debt to our friends and coworkers is considerable. Yet, none of them is responsible for our imperfect interpretations of their contributions and any conclusions we have expressed. We will continue to learn and benefit from our relationships.

1
Personal Journey

Personal and Organizational Beliefs and Values

Total quality management principles are difficult to implement if the starting point for any individual is not with an understanding of personal beliefs and values. A clear understanding of what makes people act the way they do is essential if one is going to undertake a leadership role for the design, development, and implementation of total quality principles in an organization. In addition to personal beliefs and values, every organization has beliefs and values, behaviors considered acceptable or unacceptable in its day-to-day management. Usually, beliefs and values are a combination of formal policies and an informal set of rules that collectively represent a value system shaped by the actions and behaviors of employees: the actions of an operator on the plant floor, an executive secretary, a general supervisor, a Shop Committeeperson, or a corporate Vice President. Aligning personal values, as defined over time by personal beliefs, with organizational values, as exhibited in decision making and individual behavior on the job, shapes "what's OK to do and what's *really* OK to do."

How we think and react in a given situation is controlled by our own personal beliefs and values, enhanced or tempered by organizational beliefs and values. Personal truth is defined by events throughout our lifetime. What shapes our beliefs and values is based on what has influenced our thinking. Our willingness to accept change is based on a combination of our beliefs and values, what we believe to be truth and external organizational beliefs and values that we choose to accept. As we venture through life's journey, we consciously and subconsciously react to each event or situation based on how it aligns with our beliefs and values, what we believe is truth, and, to a lesser extent, organizational beliefs and values. Our personal approach to leading the UAW–GM Quality Network—that is, the General Motors' total quality management process for customer satisfaction—is based upon the events, principles, organizational beliefs and values, and personal beliefs and values that have shaped our lives, our abilities, and our professional relationships. We have each traveled a very different route to get to the same place, where we are today. Nevertheless, separately in the past and together today, we both passionately champion principles and practices that encourage and empower people throughout our respective organizations to work toward common goals that allow all to prosper and meet individual and organizational goals.

Four Generations with General Motors

Jay Wilber on the Beliefs and Values That Shaped His Participation in the Quality Network

When I think about what makes up some of my own personal beliefs and values, I'm taken back to my childhood and recollections of both my father and grandfather, who were supervisors together in a General Motors plant in Flint, Michigan.

My dad and grandfather often told me about their work. They talked about the 1937 strikes—how men who worked for them prior to the sit-down became embittered and angry in their quest for changes in the workplace and their struggles to begin a union to represent them with management. It was a hard time for both sides, and it was a time that sides were definitely and emphatically taken—"them versus us"—from both points of view. With their stories as part of my history, once removed, I was hired in as a General Motors employee in June 1965. I was the fourth generation of my family to work for this great company; my great-grandfather had been an hourly assembler for Fisher Body. I was a young man who had spent a year in a community college who now had a chance to go to work at the Chevrolet V-8 engine plant in Flint, the same plant my father had worked at from 1953 until 1972.

Hourly Employment

I'll never forget my first day on the job. The first things I noticed when I walked into the plant were the noise and the strong smell of oil and dust in the air. There was a maze of conveyors taking parts someplace. Drills were squealing, and smoke was in the air everywhere I looked. I was both scared and excited. In those days a new-employee orientation process did not exist.

I remember being assigned to my first job: hand loading parts into a transfer line used to machine the contact face of an exhaust manifold and drill the bolt holes. My job was to take the parts from a gondola and put them into a carrier for entry into the machine. I was not told what the part was being used for or what the overall process was to accomplish. I barely knew where I was in the plant.

My parents had always encouraged me to go to college, but there really was no money for me to go away to school. Seven children to raise and only one parent working outside the home was all my wonderful parents could do. Like so many others in Flint at the time, I decided to attend the local community college. My father and I discussed a skilled-trade apprenticeship for me. He said it would be great to have that experience to go along with my formal education. As a result I took the apprentice test and scored high enough to start my apprenticeship in September 1965. I forgot my lofty plans to become a scientist or doctor. I completed my apprenticeship and became a journeyperson in June 1968. During that time I developed a diverse background and experience with machine tools and various machining operations.

I worked at my first job for approximately five weeks when I was transferred to the *finished end* of the department. My new job assignment was to load finished exhaust manifolds to hooks on a passing monorail. The conveyor hooks were color coded, but the parts were not. The trick was to look at the part and know from experience which part went on which hook. I had no experience on the job and minimal instruction, so I had to learn fast. Putting the wrong part on a certain color-coded hook could result in the wrong manifold getting assembled on an engine. My feedback was loud and direct. It came from an assembly line repairman who had to remove the wrong manifolds. His instructions to me were clear after he would walk from the assembly line to my work site to inform me he was not happy with my learning curve. It took me a couple of days and a number of visits from the repairman to get this new assignment down pat and to eliminate the necessity for his visits to me.

In the area of my new assignment, workers were using rotating power drivers on several assembly benches to insert three threaded studs to a variety of exhaust manifolds. These studs were used to attach the exhaust pipe to the exhaust manifold. Certain manifolds called for the installation of a *heat tube* (emissions control component), which required that an additional employee be assigned to work with the stud assembler. Occasionally my supervisor asked me to assist the stud driver and install the heat tube. One day the power driver operator was sick and did not report to work. My supervisor assigned me to install the studs as well as install the heat tubes. Naturally, I did the assignment as instructed and was able to keep up with the requirements of the job to which two people were usually assigned. Another employee in the department called for his union representative and claimed my supervisor had violated a provision of the contract dealing with workload and workpace (Paragraph 78 of the 1964 GM–UAW National Agreement) by assigning me to do both jobs. I was still a new employee and did not understand the objection. I had no problem keeping up with the pace, but it later became clear to me that it would have been difficult for some of the older employees in the department to do the work. My youth and energy were soon to be used on a more difficult assignment.

Joining the Management Team

In April 1969, I was promoted to Junior Process Engineer and assigned to the tool engineering department. This meant that I was no longer represented by the union because I was part of management. The job was to work with another tool engineer and assist machining departments to determine appropriate cutting tools, as well as experimenting with new machining processes.

The following year, as a 23-year-old husband and father of a 3-year-old son, I was promoted to Supervisor–Skilled Trades and was assigned to supervise activities on the third shift (9:30 p.m. to 6:00 a.m.) in the cutter grinding department. The day I started supervision, my father removed from his wallet a folded, typewritten piece of paper and gave it to me. He said my grandfather had given him that same piece of paper.

Don't Quit

When things go wrong, as they sometimes will,

When the road you're trudging seems all uphill,

When the funds are low, and the debts are high,

And you want to smile, but you have to sigh,

When care is pressing you down a bit,

Rest if you must, but don't quit.

Life is queer with its twists and turns,

As everyone of us sometimes learns,

And many a failure turns about,

When he might have won had he stuck it out;

Don't give up though the pace seems slow

You may succeed with another blow.

Success is failure turned inside out,

The silver tint of the clouds of doubt,

And you never can tell how close you are

It may be near when it seems so far.

So stick to the fight when you're hardest hit,

It's when things seem worse,

that you must not quit.

My father told me to read it, understand it, and think about it, especially when I was challenged (he assured me I would be) in this new facet of my career.

This was my first supervisory assignment, and I learned the position the hard way. The superintendent for the skilled-trades area assigned me the responsibility for supervising 43 journeyperson cutter grinder employees as well as some employees-in-training. He warned that they were notorious for wasting time and that the situation had to be corrected. My superintendent let me know, in no uncertain terms, that my job was to straighten up the mess and make sure the employees put in a full shift's work. I spent most of the first few days watching some of the employees in the area. For the most part, they were busy and maintained the flow of sharpened tools for production operations. However, there were a few journeypersons who appeared to be wasting time; I challenged three of them by disciplining each with a written reprimand.

That decision festered for about three or four days before its consequences surfaced. I discovered that all of the cutter grinder employees were at their jobs, diligently at work. Unfortunately, there were only a few sharpened tools resulting from their efforts. It was obvious that I had a slowdown on my hands, and it resulted from my approach in dealing with the problem. Of course, the same superintendent who had challenged me to deal with the laggards was the first one to tell me to fix the mess. It had taken me less than two weeks on the job to close the plant down due to lack of tools. The slowdown and the shutdown had certainly made its point. I reversed my decision on the three reprimands and removed them from the employees' records. Then I asked them to help me learn their jobs, and they agreed.

Over the next three months, I had each of those 43 skilled-trades journeypersons cutter grinders show me what his job was (there were no women in my department at the time) and how he did it. It was the best decision I ever made. I learned firsthand what teamwork is and what gets the job done and that approaching problems from the root cause perspective rather than a knee-jerk emotional reaction more often than not results in a better solution. Instinctively we ran to the contract and attempted to enforce each provision to the letter. However, although the contract is the legal, binding agreement that defines the rules and working relationship between management and the union, it cannot take into account the diverse nature of a plant population. It is incumbent upon union and management leadership to stretch beyond provisions and paragraphs to try to understand each other's point of view. Early plant experiences shaped my own personal set of beliefs and values, which I then carried with me into the workplace.

Joining Labor Relations

In the spring of 1972 my career took a major change in direction when I was offered an opportunity to work in the Labor Relations Department at Chevrolet Flint Engine. During these early years I was also starting to build relationships that have grown over the years and are with me to this day. Cal Rapson was the UAW committeeperson who had represented an employee I had disciplined for wasting time. One month before I joined the Labor Relations Department, Cal was elected to represent Skilled Trades employees on the plant shop committee. I recall the first grievance that Cal and I bargained together. Cal withdrew the case, and I mistakenly, if not arrogantly or naively, commented that it was obviously a case of superior bargaining on my part that caused him to withdraw the grievance. I was wrong. I did not see it as a gesture of working together. Cal withdrew the grievance in an attempt to establish a working relationship. Cal has had a long and exciting career with the UAW. He has gone from a District Committeeperson all the way to Administrative Assistant to Vice President Steve Yokich in the GM Department of the UAW at Solidarity House in Detroit. He is a good friend, and we have learned a lot together throughout the years of our working relationship.

Labor Relations before the Network

During those early years in Labor Relations at the Engine Plant, problem solving was not at the forefront of our thinking. Basically, we were in a win-lose mindset. The union wanted to win at management's expense; management wanted the win at the union's expense. There were a few areas we agreed on which, for the most part, were not issues that would have really made a difference in the workplace. We focused on investigating discipline situations or contractual violations. Each side tried to put together the best case and prevail over the other's set of facts. There was an adversarial atmosphere in the bargaining room; call it "positioning bargaining." However, because both sides were obligated to resolve problems, there was respect for the job that each had to do. There was a whole culture inside a culture, language inside a language. The word f_{---} was used frequently as a noun, adjective, and verb; some sentences contained the word four or five times. Personal attacks were frequent but not long lasting, and strangely—ultimately—they were not taken personally. This is far different than the relationship we see today.

A Snake in the Desk. Not everything that occurs in Labor Relations is necessarily contractually related, and we have had some unusual circumstances occur. I was working the second shift in Labor Relations and received a telephone call from a supervisor, Daryll Smith, who was a second-shift supervisor in the cutter grinding department, the same cutter grinding department where I started my supervisory career. Daryll asked me to come down to his office because he had a snake in his desk drawer. I asked if it was a rubber snake, and he said no, its tongue was flitting in and out and the sound that it made sounded like a live one. I didn't know what he expected me to do, but I went to take a look. Daryll was standing at his desk pointing at the drawer. I carefully opened it just enough to see inside, and sure enough, coiled in the drawer with the markings of a diamondback rattler, was a snake moving its head in a threatening way. I immediately shut the drawer.

The two of us decided that we needed to get the drawer out of the desk, and the snake out of the plant. We took a burlap bag, normally used to store dull cutting tools, to wrap the drawer and keep the snake trapped inside. The plan worked. We removed the drawer and the snake and proceeded to plant security. We informed the officers that we had a snake in a drawer and gave them the background. They didn't have anything to put the snake in, so we went to the medical department where they had some large plastic bags we thought would be appropriate for the transfer. By this time word had spread throughout the plant that there was a snake in the supervisor's drawer and he was currently trying to get it out of the drawer and out of the plant. As we left the plant hospital and prepared to make the exchange from the drawer to the bag, about 40 employees gathered in a semicircle observing the event. Daryll rolled back the burlap bag, and I was poised for the transfer, standing there with the plastic bag opened. The snake started out as planned; but unplanned, the snake took off up my arm and then down onto the plant floor. Those 40 employees scattered in every direction, and the snake and I were the only two left. The snake was moving along a wall made of hollow partitions; one of the floor plates that connects the partitions together was missing. My fear was the snake would slip into the hole, disappear, and come out in one of the offices the next day. I grabbed for the snake using the method I was taught in Scouts, but the approach did not work, and the snake turned and bit me. Fortunately, after consulting with a resident herpetologist of the University of Michigan, we determined the snake was a nonpoisonous fox snake.

The plant reported the incident as a "near miss," the traditional wording used any time a close call would occur in the plant. This time, however, the emphasis was on the snake's condition, not mine. It was reported that the snake was doing fine, in spite of biting my finger. The nonpoisonous reptile became a new resident of the University of Michigan's Herpetology Lab. The following week in a meeting with the local plant union leadership, I was given a snake bite kit and advised that I should carry it with me at all times in the event that the incident was to be repeated. Circumstantial evidence suggested that two employees of the cutter grinding department had been fishing in a lake in Alabama the week before the snake was found in the drawer. We also learned that fox snakes only live in southern states. We were in Flint, Michigan. However, there was not enough hard evidence to proceed with a discipline case. Besides, the snake was doing well.

I know this is a humorous story, but there is an important lesson here: The snake was brought into the plant not as a joke but as a spiteful act. The men who brought the snake into the plant disliked the supervisor and knew he had a great fear of snakes. This event could have caused severe injury. Daryll Smith could have hurt himself or someone else in those first few moments of fear, and fortunately for me, the snake wasn't poisonous. The point is that the environment was a we-they situation, and the gulf between the two factions seemed bottomless at times.

They Shoot Supervisors, Don't They?

Another example of the extremes to which explosive behavior can go happened while I was working the second shift at the Engine Plant in Labor Relations. I received a call that a plant security officer had confronted an exiting employee just minutes after he had shot at three supervisors in the plant, one of whom was severely wounded with a leg injury. The employee was upset because he had been disciplined for an infraction of company rules, and he returned to the plant with his 44 Bulldog Magnum to shoot his supervisor. The plant security officer was aware that the event had occurred and had a description of the employee. He carefully and professionally talked the employee into turning over the weapon. Events like this have a chilling effect on a plant, and many times reflect the environment in which people are working. This is not to suggest that this employee shot his supervisor, or was justified in doing so, as a result of being unhappy with his work situation. But creating and building a supportive environment will go a long way in reducing tension in the workplace and hopefully reducing the potential for explosive situations such as this.

The Grand Experiment

While I was working in Labor Relations at the plant, a significant, career-altering experience occurred. It involved a series of grievances that had been filed in 1975 protesting the outsourcing of skilled-trades work associated with the installation of equipment for the new Chevette four-cylinder engine. The cases were appealed through the local grievance procedure and were referred to Chevrolet Central Office, Labor Relations, for resolution. Pat Crane, Director of Labor Relations for the Chevrolet Motor Division at the time, along with Don Hadsal were assigned to investigate the contracting cases. Pat and Don spent some time at the plant going through our investigation, which was thorough and prepared them well for the argument that the majority of the work associated with the project had actually been either performed or was scheduled to be performed by Skilled Trades employees at the Flint Engine Plant.

During this time I got to know Pat and Don well; Pat spent time with me touring the plant. I took him through the entire Chevette four-cylinder engine manufacturing process, which I knew extremely well both because of my prior skilled-trades experience and my work investigating the subcontracting cases. As a result of our work together and my experience and background in Labor Relations, Pat subsequently recommended me for the corporate Labor Relations staff, assigned to the wage administration section. It was a highly unusual move; normally, people who were destined to become members of the corporate Industrial Relations staff first went through a divisional staff Labor Relations assignment. So, in 1978, I joined the corporate Industrial Relations staff in Detroit. When I arrived at my new job, I found my reputation had preceded me; I had been dubbed *the grand experiment*.

My work experience, coupled with my 10 years of night school to earn a bachelor's degree in business administration from the University of Michigan, helped me secure this opportunity. I now had the responsibility for investigation of new technology cases and wage and classification cases, as well as an occasional skilled-trades demarcation case, which were appealed through the grievance procedure to the corporate labor staff for resolution.

The Beginning of Trust.   It was during this time that I first met my current partner, Tom Weekley. Together we were able to resolve a number of plant-related employee grievance issues with very little difficulty. We didn't allow ourselves to get caught up in the union-management politics frequently associated with skilled-trade lines-of-demarcation issues. We looked at the facts and made decisions based on them. Little did we know at the time that we would be coming back together in 1990 to work on General Motors' Total Quality Process, the Quality Network.

Over the next several years I participated in labor contract negotiations on a national basis (1979, 1982, 1984, and 1990) between General Motors and the UAW. I was a subcommittee chairperson for a number of different bargaining committees and was a chief negotiator for GM of Canada and the Canadian Automobile Workers union (CAW) negotiations in 1987. I was responsible for the GM–CAW Master Agreement provisions, with the exception of key economic issues that were the responsibility of the Vice President of Personnel, Rick Curd.

While in Canada I worked with Suzuki, a Japanese auto company, which eventually signed an agreement with General Motors of Canada to form a joint venture, CAMI. It gave me an opportunity to learn about a Japanese production system and develop a better understanding of the Japanese culture. Suzuki's production system is similar to Toyota's. My experience with Suzuki foreshadowed my involvement with the Quality Network, which espouses many of the tools, techniques, and production processes learned from General Motors' joint venture with Toyota, NUMMI.

An Emerging Philosophy

During my life, a number of people and events have influenced my own personal beliefs and values. One thing I have concluded: There truly needs to be a process in place that results in continuous improvement in the way people are being treated in organizations across America. Hopefully, this book will provide insight for leaders that will inspire a new level of awareness and sensitivity.

We should not look at our history in a negative sense. It is important for an organization to build on its strengths, but it must also recognize and eliminate weaknesses. Organizations must understand that there are weaknesses and that the true strength of any company lies with the men and women that design, engineer, and manufacture the products or services of the enterprise.

My personal beliefs and values have been shaped by the events of my life. I have been influenced by individuals who treated me with dignity and respect, whom I trusted and cared for. I have been influenced by those whom no one trusted, but it takes all kinds to shape one's value system. In today's world we have to value people for their ideas and innovation. We must give trust before we can expect to receive trust in return. We have to understand and commit ourselves to never allowing issues and problems to rise above relationships.

The Shaping of a Workers' Advocate

Tom Weekley on the Events That Brought Him to Quality Network

Blue-Collar Beginnings

My personal beliefs and values have been influenced by a vast array of experiences that have molded my life. In the latter part of my senior year in high school, I was able to secure a machinist apprenticeship at Central States Can Corporation in Massillon, Ohio. I attended school in the morning and worked on the apprenticeship program in the afternoon. When I graduated from high school, I applied for an apprenticeship at Chrysler Corporation in Twinsburg, Ohio. In 1965, I passed all of the tests and started in the die maker apprentice program the day after my eighteenth birthday. I loved the work, I loved the atmosphere, and I immediately set the goal of becoming a tool and die designer for Chrysler.

There was a long-established union at Chrysler, and the work rules were clear and well defined. The apprenticeship honed my mechanical skills and gave me a broad view of people who worked in the plant each day representing a true cross section of our society. I was also exposed to several labor disputes that resulted in strikes. When I finished my apprenticeship, I would have been assigned to the second shift based on my seniority status so I applied for a tool and die journeyperson position at the new General Motors fabricating plant in Lordstown, Ohio. I began my career with General Motors on March 7, 1970. I was hired in as nineteenth employee in that plant and worked there while the roof was still being completed and the floors were finally being installed. Because of my draw die experience, I was immediately put to work on the inner door draw dies for the new Vega subcompact car introduced by General Motors in the early 1970s.

The Awakening

My first several days on the job were a rude awakening. Since the plant was new, the union was not yet recognized as the bargaining agent for the employees at that plant. Situations occurred that I had never experienced before and didn't think could ever happen. It was during this time that I came to understand the need for workers to have input into their jobs and how important it is for management to listen to the experts that they hire. I soon found that the work environment was dramatically different from the one I had experienced at Chrysler. Since the union had not yet been recognized, management had complete control over every aspect of a worker's life. Regular breaks were not recognized. Many times I had to take a coffee break inside a die that I was grinding on rather than being able to take a few minutes to rest and relax. The pressure of production start-up began to get greater, and with it came greater pressure on workers. Extended hours and close supervision began to take its toll on morale.

Starting the Journey for Justice

The situation led me to seek out the union organizer in the plant. I obtained union authorization cards and began to ask people to sign the cards to authorize a union election. At the time, I had no intention of being involved in the union; I was taking engineering courses in order to become a tool and die designer. After the election was held, the union was certified as our bargaining agent, and many of the men I worked with asked me to run for committeeperson. I told them I had no experience at being a grievance procedure representative and committeeperson; I didn't know anything about the contract. Many of my fellow workers insisted, so I ran for committeeperson and was elected overwhelmingly, at age 22.

Within several months, I was elected as part of the shop committee or bargaining committee and led several important policy-setting movements for the fledgling local union. The adversities experienced in the plant and the injustices I saw gave me the opportunity to lead the bargaining unit and change things for working men and women in the plant. We went through many major crises during the late seventies and early eighties because the work environment was based on an antagonistic, see-who-can-win-at-any-cost type of atmosphere.

The plant Personnel Director was a very loyal General Motors person, but one who had little respect for union leadership. Out in the plant the prevailing attitude was: Let's teach this Personnel Director a lesson. Les Bryan, the UAW International Representative led the shop committee on a walk through the plant. In those days the guards followed every step of the way. Lester told us not to put on our safety glasses, to just walk through the plant. A guard came up and said to us, "Mr. Bryan, you need to put on your safety glasses," and Lester told him, "Don't worry about it, we'll fix it." And so, we kept on walking without our glasses. The guard came up again, and again we told him not to worry about it, we'd fix it. We kept walking, without glasses, and pretty soon the guard radioed the PD (Personnel Director) who showed up, approached Lester, and said, "Mr. Bryan, we need you to put on your safety glasses," and Lester said, "Well, we'll fix it." He kept on walking, and all of us kept on walking with him. Everyone in the plant knew what was going on. Finally, the PD said, "Mr. Bryan, we're going to have to ask you to leave the plant if you don't put on your safety glasses." Lester looked at him and said, "Well, I told you we would fix it." The Personnel Director said, "What does that mean? Are you going to put on your safety glasses or not?" Lester said, "Well, that's enough of an answer, isn't it? We'll fix it." The PD said "No, that answer is not good enough." Then Lester proceeded to explain to him that that's the kind of answer he had been giving us all the time, and if he, the PD, didn't like that kind of answer, why would he use it on us? We had incident after incident like this that became simply a test of wills.

The Significance of Coffee

As we were defining our relationship, big stands were sometimes taken over seemingly small issues. When I was first elected committeeperson, I got a committee call: People were being told they couldn't take coffee cups away from the break area to their job or, for that matter, anywhere else in the plant. I went out to my district, along with the shift district committeeperson, and told the people to go ahead and take their coffee cups with them back to the shop, to be sure not to allow their actions to interfere with production, and to be sure they threw their coffee cups away in the proper place. Both the second-shift district committeeperson and I were then warned by Labor Relations that everyone was going to be disciplined. We were to be disciplined as well for telling people to defy orders. Ultimately, since everyone in the plant had earned a discipline, management had to back down and take a more rational view—allowing people take a drink of coffee during production lulls. Some of these confrontations seem petty today, but they were serious statements of the rights of individuals versus the rights of the boss, and they reflected the win-lose mentality that was prevalent at the time.

Our First Walkout

I was a district committeeperson for the first strike at the plant. I was told to go up front, that I was being disciplined. Turns out, I was being suspended for my involvement in a committee call on a health and safety issue. I had told management that we were not going to do the job because someone was going to get hurt. When they took me up front, all the employees on the third shift began to walk out of the plant, and a three-day wildcat strike ensued. It came about because of the lack of concern and understanding for employee safety as well as the entire membership's frustration at not getting their grievances addressed and their concerns listened to.

Elected Chairperson

At the next union election, at 23 years old, I was elected Chairperson of the Shop Committee, heading the entire bargaining unit for UAW Local 1714, which represented workers at the Fisher Body Fabricating Plant. It was an awesome responsibility at that age. I was young, it was a new local in a new plant, and there was not much respect either for me or for the union I represented. When I was elected Chairperson, the Personnel Director called me out in the hall and stated his position concerning the union. He said, "When I was in college, I dated the girlfriend of one of the basketball players. The basketball player found out about it and caught me outside and started a fight with me and was just beating me up. But, I kept getting up. Even though I was a lot smaller, I kept getting up. Ultimately I wore him down and I won the fight." He said, "So, I take that same approach with the union. Someone may be bigger or stronger, but if I hang in there long enough, I can win." So I told him, "Well, that may have worked in the past, but you're dealing with a stubborn, red-headed Irishman now, and I can hang in there longer than you can. Besides, I'm younger, and I'll be around a lot longer than you."

On another occasion in a shop committee meeting, the PD looked across the table at me and said, "I don't know why this membership would elect a boy to do a man's job, but I guess we'll have to deal with you." Of course, this was said in front of all my peers on the shop committee. The role each of us was going to have to play had been defined. The incident was broadcast throughout the plant via the informal, word-of-mouth network within minutes. A we-they attitude had been established.

The Lordstown Reputation

Incidents like this were numerous and led to continual strife at Lordstown. The plant became the subject of many case studies and articles examining the new labor force and the problems that we had at the entire Lordstown complex. Many times we established strike deadlines and stayed in negotiations for weeks, sometimes not leaving the plant for two or three days at a time. During all of these confrontations both sides were looking at ways to win the confrontation rather than directly find a solution to the problem.

I was fired and suspended from General Motors several times for actively protecting the interests of the workers. On one occasion I was called to a press line where a large press was being used to run a very small die and workers had to actually walk inside the stamping press in order to load parts. Previously I had settled a grievance establishing that slides and long hooks would be used so operators could slide the parts in and use the hooks to position the parts properly, thereby eliminating the need for workers to enter this very small die. When I addressed the general supervisor, he told me there was no time for that, that we needed to load these parts quick. He told me, "I'm giving a direct order to all employees to run it without the sliders or hooks." This was a severe safety hazard. If the press had rolled over and the employee had not completely left the interior of the die, the odds were very good that the employee could be severely injured.

I told all the employees on the job that they could refuse the job. They should not go inside the press for fear for their safety. A foreman who had been part of a private conversation among Labor Relations Supervisors came up to me and told me, while looking the other way, that they were going to get me by disciplining all the employees who refused to do the job. In their opinion this would make me look bad politically. Now, I have a black belt in karate and had recently been in a major championship fight. Most of the employees in the plant knew of my black belt status. I went around to each employee on the job and told him or her, "Look, if management comes around and give you orders to do the job, tell them you are more than happy to do the job, but you are afraid to because I've threatened that, if you go inside that press, I am going to physically assault you. That way, you won't be disciplined and yet you still won't have to go inside the die." The Labor Relations supervisor went around and began to give everyone direct orders to do the job. Each worker he confronted told him he or she was afraid "Red" (my nickname) would physically assault him or her. The supervisor called plant protection and the local police to come in and escort me out of the plant because I was physically threatening people within the plant. Well, they did physically escort me out of the plant. However, in the meantime, an International Union Representative who had been meeting on grievances next door at the assembly plant was notified of the problem. He came in and called GM management in Detroit. The situation was corrected: The grievance was complied with, and I was reinstated from the suspension. Incidences like these illustrate the adversarial nature of the relationship between the union and management at that time. It is helpful today, when things seem to bog down and progress is not as rapid as we would like, to remember the way we used to operate.

"We Didn't Know"

We used contractual means to make our point and get management to listen. There was an overhead monorail attaching the fabricating plant and the assembly plant at the Lordstown complex. The fabricating plant shipped parts across and kept the assembly plant running. We had over 300 grievances on legitimate issues in the material handling area that fed the overhead line system. There was no action on these cases. So, one day at a shop committee meeting, I told all the shop committeepersons that they should begin to go through all the various grievances we had and whenever management began to ask questions, tell them "we didn't know." At the meeting we raised issues that had all been raised previously; management asked questions, and we said,

"We didn't know." Finally the Labor Relations supervisor said to me across the table, "You need to investigate these issues. How can we settle them when you don't have the facts?" I asked him to give us a break, and he left. All the committeepersons asked me what I was doing. I told them that the Supervisor wanted us to investigate the cases and get the facts, so go out and investigate the cases.

Now, I was well aware that the National Agreement allowed all members of the shop committee to go out into the plant, take people off the job, and investigate cases. We all went out to the overhead monorail system and took the hourly operators off the job. I took them on committee call. After about 15 minutes, the Labor Relations Supervisor came out and wanted to know what was going on. I told him that we were doing what he had asked us to do, investigate the cases and gather the facts. He stood around impatiently for about 15 more minutes. At this point a half hour had gone by, and, in another half hour, the neighboring assembly plant would be out of parts. Finally, he came up and asked if we were done investigating yet. I told him, "No, we are not." He said, "Well, we're going to have to replace employees." This was fine with me. As he replaced employees, we would take them off line on committee call to thoroughly investigate the cases. With only minutes left before the assembly plant would have shut down, he came to me and told me they would take care of the legitimate grievances; he would sit down and work this out with me. I agreed, and we went back in and worked out the issues. It took that kind of confrontation basis to get things done.

The Unknown Pickets

A final example of the atmosphere in which we were working in my early years at General Motors: Later in my term of office as Chairperson of the Bargaining Committee, a group of people became so frustrated that they staged a wildcat strike, putting bags over their heads to picket outside the plant so that they could not be identified. The PD went up to them and got right in their faces, only inches away, screaming at them, cursing them, saying things about their mothers— anything he could do to try to provoke them into a fight. At the same time he was trying to identify them in some way since he knew he could not touch them. After the picket line had stood for several hours, management found an obscure law originally used against the Ku Klux Klan, forbidding Klansmen from wearing hoods. The PD notified the local sheriff's department to stir up some action. Fortunately, we were warned by the sheriff's department, and we convinced the employees in the picket line to leave the line before the sheriff had to arrest them. Incidents like this were carried out by average, nice American workers who were so frustrated at their inability to be heard that they resorted to radical and drastic means. All of these stories point out the need for union and management to work together to establish an environment in which people can air their concerns and feel that someone is listening, where workers become partners with management to help the business run effectively and efficiently, ensuring long-term job security for everybody.

Soon after being elected Chairperson of the local union bargaining unit, I also was elected as Recording Secretary of a large international UAW subcouncil, representing all of the trim, cut and sew, fabricating, and hardware plants in the United States. Within several months I was elected as Chairperson of that national subcouncil. This was my first opportunity to broaden my service to people and expand it on a national level. After several years as Chairperson and being consistently reelected by wide margins, in both my local union and the national subcouncil, I knew that the rest of my life would be dedicated to the advancement and the causes of working men and women throughout General Motors and if possible, the world.

Blue-Collar Blues

My reputation was set: I had been suspended and discharged several times from General Motors for my activist role supporting people and felt an overwhelming call to crusade and fight for justice in the workplace. The Lordstown, Ohio, complex had a national reputation for labor disputes and especially for what was called in the seventies "the blue-collar blues." All our extended labor disputes, in my opinion, were over issues that did not warrant the kind of action that we were forced to take. The issues involved were basic, common, everyday rights that should be accorded people in the workplace.

As a local union Chairperson responsible for the bargaining committee and all collective bargaining within UAW Local 1714 at Lordstown in the early seventies, I found myself constantly fighting for a win in the membership's eyes no matter what the cost, much the same as my counterpart fought for a win in the corporation's eyes no matter what the cost. It wasn't that I didn't care about General Motors Corporation. I did understand that GM had to survive if I was to have a job along with all the people that worked with me. However, I saw the issues in the plant as such blatant violations of the workers' rights that all concern for the corporation was laid aside. I'm sure that my counterparts in management at that local level felt under such pressure to hold down "union gains" that they, too, wanted to win in their leaders' eyes, whatever the cost. We had many bargaining sessions that degenerated into personal attacks across the bargaining table, serving no real purpose other than to make the situation even more volatile. Many of my suspensions from GM resulted from my taking a stand on worker safety and other issues rising from sheer frustration and the perception that management did not care about or would not listen to legitimate concerns of the membership I represented. I spent many a sleepless night worrying about whether I would have a job, be able to support my children, based on my union involvement and interference with management's agenda and disregard for the membership I represented. The directives to management counterparts at the local level to win at all costs led to many abuses, and the response I encouraged, in many cases, severely hindered management's efficiency and effectiveness. This perpetuated the cycle of distrust and adversarial relations. However, from my point of view, there was no viable alternative. In many situations the grievance procedure was not used properly and served more to fuel the frustration rather than facilitate finding simple settlements for the issues that faced us.

One Person Can Make a Difference

When a young Labor Supervisor named Bill Malone took over the reins as my counterpart for bargaining sessions, the relationship and work environment at Lordstown began to change. He was a man who kept his word. There were many occasions, I know for a fact, when he put his job on the line based on commitments that he had given us, whether they were written or verbal. With that kind of assurance, I felt comfortable in sitting down and looking at solutions that benefited both the membership I represented and management. I knew what we agreed on would be carried out. Bill Malone, single-handedly, turned the relationship at our location from one of constant antagonism to one of cooperation and concern for workers and for the corporation that they worked for. He placed an emphasis on what was right in any given situation rather than on who could win or lose. In this environment of integrity and concern, it was easy to see how an individual in a position of leadership who is willing to objectively look at the rights of all concerned could make a real difference. Since then, I have seen many cases of individual leaders standing up for what is right rather than what is expedient, what benefited all involved parties rather than furthered a personal career. One person *can* make a radical difference in a situation that seems impossible.

Change in Direction

My value system found reinforcement in the work I was doing for the union. It was at this point of my career that I felt a call to the ministry and resigned my positions with the UAW both locally and nationally. My family and I moved in blind faith to Springfield, Missouri, where I attended Bible college. I planned to become an ordained minister and thought my life would continue in this new direction. Originally I envisioned my future as an engineer and moved from that arena into one of worker advocacy, and then to the ministry.

Joining the International Union

While in Springfield, I was called by UAW President Douglas Frazier. He asked me to join the national United Automobile Workers Union staff. I agreed and was assigned to the UAW Skilled-Trades Department in technological advance. I worked in the General Motors system on lines-of-demarcation cases (Skilled Trades job assignment disputes). During this time two significant things happened: I met Jay Wilber, who was to become my counterpart in the Quality Network in 1990, and found him to be fair and a man of integrity. We worked on Skilled Trades' disputes together, and, like Bill Malone, Jay worked to settle cases on their merits and looked for ways working men and women could contribute. At the same time, he was able to maintain the integrity and the strength of the supervisors and local plant management.

The second thing that happened was that I was accepted as a member of the Society of Manufacturing Engineers, Robotics Institute of America (RIA), and co-chaired RIA's Human Factors Committee. These opportunities exposed me to publications and presentations on labor and management principles pertaining to technological advancement.

Further during this period, I continued my studies and finished a bachelor's degree in Bible studies and on my own time became an associate pastor at a local church. During that period, I grew in understanding of people and became much more effective in my ability to represent people in every area of their life.

Soon after starting work in the UAW Skilled Trades Department, a new Vice President, Stephen P. Yokich, was elected. He promoted me to a coordinator level within the Skilled Trades Department and later named me as his Assistant Director. Through these appointments I participated in various aspects of negotiations in the automotive industry as well as other distinct industrial cultures. I negotiated agreements and worked with international representatives in almost every major industry in the United States and assisted in negotiating apprentice programs at Mazda and NUMMI with Japanese counterparts, broadening my understanding of labor relations on a worldwide basis.

After several years as Assistant Director, I received a call from the Assemblies of God, Michigan district, asking if I would assist a small church in Marlette, Michigan, that was having financial difficulties and could not afford to pay a pastor. I took a leave of absence from the UAW and began to pastor the church in the upper thumb area of Michigan.

When my leave of absence had elapsed, I returned to the UAW as Assistant Director in the Skilled Trades Department. I was fortunate during that period to be appointed to the Federal Committee on Apprenticeship by then Director, Elizabeth Dole. This appointment broadened my understanding of apprenticeship and skilled trades issues in the United States. During this same period, I earned a master's degree in science of administration that truly paved the way for future involvement in management systems and provided a foundation for my doctoral studies in process management.

Handed the Reins

In 1990, Steve Yokich, Vice President and Director of the General Motors' Department, asked me to move to the General Motors Department and assume the Assistant Director's responsibilities for the Quality Network. The Quality Network had been jointly established as the process management system for General Motors. However, it was floundering due to lack of cohesive direction and total commitment by both parties. My directive from Vice President Yokich was to make the process work and make it responsive to the needs of the union members that we represented, as well as the company.

Forging a Partnership

Jay Wilber had been named management Executive Director of the Quality Network just before my appointment. Together we began to forge a new partnership for the UAW and General Motors; working together toward total quality and quality processes in plants throughout General Motors. Upon moving to the General Motors Department, I sensed a need for additional expertise and knowledge regarding process management. As a result, I began to read and view everything I could from any expert in the field. I attended several W. Edwards Deming seminars and began my Ph.D. studies in management and labor relations with the focus on process management. Dr. Deming helped guide my studies as adjunct on my Doctoral Committee. I attended presentations by other companies that were experimenting with different process management systems and different workplace processes, such as Xerox, Federal Express, Ford, Mazda, NUMMI, and others. In just a short time, I gained real insight into the principles needed for effective business practices but, more important, principles that are needed to allow people to become an integral part in those business practices.

Early in our new relationship Jay and I determined that we would do what was right for each situation. The lessons that each of us had learned early in our careers and childhoods would be the foundations on which we would work together. This meant that justice, truth, and honesty would be our foundation for moving forward and that the trust between us needed to be unwavering.

Jay and I have had very similar backgrounds on opposite sides of the fence. Yet we both envision a coalition between labor and management that allows both entities to prosper without either giving up the rights and the responsibilities that our respective organizations require. Jay is a strong leader for General Motors Corporation. I am a strong leader for the UAW and the members that pay my salary each week. Our efforts together are based on and depend upon both of us being strong leaders, yet both of us being fair and just in looking for ways that help both sides fulfill their goals.

Common Ground

The remaining chapters of this book will discuss how we, in spite of our diverse organizational backgrounds, have formed a partnership that constantly seeks a win-win resolution of problems. This effort will not be a point-counterpoint approach but will try to describe, in our opinion, the common ground where joint parties—workers and management—can harmoniously pursue total quality and process management without fear. We also believe that we must reflect, through our personal behavior, our *beliefs and values* and inspire our organizations, General Motors and the UAW, to do the same.

2
Historical Look at GM, UAW, and Quality

The Sun Rises Over Detroit

The Start of the UAW–GM Relationship

The importance of quality, particularly product quality, to business success and job security has been evident to the leadership of both General Motors and the United Automobile Workers union since their founding. Prior to the company's relationship with the United Automobile Workers, General Motors' leadership recognized that quality could be achieved only by all parties working together. In a letter to "All Employees In General Motors Factories" dated October 15, 1934, Alfred P. Sloan, Jr., then President of General Motors Corporation, wrote:

> Recently I sent you a pamphlet outlining the policies governing General Motors relations with factory employees. In that pamphlet it was said that the relationship between management and employees "requires a harmonious working together to the end that the quality and cost of the product may be such that the business will prove continuously successful and will survive." What this means is that we have got to make products which the public will buy, and we can do it only by all working together with that in mind. The

buyers of our products are our real bosses. They are the ones who
provide the money for the wages of every one of us. We must satisfy them or lose our jobs....General Motors has been able to grow
and provide more jobs only because we have had products of good
quality at satisfactory prices. This has been possible because
General Motors employees and management have worked
together.[1]

Sloan finished his letter:

The spirit of fairness and cooperation in our relations with one
another is necessary. It is only by real teamwork that we can maintain the quality of our products and satisfy the buyers upon whom
all of us depend for our livelihood.[2]

When Sloan sent this letter to all General Motors employees, independent unions were organizing workers in various auto plants.
Teamwork, product quality, and satisfied customers, all characteristics
of a total quality system, were not foremost in the minds of union
organizers. They were concerned with the quality of the work procedures and practices, as well as the relationship between the worker
and the company. At the time, the relationship between the unions and
management was adversarial.

In 1934 the American Federation of Labor (AFL) agreed to hold the
first national conference of the United Automobile Workers Federal
Labor Unions. Two hundred delegates convened in Detroit, Michigan,
in August of 1935. The employees in General Motors factories had
begun their fight for representation.

The Sit-Down Strike

The relationship between General Motors management and automotive workers in its plants began to formalize when, on February 11,
1937, the company agreed to negotiate with the union after a bitter 42-
day sit-down strike at Fisher Body Plant No. 1 in Flint, Michigan. As
the workers formulated a list of their demands, they also composed a
song that captured their spirit and confidence:

These 4,000 Union Boys

Oh, they sure made lots of noise,

They decided then and there to shut down tight.

In the office they got snooty,

So we started picket duty,

Now the Fisher Body shop is on strike.[3]

A one-page agreement resulted—the first contract between the union and one of the Big Three and the first of many formal agreements between the UAW and General Motors.

A definitive history of the UAW or General Motors is clearly outside the scope of this book. However, the following discussion provides some background information about these organizations since one is a standard for unions around the world and the other, in the minds of many people, is the embodiment of corporate America.

A Democratic Institution

Tom Weekley on the International Union,
UAW

The UAW is designed to represent as pure a democracy as possible. When you look at the history of the UAW union, you will find that it is one of the most scandal-free organizations in our country. Funds are closely monitored and guarded. Terms are limited, open elections are required, and each member gets to vote. Even the national leadership has to run for office and be elected by delegates from the local unions. This is very similar to the way our electoral college works within the framework of the U.S. Constitution.

Our structure causes union leaders to be dependent upon political realities, while it holds them accountable to the membership they represent. At the local level, leaders can easily be removed from office for not acting according to the wills and desires of their membership. Local union leaders are elected to handle the business of the local union as well as bargaining for that local union. The vote is the currency of position and responsibility in the UAW.

A Fight for the Vote

The UAW's reliance on and dedication to an elected leadership have a long history. In the early days of union organizing, the AFL had organized separate unions for individual crafts and skills. Machinists and blacksmiths could work for the same employer but be in different unions. Management could easily manipulate workers in several fragmented unions. There was great strength in craft union traditions; so much so that in 1917 the AFL suspended the Carriage and Wagon Makers Union for violating these traditions by attempting to organize across craft lines. The union responded by changing its name to United Automobile, Aircraft, and Vehicle Workers and continued organizing. During the 1920s, the AFL was directly chartering some local unions for auto workers. As a number of local charters increased, the auto workers requested that an independent union be established specifically to represent all automotive workers. The AFL leadership feared the impact of industrial workers within their organization; however, they finally relented and granted a charter on the condition that the leadership for the new union be appointed, not elected. This would allow the AFL to control the new Executive Board and, therefore, the new union, thereby removing a potential political threat. In June 1934, the AFL agreed to hold the first national conference for the United Automobile Workers Federal Labor Unions. It was over a year later when the conference finally was held in Detroit in August 1935. At the conference the 200 delegates were led to believe that they would be electing members of their Executive Board. Dissension began immediately when AFL President William Green appointed a member of his staff, Francis Dillon, as the first President of the UAW. It was clear to the early delegates that the AFL wanted to control their union. The founding members of the UAW knew they had strength in their numbers. They believed it was right to unify all automotive workers in one union, regardless of their specified craft or level of skill. The labor movement was changing, moving away from craft unions and toward large industrial unions. Over the next 18 months, tens of thousands of auto workers joined this large, new industrial union.

The following year, in April, the UAW met in South Bend, Indiana, for its second convention. Delegates voted to raise $250,000 to fund a massive organizing and membership campaign and demanded autonomy from AFL governance and freedom to elect their Executive Board. They won this right and elected Homer Martin, an auto worker and ordained Baptist minister, as their new President. They also joined the newly established Committee for Industrial Organization (CIO) in the hopes that this action would press the leadership of the AFL to aggressively pursue organizing the industrial sector. The UAW, philosophically aligned with the CIO and its industry-based leadership, began mass organizing and recruitment efforts. They gained momentum in their campaign with the use of the "sit-down strike." As mentioned earlier, this technique spurred the management of General Motors to become the first automotive company to recognize the UAW as the collective bargaining agent for GM workers. From its inception, the UAW has seen itself as a body representing the worker, skilled or nonskilled. It fought for the right to govern itself democratically, and it has maintained this style of administration. The power in the UAW today still lies in the vote. Leadership on the plant floor and nationally is dependent on how well workers feel they are being represented.

Regional Representation

The United States is divided into 12 different UAW regions for purposes of geographical representation. Each region is led by a Regional Director who appoints staff members that assist the local unions in bargaining. The Regional Directors are elected by delegates from each local union, again assuring just representation. A region will contain any number of represented companies, including all three of the Big Three. These directors sit on the Executive Board of the international union and formulate policy governing actions of the international.

Union Structure: A Parallel of the Corporate Structure

The local unions are autonomous bodies, able to spend funds, purchase property, and make decisions, much the same as an individual plant within a corporation. The 12 regions act much the same as divisions within a corporation, each one assisting at its individual locations within its region, just as individual General Managers or Vice Presidents assist the various locations within their divisions of the corporation (Fig. 2-1).

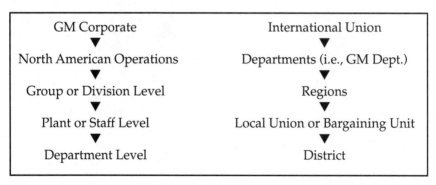

GM Corporate	International Union
▼	▼
North American Operations	Departments (i.e., GM Dept.)
▼	▼
Group or Division Level	Regions
▼	▼
Plant or Staff Level	Local Union or Bargaining Unit
▼	▼
Department Level	District

Figure 2-1

The duties of local union leaders parallel those of their management counterparts who make decisions on the basic day-to-day operations in the plant. Union leaders at the local level make decisions about the basic day-to-day operations of the union and make collective bargaining decisions that affect the membership at that particular location. Internationally, Regional Directors, along with the international officers who are elected every three years at the union's national constitutional convention, establish policy for the entire union much as corporate officials establish policy for the entire corporation. Local unions relate more closely to their regional officers than they do to the international officers, again paralleling their plant management counterparts who tend to be more open to and influenced by divisional conditions and requirements than to corporate policies in general.

The number of delegates to the national convention is based on the per capita voting strength of each local union. Delegates run at large within the local union. In most cases they are not officers within the local union but are local members who have chosen to run. The major actions of these delegates to the convention are:

- To elect, by the entire delegation, UAW officers who serve for a three-year term: President, Secretary-Treasurer, and Vice Presidents
- To elect Regional Directors by delegates from their respective regions
- To adopt constitutional amendments, resolutions, and officers' reports

Elected officers and Regional Directors compose the UAW's International Executive Board, the union's highest authority. Like the government of the United States, top leadership can be voted out—in this case every three years. These constitutional conventions are lively and energetic. Various factions use these gatherings as a forum for debate on controversial issues. Certainly joint processes have sparked a number of vigorous exchanges as we moved from a confrontational relationship with management.

Basically, the union is a large corporation that has various divisions or regions that in turn are made up of various individual locations or local unions. The major difference is in the manner in which leadership is named; in the UAW leaders are elected. The common misconception among those not familiar with the intricate workings of the union is that the union leadership is made up of a number of appointed "goons" that simply react based upon their own individual self-interests. The truth is that the UAW structure itself prohibits this from being the case since each elected leader has to answer to the members he or she represents whether it be at the local, regional, or national level.

The International Staff

There are some appointed staff members at the national and regional levels that do not have to face elections; elected officials appoint these "international representatives" much the same as corporations who elect their top officers but fill lower staff positions based upon individual qualifications and accomplishments. International Representatives are actually employees of the International Union; the Co-director of the UAW–GM Quality Network is a staff position in the General Motors department. Staff members are subject to stringent policies established by the UAW membership. They are liable for their financial decisions (that is, their fiduciary decisions) as well as their moral and ethical conduct. Additionally, national labor relations laws govern their actions, assuring that individual members can, within the compliance of the union or, if necessary, with outside assistance from the U.S. Department of Labor, appeal or challenge decisions that they consider improper. The UAW has established a totally independent public review board to which any member can appeal a decision of a UAW leader for final and binding resolution. The expenses for the hearings are paid for out of the UAW general fund; challenging a position or decision does not cost a member anything. This outside appeal board is made up of priests, rabbis, college professors, and other people whose motives to serve are based on an honest desire to see justice prevail and not on any tie to the International Union, thus ensuring the democratic process.

Counterparts

UAW leadership and the management of General Motors operate in a similar manner, although the union's goals and motives are governed by political, moral, and people considerations, whereas the corporation must also consider their obligations to shareholders and their customers. Within the joint union-corporate process, it is very easy to team up the various layers of union leadership with counterparts from the management leadership. In the joint leadership within General Motors and the UAW, the GM CEO and President and the UAW Vice President of the GM department are counterparts. This relationship extends right on down the line to the local plant level where the

President of the Local and Chairperson of the Bargaining Committee are joint partners with the Plant Manager and Personnel Director in operating joint programs at the local or plant level. These established relationships lend stability to the organization when changes in leadership occur. The structure itself establishes functional leadership positions, which are filled according to union and management processes as previously discussed. A turnover of all union and management leadership at the same time cannot occur.

Leadership on the Plant Floor

The UAW structure under GM basically places all bargaining responsibilities into the portfolio of the Chairperson of the Shop Committee. The Chairperson is the leader for the shop committee members who are elected at large from the plant. The number of shop committee members is based on the plant's population, and they represent all the various segments within the plant in bargaining sessions. The President and officers within the local union handle most administrative functions and act as political liaisons with various organizations. The UAW–GM structure as it relates to the President's role differs from other organizations in which the President would be the chief bargainer and CEO. In fact, the UAW structure, as it relates to the President's role, differs from all other companies who have the UAW as their bargaining representatives. Bargaining sessions are normally held once a week to consider everyday grievances that may arise. Issues not settled at this level are then appealed at the next step in the procedure, which involves a regional representative. Thereafter, if the issue is still unresolved, it may be discussed with an International Representative from Detroit, along with the Chairperson of the Shop Committee and local management representatives. If it is not settled at this level, the issue then proceeds to arbitration where the UAW has an arbitration staff within the GM department that handles all GM arbitration cases. The Chairperson of the Shop Committee heads the negotiating team for all local negotiations, including the local union contract that supplements the National Agreement. It was my responsibility during the 1970s to handle all the bargaining with GM at the Lordstown Fabricating Plant.

Within the UAW International, there are several Vice Presidents who oversee the major departments. For example, one Vice President has specific responsibilities for the General Motors department and oversees all national bargaining along with all national officials from the various bodies within the GM system. All national contracts have to be submitted to the entire GM membership for ratification. Local union contracts have to be approved by the members of that particular local union and location.

Stability in the Face of Changing Leadership

There is an added benefit to those of us who believe in joint processes. Management and union leaders who have worked in an environment with joint counterparts perpetuate and assist in institutionalizing a joint system due to their familiarity with standard joint processes and the communication mechanisms that support them. A good example of this would be in the General Motors–UAW system. Many top leaders came from assignments within programs established by both union and management. As they move up the union or corporate ladder into more responsible leadership positions, they further the system of joint cooperation and understanding; for them, it's become the way they do business, and they have been rewarded accordingly.

Many appointed International Representatives and local union officials whose former assignments were with the Quality Network process are currently holding leadership positions in the UAW–GM Department. Correspondingly, many leaders in the General Motors structure have been promoted through the many restructurings that have gone on, moving into areas of ever-increasing responsibility and taking their knowledge of the joint process and their commitment with them. This perpetuates the process and helps establish more mature, long-term relationships. Certainly there will be disagreements because of the different focus of each party. Traditionally, corporate officials are rated and promoted based upon their performance as reflected in the "bottom line." Union leadership is promoted based upon the political realities of their post and the requirements of the membership they represent. The dynamics of this relationship produce areas of natural agreement and also areas of natural disagreement. The key to the joint relationship is the desire on both sides to work together on things that can further the goals of both entities. On areas of disagreement, both sides must constantly look for compromises that allow both parties to efficiently and effectively coexist.

It's Not What You Hear

This complicated matching structure within both bodies is very seldom reported in the media's coverage of the interaction between the

UAW and General Motors. Most often, areas of disagreement are held up as the norm, and the demanding, day-to-day operations of plants and locations that are driven by joint processes and a commitment on the part of joint leadership to work together are overlooked. Consider the impossibility of individual work contracts with each employee in a corporation the size of General Motors. A single entity like a union is a necessity in labor and management relationships, and this relationship can mature and grow without compromising either organization's basic goals and responsibilities.

Just the Facts

*Jay Wilber on General Motors
Corporation*

Changing the way an organization runs its business is a challenge at best. Consider the challenge when the organization is over 80 years old and is considered one of the largest corporations in the world. To understand the magnitude of General Motors' transformation into the twenty-first century, it is necessary to get a grasp of its size, its institutions, and its culture. General Motors has operations in 53 countries and worldwide employment averaging 711,000. Best known as a full-line vehicle manufacturer, GM had worldwide factory sales in 1993 of more than 7.8 million motor vehicles, of which approximately 4.7 million were sold in the United States. GM manufactures and sells cars and trucks worldwide through a variety of nameplates, including Chevrolet, Pontiac, Oldsmobile, Buick, Cadillac, GMC Truck, Saturn, Opel, Vauxhall, Holden, Isuzu, and Saab. In 1993, GM's market share was 33.2 percent of the total U.S. vehicle market and 18.2 percent of the worldwide vehicle market. As of December 31, 1993, there were approximately 8665 GM motor vehicle dealers in North America and approximately 9200 dealers overseas.

In order to maintain the leveraging size and knowledge of a viable worldwide organization, General Motors also has other substantial business interests. GM's Delphi Automotive Systems (the name was changed in February 1995 from Automotive Components Group Worldwide) is a major supplier to GM, but it also supplies components and systems to every other major automotive manufacturer. General Motors Acceptance Corporation (GMAC) and its subsidiaries provide financing and insurance products to GM customers and dealers. GM Hughes Electronics Corporation (GMHE) is a specialist in automotive electronics, commercial technologies, telecommunications, and space and defense electronics. Electronic Data Systems (EDS) is a world leader in applying information technologies and has helped General Motors' internal operations prepare for the twenty-first century information management. EDS is pursuing an ever-increasing customer base outside GM, around the globe. The GM Electro-Motive Division is the second largest producer in the world of diesel-electric locomotives, and Allison Transmission is the largest U.S. producer of heavy-duty vehicle transmissions. In total, GM's 1993 worldwide sales and revenues were $138.2 billion.

Why the Focus on the U.S. Auto Industry?

The American economy cannot exist on jobs focusing on making hamburgers or pizza; rather, it must have, as its industrial foundation, good, high-paying jobs. Traditionally, the U.S. automotive industry has provided these jobs. Although we recognize that General Motors is an international company competing in the global marketplace, for our purposes we will focus on the domestic automobile business and GM's role and responsibility within this vital and viable American industry.

Economic Contributions.   The domestic motor vehicle industry is a major factor in the U.S. economy, in terms of the value of its output, the jobs it creates, the income it generates, and the taxes it pays:

- Over the last three decades, spending on new vehicles has averaged 4.4 percent of the U.S. gross domestic product (GDP).

- Collectively, the members of the American Automobile Manufacturers Association (AAMA)—GM, Ford, and Chrysler—employ over 600,000 U.S. workers in auto-related jobs, making the motor vehicle industry the largest employer among U.S. manufacturing industries. In addition, AAMA members support 900,000 jobs in the supplier industry, so that, in total, AAMA members support 19 out of every 20 jobs related to the production of cars and trucks in the United States (Fig. 2-2).

- The sale and service of completed vehicles generates further economic activity. This includes the 18,000 dealer franchises employing 650,000 people that sell and service the products of the domestic automobile industry and the more than 300,000 repair and service facilities that help to maintain the U.S. vehicle fleet.

- Among the three domestic automakers, General Motors vehicles have the highest average U.S. and Canadian domestic content at 97

Material Consumption by the Automotive Industry
(percent of U.S. total)

Percent	Material
74	Natural rubber
23	Zinc
49	Synthetic rubber
20	Semiconductors
41	Platinum
18	Aluminum
40	Machine tools
11	Steel
34	Iron
10	Copper
25	Glass
3	Plastic

Source: American Automobile Manufacturers Association (AAMA).

Figure 2-2

percent, and over 96 percent of the GM light vehicles sold in the United States are assembled in the United States and Canada.

- GM compensates its workers well for their productivity. The cost to GM for an hourly employee averages $42.72 per hour worked, about twice the average for all manufacturing firms.

- In 1993, GM paid nearly $4.3 billion in taxes, or $6.03 per share of GM common stock, to U.S. and foreign tax authorities. Also, customers purchasing GM products paid $4.7 billion in U.S. and foreign taxes, including franchise, sales, use and other local taxes, federal excise taxes, import duties, and value-added taxes. In addition, GM withheld and remitted to the U.S. government $4.2 billion in federal income taxes and social security taxes from its U.S. employees' wages (Fig. 2-3).

The auto industry also invests heavily in the research, development, and technology that helps drive the economy and is one of the most important industrial consumers of the products of other high-tech industries:

- The entire motor vehicle and equipment manufacturing industry accounted for 11.7 percent of all corporate R&D spending in the

Taxes Generated by GM Activities, 1993
(Dollars in millions)

Taxes Payable by GM to U.S. and Foreign Tax Authorities

Income taxes	$ 109.5
Payroll taxes	3,102.9
Property taxes	603.7
Federal excise taxes and import duties and/or taxes	271.6
Miscellaneous taxes	129.4
Franchise, sales, and use taxes	65.4
Total	$4,282.5

U.S. and Foreign Taxes Paid by Customers Purchasing GM Products*

Franchise, sales, use, and other local taxes	$1,203.6
Federal excise taxes and import duties and/or taxes	3,529.4
Total	$4,733.0

Employee U.S. Federal Income and Social Security Taxes Withheld by GM

Federal income tax	$2,899.3
FICA tax	1,289.7
Total	$4,189.0

*These taxes represent only those taxes paid by customers that are collected by GM and remitted to the appropriate tax authorities.

Figure 2-3

United States in 1991, according to the National Science Foundation. Worldwide R&D spending at GM alone has averaged nearly $6 billion per year in recent years.

- A GM car today with the newest engine control systems and state-of-the-art safety systems—antilock brakes, traction control, and air bags—has about five times the computing power of the onboard guidance system used in the 1969 Apollo moon shot. GM's Delco Electronics subsidiary, which built the Apollo system and is now providing electronic systems for cars, is the nation's largest single producer of microprocessors.

The importance of the domestic auto industry does not rest solely on the role it plays in the economic success of the nation. The industry and its unions have also tried to play a leadership role in many areas of corporate responsibility, ranging from the quality of products and services we provide to the ways we operate our facilities and the nature of our relationships with our employees and other stakeholders. The following sections provide examples of how GM is approaching challenges in these areas.

Industry Trends.   The domestic auto industry's continuing economic importance is proof of its ability to adapt to change. Competition provides the catalyst that drives the industry forward and challenges it to cope with the complexities of a global economy. The Big Three U.S. automakers held the *Drive American Quality* event in Washington, D.C., to display American automobiles to our government leaders. Owen Bieber, UAW President, and the CEOs of the Big Three, Jack Smith from GM, Bob Eaton from Chrysler, and Red Poling from Ford, were there as well as Labor Secretary Reich. They test-drove the best we all had to offer. At this event, President Bill Clinton underscored the importance of the automotive industry in America and its progress over the past few years:

> These cars are what is best about America: increasing productivity, increasing quality, and gaining market share back. The people who make them are the people who deserve our support, and this administration is determined to give it to them.
>
> Last year the auto industry production was 5.6 percent of our Gross National Product. In 1992, vehicle and parts manufacturing directly accounted for 4.6 percent of our manufacturing employment. During the first quarter of this year, the Big Three accounted for two out of three auto sales in the United States, with the American cars gaining market share in 1993. This did not happen by accident. It required investment, it required reorganization, it required some reductions in spending. Over the last three years, $73 billion have been invested by the Big Three. Since 1981 quality has dramatically improved. The number of customer-reported defects is down by 80 percent. And many of our American cars, by any quality measure, are better than their foreign competitors today.[4]

Productivity and Quality Improvements.   In the mid-eighties, the combined effects of an overvalued dollar and the significant productivity advantage enjoyed by many Japanese manufacturers placed U.S. auto manufacturers at an estimated cost disadvantage of $1500 to $2500 per vehicle. The industry responded by improving productivity and quality much faster than its foreign competition thought possible, which has contributed to recaptured domestic market share.

■ Today, the cost disadvantage from productivity has generally disappeared, largely because productivity of the most efficient U.S. plants is about the same as the most efficient Japanese plants and superior to those of Daimler Benz, BMW, and Volvo. Getting the health care costs of domestic automakers more in line with those of the U.S. operations of foreign-based manufacturers would further reduce the cost disadvantage.

■ The U.S. industry also has succeeded in virtually closing the quality gap vis-à-vis overseas competitors. In 1981, the average North American–produced passenger car had about seven problems reported after 90 days of ownership, while owners of Japanese-built cars reported an average of two problems per vehicle. In 1993, the gap between the average GM car and the average Japanese car was less than one-sixth of a problem per car.

■ Since J.D. Power and Associates began giving awards for quality to the top three plants in 1990, only GM and Toyota had won the awards through 1993.

The improved quality of American vehicles, together with the superior value that American manufacturers are now able to deliver because of enhanced productivity, is reflected in a turnaround in market shares. After 10 years of losing ground to foreign nameplates, AAMA members' share of light vehicle sales rose to 73.9 percent in the United States and 72.1 percent in Canada in 1993, up from 72.2 percent and 69.3 percent, respectively, in 1992.

Expanding Role of Exports. Even more dramatic, the U.S. industry is positioned to become a larger player in export markets. With the trend toward more favorable economic and trade policies here and abroad, the United States has become the lowest-cost production site in the world for many types of vehicles. These factors have helped to fuel a fourfold increase in exports by GM, Ford, and Chrysler since 1986.

In 1993, GM remained the largest exporter of vehicles from the United States by sending 109,760 fully assembled and 22,920 partially assembled vehicles to markets outside of North America. Exports from GM's Automotive Components Group Worldwide (now known as Delphi Automotive Systems) increased 10 percent in 1993. Indeed, GM is becoming more reliant on export sales for growth, mirroring the experience of U.S. businesses generally. Since 1988, approximately 70 percent of U.S. economic growth has come from expanding exports to international markets.

Currently, the Middle East is GM's largest vehicle export market, followed by Europe and Latin America. In addition, initiatives are

under way to expand into the former Soviet Union, other former
Eastern Bloc nations, China, and Africa and to increase GM's presence
in Japan and South Korea. With a mature U.S. market and many of the
countries in the European Union in recession, the fast-growing Latin
American and Asia-Pacific markets have become increasingly attractive.[5]

Managing the GM Giant

The General Motors Board of Directors, elected by GM stockholders
and chaired by John G. Smale, oversees the global decisions of this
immense and influential corporation. The day-to-day management of
GM operations is accomplished through a series of *strategy boards* with
CEO and President John F. Smith, Jr., at the helm of the President's
Council.

The days when independent, powerful leaders focused only on their
part of the business are gone as GM can no longer afford the luxury of
competing with itself. Today we are rewarding and recognizing managers who focus on external competition and customer satisfaction
and not those who try to make themselves look good at the expense of
others or at the expense of suboptimizing the total system. A spirit of
teamwork and partnering to maximize the capability of the entire system has replaced the former "lone ranger" approach.

From the Minds of Many. GM is managed by several Strategy
Boards chaired by a top executive. Those boards are identified in Fig. 2-4.
North American Operations (NAO) currently presents the greatest chal-

Strategy Board	Chairperson
Global	CEO and President
North American Operations	President of North American Operations
Delphi Automotive Systems	President of Delphi Automotive Systems
GM Europe	President of GM Europe
International Operations	President of International Operations

Figure 2-4

lenge and opportunity for GM to leverage its immense intellectual capability. As a result, we will focus our discussion on NAO.

North American Operations.   General Motors' North American Operations accounts for the largest vehicle customer base of any of GM's worldwide organizations (5,198,000 of a total 1993 worldwide sales of 7,785,000 units). The sheer size of NAO requires a different management approach and philosophy than has been prevalent in GM's recent past. No longer can one individual make all the decisions for each sector of NAO's operations without considering the impact such decisions will have on the entire NAO system. As such, the NAO Strategy Board, led by NAO President Rick Wagoner, has become the decision body for all U.S. vehicle, engineering, manufacturing, and marketing operations. Figure 2-5 lists the GM groups represented on the NAO Strategy Board.

NAO has four primary vehicle manufacturing business units plus a sales, service, and marketing unit, as depicted in Fig. 2-6. The objective for these business units is "to satisfy the customers' vehicle and service needs and wants profitably."

In order to maintain consistency across these units in terms of such things as vehicle engineering methodology, planning, finance, purchasing, and personnel matters, support units have been established as depicted in Fig. 2-7. The objective for these support units is "to support business units in satisfying customers through the development and application of effective and efficient common business processes."

North American Operations Strategy Board

President and Chairperson, NAO Strategy Board
NAO Planning
Midsize and Luxury Car Group
NAO Business Support Group and GM of Mexico
NAO Personnel
Worldwide Purchasing
Small Car Group
NAO Vehicle Development and Technical Operations Group
GM Powertrain Group
NAO Finance
North American Truck Group
North American Vehicle Sales, Service, and Marketing Group

Figure 2-5

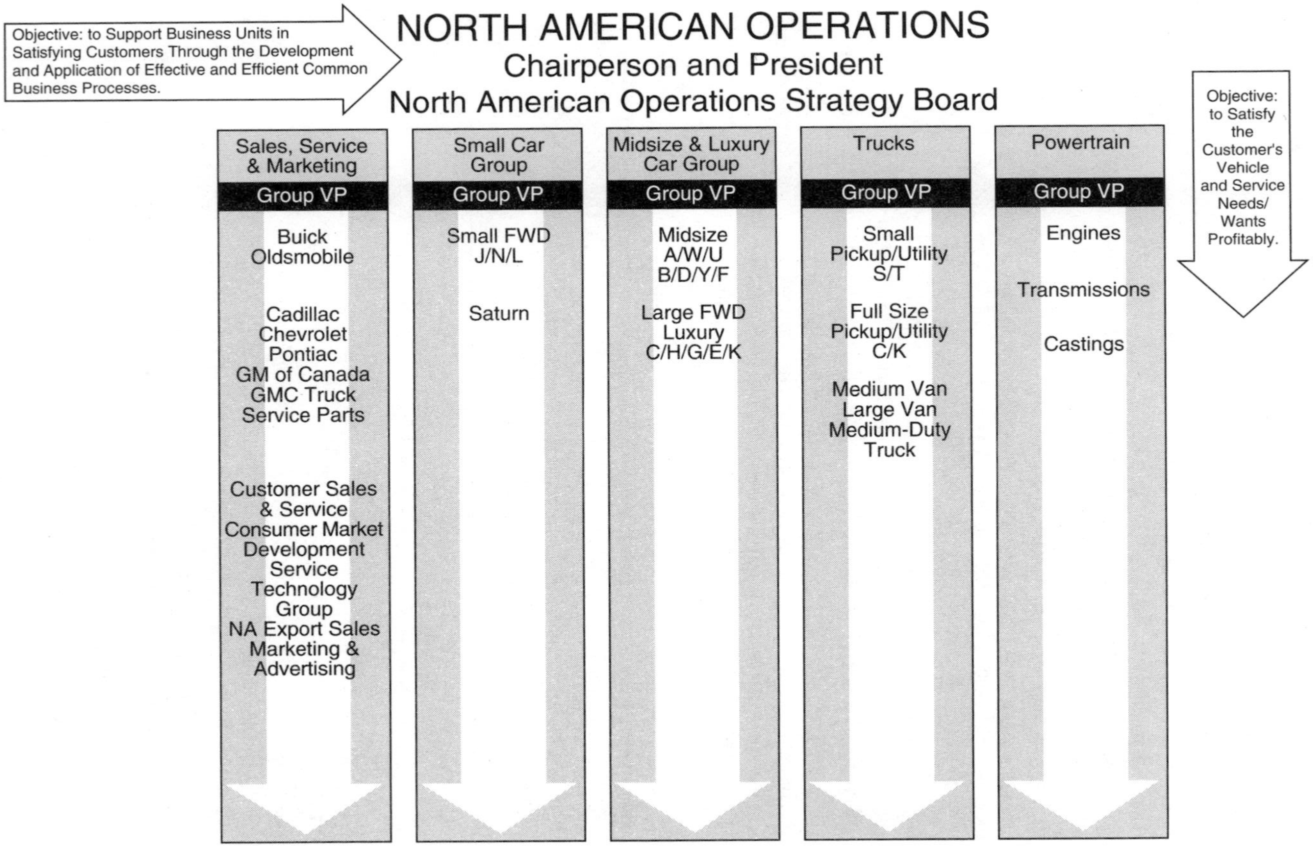

NORTH AMERICAN OPERATIONS
Chairperson and President
North American Operations Strategy Board

Objective: to Support Business Units in Satisfying Customers Through the Development and Application of Effective and Efficient Common Business Processes.

Objective: to Satisfy the Customer's Vehicle and Service Needs/ Wants Profitably.

Sales, Service & Marketing	Small Car Group	Midsize & Luxury Car Group	Trucks	Powertrain
Group VP	Group VP	Group VP	Group VP	Group VP
Buick Oldsmobile	Small FWD J/N/L	Midsize A/W/U B/D/Y/F	Small Pickup/Utility S/T	Engines Transmissions
Cadillac Chevrolet Pontiac GM of Canada GMC Truck Service Parts	Saturn	Large FWD Luxury C/H/G/E/K	Full Size Pickup/Utility C/K	Castings
Customer Sales & Service Consumer Market Development Service Technology Group NA Export Sales Marketing & Advertising			Medium Van Large Van Medium-Duty Truck	

Figure 2-6

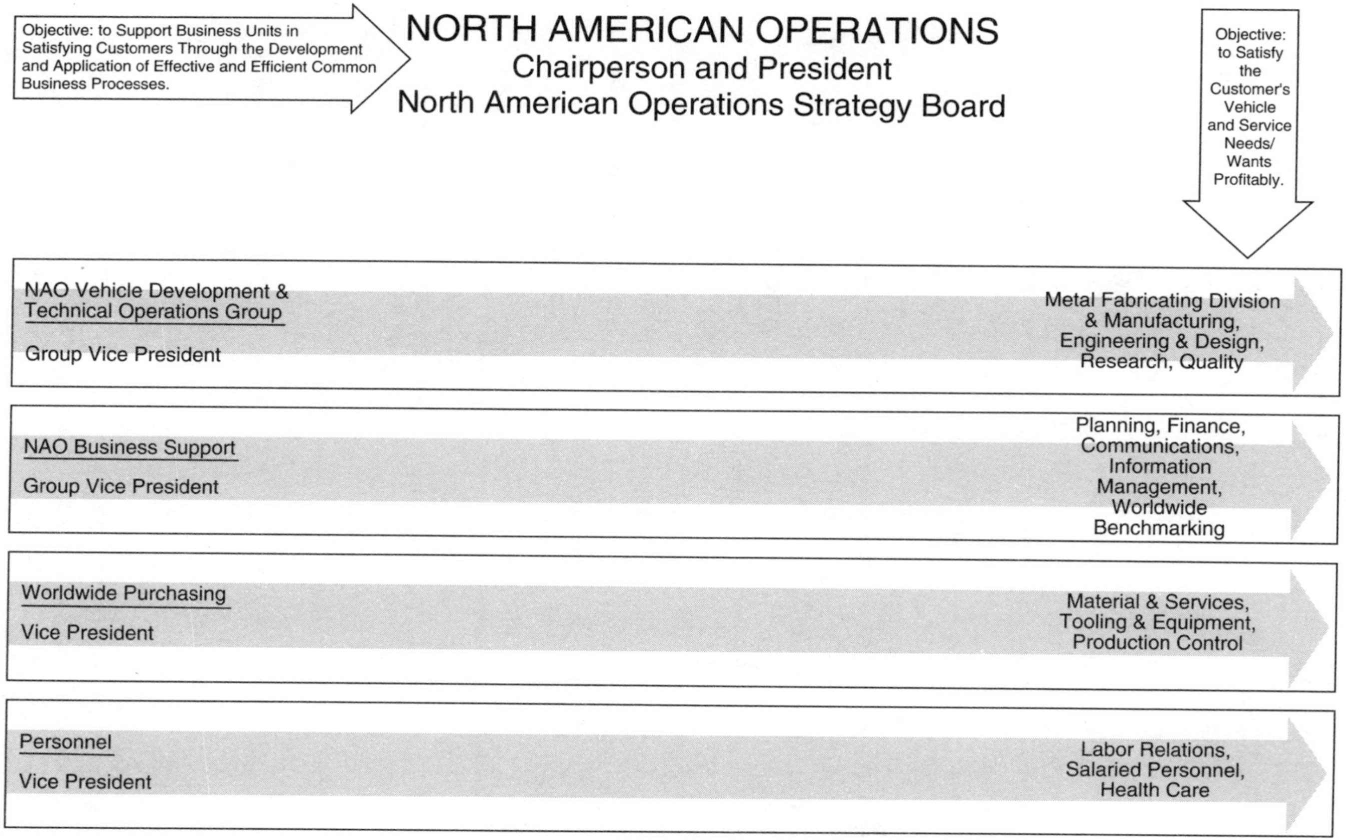

NORTH AMERICAN OPERATIONS
Chairperson and President
North American Operations Strategy Board

Objective: to Support Business Units in Satisfying Customers Through the Development and Application of Effective and Efficient Common Business Processes.

Objective: to Satisfy the Customer's Vehicle and Service Needs/ Wants Profitably.

NAO Vehicle Development & Technical Operations Group

Group Vice President

Metal Fabricating Division & Manufacturing, Engineering & Design, Research, Quality

NAO Business Support

Group Vice President

Planning, Finance, Communications, Information Management, Worldwide Benchmarking

Worldwide Purchasing

Vice President

Material & Services, Tooling & Equipment, Production Control

Personnel

Vice President

Labor Relations, Salaried Personnel, Health Care

Figure 2-7

41

These business and support units work together, mindful of the required internal-external, customer-supplier relationships. The interrelationships of the business and support units are depicted through the marriage of Figs. 2-6 and 2-7 into what is referred to as the "Basketweave" organizational structure, as shown in Fig. 2-8.

The NAO Basketweave structure is the result of a series of organizational refinements accomplished over the past decade of reorganization. GM has recognized that customer satisfaction can result only from a well-organized team focused on external competition. Pontiac competing against Chevrolet and vice versa made the internal team allegiance stronger but failed to focus our resources on the true competition—Ford, Toyota, and so on.

The critical factor in the NAO Basketweave structure is the success of the customer-supplier relationships defined at the intersection of the horizontal and vertical weaves or at the interface points between the business and support units. For example, how does the NAO Vehicle Development and Technical Operations Group interface with each of the business units to ensure the learning that occurs from project to project is retained through organizational memory and shared across all business units? Successful implementation of common systems and processes is contingent upon learning being transmitted across well-defined intersection points and relationships.

The single greatest challenge in an organizational structure of this nature is getting everyone to understand the necessity of optimizing the total system. For example, Chevrolet Marketing in the Small Car Group may have to be willing to forgo a new Chevrolet car model because research suggests the money and/or resources would be better utilized in developing a new GMC truck for the North American Truck Group. In the past, strong nameplate marketing management for Chevrolet would have possibly preempted the resources away from GMC Truck, and that would have been the end of the discussion. Today the right decisions are being made to optimize the total system.

Obviously, in a company the size of General Motors and in a business sector the size of NAO, not all of these critical relationships have been defined, nor are all the decision makers in harmony, but the learning that has occurred has resulted in a much better understanding of the necessity of optimizing the total system.

Delphi Automotive Systems. On February 13, 1995, GM's Automotive Components Group Worldwide moved to unify its divisional names and clarify its identity by changing its name to Delphi Automotive Systems (Delphi-AS). It is composed of six operating divisions and three regional marketing units (Europe, Asia-Pacific, and South

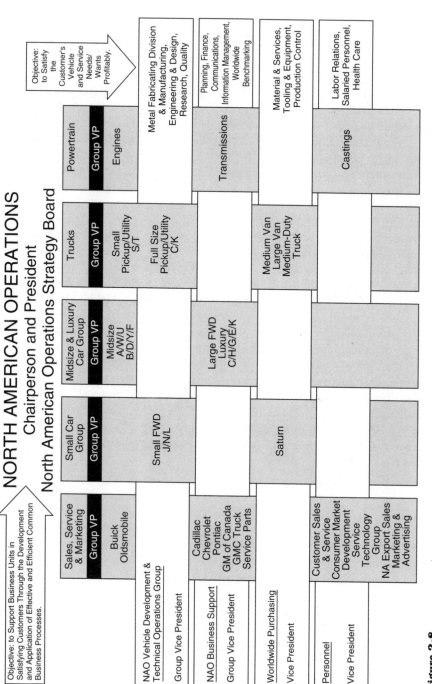

NORTH AMERICAN OPERATIONS
Chairperson and President
North American Operations Strategy Board

Objective: to Support Business Units in Satisfying Customers Through the Development and Application of Effective and Efficient Common Business Processes.

Objective: to Satisfy the Customer's Vehicle and Service Needs/ Wants Profitably.

	Sales, Service & Marketing	Small Car Group	Midsize & Luxury Car Group	Trucks	Powertrain
	Group VP	Group VP	Group VP	Group VP	Group VP
	Buick Oldsmobile	Small FWD J/N/L	Midsize A/W/U B/D/Y/F	Small Pickup/Utility S/T	Engines
NAO Vehicle Development & Technical Operations Group — Group Vice President				Full Size Pickup/Utility C/K	Metal Fabricating Division & Manufacturing, Engineering & Design, Research, Quality
NAO Business Support — Group Vice President	Cadillac Chevrolet Pontiac GM of Canada GMC Truck Service Parts		Large FWD Luxury C/H/G/E/K		Transmissions
					Planning, Finance, Communications, Information Management, Worldwide Benchmarking
Worldwide Purchasing — Vice President		Saturn		Medium Van Large Van Medium-Duty Truck	Material & Services, Tooling & Equipment, Production Control
Personnel — Vice President	Customer Sales & Service Consumer Market Development Service Technology Group NA Export Sales Marketing & Advertising				Castings
					Labor Relations, Salaried Personnel, Health Care

Figure 2-8

43

America). Delphi-AS accounts for the second largest portion of GM's manufacturing operations in North America. Although it is a separate business sector to allow for a global focus, Delphi-AS is inextricably linked to NAO's success. Delphi-AS is the single largest component supplier to NAO, and it is one of GM's greatest assets. It employs over 172,000 people at 190 locations in 31 countries. In 1994 Delphi-AS sales totaled $26.1 billion. Close partnering with the Delphi-AS allows NAO to leverage technology, processes, systems, and people across NAO business units. High-volume components and systems utilization reduce development cost and leverage high volume for capital utilization.

Delphi Automotive Systems is lead by Senior Vice President J. T. Battenberg III, who also is President of Delphi-AS and chairs its Strategy Board. This Strategy Board functions much like the NAO Strategy Board except that it has a worldwide focus. Figure 2-9 depicts the Delphi-AS organizational structure.

The business units depicted by the vertical bars—Delphi Chassis Systems, Delphi Packard Electric Systems, Delphi Energy & Engine Management, Delphi Saginaw Steering Systems, Delphi Harrison Thermal Systems, and Delphi Interior & Lighting Systems—are the divisions of Delphi Automotive Systems, and they produce a broad range of components and systems for GM's worldwide operations. Delphi-AS is also a major supplier of automotive components to other vehicle manufacturers all over the world.

The horizontal bars represent lean support activities made up of a small number of representatives from Delphi-AS headquarters, with the lion's share of the representation coming from the divisional staffs such as financial, manufacturing, and quality. Several cross business unit task teams have the responsibility to leverage the Delphi Automotive Systems resources to maximize the system and opportunities.

The Action Is at the Intersections

The key success factor to these critical and major pieces of GM's total system lies with the organization's ability to define required internal relationships. These relationships (internal customer-supplier) can be seen in Figs. 2-8 and 2-9 where the horizontal and vertical organizations cross. However, NAO and Delphi-AS must also interact to define the customer-supplier relationships required. This interaction adds a third dimension to these two-dimensional models. We've attempted to capture this relationship in the model in Fig. 2-10.

As you can see, this is becoming complicated. How do we maximize

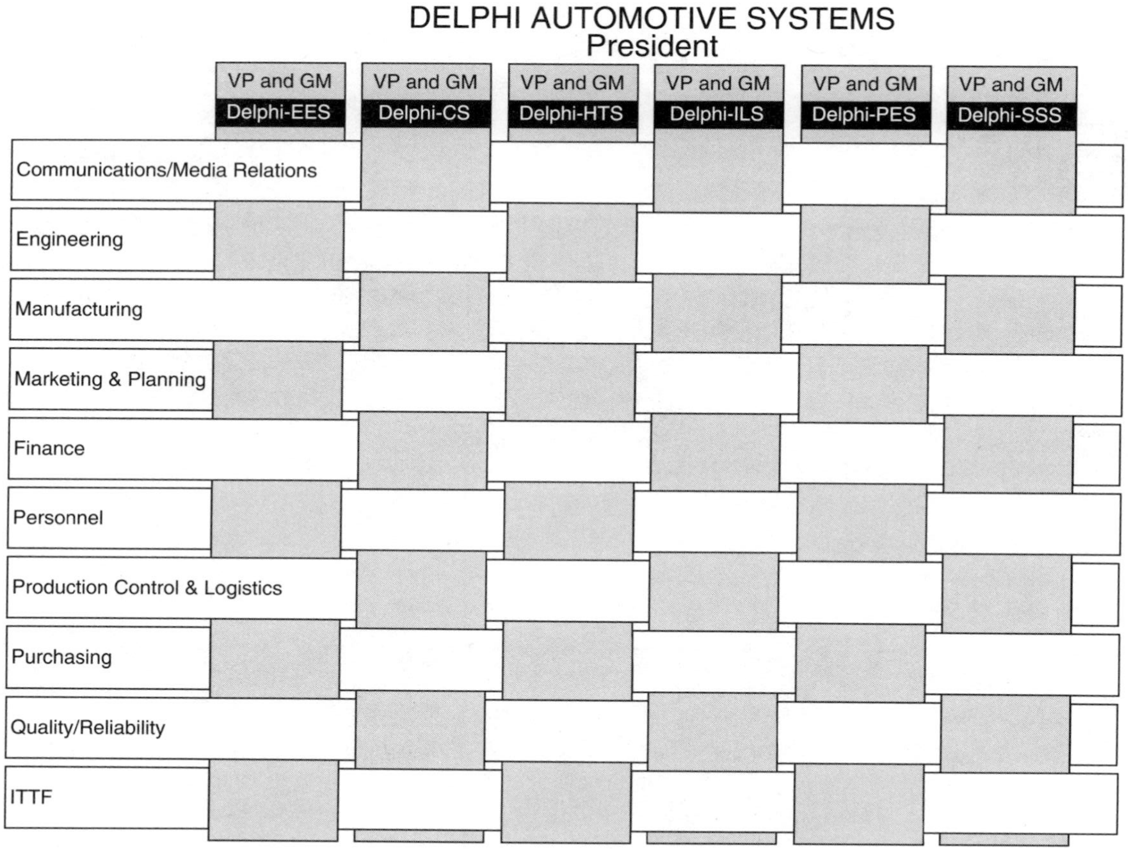

DELPHI AUTOMOTIVE SYSTEMS
President

	VP and GM Delphi-EES	VP and GM Delphi-CS	VP and GM Delphi-HTS	VP and GM Delphi-ILS	VP and GM Delphi-PES	VP and GM Delphi-SSS
Communications/Media Relations						
Engineering						
Manufacturing						
Marketing & Planning						
Finance						
Personnel						
Production Control & Logistics						
Purchasing						
Quality/Reliability						
ITTF						

Figure 2-9

45

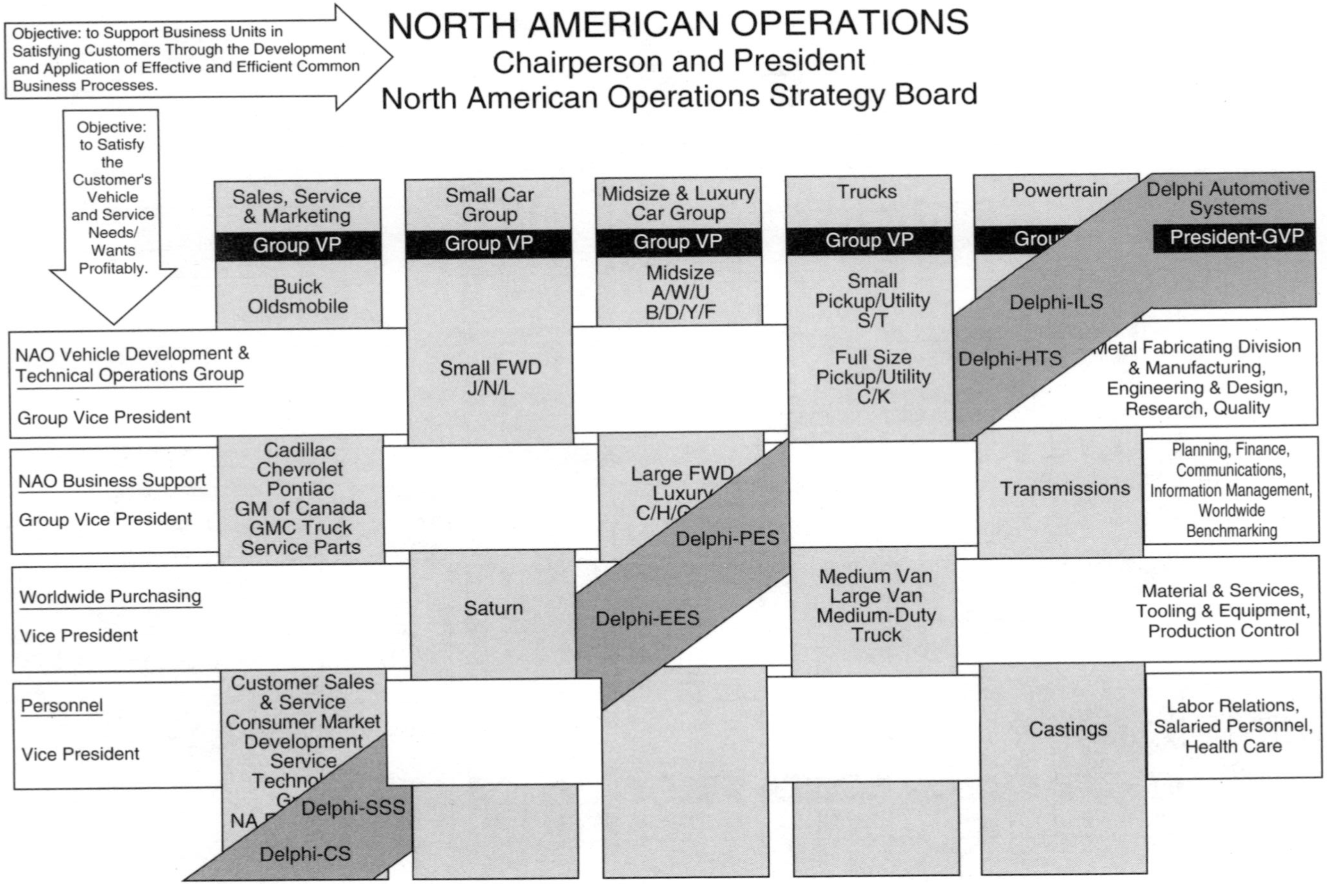

NORTH AMERICAN OPERATIONS
Chairperson and President
North American Operations Strategy Board

Figure 2-10

46

the total system, partner within the organization to define internal customer-supplier relationships, and at the same time maintain our focus on the ultimate customer: the men and women who buy our cars and trucks or utilize our services? At General Motors we are managing this process through the principles of total quality management (TQM), and at NAO and Delphi we are partnering with our unions.

How did we get from a sit-down strike in Flint in 1937 to a partnership for the future in 1995? Mostly by both parties actively formulating a framework around which to work together. Sometimes the framework could be described as adversarial, but both sides know the rules and act accordingly. As the relationship has matured and times have changed, so have we.

Quality at the Bargaining Table.   In the early years, the union bargained for wage increases, a grievance procedure, and recognition of seniority in matters of layoff and recall. However, there was another issue that was included; the earliest UAW–GM agreements specifically recognized and emphasized the importance of product quality to both parties. The 1940 GM–UAW National Agreement, which had grown to 39 pages, stated in its introduction:

> The management of General Motors recognizes that it cannot get along without labor any more than labor can get along without the management. Both are in the same business and the success of that business is vital to all concerned. This requires that both management and the employees work together to the end that quality and cost of the product will prove increasingly attractive to the public so that the business will be continuously successful.

Framing the Quality Vision.   These words, although noble in intent, described a vision that would take years to accomplish. Even though this introduction has been included in every UAW–GM national agreement since 1940, in the early years of the relationship the parties found their efforts expended on social and physical environmental issues for hourly employees. This focus took precedence over stated productivity and product quality concerns. In succeeding years programs were initiated to address social and environmental issues such as the quality of work life (QWL) programs. For the most part, such QWL programs fell short of expectations because there were no structured mechanisms linking their efforts to plans for tangible productivity gains and quality improvements. However, there were pockets of success. Early efforts were important stepping stones for future joint quality efforts since it recognized people as important assets of General Motors. Over the years various efforts addressed product quality; however, most efforts were management driven following traditional lines of thinking (e.g., additional inspection, postproduction repair, and additional supervisory involvement).

QWL Programs. Process management systems are an extension of earlier quality of work life programs aimed at benefiting the worker by making work a more satisfying experience, benefiting the company by leading to a reduction in employee absenteeism and turnover, and eventually benefiting the customer through improvement in the quality of the product that is being produced. Early work by the American Center for Quality of Working Life stated the following:

> In early 1977, in an effort to clarify the meaning of the term, the staff of the American Center for the Quality of Working Life (QWL) developed a definition of QWL improvements as "any activity which takes place at every level of an organization which seeks greater organizational effectiveness through the enhancement of human dignity and growth." This definition stresses that QWL efforts have two goals: Enhancing life at work and increasing effectiveness of both companies and unions. Toward these ends, "the stakeholders in the organization—management, union(s), and employees—learn how to work together better...to determine for themselves what actions, changes, and improvements are desirable and workable.[6]

Quality of work life became a buzzword familiar to engineers, line supervisors, vice presidents, and the workers on the plant floor. In the 1970s and early 1980s, specific and formal programs were implemented in the auto industry to establish quality of work life programs. These early attempts at workplace democracy paved the way for process management systems that offer the opportunity for workers to become part of not only the decision-making process but also all aspects of the production process. A specific awareness phase was established during which each local plant began to explore ways to involve workers in the decision-making process. Both union and management examined each other's motives and openly talked about ways of cooperating in the future. They agreed that there would be no attempt to unilaterally initiate the quality of work life program unless agreed to by the workers' representatives.

The Sun Rises Over Detroit. The 1980s brought competitive pressures not faced in the past by domestic automobile manufacturers. General Motors Corporation in particular, but all domestic auto manufacturers in general, lost substantial market share to Japanese competitors. In the past, Japanese cars were known for boxy styling, poor quality, cheap, unsafe construction, and poor handling. Today, some of these competitors are recognized as leaders in quality, styling, safety, and design.

During the gasoline shortages of the late 1960s and early 1970s, consumers switched from large, less fuel efficient vehicles to smaller, fuel-efficient cars and trucks. Japanese automobile manufacturers, who learned their lesson in earlier attempts at penetrating the North American market with poor-quality, low-value vehicles, adopted a philosophy of continuous incremental improvements to transform their products into efficient high-quality, reliable vehicles. The concept of continuous improvement advocated an ongoing effort to improve the quality through small incremental changes, ultimately leading to as close to a perfect product as possible.

Clouds on the Horizon.   In contrast, North American automobile manufacturers continued to pursue the course of occasional mass changes of their models with an emphasis on production, rather than on high quality. There was limited emphasis on recognition of the needs of workers and the impact of failure to effectively use their knowledge and talents to satisfy customers.

Market Changes.   Consumer attitudes began to change and quality became the focus as competitively priced Japanese automobiles began to offer the features desired, competing head on in most vehicle classes dominated by domestic manufacturers. In the 1970s, North American domestic automobile manufacturers found themselves beginning to compete for market share in an industry they had formerly dominated.

Ironically, prior to this period General Motors had held such a commanding market share that it was widely rumored that antitrust action was being considered. It was alleged that not only did it command nearly 50 percent of the U.S. automobile market but also at will could have driven out several of the other competitors.

A Culture for Consistency.   Japanese manufacturers realized that a high-quality product, at a competitive price, would cause a paradigm shift. The Japanese culture had also permeated the workplace, resulting in worker involvement throughout the entire manufacturing process. As a result, workers were committed to corporate missions and goals. Domestic automobile company leaders began to heed the then radical manufacturing and human factor principles advocated by W. Edwards Deming and Joseph M. Juran.

Anyone who questions the success of this total quality–people orientation approach need only look at our recent past for validation and proof. In the 1950s and 1960s Japanese products were clearly associated with the word *junk*. *Low cost, low quality,* and *low durability* accurately described most Japanese products imported to the United States or other countries. Dr. W. Edwards Deming, an advocate of statistical process control and continuous improvement, introduced his ideas to Japanese industrial leaders who grasped his long-term intent. In her book, *The World of W. Edwards Deming,* his longtime secretary Cecelia S. Kilian outlines his success among the Japanese following his initial visits there. His theories were accepted by Japanese management who began plans for full implementation of systems theory. Long-term goals would focus on providing high-quality, high-durability, low-cost goods and services. Short-term profits were sacrificed for long-term viability, survival, and profitability. Workers were referred to as "team members" and "associates" and were made a part of the decision-making process.

The Japanese commitment to people as a vital asset resulted in winning the loyalty of the Japanese worker. Certainly the social environment allowed this radical approach to managing people to evolve and be perfected. Ultimately, quality began to be everyone's goal. Training received top priority. From the concept designers, to the press operator, to the final process person, a sense of common concern and unity emerged that encouraged incremental changes in design and manufacturing, based on worker involvement. Japanese products were recognized for their quality as well as styling, fuel efficiency, and reliability. Consumers in North America became more discriminating as the Japanese automobile created this paradigm shift in quality and durability.

Effects of the Storm.   During the fifties and sixties in the United States most markets were dominated by American companies who could sell things as fast as they could be made. Production line methods pioneered by Henry Ford and others turned out an unending flow of goods with limited focus on quality. A repair, inspect, or fix-it-later mentality prevailed. Experts like Dr. Deming were given little recognition, and overall systems theory with its emphasis on long-term vision was largely ignored.

General Motors escaped major reductions in market share until the late 1980s when a series of marketing and design miscues led to a line of products that customers perceived looked alike and that were overshadowed by Japanese quality and reliability. The dominant player in the world market saw its U.S. market share drop below 35 percent in automobiles, and found customer satisfaction to be at an all-time low.

In direct relation to its market share loss, employee morale was being impacted.

In the 1970s and 1980s a gradual transition took place as the long-term vision of the Japanese began paying great dividends. Their products became recognized as having changed and were now regarded as high quality, high durability, and low cost. American industries long dominated by the well-known companies began to lose market share to their offshore quality-minded competitors. By 1990 the transition was almost complete. Many world consumers actually began to prefer Japanese goods over U.S. suppliers even in the United States.

American industry could no longer afford the "home-run" mentality that had served them so well in the past. Complete redesign and dramatic technical breakthroughs could not be counted on alone to recapture lost market share. Additionally, reduced market share eliminated the luxury of being able to have quality goals of less than 100 percent while boosting prices to cover rework, scrap, and warranty repair and replacement.

American industry found itself using outdated manufacturing, design, and engineering processes and methods, yet was reluctant to abandon the successful strategies of the past. Many long-term, well-known organizations were driven out of business because of their inability or unwillingness to change. American industry was on the decline and its industrial might threatened by an ideology that advocated continuous improvement and employee involvement.

Reacting to the Thunder.   Domestic manufacturers continued to utilize antiquated, inefficient methods and systems that did not effectively integrate the needs and requirements of the people doing the work or respond adequately to customer requirements and demands. General Motors attempted to address this issue by installing high-tech, highly automated production systems to reduce labor costs. Massive investments in automation were made to try to restore General Motors' competitive edge only to find that the performance of automated equipment fell short of expectations. Japanese competitors, however, implemented "lean" manufacturing systems that better utilized people and technology to streamline and create efficient processes through small, incremental, continuous improvements. Additionally, the Japanese experienced major breakthrough improvements and innovations as a result of their continuous improvement efforts.

The Icarus Paradox.   People, recognized today as the greatest asset of General Motors, became disillusioned and disheartened. Employees were not encouraged to provide necessary and meaningful input into the production process. Supervisors were focused on the production schedule and not necessarily on product quality. General Motors, having once had the luxury of being able to allow its divisions to compete against one another—Pontiac against Chevrolet and Buick against Oldsmobile—could no longer do so. The ability to rely on competition within itself to create a better product changed from a strength to a liability. This permitted repetitive and costly efforts to "reinvent the wheel." As outside competitors became more efficient, General Motors' internal competition became its greatest liability. Sheer size maintained dividends, but an undercutting of the foundation of the corporation began to insidiously eat away at the heart of General Motors. In his book *The Icarus Paradox* author Danny Miller likens such problems to the mythical figure Icarus, who made wings of feathers and wax and then began to fly. He was so enamored with his success that he flew closer and closer to the sun. The wax melted, the wings came apart, and Icarus became a victim of his own success.

Preserving the American Dream.   In the early 1980s, union leaders focused on the general need for worker participation in order to retain domestic jobs for American workers. This issue was critical to the union if the standard of living of the American worker was to be preserved. During the same period, a few management officials began to recognize that an overreliance on high-volume manufacturing resulted in inflexible processes that made it difficult for workers to respond quickly to the production changes necessary to meet customer requirements efficiently. At the same time, a greater recognition of people, the skills they possessed, and the processes that allowed their input began to be a greater focus of both parties. Within management, however, there was some confusion about the implications of worker participation. Some were concerned that such participation would open the doors to higher levels of union involvement in the running of the business.

A Sense of Urgency.   John Debbink, retired GM Vice President and Group Executive, Power Products and Defense, painted the picture in a speech he gave in March 1989 before the union and management leadership of his organization.

> We now have to radically change how we do business. Why are we doing this?...We've talked about our own self-interests, but we're all not really doing it just for ourselves. We're all part of a larger group, be it a union or a plant, and usually we all want to be part of a group and contribute successfully to it. You are not leaders on an

ego trip;...many of you are leaders because you sincerely want to do something better for the group, bettering other people. And perhaps there is an even greater motivation, being in this for the betterment of other people as part of a wider group. I guess you could say General Motors Corporation is one wider group we're interested in bettering, making it survive. And that survival is important not only to millions of retirees and stockholders, but we need, as a corporation, to be a survivor. We don't want to go the way of the television industry, radio, textiles, shoes, motorcycles, half the steel industry, and the subcompact part of our own industry—it's all gone.

So, we're really talking about not just the survival of our industry—we really need to translate it to survival of the United States as we know it in industrial America. If we who comprise GM ... can't do it, what major American industry can? Who can survive better than us, with our resources, our talents, and our people? If we can't do it, who in America is going to do it?

You know, right now our principal exports to Japan are scrap iron, coal, soybeans, grain, lumber, and oil. All of these raw materials. Our imports from Japan are cars, TVs, video cameras, hi-fis, machinery, and computer parts. Well, that's the classical definition of a colony. You send somebody your raw materials, they put the value-added on it, and they get the hog's share of the profit.

Think back just over 200 years. That was the mercantile arrangement we had with England. We were a colony, and we didn't like it then, and I suggest we're not going to like it a damn bit better now....We can be part of the answer. We can have an influence at a place where it counts, the place where we work.[7]

Transformation Begins.   The stage was set for General Motors to make radical, far-reaching, corporate changes. A new process to change the corporate culture of General Motors was implemented to create a "people" environment conducive to quality, not only in product but in human factors areas as well.

Notes

1. Alfred P. Sloan, Jr., letter to "All Employees In General Motors Factories," October 15, 1934.

2. Ibid.

3. Dave Elsila, editor, *We Make Our Own History: A Portrait of the UAW*, International Union, UAW, Detroit, 1986, p. 30.

4. President William Clinton, remarks by the President at *Drive American Quality* event at the National Air and Space Museum, Washington, D.C., May 25, 1993.

5. All GM data excerpted directly from *General Motors Public Interest Report, 1994*, General Motors Industry Government Relations, Detroit, MI, pp. 2–4.

6. J. Ball & L. Ozley, "Quality of Work Life: How Do People do it and not do it," *The Warton Annual*, 1983, p. 152, cited in T. Weekley, *Total Quality Management From a Joint Management and Labor Perspective*, The Graduate School of The Union Institute, Cincinnati, OH, 1993.

7. John Debbink, speech before Power Products and Defense Quality Councils, Quality Network Leadership Seminar, March 1989.

3
General Motors Moves to Total Quality

Aligning the Arrows

Where We Were in the Eighties

January through March of 1989 General Motors launched its Quality Network, its proclaimed one total quality process for customer satisfaction. A series of 10 leadership seminars was held, and each seminar focused on a particular group, such as the Power Products and Defense Group, which was led by John Debbink and his union counterpart, Jim Wagner, Assistant Director of the GM Department of the UAW. Debbink's concluding remarks concerning the current state of our business and the sense of urgency he conveyed summed up the feelings of most of the 4500 union and management leadership who participated in the seminars. The good news in 1989 was that we had a plan and a corporationwide, jointly developed quality process to use. The bad news was that we were in dire need of an overhaul. The challenge was a massive corporate culture change.

Organizational Transformation

General Motors recognized the need for a formal process management system. It also recognized that it needed its unions to be involved and committed. Very few partnerships have been formalized in the joint labor union–management arena focusing on a total quality process. The jointly developed Quality Network *is* General Motors' Total Quality Process. The unions that work with General Motors on a day-to-day basis have agreed to a commitment to product quality. This agreement wasn't taken lightly by any of the union officers for the various unions involved. If General Motors is not competitive, if General Motors shrinks as a company, the membership represented is negatively affected.

The leadership seminars were designed to bring union and management leaders together and get them started at the same time and the same place, hearing the same things. It isn't easy asking people to radically change the way they do business. Yet, that is exactly what the leaders of GM and the UAW were asking them to do. There was resistance on both sides, and it is understandable.

The organizational transformation chart in Fig. 3-1 illustrates how General Motors is moving from an old, traditional organization to a new, transformed organization, based on the Quality Network. It was this vision of the future state that was introduced at the leadership seminars. Participants came from across the corporation and represented every step of the transformation chart. Some people were almost at the top of the chart. For others this was all new—they had not begun to change and knew little or nothing about the plan. Most were somewhere in the middle. Some wanted to change, others emphatically did not, still others did not know how. While some wanted the transformation to happen quickly, others were deliberate and wanted to move slowly and cautiously. Most were caught between the two forces and were filled with doubt and fear, unable to commit to change. We are much further along today than we were in 1989, but we still have people all along the continuum. It is the nature of change.

One thing was certain in 1989, for General Motors and its union partners the imperative was obvious. As Dr. Deming has said many times, "Survival is not mandatory." Jim Wagner made it more personal. In his remarks at the leadership seminar he talked about the loss of market share GM had suffered and the resulting loss of jobs. At that time, the rule of thumb was that 1 point of market share lost meant 10,000 jobs lost. Jim spoke from 29 years of experience on the interna-

ORGANIZATIONAL TRANSFORMATION

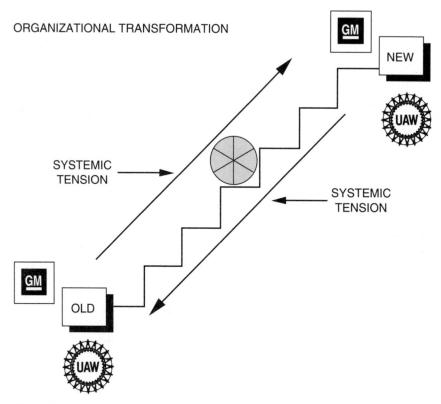

Figure 3-1.

tional staff of the UAW. He asked why Roger Penske had been able to produce over 5000 engines per year at Detroit Diesel, with a target of 10,000 for the following year, when only 1000 engines were produced under General Motors' ownership? The people and plant were the same. When Jim was the Servicing Rep for the General Motors plant in Fremont, California, grievances had exceeded 8000, and, as he put it, "we were not producing quality vehicles." Then General Motors entered into a joint venture with Toyota, New United Motors Manufacturing Inc. (NUMMI). Again, same people and same plant. Now, in a short time, they were producing a fine automobile, the Chevy Nova, first in quality. Finally he talked about how GM's Electro-Motive Division had once produced five to six locomotives per day with a work force of 13,000. At the time Jim spoke, the work force numbered 1700. And so, he asked "Why?" and proceeded to answer his own question, bluntly stating the case for change:

Because, my friends, we are not attending to business. Somebody along the line figured we were a prosperous corporation...I'm not pointing a finger, both sides are in this...and let all these jobs go. Seems to me there is a story here, behind this. You know, there's not going to be a job out there unless we have the market. There is not a corporation in this world that is going to provide you jobs if they have no market for what you are producing.

I would like to say to you now...take heed of what you see here, take it back home, apply it....Earlier a Chairman (from one of our plants) walked up and said to me, "Why, I can't take this back and tell my people about it. I won't be able to get elected." My Friends, if he doesn't take it back home, there won't be a job to get elected to.[1]

At the time that Jim was addressing the leadership of our Power Products Division, GM's market share was at a low of 36 percent, down from 47 percent nine years earlier (1987 and 1978 figures). Since 1972 North American passenger car volume had peaked at over 12 million in 1979, down to under 9 million in 1983, and back up to approximately 11.5 million in 1987, essentially the same place it had been in 1972. During this same period of flat demand, there was a 60 percent increase in the number of automotive companies manufacturing in the United States, from five to eight. Additionally, the number of auto firms selling in the United States increased from 26 to 29, a 12 percent increase. The sense of urgency was real.

Three Components of Change

There are three components of change (Fig. 3-2)[2]: The *passive component*, which includes institutionalized behaviors and habits in an internal environment that resists change; the *active component*, which advocates change; and the *enabling component*, which could be in the external environment or in a vision.

It is important that these components for change be understood. The active component really wants change; they want to transform the organization. What brings about that desire to change? Although not many people really want to change things, some people believe the change will be an improvement and are willing to work to bring it about.

Fortunately, there existed a strong active component in both the GM management and the UAW leadership. The leaders who spoke at the

THREE COMPONENTS OF CHANGE

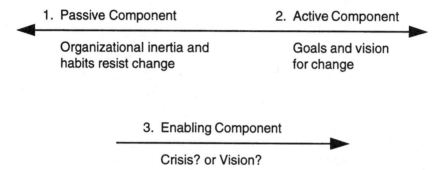

Figure 3-2.

forums had signed on for change. Some participants were also ready to move in this new direction.

Some participants, however, were hesitant and could have been considered the passive component. Most of the participants at the seminars were plant quality councils consisting of Chairpersons, Local Presidents, Plant Managers, Personnel Directors, new Quality Network Reps, and members of the plant manager's staff or union bargaining committee. For them, this was all new and needed some major explanation. Many seminar participants profiled the passive component that believes this is the way we have always done things; this is the system that's set up, so why should we change now? Often this group is committed to organizational habits that have been in the culture since its inception.

Finally, there is the enabling component, that is, some factor or event in the environment that in some way must be responded to. What brings about a desire in the hearts of people to change? Sometimes a crisis will motivate people to change, other times it is a vision of the future that says we can do things better, that we can make things better for the people and for the world that we live in. The visionaries among us hold an ardent belief that improving the world is reason enough. Leaders in successful change movements provide a vision that can capture the hearts of people to inspire necessary active change in preparation for the future.

General Motors and its unions had visionary leadership in this time of business crisis. The question is, how had this situation developed?

A Prescription for the West

In June 1981 Dr. Joseph M. Juran presented a paper, titled *Product Quality—A Prescription for the West* at the closing session of the Twenty-Fifth Conference of the European Organization for Quality Control in Paris. He wrote, "The West is in serious trouble with respect to product quality. A major reason is the immediate threat posed by the Japanese revolution in quality."[3] He graphically depicted the current state of product quality and a projected continuum (Fig. 3-3).

Juran wrote of the rapid ascent of Japanese quality and their aggressive campaign to eliminate the "Made in Japan" poor-quality image of the fifties. Quality performance during the fifties and sixties had not deteriorated, as many claimed. It was improving at a very flat rate. Juran estimated that in the mid-seventies Japan met and surpassed western quality and continued on a rapid ascent. He predicted:

> The prospect is that during the 1980s the situation will get worse, much worse. The scenario of the color TV set is being rerun in many product lines, including such essentials as automobiles and large-scale integrated circuits. The magnitude of this threat has yet to be grasped by the West.[4]

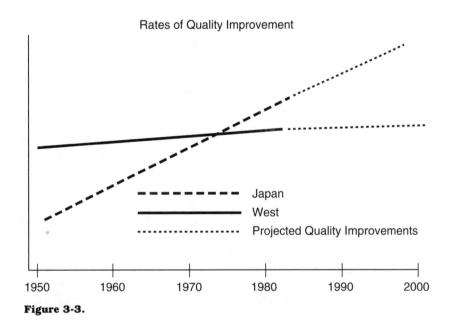

Figure 3-3.

Juran's insight is more remarkable in light of remarks he made in June 1966 in Stockholm on the occasion of an earlier European Organization for Quality Control Conference:

> In my observation, no other nation is so completely unified on the importance of good quality achievement, so eager to discover and adopt the best practices being followed in other countries, so avid in training in modern methods of controlling quality, so vigilant in regulating the quality of exported goods. To be sure, there is progress along these fronts in all countries, but nowhere else is there the broad based sense of devotion and especially the **sense of urgency** which is so evident among the Japanese. Witnessing their accelerated pace, and comparing this with the pedestrian progress of other countries, the conclusion is inescapable: The Japanese are headed for world quality leadership, and will attain it in the next two decades, because no one else is moving there at the same pace.[5]

Juran then went on to forecast that things would get worse for the West before they got better, but that ultimately the industrialized West would produce "astounding results" when clear priorities were established and quality goals were set. And, in fact, it was in the early eighties that the U.S. auto companies began to move to catch up. We had to accelerate our quality efforts and change our fundamental approach to managing the business.

Who Defines Quality?

The Japanese let their customers define how good their quality is. Today, we do the same. However, in the early eighties we defined quality using such measures as:

- Conformance to specifications
- Voice of the designer
- Voice of the engineer
- Voice of manufacturing
- Warranty costs
- Limited voice of the customer
- Adherence to schedule

These measures often conflicted with each other, and the limited voice of the customer came by way of complaints after the fact.

Customer, for our purposes here, includes both the internal customer in the production chain and the external or ultimate customer, the purchasers of our products and services.

99.9 Percent Quality

What would your customers think if you guaranteed to supply them with goods and services that have a 99.9 percent conformance to specifications? The list in Fig. 3-4 has been used in many presentations to make the point that the customer doesn't care about specifications. The customer defines quality.[6]

Looking at the last item, this means that at least 22 parts would fail on every GM vehicle, based on 22,000 parts per GM vehicle. Each of these parts is involved in a specific process for installation, a process seemingly designed not to create defects. These parts range from a critical brake line, ignition electronics, or a simple bolt that rattles in the door frame. Clearly, 99.9 percent is an unacceptable measure of quality.

In 1984 the American automotive industry had lost its quality advantage over the Japanese. The headlines reflected the belief that

---

99.9% Conformance to Specifications

- At least 20,000 wrong drug prescriptions per year
- No electricity, water, or heat for 8.6 hours per year
- No telephone service for 10 minutes per week
- Two short or long landings at each major airport per day
- 500 incorrect surgical operations performed per week
- 50 newborn babies dropped at birth each day
- 22,000 checks deducted from the wrong account each year
- 2000 lost articles of mail per hour
- At least 22 individual failed parts per GM car based on an average of 22,000 parts per GM vehicle

Figure 3-4.

U.S. quality had slipped and the future of the American automotive industry was at risk. The question was, would the Big Three survive?

- *U.S. News and World Report,* March 8, 1992: "Can Detroit Ever Come Back?

- *The Detroit News,* July 12, 1983: "Will U.S. auto producers survive to 2000?"

- *The Detroit Free Press,* March 12, 1983: "Can U.S. auto workers compete with Japanese?"

- *Chicago Tribune,* January 5, 1984: "Survey finds quality drives buyers from U.S. cars."

- *The Detroit News,* March 22, 1984: "U.S. auto quality has far to go."

- *The New York Times,* February 1, 1984: "Japan Auto Success Analyzed."

As bad as it was for the industry, General Motors got its own share of attention. We were making money; it was not a bad year. However, the following headlines foreshadowed problems to come. They reflect General Motors' dependence on technology to solve all ills and move us on to the twenty-first century:

- *The New York Times,* October 20, 1984: "GM `Factory of Future' Will Run with Robots."

- *Business Week,* January 23, 1984: "Can GM Solve its Identity Crisis?"

- *The Detroit Free Press:* GM's Customers the least satisfied among Big Three."

- "Auto Automation: To Battle the Japanese, GM Pushing Boldly into Computerization."

- *The Detroit News,* August 31, 1984: "GM plans push to equal Japan in production costs."

The good news is that 10 years later, we have responded. Current headlines reveal that, unlike in 1984 when we were in a catch-up position, we are now challenging the competition:

- *Automotive News:* "Japan sales slide continues."

- *Business Week,* January 10, 1994: "Value Will Keep Detroit Moving. Big Three quality and prices have put a dent in imports."

- *USA Today,* March 3, 1994: "Automakers step on the gas to meet demand."

- *The Wall Street Journal,* February 17, 1994: "New Japanese Cars All Seem to Look the Same—Boring."
- "Analysts: Big 3 in High Gear."
- *The Detroit News:* "Consumers shift allegiance. Market trends: Loyalty to imported cars erodes as U.S. automakers keep quality up, prices down."

How did we change? What did we do?

Creating a Quality Culture

F. James McDonald became President and Chief Operating Officer of General Motors on February 1, 1981. He later wrote about the quality strategy the corporation took on early in his leadership to begin addressing the quality challenge:

> In 1981, General Motors (GM) set out to make quality its number one operating priority. More than a slogan, this represented a total commitment by top management to create an ongoing quality culture. Fostering a new culture in the largest industrial corporation in the world, with more employees than the U.S. Navy and Marines combined, with more facilities and assets than most third-world countries and with thousands of suppliers whose culture must change with GM's was an immense task.[7]

McDonald stressed three key approaches upon which this cultural change was to be built: technology, training, and teamwork: technology to be capable of conforming to precise specifications; training as an investment in the talents and commitment of GM people, especially in the areas of state-of-the-art readiness to use the technology and in quality decision making; and teamwork through quality of work life groups, shared knowledge, and continuous improvement. There was one other ingredient as well: management consistency. McDonald felt it was management's responsibility to lead by example, or "walk like it talks." Any regression from absolute quality standards on the part of management would spread throughout the organization like a shot. Yet, early in the 1980s the customer had not yet been written into the quality formula.

Corporate leadership signaled its commitment to quality when, in 1981, it named its first Vice President for Quality and Reliability who reported directly to the President of GM. Quality was now visible and out front, demonstrating its prominence as a top corporate priority.

Our Small-Car Project

In 1982 a commitment was made to manufacture a small, domestically produced automobile. The following year this car got a name—Saturn—and GM and the UAW revealed plans for a Joint Study Center targeted at designing an unprecedented union-management partnership for the Saturn project. The Saturn added a sixth nameplate to GM's North American passenger car lineup. Created as a separate subsidiary, the Saturn Corporation was to be a learning lab to utilize new manufacturing techniques and systems and a new worker-management relationship to build the next-generation, world competitive automobile.

A Cross-Industry Study

During the summer of 1982, General Motors conducted a needs analysis of the current state of quality in the corporation. One hundred fifty managers from across the organization met and discussed major quality issues including the gap between customer expectations and actual performance in the areas of quality, reliability, durability, and performance. Based on the meeting, Corporate Quality and Reliability commissioned a study to investigate companies outside General Motors: *General Motors Quality and Reliability Cross-Industry Study.* The purpose of the study was:

- To discover how and why other companies were successful in achieving high-quality standards
- To confirm our belief that strategies they had in place could also be used by GM
- To save time and money for GM by learning from the experience and accomplishments of others
- To enrich Study Team members through exposure to these quality companies

Between June and August 1983 GM Study Teams, made up of three to four managers, a Quality and Reliability representative, and an outside consultant, visited Boeing Commercial Aircraft, Cincinnati Milacron, Deer and Company, GE Medical Systems, Hewlett-Packard, IBM, Maytag, Rockwell International Automotive Operations, Texas Instruments, 3M, and Western Electric/Bell Labs. The report was published January 26, 1984; four key success factors for quality were identified: management commitment, people development processes, quality performance processes, and customer satisfaction. In spite of diversity in size, geographical location, type of products or services and organizational structure, the study concluded that the 11 companies visited all focused on quality in everything they did. Some stressed technology, some people development, some organization approaches, and others cultural issues. No matter what the focus, all believe that quality can be realized throughout their organizations when top management leads the way. Quality can be linked directly to marketplace success. Customer satisfaction through high-quality products and services will lead to short- and long-term increased and sustained profitability and, therefore, job security.[8] The study acted as a catalyst; quality steering committees, quality councils, quality improvement teams, and so on, sprouted up everywhere.

NUMMI

During this same time we also looked at the competition. We studied the Japanese and, by 1983, launched an agreement to form a joint venture with the Toyota Motor Company to produce a small Chevrolet automobile in the Fremont, California, assembly plant previously operated by General Motors. In 1984 the plant opened under the name New United Motor Manufacturing, Inc. (NUMMI), and immediately achieved the top quality rating of any General Motors plant.

GM Readies for the Quality Network

General Motors was working on four fronts to transform itself. First, we were learning from our competitors by working with Toyota at NUMMI: a UAW–GM work force, Toyota and GM management, the Toyota Production System. Second, we created our own experiment by charging 99 employees representing a total cross section of the corporation—union and management, line workers, executives, Skilled Trades journeypersons, engineers, training professionals, union leaders, corporate support staff representatives, and so on—to design the perfect automotive manufacturing company, Saturn. Third, we benchmarked quality leaders in highly competitive industries, looking for key quality success factors that could migrate into GM. And finally we studied the individual groups and divisions within General Motors who had developed their own quality programs. They had been consulting with W. Edwards Deming, Joseph Juran, and Philip Crosby and had studied Shewhart, Taguchi, Ishikawa, Feigenbaum, Imai, and many others.

Implementation of the various quality efforts was inconsistent and unbalanced across the corporation. Different groups favored different philosophies. In 1982 Dr. Deming began his work in General Motors with Pontiac Motor Division. His philosophy, then 10 points, was implemented in an assembly plant in Pontiac, Michigan. In 1983 Dr. Juran worked primarily with GM of Canada, Oldsmobile, and GM Truck and Bus, increasing quality awareness in these organizations. In 1983 and 1984 GM Truck and Bus also worked with Philip Crosby, whose four absolutes for quality management greatly influenced its organization as well as Chevrolet and several GM component divisions. GM's President, all corporate Vice Presidents, and general managers attended the Crosby Executive Quality Council. We were all working diligently toward the same goals—high quality, low cost, and elimination of wasted time, talents, and materials—but we were not aligned. The individual groups and divisions committed to various quality directions and could not or would not reconcile other ideas. With each unit charting its own course, we were creating duplication of efforts and seemingly conflicting procedures and practices, and we were producing waste. We were energetically committed to our improvement efforts, each unit to its own effort, and were working at cross purposes to each other. This independent, competitive nature had been the management strategy espoused by Alfred Sloan in the twenties and thirties and had served us well, especially when there were few external competitors and there were customers lined up to buy our product. This style of management did not and could not work in light of the changing times. It is easy to say but difficult to accomplish: We needed a major paradigm shift. Levels of readiness throughout the corporation were all over the map.

The Worker's Role in Quality in 1983

Although traditional organizational structures and bureaucracy hindered radical change, efforts continued to better train workers and utilize their ideas in the manufacturing process. One of the eight management objectives presented at the April 1983 General Motors Executive Conference was *Strengthen Employe* (sic) *Relations*. The strategy for doing so was to *Expand the Quality of Work Life Program*. However, distrust on the part of General Motors workers created political pressures within the UAW that hindered union leaders' ability to fully participate in new processes. The overall lack of success of quality of work life (QWL) efforts left workers skeptical that they could work with management. Such distrust was evidenced by the creation of new caucuses and special-interest groups within the union structure. Quality of work life programs had allowed input from all parties but did not have the broad-based support and commitment to address critical processes throughout the corporation. Although successful in some areas of the corporation, QWL generally floundered without active and consistent commitment and support of both union and management leadership. Responsibility for implementation was at the discretion of individual locations. QWL lacked uniform plans and processes; there was consequently great variation in the results. Union leadership responded to their membership when accusations were made that employee involvement programs, specifically QWL, were being used to add more work and eliminate jobs. *Productivity* became a nasty word, guaranteed to provoke an argument if uttered.

QWL guidelines had been established in the 1973 UAW–GM National Agreement to formalize programs designed to improve working conditions on the plant floor and to invite union workers to participate in management decisions that affected their jobs. By extension, QWL was to improve product quality and working relationships. By fall 1983 large and small union locals abandoned this joint program. Don Ephlin, UAW Vice President of the GM Department at the time, was so upset at the misuse of these programs by plant management that he recommended a large local in Indianapolis pull out of the QWL program there, even though Ephlin was a strong advocate of such programs. In a *Detroit Free Press* article November 10, 1983, a UAW official who asked not to be named stated, "Ephlin is seeking an understanding with the corporation that these programs must meet the national guidelines, and where the programs aren't working, they should be shut down."[9]

Union officials at a truck and bus plant in Indianapolis, Local 23, ended their program shortly after it was instituted:

> "We only had the program for about a month," said Bill Hayes, president of Local 23. "It just caused too many problems internally for the union and for our members. It seemed like it was only designed to pit worker against worker to eliminate jobs."[10]

Many union members saw cooperative union-management programs such as QWL as a way for management to increase productivity by finding ways to eliminate jobs. Management, on the other hand, viewed these programs as a threat to its ability to control the business. The possibility of a wholesale pullout on the union's part loomed menacingly over the heads of enlightened leadership who advocated union-management partnerships as a win-win proposition. This was a valuable lesson learned. Other joint programs, such as Employee Assistance, Health and Safety, and Apprenticeship, showed that joint decisions can elicit a much broader base of support, creating an atmosphere of excitement and mutual commitment. These programs were national in scope and were recognized in the National Agreement. Quality of work life, however, did not have the apparent singleness of purpose of these other joint processes.

Quality Initiatives

In spite of these areas of discord, both union and management leadership recognized they had to do something about quality. Joint processes, such as QWL, had been written into a succession of National Agreements. GM management sponsored several quality programs: Targets for Excellence, General Motors Quality Ethic, GM Mark of Excellence, and GM Quality Institute.

- *General Motors Quality Ethic,* presented in Fig. 3-5, was first issued in 1984 by F. James McDonald, President; it put quality in focus for GM. The new ethic then defined four customer-focused components:

  Quality: Conformance to requirements and specification that meet customer expectations

  Reliability: Measure of ability to perform an intended function for a given period of time under specified environmental conditions, in a manner that meets customer expectations

  Durability: Measure of ability to perform an intended function without requiring overhaul or rebuild due to wearout, in a manner that meets customer expectations

  Performance: The achievement of system requirements that meet market expectations

- *GM Mark of Excellence*

- *General Motors Quality Institute* was established in 1984 to meet the quality education demands of General Motors' groups, divisions, and staffs. As mentioned earlier, GM first put its top executives through (Philip) Crosby Executive Quality College before creating

---

General Motors Quality Ethic

QUALITY is the *Number One* operating priority in General Motors.

Our goal is to give quality top attention—top status—and top dedication in every decision we make—every action we take and move we make.

This philosophy is to be implemented at every General Motors location by adherence to the following six quality mandates:

1. Every GM product must be the unquestioned quality leader within its market segment as perceived by the customer.
2. Every manager in General Motors must develop a strategy and an action plan to carry out the first mandate.
3. Every member of every unit must understand that the cost of quality is the expense of doing things wrong.
4. Every GM employee must recognize that quality means *total conformance to specifications and procedures* that will result in satisfied customers. Well designed and fully implemented process control systems will be a part of our procedures.
5. Top management at General Motors must become involved in the organization and the management of quality programs.
6. *Every employee* at General Motors must become actively involved in the implementation of a new quality ethic. *Everyone on the team* must be committed to quality.

Figure 3-5.

its own quality college for hourly and salaried employees, licensed by Philip Crosby to teach his philosophy. The purpose of the institute was to be a quality leadership resource to assist General Motors in quality decision making and in creating a customer satisfaction focus.

- *Targets for Excellence* (TFE): A problem resolution, assessment, and development process, introduced in 1987, designed to strengthen GM's supplier network with suppliers of production and service parts, including GM manufacturing locations. TFE consolidated into one and replaced several previously used supplier rating programs. It stressed continuous improvement in five key assessment areas of the business:

Quality
Cost
Delivery
Management
Technology

GM teams from purchasing, product engineering, manufacturing, and quality control activities conduct supplier assessments, the results of which are shared with the suppliers and GM operating units in North America. This new system eliminated multiple visits by different GM organizations. A Targets of Excellence award was presented to suppliers who achieved superior ratings in the five assessment areas.

GM employees, both hourly and salaried, had extensive exposure to quality-related subjects. All of these efforts were aimed at improving quality and thus satisfying customers. Unfortunately, due to the complexity, diversity, and size of General Motors, the results were often inconsistent, and efforts were duplicated. The focus on customer satisfaction was not coordinated. All of the programs were aimed at the same target, but they did not align. There was not a single, consistent approach that would result in a total strength greater than the sum of the individual efforts.

Basic Concepts

The *Quality Network* began with a recognition by the leadership of General Motors that there was a need for a corporatewide change in the way people were viewed and treated, as well as a need to focus on the entire business system, if the ultimate corporate goals were going to be fully realized. A work force trained to be disenfranchised and excluded from the decision-making process could not be expected to respond with heartfelt support to a call for greater quality and efficiency.

At the same time, GM management recognized that standard methods of operation were necessary throughout the organization to promote efficiency and competitiveness in a world market. In order to overcome the competing factions within GM, it would be necessary to develop a unified process for customer satisfaction, focused on people, teamwork, and continuous improvement. How could these seemingly unrelated goals of treating people as full partners and establishing "one GM way" be accomplished?

Joint Efforts

In July 1985, a joint committee composed of International Union and management representatives was formed to study the issue of a sustained product quality process. Initially the committee's charge was to study one approach, the Philip Crosby quality process, that was prevalent within General Motors. A number of concerns from various locations had been raised regarding lack of jointness and limited union participation and worker involvement. A representative of the Philip Crosby Associates participated in the investigative stages of the study.

The committee produced *The UAW–GM Joint Quality Study* in March 1986. The report concluded that the Crosby process did not adequately recognize the need to involve the union structure in identifying appropriate members of a plant-level quality implementation team. Additionally, the workers' role in the process was solely to identify problems; they were not involved in the resolution of problems. Further, there had been no attempt to communicate or explain the massive cultural and systemic changes that the Crosby process espoused. Early in their examination, committee members determined that the study should be expanded beyond the Crosby quality process. They identified several quality programs that were being implemented throughout the corporation, many based on W. Edwards Deming and Joseph Juran. All these efforts had begun before a joint agreement was reached on what was needed at GM to accomplish product and service quality improvement and job security.

> Our study led us to conclude that for meaningful product quality improvements to be made at manufacturing levels, significant organizational changes must occur. New roles and responsibilities need to be defined for managers, workers, supervisors, union representatives and others. For these roles to effectively merge and be fulfilled, other changes must also occur. Training needs to be provided. Responsibility and authority must be redefined. Tools, equipment, machinery, processes, material and parts must be able to produce quality products. In short, an enormous cultural and systems change needs to occur which will require jointness, collaboration, commitment, support and financial resources....Attitudinal changes will be required....While the task is recognizably enormous, we are convinced of its absolute necessity.[11]

The committee's report, issued in March 1986 to UAW Vice President and Director of the GM Department Don Ephlin and Vice President Industrial Relations of General Motors Alfred S. Warren, Jr., recommended a national joint quality conference to determine who does what and why. The committee stressed that its recommendations were not intended to replace quality efforts already under way. Rather, the committee intended these learnings to be the foundation of a jointly developed, unified quality process.

General Motors Production System

As a joint plan to consolidate quality efforts was being proposed, GM leadership was also considering merging the best practices of GM production processes, as well as lessons learned from our joint venture with Toyota, into one General Motors Production System. The GM Production System (GMPS), depicted in Fig. 3-6,[12] was an integrated process designed to utilize the talents of GM people to convert ideas and resources into world-class products and services at the least cost.

The GMPS Task Team, chaired by Dick Donnelly, was formally introduced December 9, 1986, in a letter from Group Vice President of Power Products, Don Atwood, Group Vice President of C-P-C (Chevrolet-Pontiac-GM of Canada) Lloyd Reuss, and Group Vice President of B-O-C (Buick-Oldsmobile-Cadillac) Bob Stempel to the

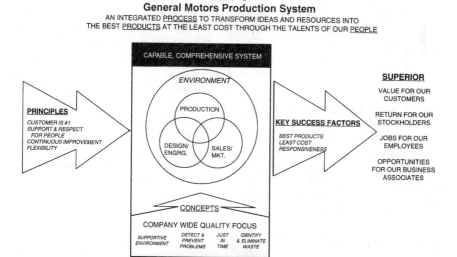

Figure 3-6.

leadership of General Motors—Divisional General Managers, General Operating Officers, Group Executives, Staff Executives, and Heads of Staff Sections:

> Development and implementation of this new production system will be a major effort, ultimately requiring involvement of most functions within every operating unit in North America....It is essential that all operating units give this program top priority.
>
> Your effort in creating a team environment for this program that builds on the collective strength of the total organization, while maintaining the concept of our decentralized structure, is required to meet the competitive challenges and assure our long-term success.[13]

We had begun to see that we had to work together for the mutual benefits of all. Each group and division had its own way of designing and building a car. Now, the groups were being asked to come together and create one common production system to be followed by all. The transition to total systems thinking had not yet taken place, however; we were still clinging to our decentralized structure.

It was through the consolidation efforts of this production system task team that many total quality strategies were introduced to the entire corporation. Strategies such as a customer focus–voice of the customer, variation reduction, process management, measurement and feedback systems, quality function deployment, and other critical continuous improvement strategies began to help paint the picture of a total quality system appropriate and necessary for the whole corporation. The paradigm shift that we discussed earlier was starting to move. We were beginning to see that we had to work together to satisfy our customers. They are the arbitrators of our quality.

Voice of the Customer

We were beginning to ask ourselves some very important and fundamental questions. Properly applied, a customer focus results in higher-quality products, lower costs, increased market share, increased profits, and job security. We realized that quality improvement is brought about by a change to a customer-driven Total Quality System. A customer focus asks:

- Who are our customers?
- What are their expectations?
- Are we meeting our customers' expectations?
- How do we know?

Converging Forces

A joint study had recommended a national quality conference look at all the best practices in use and valuable lessons learned in order to come up with one quality system for General Motors. A cross-industry study identified the value of a "quality culture" with a customer focus and key success factors that focused on people development, management commitment, and quality processes. The quality experts' influence was evident throughout our organization; everyone was talking about customer involvement—both internal and external—by the total work force, visible leadership commitment and responsibility, and process management and control. Experience with the Toyota Production System at NUMMI led us to undertake the creation of the General Motors Production System, geared to improving efficiencies and effectiveness and being applied across all the groups and divisions. If we truly believed that we had the best system, we certainly would want everyone in General Motors to have access to it and be part of it. Total quality philosophy, tools, and techniques were being introduced throughout General Motors; they were called by different names, applied in different ways, came from different sources, but were aimed at the same thing—satisfying the customer. We started synthesizing all these endeavors when we finally met in Toledo, Ohio, in 1987.

The Vision

Having a clear vision of desired change is a powerful tool. Vision helps to overcome resistance in the internal environment that resists change, and vision also creates a stronger positive force for change. It begins with a vision. As we had learned from our studies, enlightened leaders of successful organizations have a vision for their companies: The company can be more caring for people and can continue to lead the world with the best products, processes, services, and relationships. However, people must trust that they can support that vision.

This is where the total quality journey begins, with a vision. It empowers people; it gives people the opportunity to make decisions on their jobs. Each of us at one time or another has been in a situation in which we knew a better way of doing something, but because the process said this is the way we do it, our idea wasn't considered. It was frustrating. There are thousands upon thousands of people who run into the same frustration every day. Management has to provide processes that are designed to bring about improvement. How does management do that? By involving everyone who works on the job and bringing in new ideas. Not change for the sake of change but change that actually makes things better for everyone and improves the system.

A total quality process has a very simple hierarchy. It starts with leadership doing the right things. Process management ensures the right things get done right. People are recognized as the heart of any process and must be provided the opportunity and support to follow through on their job in the right way. It was with this understanding, albeit not expressed in a unified voice, that General Motors formally embarked on creating its total quality process for customer satisfaction.

The Toledo Accord

In February 1987, continuing joint improvement efforts were brought into focus when General Motors and UAW leaders met at a quality strategy conference in Toledo, Ohio, to discuss quality and the necessity of changing past practices and relationships. Each group or division in General Motors was invited to present its quality plan to the leadership. These presentations clarified the need for a single joint quality system for the corporation. This system would have to address each division's or group's needs, as well as the union's.

The resulting actions reflected more of a joint partnership, addressing each other's needs while working together on participative processes. This effort not only met the self-interest of both parties, brought forcefully to the fore by economic pressures, but also demonstrated a maturing relationship between both parties. Each recognized that its future depended upon working with one another in areas previously considered to be solely management concerns or union concerns, with a strict line of demarcation between the two. The meeting resulted in what became known as the Toledo Accord (see Fig. 3-7) which envisioned a new partnership in addressing processes, engineering and manufacturing methods, and the working environment throughout General Motors. This broad understanding formed the foundation for a total quality management initiative titled the *Quality Network*—one process for managing General Motors, jointly developed by GM and UAW leadership, encompassing participative management at all levels of the corporation.

First Steps

The Toledo Accord paved the way to a corporate focus on people and process improvement. The purpose of this process was to promote

---

THE TOLEDO ACCORD

The undersigned leadership of General Motors and the UAW is jointly committed to securing General Motors position in the market and the job security of its employees in every phase of the corporation through an ongoing process of producing the highest quality customer valued products. The parties agree that the production of world-class quality products is the key to our survival and jointly commit to pursue the implementation of the following jointly developed quality strategy:

- Ongoing UAW/GM top leadership commitment and involvement to a corporate quality strategy.

- Voice of the customer is understood and drives the whole process.

- Ongoing education and training to support the quality improvement process.

- Communication process to support the quality process.

- Create a plan and structure for a joint process for implementation.

- Total involvement for continuous improvement and elimination of waste.

- Reward system which supports the total quality process.

Signed by Robert Schultz, W. Blair Thompson, William Hoglund, Alfred Warren, John Debbink, Donald Ephlin, Donald Atwood, Charlie Best, Charles Katko, E. M. Mutchler, E. Czapor, Robert Stempel, L. C. Reuss, J. McDonald, and Robert Walker

---

Figure 3-7.

higher quality and more effective and efficient operations through a recognition of the value of each person working at General Motors Corporation by:

- Listening to employees' suggestions or complaints and responding to them

- Respecting people as a valuable asset rather than as a simple necessary commodity

- Caring about the work environment because it was the right thing to do, not because it was required by contract or law

- Letting employees share in the pride associated with a job well done

- Recognizing employee representatives as legitimate spokespersons for their members and including them in the business decisions affecting union members

This represented a radical departure from the practices of the past but became an obvious step in retaining a "world-class" image in the world market.

The model seen in Fig. 3-8 was created to depict the early elements of the Quality Network. A joint task force was named to create an identity for this first-ever, corporatewide joint quality effort. The

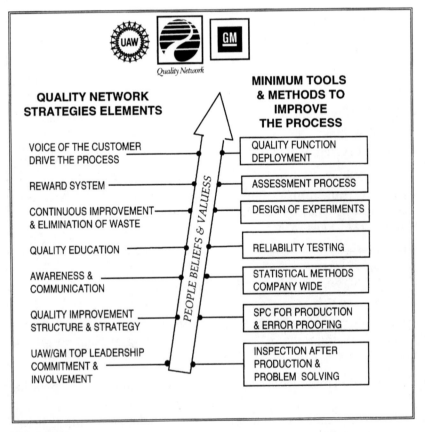

Figure 3-8.

resulting logo, as shown in Fig. 3-8, captures the ideas, philosophies, and themes of the Quality Network. The UAW is represented by the circle, and GM is illustrated by the outlying square, each reflecting the shape of its respective logos. The circle and square design interrelationship along with the use of the UAW and GM logos represents the teamwork and cooperation pledged by the two parties. The UAW–GM Quality Network's journey to continuous improvement is depicted by the curving white line. The model also shows the seven strategic elements of a joint quality process identified as foundational strategies as well as their corresponding tools and techniques. Later this same year the General Motors Production System was merged with these strategic elements to create the Quality Network. General Motors in partnership with its unions was aligning its quality efforts into one total quality process for customer satisfaction.

A Common Goal

Previous efforts at participative management gave valuable insights into the obstacles that a total joint process might face. The architects of the Quality Network realized from the beginning that top leadership commitment across the board had to be in place. They did not want a repeat of the disharmony caused by unsuccessful quality of work life programs. Quality and customer satisfaction provided a comfort zone for union and management to work together, a common goal that both parties did not have to fight about.

Voices of Divisiveness

Union leaders were criticized by members of their own union for addressing issues that traditionally had been concerns of management. Charges of "getting in bed with management" were not uncommon. Conversely, management officials were criticized for "selling out" to the union because of their efforts to invite the union to be full partners in the business. These reactions mirrored traditional viewpoints based on a history of union-management militancy and distrust. However, times and the marketplace had changed. So had the way business was going to have to operate to survive. Change was inevitable, and both parties recognized the necessity to manage it and turn it into an opportunity for growth, prosperity, and security.

At a constitutional convention top union officials received the support of delegates for joint programs. This support was based upon the compelling argument that early input into the decision-making process gave workers some say in their futures and the future of the company. Both union and management leaders made it clear to their constituents that neither party had "sold out" to the other, that the decision to address mutual concerns jointly would benefit everyone involved.

All in the Same Boat Together

At a Quality Network training workshop, Horst Schulze, Chairperson of the Ritz Carlton Hotel chain, gave an excellent example of why both parties must jointly address future issues. He began by saying that he did not understand why unions and companies could not work together. He likened the issue to two people sitting in a boat in the middle of the ocean with no chance of rescue. Suddenly, the boat develops a leak. The management representative turns to the union representative and orders the individual to fix the leak. The union official responds by saying that management should fix the leak since they caused it. The management official then rationalizes that the problem was the union's fault because of faulty workmanship. The union official counterargues that if management had authorized proper preventive maintenance and upkeep, the leak would never have happened. Charge is answered by countercharge until ultimately the boat sinks. The moral, obviously, is that management, workers, and their representatives are all in the same boat together. We can argue, as in the past, about cause and effect and sink; or, we can work together, address mutual concerns, and save the ship.

The Quality Network

The UAW–GM Quality Network represents a departure from the antagonistic cycle Schulze talks about. The Quality Network has an established process and environment for joint decision making and action. Following the Toledo Accord, top UAW and General Motors officials, led by Don Ephlin and Bob Stempel, were charged to create the vision for the Quality Network and design the framework for the process to be presented to their respective leadership.

Formal Recognition

Based on the work done in this historic meeting, the Quality Network was formally recognized in the 1987 National Agreement. The

National Agreement is the binding contract between the UAW and General Motors that governs how these two large entities conduct business with one another. It is, if you will, the body of law agreed to by both sides. When an item is included in the National Agreement, it is binding on the part of both parties. For the Quality Network to be part of the National Agreement moved it from a nice idea to a fact of life. It was official; GM and the UAW would work together on quality. The contract read:

> During the course of 1987 negotiations, General Motors and the International Union, UAW, held extensive discussions about the subject of product quality. There was recognition on the part of both parties to the National Agreement that the cornerstone of job security for all General Motors employees is the production of highest quality, customer-valued products. This is reflected in the extensive efforts both parties have devoted to the subject of quality both on the national and local levels, exemplified by the formation of the UAW–GM Quality Network....[14]

The 1990 GM–UAW National Agreement further defines the role of the Quality Network. Document No. 119, *UAW-GM Memorandum of Commitment to Product Quality,* states: "General Motors process for total quality is the Quality Network—the one process for customer satisfaction. Although Management has the ultimate responsibility for the Quality Network, it is recognized that UAW leaders and members are valuable partners in the development of the process, the action strategies, and its implementation plans."[15]

In 1988 the *General Motors Operations Procedures Manual* formally recognized Quality Network as the corporatewide quality effort eliciting total employee involvement:

> The Quality Network provides a framework, or process, for each employee to become directly involved in quality improvement and satisfying customers. It is one process and one system....The Quality Network is a process that links together all existing efforts to improve quality and customer satisfaction, encompassing a broad spectrum of elements...throughout the business."[16]

The UAW and GM jointly announced the formation of the Quality Network in a *Fortune* magazine supplement (September 28, 1987) titled "Quality: The Competitive Edge." Signed by Don Ephlin, then UAW Vice President and Director of the GM Department, and Bob Stempel, President, General Motors Corporation, the ad read, "For General Motors, Customer Satisfaction is the Master Plan." It also said, "General Motors and the UAW are jointly committed to achieving

excellence. And quality people are the foundation of this commitment." The two men followed this announcement by appearing
together at the American Society for Quality Control's (ASQC) Fourth
Annual National Quality Forum where they publicly talked about
management's and labor's quality partnership.

> DON EPHLIN: In the past decade the roles of both union leaders and corpo-
> rate managers have changed dramatically. Union people used to be rel-
> egated to strictly a reactive role. Our job was to handle grievances and
> say no at every opportunity. I am happy to say that this has changed.
> Union people today share in many business decisions. They have
> meaningful input in all kinds of programs that affect the future of the
> corporation and the job security of the members we represent. I think
> things have changed for corporate managers too. Nothing illustrates
> this change better than the Quality Network.[17]
>
> BOB STEMPEL: Quality Network is the way we run our business and joint-
> ness is the key—jointness with the union and jointness with all our
> people. It's a people involvement process and it emphasizes teamwork
> and continuous quality improvement.[18]

Description of GM As a System

The Quality Network is General Motors' One Total Quality Management Process for the continuous improvement of the business system.
The system in question, in a global perspective, is General Motors. The
Quality Network borrows from Dr. W. E. Deming his definition of a
system: "an interconnected complex of functionally related components that work together to accomplish the aim of the system."[19]
Recognizing the North American Operations (NAO) as the profit center for General Motors and the primary component of the corporation,
then the vehicle, truck, component, and service groups are subsystems
of NAO, each with platforms or divisions as subsystems, with plants
as the subsystems to the platforms or divisions. Of course, within any
plant there are a series of subsystems or departments that support the
plant. All business units and functions are focused on optimizing
NAO. As is evident from the decentralized structure we operated
under in the past, thinking of General Motors as one total system with
large and complex subsystems is a major departure and one that takes
getting used to.

Quality Gurus and the Silver Bullet

As General Motors' Total Quality Management Process, the Quality Network draws heavily from many recognized quality experts, such as Joseph M. Juran, Philip B. Crosby, and, in particular, W. Edwards Deming. The methods of these quality experts have been tried and proven worldwide. It is widely recognized by such experts that systems must be addressed as a *whole* to bring about long-term and lasting change. Short-term "quick fixes" cannot provide the lasting quality improvements necessary to compete in today's competitive world. The quick-fix or silver-bullet approach only results in "programs-of-the-month" that do not encourage long-term employee commitment to change. Thus, the Quality Network encourages the establishment of standard processes and designs to ensure long-term change. More significantly, it emphasizes incremental improvements through employee suggestions rather than a search for the "silver bullet" to bring about system changes. Taken together, these result in system change.

Putting Meat on the Bones

Following the Toledo Accord union and management leadership met to build on the foundation of the accord. The result was a compilation and integration of the knowledge, techniques, and experience of quality experts, union leaders, managers, supervisors, shop floor operators, job setters, and support functions. The Quality Network is soundly based on total quality principles and General Motors cultures. We recognize that each plant, each division, each group in GM has its own particular style and characteristics, just as there are common traits in the nameplates we offer as well as distinct looks and feels to each. Cadillacs are different from Bonnevilles, Grand Ams differ from the Chevrolet Camero, and the GMC Suburban from the Chevy S-10 Pickup. However, there are basics to all our car lines that are adhered to in each model, both in technology and design. Quality, safety, reliability and durability, and comfort are some that factor into every design we create.

The balance between individualism and common systems creates a dynamic within the Quality Network that gives it life and propels it forward. However, it is always grounded in quality tenets that remain constant. Utilization of their proven techniques within the confines of a one-system approach to management provides GM and its workers the opportunity to form a partnership on quality that benefits all parties involved both as an institution and as individuals within the system.

Notes

1. Jim Wagner, Assistant Director, GM Department, UAW (since retired), remarks at the Power Products and Defense Quality Network Leadership Seminar in Grenlefe, Fla., February 13 and 14, 1989.

2. Jim Kowalick, *Organizational Excellence Beyond Total Quality Management: Building the Robust Organization*, Renaissance Leadership Institute, seminar in Warren, Mich., Oregon House, Calif., October 26–28, 1994.

3. J. M. Juran, reprinted from *Management Review*, June and July 1981. Published by AMACOM, a division of American Management Association.

4. Ibid.

5. Ibid.

6. Bruce Brocka, and M. Suzanne Brocka, *Quality Management: Implementing the Best Ideas of the Masters*, Business One Irwin, Homewood, Ill., 1992, p. 3. The Brockas attribute this list to "anonymous." We added items 6, 7, and 9 to their list.

7. F. James McDonald, "Creating a Quality Culture," *The Quality Circles Journal*, March 1987, pp. 56–57.

8. General Motors Corporate Quality and Reliability, *General Motors Quality and Reliability Cross-Industry Study Report 1983*, 1984.

9. James Risen, "Job-Quality Plans Abused, UAW Says," *Detroit Free Press*, November 10, 1983.

10. Ibid.

11. UAW–GM Joint Quality Study Committee, *UAW–GM Joint Quality Study*, a report to D. Ephlin and A. Warren, March 1986. pp. 2–4, App. A, p. 1.

12. Chart in Fig. 3-6 is from the *Fiero Production System*, a General Motors manual of procedures and practices, December 1, 1985.

13. Donald Atwood, Lloyd Reuss, and Robert Stempel, letter regarding the General Motors Production System, December 9, 1986.

14. *GM–UAW 1987 National Agreement*.

15. *GM–UAW 1990 National Agreement*.

16. General Motors, "Quality Network," *General Motors Operating Manual*, No. OP-34, 1988.

17. Don Ephlin and Bob Stempel, excerpted from videotaped remarks at the Fourth Annual ASQC Quality Forum, November 11, 1988.

18. Ibid.

19. Dr. W. Edwards Deming, *The New Economics for Industry, Education and Government*. This quote was from seminar material distributed by Dr. Deming during his July 14–17, 1992, seminar and precedes the publication of his book with the same title. The material can be found in "Introduction to a System," Module 3, p. 46.

4
Framework for a
Quality Network

What's in a Name?

There are as many different definitions of *total quality* as there are names to describe them and people to champion them. This can present a problem, especially to an organization as large and geographically scattered as General Motors. Total quality, total quality management (TQM), agile manufacturing, synchronous organization, simultaneous manufacturing, lean production, total quality control (TQC), total quality leadership (TQL), continuous quality improvement (CQI), virtual organization, process management, reengineering. Which one is best? What's the latest cure for what ails us? What's the latest book on the best-seller list? Which way does the boss favor? Which is currently being denigrated in the latest business periodical for not working? Is TQM really dead? What's wrong with lean production?

Some of these names represent large, overarching philosophies, total if you will, and others hone in on specific improvement techniques. Putting buzzwords and favorite approaches aside, they are all aimed, to a greater or lesser extent, at making work more effective, efficient, and flexible to meet customer needs through effective processes and concern for people. When the commonalities of all these quality axioms are identified, each variation is far more alike than different. Total quality is a philosophy and set of guiding principles that form the foundation of a business system for an organization, any organization, dedicated to achieving total customer satisfaction through continuous improvement of products, services, processes, and relationships.

General Motors is the global business system to which we belong. In General Motors, Quality Network is the name of our total quality process to continually improve this business system, to optimize the total system by continually improving the interdependent components that constitute the system. North American Operations (NAO), Delphi Automotive Systems Worldwide (Delphi-AS), and GM Europe are just three of the large subsystems that form General Motors.

Identifying Commonalities

The key for the designers of General Motors total quality process was to focus on the common strengths of each quality approach and study the differences for validation and merit. We avoid using "quality program" to describe all these efforts because programs have an end, and there is no end to quality work. This fact is stressed in all that we do. We discovered that quality philosophies are strong proponents of five focus areas:

- Systems orientation
- Customer focus
- Broad definition of *quality*
- Continuous improvement emphasizing process management
- People involvement centering on leadership and teamwork

There are different approaches to these focus areas, and their fundamental characteristics can be grouped differently—by which tools to use or which techniques seem most appropriate. We can all spend a lot of time arguing over nuances and missing the main point. We agree with Dr. Juran who stated on his *Last Word Tour* in Detroit, April 11, 1994, that it is very important, when you are discussing quality, that everyone understands clearly how you are defining *quality*. This is also true here of *total quality management* (TQM). Dr. Deming, when asked if he was a proponent of total quality management, said he had no idea what it was, yet much of its tenets come directly from his teachings. So, before we look at the specifics of Quality Network, we need to look at the broad-brush principles that form the basis of our total quality philosophy. As will become apparent early in this explanation, these five focus areas overlap and interact in such a fashion that they cannot be clearly distinguished from each other. In order for a system to satisfy customers, it needs a continuous improvement mindset, on the part of leadership and workers, that looks to process management as the means to improve process quality and thereby improve the output of the process that will satisfy our customers. The focus areas we have identified merely serve to convey what we have learned and used to establish our total quality system.

System Orientation

A systems orientation is paramount to the way we look at our business. We can think in terms of systems or not—we have the choice. The point is that the world is made up of systems and subsystems, and that is not going to change. We choose to use Dr. Deming's definition of *system* as "an interconnected complex of functionally related components that work together to try to accomplish the aim of the system."[1] Probably one of the easiest ways to understand how interrelated components, or subsystems, relate to the whole is to look at the human body. The nervous system, cardiovascular system, digestive system, immune system, respiratory system, and so on, all work together to operate the human body. Each has a job to do, and each is dependent upon the others. Each is an integral part of the whole. When one subsystem breaks down, the entire body is affected. Conversely, what is done to the system in one area acts upon the others. A global example of this interrelatedness was the recent eruption of a volcano in the South Pacific that, in turn, influenced weather all over the globe. Certainly we, in Michigan, felt the effects. Total quality manages the whole system, looks at the big picture, and balances requirements and resources accordingly.

The focus must be on *all* systems, not just some systems. If a company and its people understand these principles, commitment becomes a natural process, resulting in a total quality organization. From product conception to final delivery, there will be teamwork and cooperation, and all operations will be in sync. This has permitted the Japanese automobile manufacturers to deliver cars faster and operate more efficiently. If it only takes from one to two days for an automobile to be processed through an assembly plant, why then does it take six or seven weeks to deliver that car or truck? It is because the U.S. automotive manufacturers are not currently process management organizations.

A System Will Not Be Divided

For leaders in almost any capacity it seems that the road to better efficiency is to break down any system, whether that be a company, a recreational organization, an educational institution, or an automobile factory, into individual components and then improve the efficiency of each individual component. It seems logical, yet what happens is that instead of increasing the efficiency of the overall system, you have many individual components that are operating at peak but when put together don't efficiently interact. Therefore, individual efforts must be focused on the effectiveness of the entire system.

To clarify this, let us look at an example from the automotive industry. Somewhere in the world a manufacturer is building the "best part." There are several manufacturers who produce various parts considered to be the "best." If we were to take the acknowledged best component(s) from every automobile part manufacturer in the world, such as the best fuel injection system, the best pistons, or the best windshield wiper motors, and try to put them together, they would not work. They were not designed as a system.

Dr. Deming uses the example of an orchestra to help one understand the necessity of systems thinking. There are many individual instruments that make up an orchestra, and the same type of instrument has many different parts within a particular section. All of the musicians must be able to play their instrument at the right time, playing the exact part, for the entire orchestra to sound harmonious. Though the cymbals may play only at certain times, their part is crucial in the overall performance. The violinist, who may play throughout the entire performance, is not considered more important than the musician playing the cymbals who performs only occasionally. The musician playing the cymbals does not sit in his or her chair hoping that the violinist or the cellist or the flutist makes a mistake so that the moment to play the cymbals is more effective. The entire orchestra works together as a complete system in order to produce a pleasing and professional performance. A recognition of the fact that the entire system must be addressed when making quality improvements is an absolute necessity if such improvements are to be effective.

A company that chooses to attack its quality problems by instituting departments that work on parts of a system, such as design, engineering, or manufacturing, but do not work as a team will suboptimize. Dr. Deming's definition and examples make it very clear that the establishment of a total quality system must be based on the principle of looking at entire systems (for example, entire corporations or divisions) rather than individual system components. In order to do this, it is critical that the aim and direction of the system overall be clearly established, understood, and communicated. If the mission and goals of a corporation or business are clear and concise and properly address the needs of all the stakeholders, then success will be greater together than the sum of any individual successes. That is the purpose of total quality management systems—to bring together all the components of diverse, large, and complex systems for the purpose of providing customer satisfaction.

The General Motors System

General Motors, as we have stated, is our business system. North American Operations (NAO) is a primary subsystem. It is in NAO where the Quality Network is jointly administered by GM and UAW leadership, which also administers the Quality Network for our Delphi Automotive Systems Worldwide. These organizations are composed of large subsystems. NAO is made up of car, truck, and service subsystems: Midsize and Luxury Car Group; Small Car Group; North American Truck Group; Powertrain; Sales, Service, and Marketing; NAO Vehicle Development and Technical Operation Group; NAO Business Support; Worldwide Purchasing; and Personnel. These are made up of platforms and divisions and staffs. The vehicle platforms are divided into plant locations that, in turn, are composed of departments and staffs that support the plants. Delphi Automotive Systems is made up of six divisions, each of which has several plants, departments, and staffs.

As we have worked inside this system, we have watched systems thinking drive General Motors, and our North American Operations in particular, shaping through systematic reorganization directed at fine-tuning the system. Over the last decade we have continually refined the organization to focus on the customer. Where we have uncovered barriers and run into roadblocks, we have modified our structure and practices to reconcile our operating philosophy with our aim, customer satisfaction. Our response has been and will continue to be intelligent because it is based on knowledge and customer requirements.

We have come to understand that all business units and functions, no matter how small the subsystem, should be focused on supporting the aim of the system. For example, by optimizing NAO, we are furthering the aim of General Motors. Another way to look at it is that subsystems are internal customers. They have requirements based on goals they are aiming at. These goals should support the larger system's aim. A systems orientation looks at the relationship between the different subsystems as a customer-supplier chain. Our dealer system and supplier base are integral parts of our system. Nonsystems thinking promotes behavior characterized by "over-the-wall" and "hand-off" and "turf" mentalities.

Systems thinking requires looking at the big picture and often requires help from the outside for full understanding. A common mistake is to try to understand a system by analyzing it piece by piece, "taking the watch apart." When we try to take a system apart, it loses its essential properties, and so do its parts. It is no longer a system. The dynamic interactivity is gone. It is true that we need knowledge of the subsystems, but especially in their roles or responsibilities with regard to the larger system they occupy. An automobile cannot be understood by looking at a tire, spark plug, piston, or fuel tank. It must be seen as a whole and then improved as a whole. Yes, we can design better parts—the antilock braking system (ABS) is a good example. But it had to be designed with the whole car in mind. How would such a new system impact handling and the functions of the steering mechanisms? We developed a videotape for police officers driving our Chevrolet police cars with ABS brakes. The improved stopping characteristics changed the way the vehicle performed. A spin around a 180-degree turn had to be accomplished differently than in the past.

The old story of three people who are blindfolded and asked to describe the elephant they are touching is a wonderful example. One has the tail, one the trunk, and one the leg. How could each know what they were touching without seeing the whole? What would be the loss should they try to take apart that elephant to understand it?

The NAO Team

For General Motors, a systems orientation is a major culture change. It's all about abandoning internal competition, which had been the heart of our management style in the past. Beginning in 1908, Billy Durant began acquiring a number of existing automobile companies and created General Motors. After several turbulent years, Alfred Sloan was elected President in 1923. The company he inherited to run was still composed of independent-thinking automakers: 5 passenger car divisions and over 12 parts and accessories subsidiaries. Sloan believed that each operating unit should run its business separately. The corporation provided strong and clear strategic direction, financial control, and policy coordination. Not unsurprisingly, Sloan met with resistance. These strong roots in General Motors' culture have caused a slow journey to where we are today. These roots still have some influence on decisions and behaviors.

One of our corporate objectives for 1995 is *Build the NAO Focus/NAO Team,* stressing common systems and processes throughout the company. In the past, internal competition caused duplication of effort and resources and took our attention from our true competition and the customer. This objective is intended to place specific focus on defining the *aim* for our North American Operations while building teamwork across the entire organization. While the Japanese were studying the American customer, we compared GM plants against one another. We offered the customer what we thought he or she wanted. We are changing a strong cultural practice and are moving away from internal competition. We are now focused on NAO as a single team.

A Customer Focus

Today we say we are in the business of satisfying and encouraging enthusiasm in our customer. Not so a few years ago when some felt we were in business only to make a profit, produce a good return on investment, have a favorable bottom line. We now understand all of these things will come about if the customer is satisfied, if the customer perceives he or she received quality and value. Customer value is the relationship between quality and price. The higher the quality and the lower the price, the higher the customer (perceives) value. In this case we are talking about the ultimate customer.

However, in the broader sense we look at the customer as anyone or any entity that is affected by the system. This includes all people in the value chain. The process of producing and selling a product or service creates a long line of internal customers and stakeholders, all of whom ultimately impact the final or ultimate customer, the person who buys and/or uses our products and services. We must know who our customers are and listen carefully to them in order to be able to meet their expectations. The ultimate customer's product ownership or service experience is the result of a total system. The ultimate purchaser of the product or service does not distinguish internal customers, suppliers, dealers, and so on from the product but views, in our case, the vehicle experience or service experience with General Motors.

It is important for each member of a system to understand that he or she has a strong personal link to the ultimate customer. This is not often easy to do. We are using pipeline studies and process modeling to study processes that need to be streamlined so that waste is eliminated and the customer is satisfied. An example of this would be the process to deliver a car from ordering at the dealership to delivery at the dealership. Our current average time is approximately 60 days from when the customer signs the order until he or she drives away in a new car or truck. Toyota does it in a little over 14 days. Both of us manufacture the car in 2 days, and both are targeting 3 days as the ideal. A small portion of the order processing time is accounted for by transportation from the assembly plant to the dealership. The rest of the time is paperwork processing. Orders are preferenced, aligned, assigned, targeted. There are short-term forecasts, long-term forecasts, build and materials restrictions, production plan controls. This list goes on, and the customer waits. Hundreds of GM people are involved in these processes, and many do not draw a direct connection with the work they do to the ultimate customer awaiting a new vehicle. We need to take the waste out of the system and eliminate as much non-value-added work as possible. This is good for both the customer and General Motors because it will cut down on wasted time, talents, and materials. The people impacted can then be redeployed to more meaningful work assignments. There is nothing worse than maintaining a task or assignment that adds no value for an internal or external customer.

The Customer in Our Vision

The corporate vision for General Motors is:

> General Motors—World Leader in Transportation Products and Services. We are committed to Providing Total Customer Enthusiasm through People, Teamwork, Technology, and Continuous Improvement.

The North American Operations (NAO) Strategy Board set its vision:

Total Customer Enthusiasm:

- Business begins and ends with the customer.
- Customer values are embraced throughout the product owner-ship cycle.
- Customer enthusiasm is the ultimate objective.

The system must establish an operational environment that provides for continuous quality improvement and results in total customer satisfaction and ultimately total customer enthusiasm. Every element of the organization is geared to satisfy the customer. *Satisfy* is defined as meeting and exceeding the needs, wants, and expectations of customers, resulting in repeat sales, owner loyalty, and new sales. *Enthusiasm* takes it a step further, using innovation and creativity to excite and delight. We need to be out in front of our customers, offering them something they do not know they want until after they have it. We call this concept the *Total Ownership Experience,* a notion inspired by Ron Haas, GM Vice President of Quality and Reliability. It captures the essence of our leadership initiative "Create an organizationwide customer focus."

Who Are General Motors Customers?

We have been talking about the satisfying and enthusing of the external or ultimate customer as the force that is driving our business system. However, there are many more customer groups we serve. General Motors has an obligation to our many customer groups to succeed—its employees, shareholders, unions, suppliers, dealers, the communities in which it exists, the environment it affects, the industry to which it belongs, and our ultimate customers, the purchasers and users of General Motors products and services. Many customers belong to several of these customer groups. It is not uncommon for a purchaser of a new vehicle to be an employee, union member, or a shareholder who lives in the community in which he or she is employed and is therefore affected by the environment surrounding the community. This list is clearly not all inclusive. Consider the child who runs out into the middle of the street after a misthrown baseball. The quality and performance of the braking system of the car that happens along at that instant are critical to the child, a customer of the system. Our system must:

- Provide a safe and healthful workplace for our **employees,** where they have joy in their work, are confident in their job security, and are proud of the products and services they produce.

- Work in concert with our **unions** to support their efforts to ensure job security and sustain a comfortable standard of living for their members.

- Ensure that our **shareholders** receive a fair return on their investments, and such consideration must be part of the overall aim of the system. It must be noted that General Motors shareholders include pension plans of many large organizations, and many depend on

GM business performance for their livelihood. Decisions made by the company have a profound effect on them.

- Develop long-lasting relationships with its **suppliers,** establishing relationships that provide stability to their businesses and help improve the quality of their products.

- Produce exciting and highly valued products and services for its **dealers** to sell and to offer. Dealers should receive products that require little initial service. Furthermore, dealerships should be well equipped and have trained personnel to provide effective service and customer satisfaction.

- Maintain a strong and healthy business which helps finance and sustain growth in a **community** as well as support communities as they attempt to meet the needs of their citizens. The community must be considered as a company that makes long-term plans. In many cases, businesses and incomes within a community depend on the decisions made by larger employers within their boundaries. General Motors has consistently ranked among the top corporations in the United States in terms of philanthropic contributions. These contributions include grants and in-kind donations to educational institutions, health and welfare organizations, civic and community programs, cultural organizations, and other causes. In 1993, combined worldwide contributions of GM and the GM Foundation were over $54 million. Increasingly, GM is relying on community partnerships to address a broad range of issues, such as educational quality, safety, the environment, diversity, and cancer research. Quality Network's *Employee Excellence Development* Action Strategy works with communities on adult literacy programs.

- Improve products and processes that will contribute to the betterment of the **environment,** for the good of all. This means that as the needs of all the various elements of the system are balanced out, the outcome must have a positive effect on the environment. General Motors and its employees are active in many national and local programs to promote environmental quality, conservation, and automotive safety. This is consistent with our belief that educating the public about environmental, conservation, and safety issues is an integral part of our corporate responsibility. Since 1989, GM has participated with the University of Michigan and local schools to implement GREEN (Global Rivers Environmental Network) projects throughout the United States. GREEN helps students learn about local environmental issues and how to take effective action to resolve problems. Through GREEN, teachers are taking their students to local rivers and teaching them how to monitor water quality, analyze watershed usage, identify the socioeconomic determinants of river degradation, and present their findings and recommendations to local officials. GM is also involved in GREEN projects in Canada and Mexico. The Quality Network *Conserve Resources/Prevent Pollution* Action Strategy is concerned with both product and process environmental issues, such as emissions control of our products and our plants, recyclable materials in our manufacturing process, and targeting "zero-landfill of packaging waste" efforts.

- Support and sustain a strong and healthy American automotive industry. Its sheer size and influence on the nation's job base and economy cannot be understated. Frequently the target of criticism, the automotive industry truly is the engine of the American economy. The economy of the United States cannot survive on pizza makers and hamburger producers alone, although these businesses are important. We must have a strong industrial base providing good, high-paying jobs. High-paying jobs create money to be exchanged in the economy. It is the "velocity of money" (Economics 101) that sustains economic growth and prosperity. Without money in the economy, business will not flourish. The question becomes, "What industry is better positioned than the auto industry to make this contribution to the American economy?" Pizza making? Hamburgers? The service sector? The government (no tax revenue, no government jobs)? And so on....

- Create and provide superior products and services for the **ultimate customer,** meeting and exceeding requirements and expectations while providing excitement and delight. Successful businesses are customer focused. The overall obligation to the customer requires that a corporation exceed customer expectations and provide new and innovative concepts that are considered desirable by customers. Dr. Deming points out clearly that it is necessary to anticipate customer needs because the customer really has no voice in the process, the customer is not in a position to know what he or she may want. For example, how would a customer have known, in 1965, that he or she would be demanding air bags or antilock brakes 30 years later? At the same time Deming holds that the customer is the most important part of the production line. Who are we making the product for? If there are no customers, would there be a business? If customers are dissatisfied, they will leave, and then where will the business go? To the competition. What is the cost to business to replace a defective part or correct a mistake? What is the cost of replacing a customer as a result of faulty work or service? Therefore, quality should be focused on the customer's current needs and those in the future. Businesses decide what they are going to produce and provide to the customer. The only voice the customer has is in the choice of whether to purchase the product or not, whether to use a particular service or not. An important element of customer enthusiasm is in the area of safety. Over the past 10 years, GM has initiated many efforts to educate drivers about safe driving practices. GM has also applied its extensive research on safety to address nonautomotive, as well as automotive safety challenges. The *GM Owner's Manual* devotes over 60 pages to proper restraint system use and driving techniques. GM has distributed hundreds of thousands of brochures on safe driving techniques to schools, safety organizations, the law enforcement community, and to the general public. The correlation between drinking and driving ability and the proper use of safety belts were among the topics covered in videotapes that GM produces and distributes to all primary and secondary schools in the United States. In April 1993, GM sponsored a one-hour network television special titled, *The Ultimate Driving Challenge*. The program demonstrates the importance of driving behavior in avoiding crashes—9 out of 10 of which are attributed to driver error.

Quality and the Ultimate Customer

Dr. Noriaki Kano, a student of Kaoru Ishikawa who was the father of quality control in Japan, perceives three categories of quality attributes, as shown in Fig. 4-1, that are related to satisfying the ultimate customer.[2] There are two aspects of quality that previously have been looked at separately and by two distinct groups. Market research, for one, rates customer perception. Design and engineering looks at product and service attributes. Customer perception of a product or service ranges from dissatisfied to satisfied. Product-service attributes are measured on a scale from insufficient to sufficient.

Kano looks at customer satisfaction in relation to defect reduction and conformance to specification. He learned that the customer, if he or she purchases a product that meets specifications, is neither satisfied nor dissatisfied. The customer expects the product to meet specifications, the customer expects the product to do what it is supposed to

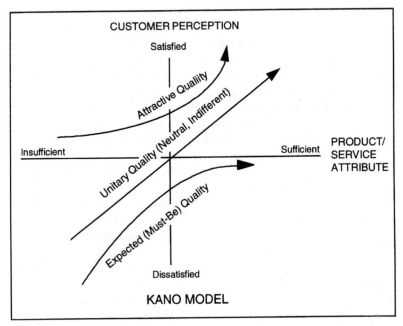

CUSTOMER PERCEPTION

Satisfied

Attractive Quality

Unitary Quality (Neutral, Indifferent)

Insufficient

Sufficient

PRODUCT/
SERVICE
ATTRIBUTE

Expected (Must-Be) Quality

Dissatisfied

KANO MODEL

Figure 4-1.

do. Thus Dr. Kano developed his model depicting the three categories of quality attributes relative to customer perception:

- *Expected quality:* This is "must-be" quality, basic quality. Continuous improvement will cause a leveling off or neutral reaction to this quality attribute. When the attribute is insufficient, not delivering, the customer is dissatisfied. When the attribute delivers, or conforms to requirements, the customer is more satisfied to a point of neutrality. A vehicle must start immediately, must be easy to enter, and must have comfortable seats. Improving basic quality will result in lower warranty costs but will probably not generate new sales.

- *Unitary quality:* This is "got-to" quality, stated and direct performance quality. The more this quality attribute is improved, the better the customer will like it. Continuous improvement is likely to generate sales. Fuel economy is such an attribute.

- *Attractive quality:* This is exciting quality, unexpected and latent, deep in the heart of the consumer. Continuous improvement of attractive quality generates a growing satisfaction on the part of customers, at a greater rate than unitary quality. When attractive quality is insufficient, the customer is neutral. Attractive quality is revenue producing—new features, new services. In the automotive industry attractive features of today rapidly become basic "must-have" features tomorrow: strategically placed cup holders, remote locks, cruise control, stereo radios and tape decks. Prototype cars today feature satellite guidance systems. Will these be standard tomorrow? Color TV in the early years excited customers—even at minimal performance it was still considered a plus.

Dr. Kano uses the color television to further illustrate his point. The attribute of safety is expected, basic. The attribute of electrical consumption is an example of unitary quality. The lower the consumption, the higher the satisfaction. Finally the advent of the remote control is an attractive quality. A television with a remote control used to be an example of an attractive quality. If you didn't have a remote control, you were not dissatisfied, you were neutral. The customer began to get excited with a simple remote control. However, as the customer gets more and more accustomed to innovative features, attractive attributes tend to become expected. The relationship of the customer to quality is dynamic and living. Being basic couch potatoes, we would be lost without our remote control and would never consider buying a TV without one.

What Does the Customer Really Want?

Organizations must ask this question continually. Are we in the business of transporting people or selling buggies? Do we manufacture carburetors, or are we in business to provide fuel delivery systems? Dr. Juran cites the invention of hair spray as the result of an individual recognizing, when his store was out of hair nets, that his customers did not really want hair nets, they wanted to be able to control their hair. Typewriter companies have gone out of business because they failed to realize that their customers didn't want typewriters, they wanted to be able to manage, or process, language for communication purposes. Remington, Smith Corona, and IBM all made great typewriters. Which company moved aggressively into the data and word processing field? The most perfect typewriter in the world today, in 100 percent conformance to specifications, is still obsolete for the most part. Clearly there are places in the world where there is no electricity and a manual typewriter is a cherished possession. These examples help explain Dr.

Deming's insistence that the customer has no voice, does not know what he or she wants. Management must make predictions and be ready for the customer. For the most part we must look to the function or service our customers want to perform. What will our customers be able to do, after they purchase our product or use our service, that they could not do before, and how do they feel about it? Can they get from point *A* to point *B* in a fashion that satisfies their needs? Do they need to haul cargo, transport cub scouts, haul a trailer? How do we know what the customer wants if the customer does not know?

In an effort to explain to Dr. Deming what we meant by the "voice of the customer" (He had, moments before, stated rather soundly that "the customer has no voice"), we used his opening shot at the overhead projector to make our point. Dr. Deming has said, "I would not dignify the company who made that lantern machine with a purchase—it's a piece of junk." We asked him what he would change. He told us in no uncertain terms. We said that's what we mean by the "voice of the customer."

Quality Function Deployment

Quality function deployment (QFD) is a methodology for translating customer needs and wants into requirements and deploying them throughout the product design, manufacturing and assembly processes, education and training, and all aspects of our business. It helps determine the performance levels of all product attributes and functions necessary for customer satisfaction. The QFD method helps set priorities, identify critical characteristics, and set specific targets. It links the customer of today with the product of tomorrow. A basic tenet of Ishikawa's quality philosophy is that marketing is the entrance and exit of quality. Market research tells us what customers like and don't like, how they are using our products, what attributes fall short of expectation, which attributes are winners, and which are losers. The marketing organization gathers product data and circumstantial data in the customer's language. QFD translates this data into the various languages of the business. Technical language, design language, and production language all must communicate with each other, driven by the customer.

More on the Internal Customer

There is an obvious obligation to employees to provide a safe and healthful workplace, along with job security and the opportunity to contribute to the overall success of the system. The primary point here is that employees are the customers of the process. Customer satisfaction for both external and internal customers is a concept that is often misunderstood. External customer satisfaction is easier to understand. It is satisfying the users of the output of the process or the company's ultimate customers who buy the products or services. Total quality is just as concerned with internal customers and internal customer satisfaction. Due to traditional thinking, internal customer satisfaction is a more difficult concept to understand. After all, they have a job, they're getting paid, why do we have to worry about satisfying them? The answer is simple: People are our competitive advantage. They add the value. Everyone, every process, every function has a local customer. An internal customer is the next person in the process, the person who uses the output of your work. For example, when a manager sits down at his or her desk and roughs out a letter, there are certain requirements that have to be met in order to get the job done. The secretary is the customer of the output at that point. She or he has to be able to read the writing and understand its content. Only then can the letter be typed, making sure the spelling and the grammar are correct. The operator of a transfer and/or machinery line is the customer of the job setter, the person who changes tools, dies, and so on; both are dependent on requirements that can be traced back to engineering specifications and design requirements.

Our Dual Role

Most of the time each of us switches back and forth between being a customer and being a supplier. There's a lot of confusion about what it means to satisfy the internal customer. Why the focus on customer satisfaction? What about the people we work with every day? The next person in line is really every person's customer. Meeting the needs of the internal customer is not some "warm-fuzzy" idea that coddles the employee. It is a sound business practice. The employee-customer relationship needs clearly defined requirements to fulfill what is expected of him or her. Employees need the proper tools, equipment, systems, training, information, and environment to do their jobs in the best manner with the best results. Safety and ergonomic issues are critical elements in the equation. Our processes must be designed to include the operators up front and foremost. Andrew Carnegie is quoted as saying that if you took away his people, grass would grow on the floors of his factories. If you tear down his factories, his people would build new ones. Employees are the customers of leadership. This is true for management and union leadership, although this understanding is more clearly built into the union structure. Management is there to put all the resources in place so that employees can do their jobs.

What Do We Mean by Quality?

When we studied the works of the quality experts searching for the one, true, clear definition of quality, we found facets of quality, but not one detailed definition that said it all. In fact, quality is usually defined by telling us what characteristics are present or are lacking in a quality product, service, process, relationship, organization, and so on. We are also given various ways to measure the various aspects of quality. Again, no one definition and no one measure. It is necessary to look at the broad view of quality as espoused by the three quality proponents most prevalent at General Motors to understand the principles, structure, tools, and techniques of the Quality Network.

Dr. Juran describes product or service quality as "fitness to use," how the product or service successfully serves the purpose of the user. He looks at quality from two views: income-oriented quality and cost-oriented quality. *Income-oriented quality* is aimed at satisfying customers' needs, is competitive, and produces revenue for the company. In this understanding, higher quality often costs more, but also creates more income. The luxury options in our vehicles are an example of this. Leather interiors cost more than vinyl and bring more money into the company.

Conversely, the higher the cost-oriented quality, the lower the costs to the company. Here quality means freedom from dissatisfiers: defects, failures, redoing, scrap, and all forms of waste. Juran holds that quality is management's responsibility. The Quality Network focuses on satisfying the customer and is concerned with both cost-oriented quality and income-oriented quality. Income-oriented quality is shaped by the voice of the customer translated into the system through such strategies as quality function deployment.

Dr. Deming was not concerned with the luxury aspects of quality. He did believe defining quality is difficult and that it can be defined only in terms of the agent who is judging quality at the time. Quality, like beauty, is in the eye of the beholder. The customer, or final beholder, is the decisive arbiter of quality. And since, with every new product and service offered, the customer is learning and changing, so too has our understanding of quality got to be redefined on an ongoing basis. Walter A. Shewhart, Deming's teacher and colleague identified the innate difficulty in defining product or service quality: "The difficulty in defining quality is to translate future needs of the user into measurable characteristics, so that a product can be designed and turned out to give satisfaction at a price the user will pay."[3] An essential component of Deming's understanding of quality is value, what the customer is willing to pay and the market is willing to bear. Therefore, it is critical to keep cost to the customer down since the competition will be doing the same. The product or service offered is the output of the system and reflects the costs inherent in that system. To improve the cost element of the system's output, the system itself must be improved. Dr. Deming is known for his tenets on variability and his conviction that productivity improves as variability in the system decreases. Quality controls are used to reduce variation, thereby improving quality and decreasing costs. Inspection of incoming or outgoing products or services is too late and expensive, often allowing defects and errors to be passed along to the customer.

Philip Crosby talks about conformance to requirements, which is measured by the cost of nonconformance. He feels that the customer deserves to receive exactly what was promised by the producer. We should not be in the business of producing defects; therefore, we should have a performance goal of zero defects. In Japan this is an engineering strategy whose implementation is management's responsibility. In the United States, *zero defects* (*defect-free*) was used to motivate workers, was left to the workers to implement, and failed. Quality management, to Crosby, means prevention; he believes all nonpreventative techniques, including the practice of inspection, have no place in a quality system. Errors cannot be tolerated.

An in-depth study of these three quality experts' views would reveal many commonly held beliefs and some divergent thoughts. However, all three agree that management must take a leadership position and be responsible for quality. Juran urges leadership to make quality the top priority in business processes. Dr. Deming declared that quality was made in the boardroom and that management is fully responsible for over 90 percent of all quality problems. Crosby holds that quality be the first among equals, that quality improvement is a process that should be permanent, ongoing, and lasting.

Big Q, Little Q, and Total Q

The way the Quality Network has been looking at quality is "Big Q/Little Q." Big Q is the macroview, reflects organizational excellence, and adheres to the belief that quality is anything that can be improved, and that everything can always be improved. Big Q is the driver of process management and a continuous improvement mindset. Little Q is a microview, specifically concerned with product or service quality. Total quality looks at the entire system, Big Q, knowing that product and service quality are encompassed within the big picture. Product and service quality will result from an excellent organization. Big Q targets improvement efforts in all products, goods, and services, whether for sale or for internal use. All processes, functions, and facilities should be scrutinized for improvement opportunities. Big Q pertains to all industries—manufacturing, service, government, nonprofit, and so on. Big Q defines the cost of poor quality as all costs that would be eliminated if everything were perfect. Little Q specifically describes the quality of manufactured goods and the processes, functions, and plants that are directly associated with their manufacture. In this case, the cost of poor quality is associated with product defects. Little Q is concerned with the quality of the output of the system, the quality that meets the customer.

The Relationship between Quality and Cost

Total quality points up some interesting relationships between quality and cost. Let's take a look at a quality cost quadrant (Fig. 4-2) used by Dr. Jim Kowalick.[4] Total operating costs are plotted from top to bottom on the Y axis with low costs at the bottom and high costs at the top. Quality is plotted across the bottom on the X axis with low quality on the left and high quality on the right. Quality in this case is as the customer perceives it.

If you are building low-quality, low-cost products, most people would classify that as junk. This was what most people felt "Made in Japan" meant in the late 1950s and early 1960s. The products don't cost much, and they don't work. If you're building low quality at high costs, it is called "idiocy." You are spending more and more money to do less. High quality at high costs reflects the belief that you have to spend money to get higher quality. Organizations in this quadrant spend money reactively, with downstream inspection and expensive countermeasures. Intricate inspection processes are put in place because these organizations expect things to go wrong and do not want the wrong things in the hands of the customer. Reactive countermeasures in the automotive industry include recalls, scrap, rework, customer assistance help services, and warranty costs. Total quality

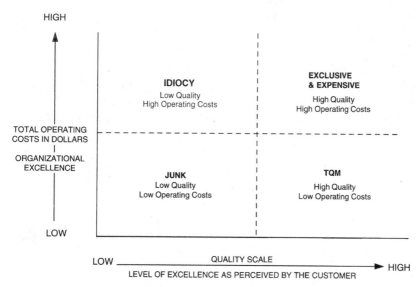

Figure 4-2.

asserts that as you improve the quality of your processes, your costs drop and your product quality increases—thus it is possible to become a high-quality, low-cost producer. This is where we want to be. Proactive policies spend dollars to ensure things do not go wrong. Quality is designed into products and processes. Continuous improvement efforts eliminate waste and variation. Both high quality and low costs are needed to be competitive in today's global market.

This same cost/quality model can be used to point out another difference between total quality and the traditional approach to the cost-quality relationship. The traditional view starts in the high-cost–high-quality quadrant. The organization plans to spend as much capital as necessary to achieve high quality, then step by step, incrementally reduce costs. The problem with this approach is if you have already installed a line, locked everything in concrete, and then find the ventilation and the flooring to be intolerable to the people that work there, the costs to go back and change it are exorbitant. There is also much resistance to make such a change, even if it is the right thing to do. A total quality view is to plan up front to be a low-cost–high-quality producer by using quality processes and policies. It is, therefore, very important to understand that preplanning costs are inexpensive when compared to the tremendous costs to change plans after the fact.

What Can Total Quality Get You?

There is a maxim that has been used often: fast, good, cheap—you can have two out of three. If you have it fast and cheap (at a low cost), it won't be good (right). If you have it cheap (at a low cost) and good (right), it won't be fast. If you have it good (right) and fast, it won't be cheap (at a low cost). Total quality attempts to tackle each of these three areas in order to improve all: to deliver the best product or service in a timely manner at the lowest possible cost; in other words, better, faster, and cheaper.

What about Fast?

We've discussed better: product and service quality, particularly as defined by the customer. The more time it takes to get a product or service to market, the higher the cost both in organizational expenses and resources and in opportunities lost by missing the boat with the customer. Chrysler jump-started the minivan market, and the competition was slow in getting onboard. The influence that total quality and process management thinking has on the time required to bring a product to market becomes very evident. More time is spent in planning and product definition phases. This extra time is rapidly gained back in the product design phase. Real savings are then gained in the reduction in product changes. Process management works to eliminate production changes through prevention. Imagine the cost savings if you spend time eliminating problems at the conception of the design rather than during the production phase. Product quality is likewise enhanced. In an effort to eliminate production problems, GM car and truck platforms are implementing a process whereby employees work on a particular operation with the engineers before the lines are planned or even before the assembly portion of the operation is put on paper. It is producing great results. Hundreds of assembly line subprocesses for new-car production have been improved and refined in these production line laboratories in the assembly plants run by the people who will eventually be putting in the lines and operating them. Figure 4-3 visually demonstrates this concept.[5]

Cheaper

It is a question of warranty costs versus design-it-right-the-first-time, and all the cost issues between these two points. Figure 4-4 represents the cost due to defects at each stage of the product development

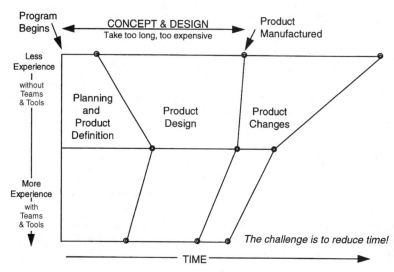

Figure 4-3.

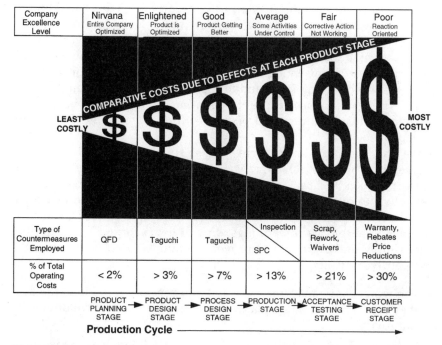

Figure 4-4.

process.[6] The later in the product cycle that defects occur and are addressed, the more costly the intervention becomes. If we direct our attention to those things we want up front, we will not be spending all our time on those things we don't want, such as defects, downstream in our process.

Early-stage countermeasures prevent higher costs in later stages of the product cycle. A company's level of process management excellence is easily determined from where they are accumulating defect costs and the type of countermeasures they are applying to prevent such costs. Warranty costs are an excellent measure of a total quality focus or lack of focus. When the majority of the problems surface with our customers, warranty costs are high, and those defects are extremely expensive to General Motors.

Designing in quality is not the only cost factor addressed in a total quality system. Process management addresses continuous improvement throughout the production process.

Continuous Improvement

Continuous improvement is a mindset, a way each of us should approach and perform our job. Therefore, continuous improvement is everyone's job, and it requires an understanding that however you are doing your job today is the worst way of doing it; tomorrow you will do it better. It is not enough to maintain high standards or levels of attainment. These standards and levels will not be high enough in the near term. The Japanese concept of continuous improvement (*Kaizen*) is people oriented, directed at people's efforts from the worker to top management.

We had the pleasure of being guest speakers at the Utah State University College of Business, May 4–5, 1994. Masaaki Imai, author of *Kaizen: The Key to Japan's Competitive Success,* was also featured as the keynote speaker. We all had dinner together, which provided us with a wonderful opportunity to discuss the world of quality. During the seminar Imai told us three things we will never forget. They sum up very simply the continuous improvement mindset Imai feels is Japan's competitive advantage:

- The worst shape machine tools and equipment will be in is the day they arrive at a Japanese plant—thereafter they will be continuously improved.

- Everyone should view the way they do the job today as the worst it will be because it can be continuously improved.

- If you want the right answers, go to the plant floor and look around, listen, and coach. He says, "Go to GEMBA," which means "go to the plant floor," the subject of his next book.[7]

Continuous improvement requires process-focused thinking. A process is a series of activities executed on an input and resulting in an output, or result, that meets a predetermined customer requirement. In order to improve the results, the processes must be improved. Process management is a methodology to continuously improve a process by increasing its efficiency and effectiveness. There is a fundamental principle underlying all process improvement efforts: You cannot improve results. The only thing that you can improve is the process. This becomes a stumbling block in interacting with people on a plant or office floor. They ask, Why should we be involved in doing anything jointly? Why should we get involved in worrying about how management sets things up? These critical questions must be understood by all. An individual can produce only the best that the process will allow. This is an indisputable fact. If people have input from the beginning when the process can be changed, then the quality of the output of the process improves, creating a win-win situation for both the employee and the company.

Continued Excellence

Continuous improvement is a philosophy of excellence that holds that everything can be improved. It stresses a relentless quest for perfection in small, steady, incremental improvements. It recognizes that quality is an unending journey, and attainment of goals and targets is merely a milepost along the way. Continuous improvement is seemingly in conflict with America's love of championing the rugged individual. We are a results-oriented society, impatient to get to the end. It is difficult for us to image no end in sight. Don Ephlin put it this way:

> Americans are fascinated by the big jump, the quantum improvement. We like those slam dunks, those hail Mary passes, those Olympic records and the home runs. There's nothing wrong with home runs whether you're negotiating new labor contracts or finding a way to improve a metal stamping. But there's another kind of improvement that's not so dramatic. It's like getting a base hit in a baseball game. It isn't always the team that gets the home run that wins. Often it's the team that gets the base hits steadily and consistently. That's what we're looking for at General Motors too. We want those steady, small improvements every day, every week, every year. It's reducing waste by a small amount every day, increasing quality by a small amount every day. Those gains really add up.[8]

Continuous improvement supports lifelong personal and organizational learning. As processes are improved, the learning that takes place becomes institutionalized and contributes to an expanded core body of knowledge.

Reduction of Variation

A powerful way to manage and improve any process is to understand the theory of variation. Variation occurs in all processes. The first step in managing any process and reduce variation is to consider the source of the variation, that is, to distinguish between common cause and special cause variation. Common cause variation is inherent in the way the process is organized and operated. Common cause variation is present in a stable process that is "in control," whose output is predictable. Since it is advisable to try to improve only processes that are in control, the distinction of these two sources of variation has great significance with respect to continuous improvement efforts. A serious loss can occur, according to Dr. Deming, when an outcome is treated as though it occurred from special cause variation when its source was common cause variation. Mistake number 2 is to do the opposite, treating a special cause result as though it were common cause. Continuous improvement efforts must distinguish between the two and take appropriate action. Mary Carter of Learning Designs, Inc.,[9] came up with a simple illustration to convey the difference. When you are driving your car down a road, there will be some movement, or variation, from side to side within your traffic lane. The steadier you are in the center of your lane, the better, but there is no harm done with a little waffling. This is common cause variation. Suddenly a dog darts out from the side of the road. You veer to miss the animal and either head into the oncoming lane or off the side of the road. There may or may not be dire consequences to you, the dog, or others. The dog is a source of special cause variation. Clearly you would and should react differently to smoothing out your car handling as opposed to avoiding the dog, other cars, and a guardrail.

Statistical methodologies such as statistical process control and process capability analysis are effective tools to help monitor and analyze processes. Increased knowledge of any process is the start toward performance betterment of that process. Studying variation and applying statistical tools for data collection is a fundamental approach for all process improvement efforts from the plant floor to staff offices. We look to increase performance on our machinery, reduce error rates in reports and ledgers, reduce scrap rates and conveyance time, improve performance of computer systems, eliminate misscheduling and missed deadlines.

The Famous Red Bead Experiment

For our purposes here, the discussion on variation reduction is brief and serves merely to establish a basic approach to process management. There is no better way to understand variation and an individual's futile attempt to improve personal performance in a stable process than to experience Dr. Deming's famous red bead experiment. Anyone who has worked through the experiment will never forget the importance of process management.

Briefly, "Willing Workers" from the audience are asked to produce **white** beads for a customer. The system's rules and procedures are resolute. The foreman is there to carry out the rules. Independent inspection is used to verify results. There are **red** beads in the supply chain reaching the Willing Workers. There is no method for worker input or departure (some might call it improvement) from the proscribed procedure. The workers are helpless. Common cause variation occurs, and red beads mix with white at the end of the line. One worker may have more red beads than another, through no fault of his or her own. The person with the most red beads is judged the worst worker, the one with the least red beads is the best worker. The experiment illustrates all that is wrong with not understanding that it is the process that produces results: "zero defects" exhortations, ranking workers (or teams, divisions, plants), motivating by increased compensation, reward and punitive programs, rigid procedures, no employee input into the process, lack of supplier involvement, and others.

Dr. Deming made a chilling and uncompassionate foreman in this experiment, part of the system that kept producing the same results no matter what techniques were used to change them. As participants in a Deming Seminar and therefore observers of this experiment, we cringed as workers were chewed out for bad results, and we laughed as they tried to sneak improvement schemes in behind the foreman's back. They were always caught. The message was clear: Nothing was going to change if the process was not changed. At our seminar Dr. Deming told the story that one Willing Worker, a volunteer participant from previous Deming Seminar in Boston, became so frustrated during the experiment that he actually quit. Unfazed, the foreman, Deming, hired another Willing Worker and kept the process going, achieving the same results.

Early in the Quality Network we recognized the importance of process management and continuous improvement and the role understanding variation plays:

> BOB STEMPEL: Traditionally we thought the goal of our manufacturing and engineering was to be able to produce parts that meet specifications. As long as you were within tolerance, you had a good product. Our continuous improvement process has taught us that any variation from the nominal, any variation at all, carries a cost. So the goal of manufacturing and engineering has to be to reduce the variation in every part and every process.[10]

Continuous Improvement by the Elimination of Waste

Efficiency and effectiveness are a manager's constant goals; therefore, the elimination of waste is crucial in any business endeavor. It cuts out the fat and causes work effort to be more productive. In a process management approach to waste elimination, it is important to understand that people are never considered waste but are considered valuable assets. Talents may be wasted because of improper utilization or wasted because no one listens, but people are never waste. Process management seeks to eliminate wasted material by maximizing material utilization.

Process management distinguishes the resources used by a process into two types: (1) the work that adds value to the product or process and (2) non-value-added waste. The objective is to identify and remove various forms of wasted time, talents, and materials from the process. Customer dissatisfaction is a waste; warrantees and litigation are wastes; lost sales are wastes; waivers and deviations are wastes; defective products and services are wastes; overhauling procedures are wastes; unsafe output is a waste; improper use of data from inspection and checking are wastes; poor system designs are wastes; unused talents, inputs, or employee innovation are wastes; poor or no planning are wastes; unnecessary testing, procedure "swamps," watching and waiting for something to happen, high inventories, improper and inadequate training, and ineffective practices and procedures are all wastes. Certainly, there is a need in every organization to look at waste and ways to prevent and eliminate it.

Elimination of Waste, Not People

The elimination of waste does not have to be threatening to those who are involved in areas of representation within a labor union. If process management is successfully implemented and properly utilized to modify the environment, the reallocation of people is planned well in advance—treating people properly, providing job security, and eliminating fears. People should be the focus of any necessary change in resource requirements or any other decisions involving practices and processes. When robotic manipulators and other forms of automation were coming into widespread use within the automobile industry, there was a real concern about such equipment replacing people. However, soon beneficial application of robots became evident. In a foundry there are jobs that are potentially hazardous and undesirable. Some job assignments require close proximity to high temperatures, molten iron, or fumes. Concern over job elimination was not threatening when robots were installed and an operator's job assignment changed from moving hot parts to operating a robot, using that robot to avoid a hazardous work environment. This kind of consideration is an intrinsic part of changing or modifying a process, using the improvement process to take into account the needs of the people involved.

Continuous Improvement and Problem Solving

Problems still arise in a total quality organization; however, a different approach is utilized. First of all, and most important, problems are looked at as opportunities. This requires a major shift in understanding. We need to begin to understand that even in problem situations being able to resolve the problem becomes an opportunity for improvement. We need to begin to look at problems as opportunities to get better.

Second, it must be understood that a costly solution may not be the best answer. Too many times companies inject money or install automation to resolve a problem instead of looking at a simple way to resolve it. Simplicity must become the focus.

Third, it is necessary to view the problem as "our" problem, not "theirs." If the workers or the organization have a problem, then it is not "their problem," it is really the total organization's problem. Any person that has been a supervisor knows that if there is a particular problem within the work force, that problem ultimately affects the supervisor. The same thing holds true if management is having a problem—that problem affects every person that works out on the floor. It is important to understand that as problems surface, they become "our" problems.

Finally, use the appropriate tool. There is an old saying that when the only tool you have is a hammer, everything looks like a nail. It is important to understand that if a problem is faced with the wrong tools, faulty decisions will result. Problem solving is a critical spirit in a total quality organization. Providing problem solving resources, tools, techniques, and education and training is paramount to the success of continuous improvement.

The People Part of the Process

The process management approach to waste identification and removal suggests using employees within the process as consultants. They already know the problems. Most of the time when you go out on a job, you'll find that the workers at the site can tell you right away what the problems are. As we mentioned, Masaaki Imai uses the Japanese phrase "go to GEMBA," go to the plant floor.[11]

Imai, at the Utah State University seminar, made his point by relating a story told by Dr. Deming when discussing the role of workers. Dr. Deming said if you want a good meal, talk to the chef, not the general manager of the restaurant. Likewise, if you want better quality and better answers, talk to the workers.[12]

Problems and concerns must be prioritized. Yes, making money is important for the stockholder. Yes, it is important that things be done efficiently. But, these goals should never be at the sacrifice of someone's health and safety or well-being. The entire range of products and services must be considered when looking at suggestions from people. To assist in preventing recurrence of problems requires that people be given the authority to make changes and decisions to prevent problems from happening. It may mean changing the locations of a glue dispenser to apply a little more in a given area to avoid shutting down a line or allowing workers to decide not to put parts on a vehicle that are faulty. People must have some freedom to be involved in the processes.

People Involvement— Leadership's Roles and Responsibilities

One major difference between Total Quality and other initiatives is the human element. There is a real focus on people; economic benefits are not the only criteria. One of the problems in the past, for many companies, has been a narrowly focused business plan that did not take into account the necessary "people issues" (i.e., ergonomics, health and safety, employee involvement, customer satisfaction, and so on). Decisions were made solely on a financial basis without a lot of concern for the people, made strictly as business decisions. This narrow focus has no place in a total quality organization.

Cost associated with employees injured on the job, lost time, retraining, replacement workers, workers' compensation, and so on, must also be considered when calculating bottom-line results. More important, however, is permitting processes to exist that may cause injury. No job, regardless of its value to the bottom line, can be tolerated if it is unsafe in any way. Safety and health of workers is number 1.

Total quality is very steadfast in its insistence that all stakeholders must be involved in and responsible for quality. This encompasses shop floor operators, administrative personnel, and top leadership. Leaders are charged to define the system and its aim. Leadership must make the decisions and policies that will govern quality actions, decisions to support continuous improvement efforts such as reduction of variation, elimination of waste, and system optimization. Quality is leadership's job—its most important job. This is a critical point that must be made over and over.

You cannot read any materials on business theories, and especially on total quality, that do not stress the role of leadership. Leadership sets the tone; leaders must be visionaries. Today you may be making the very best carburetors, but what will be their worth tomorrow? We have eliminated virtually all carburetors from GM engines manufactured in the United States. At one time we built the best, such as the Rochester Products Quadrajet Carburetor. Today Rochester Products is gone, and so is the Quadrajet. Leadership's behavior reflects its true value of quality in the organization. Leaders must lead by example, or "walk the talk." Our Quality Network Environmental Action Strategy Training stresses that leadership creates the environment: an environment that places quality first, total quality, leadership's responsibility. Since "support for the employee" is one of our Environmental Action Strategies, a total quality process is defined as one in which worker safety, health, and ergonomics are comprehended. Leadership must:

- *Lead the vision* to be shared and clearly communicated actively and visibly

- Communicate *a sense of urgency* for change—a driving need to transform coupled with the stated vision that lets people know where they are going and why

- *Empower* people by allocating the resources (education, training, tools, techniques, supportive environment) in an atmosphere of *trust*

- *Trust* that their people will do a good job and act in a consistent and honest manner that engenders *trust in return*

- *Take personal responsibility* to be stewards of the system, to stay the course while being flexible and receptive to feedback and innovation

Importance of a Vision

The correct focus for any organization is on the customers and people of that organization. The leader's role is to spread that vision. One of the things that leaders have to realize is that it takes a while for people to fully understand this vision. This vision, if not aggressively communicated, may take years to filter down to all of the employees. Communication of this vision is absolutely critical if companies are going to succeed. Leaders have to have the patience to allow their vision to be fully understood by those they lead, supporting others by removing obstacles and providing the necessary resources.

People Involvement—Teamwork

Without teamwork, total quality cannot function; it is an essential component of a total quality system and crucial in a continuous improvement environment. Teamwork does not happen overnight and requires a major shift in thinking on the part of management and workers, unions and management, suppliers and the company, dealers and the company, supervision and operators—in short, all people in the system. Perhaps the most challenging relationship that needed redefining for General Motors was that between our unions and management leadership.

A Change in Attitude

Total quality champions the legitimacy of the joint efforts of labor and management. This philosophy recognizes that cooperative relationships between employers and employees are worth developing and believes that every employee has the ability and the right to offer intelligent and useful inputs into decisions affecting their role and responsibility within the organization. Management, unions, and employees learn how to work better together, determining for themselves what actions and improvements are desirable and workable and can be achieved. Recognition of individual talents and opinions is balanced with the understanding that the ultimate success of most organizations depends on how well people at all levels within that organization can work together to achieve the aim of the system. *Team concept* is an integral part of total quality and typically includes activities focused on such areas as goal setting, problem solving, development of interpersonal relationships among team members, role analysis responsibilities, and team process analysis. Success relies on allowing considerable time for preparing the organization to be truly committed to change.

Possible outcomes from teamwork include improved working conditions, opportunities for personal development, cost reductions, and quality improvements in operations, processes, and physical and social environments. The Japanese have long understood that workers can contribute not only with their manual labor but can also be involved in the decision making. Such involvement enriches the worker's quality of work life by giving them an opportunity to contribute to the overall goals and objectives of the enterprise.

If a worker as an adult is a free citizen in a free society outside the workplace, why then should he or she be deprived of all these rights in the workplace? One local union President put it in a nutshell. It's stupid to hire somebody only from the neck down. Have you never considered that the most important part of the human being, the brain, ought to be used?[13] The answer is obvious and yet, there is often great disagreement on the role of developing our people. Education and training often seems expensive and indulgent to some while to others it is an investment in people that has to be made. Corporations cannot operate without people. This point is illustrated by a conversation held one evening between a prominent General Motors executive and several UAW International Union officials. One of the union officials, Bill Capshaw, was talking to Bill Hoglund, a group executive and GM Vice President, who was concerned about the JOBS Banks (job security agreement providing pay for employees retained at work in lieu of being laid off). Capshaw came up with an excellent and pointed way to illustrate the importance of people:

> If reducing the size of the corporation is going to make GM tremendous amounts of money, then why is it that we have lost employment equal to two Ford Motor Companies since 1979, and we're less productive per employee than we were with 430,000 people? I have a perfect solution. Offer the 230,000 active employees the maximum severance amount of $72,000 and for a one-time blue-light

special of $16.6 billion your dilemma is solved. You can just buy out everyone, and then all the group executives can sit around and make all the money they want to make; you won't have to worry about people.

That remark, although somewhat sarcastic, drove home the point that people are an investment and a necessity to running the business. Bill Hoglund, a GM visionary and a "people person," has always realized the significance of people in the system. But he also was a good financial man and was simply questioning the value of people sitting in a cafeteria drawing full wages with nothing to do when GM was losing billions of dollars. Organizations must constantly look for ways to utilize workers during recessionary periods. Training and reskilling in a planned approach is one constructive way to occupy idle workers' time. However, instead of looking at training as an expense, training must be considered an investment in the future, just as capital investments. People are an asset that are more important than the equipment, materials, machinery, and processes in any corporation and must be recognized as such. Value is added by the work force. Toyota has a 40-year plan for addressing the future that places high value on people. All corporations need to have that kind of vision.

Workers themselves began to see a chance, maybe for the first time in their entire working career, to be involved in the decision-making process. People who had for years been relegated solely to putting on front brake lines or involved only in feeding parts into a press were all of a sudden asked, "Is there a better way to do this? What do you think?" This immediately created an atmosphere of excitement, while at the same time, an atmosphere of doubt and lack of trust. This style in the workplace was new, and traditional, adversarial techniques die hard.

"Resistance also stems from lower-level managers' reluctance to give up power. Most team systems replace foremen with team leaders. Remaining managers must suggest and discuss rather than issue orders, which is a major cultural change for management," says Ken Norden, a manager at an old-style, dog-eat-dog GM plant in Baltimore before he moved to Shreveport. "The adjustment was a little hard for me at first. It's difficult to share the responsibility, but many managers can't who grew up in the old, dictatorial role."[14]

Middle- and upper-management personnel did not like dealing with workers' representatives on an equal basis. Many workers' representatives and workers themselves felt teamwork was simply a method used by management to weaken their bargaining powers and undercut contractual methods of improving workers' wages and benefits.

Earlier quality of work life (QWL) efforts raised an awareness within General Motors management that company methods and systems must be modified to use the knowledge and talents of its most important resource, the men and women on the job. GM people, not just technology, were recognized as key to competitive advantage. People produce, apply, maintain, modify, and improve technology. In the late seventies and early eighties the American automotive industry was comparable to the competition in technology; where we were different was how we treated people and people systems as exemplified by the Japanese Production System. The United Automobile Workers had encouraged worker participation in the decision-making process on the job for many years through contract provisions establishing quality of work life programs, joint apprentice programs, joint health and safety programs, joint time study methods, and other programs or methods. However, efforts were isolated and lacked a systems approach. They were highly and often very narrowly focused. Lessons learned from one program did not migrate to others; organizational learning did not take place. As important as these early efforts were, neither party successfully bridged the gap between worker participation in the decision-making process and traditional management responsibilities and union rights. Negotiations subsequent to 1973 continued to address joint participation, searching for a balance between specific and joint responsibilities. This evolving dialogue on jointness increased understanding for both parties.

Our Understanding of Teamwork

We have come a long way and have a long way to go. *Team concept* has created heartburn for many, and the term is not used in some of our locations today. However, the concept of teamwork is broader and has general acceptance. It reflects the internal customer-supplier relationship, provider-user, superior-subordinate, and it is collegial in nature. Each person is respected for his or her expertise and responsibility, as a contributing member who complements the team. It is extremely important that participants have a good understanding of what teamwork is all about. It does not replace individual skills or subvert personal responsibility and contribution, it enhances them. Why teams? Synergy! Team members are mutually dependent upon one another and must be mutually committed to the purpose of the team's work, all pulling in the same direction.

Empowered Teams

Empowered teams at all levels involve all the stakeholders and ask the people who know best how the job is done. Teams create learning environments. As the group moves toward its goals, individual members should learn from each other. The excellence of individual team members should be blended to create an outcome of balanced excellence that contributes to the optimization of the system and the system's aim. A team is a working subset of a larger system it serves. The output of a team's work should be an excellent product or service and more knowledgeable team members.

Teamwork Is a Relationship

Teamwork describes how you work together, a give-and-take of ideas, skills, and experience for an excellent outcome. Teams may be formally organized with published goals, a name, agreed-to norms, regularly scheduled meetings, and a sunset timeline. However, teamwork just as readily describes the style and interplay between any two or more people or entities. It is also important to understand that teamwork demands an environment in which all participants agree to disagree. "You're not a team player" should not be used to stifle lively and challenging dialogue.

Total Quality Principles at GM

The tenets of total quality, systems orientation, customer focus, Big Q/Little Q, continuous improvement, process focus, and people involvement through leadership and teamwork, are summed up in the Quality Network's *Beliefs & Values:* Customer Satisfaction and Enthusiasm through People, Teamwork, and Continuous Quality Improvement. This is the foundation of the Quality Network and was the linchpin for our total quality process.

Early Beginnings at General Motors

The Quality Network is premised upon union and management working together for mutual gain. For such a relationship to be feasible, both parties have to be equally committed to the goal of creating a climate of mutual trust and respect. Creating such a climate is accomplished through a number of mechanisms. First, all communication concerning the Quality Network was jointly announced by top leadership of both entities. The Quality Network was announced at the Seventh Annual General Motors Quality Conference, broadcast throughout the corporation on January 13, 1988, and hosted by Don Ephlin and Bob Stempel. Although this was the seventh conference, it was the first joint quality conference and set the precedent for all subsequent quality forums. Second, Quality Network awareness training was designed and delivered jointly. The Quality Network was rolled out to the corporation through a series of workshops delivered in the first quarter of 1989. Plant-level leaders from each group (Truck and Bus, Chevrolet-Pontiac-GM Canada, Buick-Oldsmobile-Cadillac, Automotive Components Group, Power Products and Defense, Delco Electronics, Technical Staffs Group, Corporate Support Staffs, and Service Parts Operations) were led through two days of interactive team building exercises as they learned about the Quality Network. Top UAW leadership and GM Group Executives presented the sessions together. Participants sat at tables in groups of 10, including the "key 4" from a plant—Plant Manager, Chairperson of the Bargaining Committee, Personnel Director, and local union President—all seated together. In 10 sessions, over 4000 union and management leaders attended the workshops together. Subsequent Quality Network materials, programs, workshops, and classes have all been jointly developed and implemented. A work environment education and training package has been designed for every location to participate in. Four strategies are presented for mutual consideration and understanding:

- Support for the employee
- Top leadership commitment and involvement
- Communication
- Cooperative union-management relations

These classes are designed to be jointly taught to groups with joint representation. Trust and respect cannot be mandated. However, much can be done in the design and execution of communication and education and training plans to help build these two critical factors.

Components of the Quality Network

The Quality Network is General Motors' one total quality management process that brings together all the components of the diverse, large, and complex system for the purpose of attaining the vision of total customer satisfaction and enthusiasm. The Quality Network provides the four elements necessary to realize the vision: a value system, a structure, a process focus for analysis and understanding, and tools and techniques for continuous quality improvement. The philosophical foundation of the Quality Network is our value system. All other elements are footed in the *Beliefs & Values* and contribute to their implementation at General Motors.

The *Beliefs & Values*

Union and management leadership understood that a common set of beliefs and values was needed to define a basis for desired organizational behavior of any cooperative relationship. There had to be a shared value system for all. A group of General Motors top officials took on the task of articulating a value system for General Motors that would govern both the decision-making process and the treatment of people. A collaborative interview process obtained the views of union and management leadership. Input from all the sources queried was startling and consistent. Most people want to be respected, trusted, and involved. Their responses reflected how people want to be treated in both their personal and professional lives and constituted a set of guidelines for successful relationships. In addition, respondents identified the customer as the final arbiter of products and services and affirmed that quality improvement is a never-ending journey.

The results were codified and became known as the *Quality Network Beliefs & Values*.[15] They provide the cohesiveness necessary for a shared vision and have been adopted and championed by union and management alike. The *Beliefs & Values* of the Quality Network provide constancy of purpose: **Customer Satisfaction and Enthusiasm through People, Teamwork, and Continuous Quality Improvement.** Following are the *Beliefs & Values* of the Quality Network, fully endorsed by General Motors and the UAW:

Customer Satisfaction through People...
- Invite the people of GM to be full partners in the business.
- Recognize people as our greatest resource.
- Demonstrate our commitment to people.
- Treat people with respect.
- Never compromise our integrity.

We believe that the people of GM and the UAW are General Motors' greatest strength. Through their dedication and commitment to excellence, our people are the key to achieving our customer satisfaction goals.

Customer Satisfaction through Teamwork...

- Build through teamwork and joint action.
- Take responsibility for leadership.
- Make communications work.
- Trust one another.
- Demand consistency in the application of this value system.

Joined as a team in a spirit of cooperation, union, management, hourly and salaried employees are working to achieve a common goal—customer satisfaction.

Customer Satisfaction through Continuous Quality Improvement...

- Make continuous improvement the goal of every individual.
- Put quality in everything we do.
- Eliminate every form of waste.
- Use technology as a tool.
- Accept change as an opportunity.
- Establish a learning environment at all levels.

The people of General Motors are committed to the concept of continuous improvement in our treatment of people and in everything we do.

The Quality Network is people, working together in the spirit of teamwork, continuously improving products, processes, services, and relationships. The *Beliefs & Values* serve as a creed for all GM employees, articulating how **all GM people** should behave as they work together to improve every aspect of the business. All decisions and actions are tested against them. This requirement allows the process to flourish and establishes what is "OK to do" in GM.

Operational Look at the *Beliefs & Values*

Practically speaking, how do these lofty people statements play out in the workplace? They change how we look at things. They change how we relate with one another. They change how we approach our business. We are moving to a total quality organization. The Quality Network focus takes on traditional management and union mindsets. The traditional approach to problems is to examine the problem only when there is a crisis, then be involved using a Band-Aid approach to resolve it. Quality Network focuses on prevention, anticipating problem situations that may arise and then implementing corrective action to prevent the situation from happening. The traditional view of the customers is that they are to be sold to, told exactly what they need, and told through advertisements what they like and do not like. Under the Quality Network, the focus is to satisfy the customer, both internal and external.

The traditional view of workers and the members who are represented by labor unions is that they are a burden. Under the Quality Network, people are looked upon as assets. This is the biggest paradigm shift that cultural change must bring about. Processes must be people focused, and the people who operate these processes must be viewed as real assets. In traditional organizations, the shop floor is viewed as the source of the problem or failure. It is not viewed as the source for improvement, the way to make things better. Shop floor methods are normally viewed as static and routine. "This is the way we've always done things; this is the way it came down from engineering; this is the way we're going to do it!" It does not matter how many seconds are wasted walking from a job to a parts bin when that bin could be set right beside the operator, saving time and making things better for the operator. "This is the way we've always done it; this is the way it's set up, and this is the way we are going to continue to do it!" The Quality Network approach recognizes the importance of productive change. "Let's move that parts bin right beside the operator. Then all the operator has to do is reach over, pick up the part, and put it in its place."

In a traditional organization success is measured generally based on end results only. In the Quality Network, you look at process improvement and improvement trends. Staff attitudes in a traditional organization are generally critical as opposed to the Quality Network where they are helpful. Solutions in a traditional organization focus on people; however, in the Quality Network, the focus is on systems. Information in a traditional organization is generally restricted or closed, but in the Quality Network it is shared.

The management approach in a traditional organization is departmental as opposed to cross-functional in the Quality Network. Focus is on control in a traditional organization. Traditional organizations focus on results instead of process and support for people as in the Quality Network. There is a status-quo, short-term mentality in traditional organizations versus the long-term, change mentality of a TQM organization. Appraisals in a traditional organization focus on weaknesses, whereas in the Quality Network the focus is on strengths of individuals and teams.

In the past, unions have been considered adversarial. Why not make them partners in the future, recognizing that they have valuable input, information, and leadership to offer? This is key to the Quality Network. Our partnership is one of the major key success factors for our quality improvement.

Training, traditionally, has been, "Do as you are told—just do it!" The Quality Network approach is very different. It is ongoing, willing to look at change, willing to update employee skills. Supervisors, who were inspectors in the past, must become coaches, facilitators, helpers in the future. They must become people who try to eliminate obstacles. They are now part of the team. Figure 4-5 sums up the shift in thinking from traditional thinking to the Quality Network and the *Beliefs & Values*.[16]

Dr. Deming and the *Beliefs & Values*

Our *Beliefs & Values* provide guidelines for organizational behavior. They were created by General Motors people, for General Motors people, to fit the unique needs and culture of General Motors. They reflect a partnership between General Motors and UAW leadership. They are designed to be followed by all GM people, union and management, and serve as guidelines for corporate behavior and for each part of the corporation. Like Dr. Deming's Fourteen Points for Management, they tell us what we should be doing. The Quality Network is not solely based on the teachings of Dr. Deming, but it does owe a great debt to him. While the Quality Network does not copy Deming, it is closely aligned with the principles and techniques championed by him. The thrust of Dr. Deming's work is to challenge management to live up to its responsibilities as leaders. He tacitly recognizes that the work force will make the improvements, but only when allowed to do so by management. The Quality Network covers a wider spectrum, extending out to General Motors' union leadership as well as its own management. All leadership is responsible to lead the quality process, just as all workers are responsible for quality within their respective scope.

Basic to the Deming philosophy is the thought that higher levels of quality, aimed at the consumer, improve productivity, decrease costs, and inspire market share, which in turn sustains the health and success of the organization. The Quality Network expresses a similar view. For General Motors, customer satisfaction and enthusiasm, achieved through people, teamwork, and continuous quality improve-

Characteristics	Traditional Union Point of View	Traditional Management Point of View	Quality Network Point of View
Problem treatment	Management's problem	Crisis	Prevent problems
View of customers	Only management can influence	Sell	Satisfy and delight
View of workers	Responsibility (health, safety, ergonomics)	Burden	Assets, greatest resource
Shop floor	Part of the business they can influence	Source of problems	Continuing source of improvements
Shop floor methods	Tedious and boring	Static and routine, minimum of skills	Meaningful and continuously improving
Measures of success	Doing what you are told	Only the end result	Improvement trends in product, process, service, & relationships
Focus on solutions	Management's responsibility	People, someone to blame	Improve the system
Treatment of information	"I'd like to know why. Why won't someone tell me?"	Confidential, restricted access	Open, honest, and shared
Focus of appraisal	Focus on weaknesses	Focus on weaknesses	Focus on strengths
Training	Part of the job	Necessary evil	Ongoing, positive contribution
Supervisors	Police	Inspectors	Coaches, team members
The way we view each other	Adversaries	Adversaries	Partners
Vehicle design	Not involved—"Why didn't you ask?"	Fix it later	Design in quality

Figure 4-5.

ment, is the master plan. John Roach, a quality consultant to the Quality Network, aligned Dr. Deming's Fourteen Points with portions of our *Beliefs & Values,* to promote a better understanding of the two within the Quality Network community. We offer this study here to do the same for the reader. There has been no attempt to determine how well our guidelines match Dr. Deming's. The judgment is left to the reader.[17] Each of Deming's points is listed followed by a short quote or two from the Quality Network *Beliefs & Values* booklet distributed within the corporation. It must be noted that there are several versions of Dr. Deming's Fourteen Points for Management. Most differ in minor word changes or the amount of detail provided. For purposes of brevity, the version of the Fourteen Points used here can be found on the rear dust jacket of Dr. Deming's *Out of the Crisis.*

Deming's Fourteen Points As Reflected in our *Beliefs & Values*

1. Create constancy of purpose for improvement of product and service.

   - The Quality Network is General Motors' total quality process.
   - For General Motors, customer satisfaction is the master plan.
   - Customer Satisfaction and Enthusiasm through People, Teamwork, and Continuous Quality Improvement.

2. Adopt the new philosophy.

   - To achieve the goals of the plan (customer satisfaction), the UAW and GM jointly commit to improve every area of our relationship. The foundation of this commitment is GM and UAW people working together through the Quality Network.

3. Cease dependence on inspection to achieve quality.

   - The Quality Network is based on continuous quality improvement. Everything can be improved. In today's competitive world, customer satisfaction is achievable through improvements in our products, our services, and the ways we treat people. Customers have many choices. We must design our improvements so that we are, and we remain, our customer's first choice.

4. End the practice of awarding business on the basis of price tags alone. Instead, minimize total cost by working with a single supplier.

   - Every person in GM—including the supplier and dealer base and the customers who buy our products—is part of our quality team.

- We believe we should have consistent and predictable dealings with all people associated with GM. No matter what business conditions exist, consistent application of this value system at all levels of the corporation is essential.

5. Improve constantly and forever every process for planning, production, and service.

   - *Make continuous improvement the goal of every individual.* Each person in GM should have the goal of continuous improvement as perceived by his or her customer. Small improvements can eventually add up to great strides in meeting our individual and common goals. Innovation and breakthroughs are part of continually improving and should focus on caring for customer wants and expectations.

6. Institute training on the job.

   - *Make communications work.* We believe that communications is the lifeblood of our success. Every person wants to understand his or her job assignment and its importance to the entire corporation.

7. Adopt and institute leadership.

   - *Take responsibility for leadership.* In the broadest sense, it's the responsibility of everyone to be a leader. We believe in leadership by example and in sharing the leadership task. The test of our leadership ability is the extent to which people are contributing and working effectively as a team.

8. Drive fear out.

   - *Trust one another.* Mutual trust binds this value system and should prevail throughout the corporation. Trust creates an openness in problem-solving relationships. And for mutual trust to flourish throughout the corporation, we must deal with people openly, honestly, and respectfully. Simply put, we trust those who trust us.

9. Break down barriers between staff areas.

   - *Put quality in everything we do.* All of us are suppliers to those who receive the results of our work. We need to continually ask who our customers are, what their needs and wants are, and how these can best be fulfilled. Our internal customer chain should be driven by the expectations of our external customers. From suppliers to the shop floor, from the office to the dealers, our success depends on our ability to care for our customers.

10. Eliminate slogans, exhortations, and targets for the work force.

    - The Quality Network is the master plan to channel the enormous talent and dedication of General Motors people.
    - The Quality Network can ensure business success for General

Motors and job security for General Motors people. Jointly conceived and implemented, the Quality Network is the process that will assist us in improving every aspect of our business.

11. Eliminate numerical quotas for the work force and numerical goals for management.

   - This area is not addressed in our *Beliefs & Values*. However, under "accept change as an opportunity...," part of our continuous improvement effort is to remain open to new ideas. Change requires the adoption of new practices and philosophies and the discarding of those no longer applicable.

12. Remove barriers that rob people of pride of workmanship. Eliminate the annual rating or merit system.

   - *Recognize people as our greatest resource.* We believe people want to realize their full potential. To do this, we must solicit their ideas, draw on their expertise, and seek their creative involvement in all phases of the business. Each person is an important resource in terms of his or her knowledge and skills.

   - *Treat people with respect.* All people have a basic dignity and should be respected. We believe people treated with respect will treat others with respect.

13. Institute a vigorous program of education and self-improvement for everyone.

   - *Establish a learning environment at all levels.* We will invest in education and training for the people of GM so that they are able to sharpen their skills and keep up with new technologies and new techniques. This is necessary to feed the continuous improvement process. That means learning from each other, learning from our competitors, and learning from our mistakes. A proper learning environment enhances our capacity to grow.

14. Put everybody in the company to work to accomplish the transformation.

   - Invite the people of GM to be full partners in the business. We believe in fully utilizing people's talents because the security of our employees is directly linked to the success of the corporation. People are first—because they are an asset, a talent, and a resource.

Our Constancy of Purpose

The *Beliefs & Values* represent our constancy of purpose. They are the criteria we use to run our business. They are a departure from the way we, union and management, dealt with each other in the past. They keep all of us on track and dedicated to constantly improving our business so that we satisfy our customers, remain competitive in the marketplace, and provide jobs for all of us. They have remained intact through leadership changes and economic up and down swings. They are the basis of all our processes and strategies. And, so far they work.

Notes

1. Dr. W. Edwards Deming, *The New Economics for Industry, Education and Government,* seminar, July 14–17, 1992, module 3, "Introduction to a System," p. 46. Dr. Deming has since published a book of the same title from a notebook he had used (Cambridge, Mass.: MIT Center for Advanced Engineering Study, 1993).

2. Dr. Noriaki Kano, Chairman of the Department of Manufacturing Science at Science University in Tokyo, presented a lecture at the GM Systems Engineering Center, October 18, 1994, titled *Quality Planning and Quality Creation: Quality in the Year 2000.* Our comments are from notes taken at this seminar.

3. W. Edwards Deming, *Out of the Crisis,* Massachusetts Institute of Technology, Center for Advanced Engineering Study, Cambridge, Mass., 1986, p. 169.

4. Dr. Jim Kowalick, Ph.D., *Organizational Excellence Beyond Total Quality Management,* a seminar delivered at General Motors in Warren, Mich., Renaissance Leadership Institute, Oregon House, Calif., October 26–28, 1994.

5. Ibid.

6. Ibid.

7. From conversations with Masaaki Imai at the 19th Annual Quality and Productivity Seminar held by the Partners in Business at Utah State University College of Business, May 4–5, 1994.

8. Donald Ephlin, Vice President UAW, Director General Motors Department, remarks at the ASQC Fourth Annual Quality Forum, October 5, 1988.

9. Mary Carter is President of Learning Designs, Inc., an instructional design firm in Auburn Hills, Mich., that has done extensive work for the Quality Network and the UAW–GM Human Resource Center.

10. Robert C. Stempel, President of General Motors, remarks at the ASQC Fourth Annual Quality Forum, October 5, 1988.

11. Masaaki Imai, remarks at the 19th Annual Quality and Productivity Seminar held by the Partners in Business at Utah State University, May 4–5, 1994.

12. Ibid.

13. Barry Bluestone and Irving Bluestone, *A Labor Perspective on American Business*, Basic Books, New York, 1992, p. 1.

14. A. Bernstein and W. Zellner, "Detroit vs. the UAW: At Odds over Teamwork," *Business Week*, August 24, 1987, p. 55.

15. *Quality Network Beliefs & Values* (QN no. 851), published February 1991.

16. The chart in Fig. 4-5 is an adaptation of a chart used by Dr. Jim Kowalick of the Renaissance Leadership Institute.

17. John A. Roach is President of Roach Communications, Inc., Grosse Pointe, Mich., and, as a consultant in total quality management and business communications, he has done extensive work for the Quality Network.

5
Implementing the Network

Public Announcement and Influence

The public announcement of the Quality Network came in the September, 1987, issue of *Fortune* magazine, though the advertisement aimed at assuring the customer of the quality of General Motors products. The *Quality Network Leadership Guide*, published January 30, 1989, states: "The Quality Network is our joint process for focusing on customer satisfaction, which is, and must be, our highest priority."[1]

The influence of our various quality experiences and learnings began to change General Motors Corporation in a way that would be beneficial to all General Motors employees and their representatives. Union and management leadership believed that if a corporate transformation were to really take place, with an emphasis on the value and responsibility of the individual, General Motors could again recapture the heart and support of America.

Umbrella Over All But Limited to Quality Focus

The implementation of the Quality Network began with an ambitious goal of becoming the overarching process for all GM programs. Reality dictated that the UAW Collective Bargaining Agreement be the main driving force in day-to-day relationships and that the UAW–GM Quality Network be a true joint process for assuring quality of product and process. Although a total quality philosophy, as we understood it, incorporates every aspect and group within a system, the initial thrust for implementation was in the manufacturing sector and, more specifically, with those activities whose work force was represented by a union. Product and service deliverables became our area of concentration.

Leadership Committed to a Joint Decision-Making Process

Past joint processes based solely on human value foundations had fallen off dramatically in their effectiveness because true joint decision making was never really achieved. UAW and GM leadership determined that the *Beliefs & Values* that formed the basis for the Quality Network would not be permitted to deteriorate and that true joint decision making would evolve. Top GM leadership was aligned in a structure that gave UAW leaders direct counterparts all the way up the corporate ladder, including the President of General Motors Corporation who, along with the UAW Vice President and Director of the GM Department, chaired the corporate quality council. Quality councils were established at the national-group, divisional-staff, and plant levels to meet regularly to plan and prepare for implementation improvement in every aspect of the corporation based on "people" values. As explained by then President of General Motors Corporation, Robert Stempel, he and the Vice Presidents of General Motors met in a series of self-evaluation meetings and came to the conclusion that they needed to do better in the "people side" of the business. The framework for the Quality Network *Beliefs & Values* emerged from these meetings, along with a commitment to make General Motors workers true partners in the business in decisions affecting them in the future. This commitment first manifested itself with the inclusion of union leadership in the final design of the company's value system. This was new territory for both the union and management, and it was not without its detractors.

Doubt among UAW leaders and members about the sincerity of the commitment to a new set of beliefs and values understandably followed. Was this just another corporate efficiency program, or was this really a sincere attempt to change the culture within GM Corporation?

Hadn't they been through this all before? Skepticism was also prevalent among management; the fear of losing their power base and authority was a factor. The basis for supervisory activities was compromised in the eyes of many. How were they going to do their jobs?

The Structure

With a value system written and adopted, albeit not universally embraced, we recognized the need for an operational structure specifically designed to communicate and address quality concerns, develop and provide critical training, establish quality processes, and conduct benchmarking studies to ensure world-class products and continuous improvement and to allay management and worker concerns. Training materials are available from numerous outside sources; however, material developed by experts within the company and compared to similar training in the field provided the best method for addressing the needs of General Motors, its culture, and its newly formed jointly administered quality initiative. There was little to nothing available to accommodate these criteria.

First a structure, the second element of the Quality Network, had to be put in place—one that would effectively oversee and guide all of our efforts. The basis for our configuration was the concept of interlocking quality councils, including all of the key stakeholders since it was vitally important for efforts to be coordinated and effective. The structure contained provisions for the establishment of necessary resources to pursue quality improvement efforts and provide meaningful direction from the highest levels of the corporation. This ensured that development and implementation was viewed by all as *one* process to be utilized throughout the entire system.

A formal structure (see Fig. 5-1), detailed in the 1987 National Agreement, called for the creation of a corporate quality council, consisting of the top GM operating officers and top UAW administrative staff members. The name of this council was changed in 1992 to the NAO UAW–GM Quality Council, reflecting a corporate restructure that created the North American Operations (NAO). The President of General Motors and the UAW–GM Department Vice President cochair this council. Originally the council met three times per year, or more often if needed, to establish directives for joint action on quality issues. Currently we meet twice a year and continue to provide direction on joint quality initiatives.

This highest-level quality council is composed of top GM executives and top officials for the UAW. Their challenge is to guide the organiza-

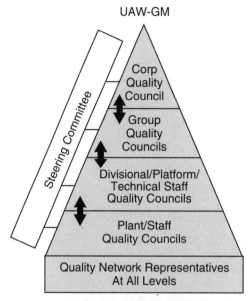

Quality Network in 1987

Figure 5-1

tion to be certain that the quality process is responsive to day-to-day issues and remains focused on total customer satisfaction. This council is an open forum where issues can be raised and discussed freely. An example of the impact that discussions at these council meetings can have is evidenced in the 1993 National Agreement, which reflects a difficult issue that was addressed and solved in council meetings. The issue revolved around the synchronous organization.

Stress in the System

Between 1989 and 1992, GM North American Operations endured operating losses requiring an emphasis on elimination of waste, efficient processes, and a more focused approach to product quality. We had to "stop the bleeding." Efforts to address these concerns resulted in the implementation of various quality improvement activities, such as the Quality Network, the Quality Network Implementation Process (QNIP), synchronous workshops, benchmarking, accelerated workshops (i.e., PICOS), lean manufacturing, process modeling, reengineering, and best practices. Some of these are processes, some activities, some programs. Some may be seen to be a subset of another. For example, process modeling is the first step in conducting a benchmarking study. Synchronous workshops highlight many Quality Network action strategies for immediate implementation on the job site. Each of these thrusts had a champion or champions. The goal of all these efforts is to streamline a process, take the fat out, do more and better work with fewer resources, work smarter, not harder—all to satisfy the customer.

Each wanted to be the savior, to proffer the one right way for General Motors to become more efficient, effective, and flexible. Unfortunately in many cases these efforts worked at cross purposes. Implementation of these activities caused confusion in some locations as they appeared to rival Quality Network efforts. In other locations activities like lean production and reengineering did not invite union involvement. Although improvements were realized in the areas of health and safety, ergonomics, and operations that affected the quality and cost of GM products and services, in many cases they caused certain jobs to be eliminated and some UAW-represented GM employees to be placed in a JOBS Bank (Job Opportunity Bank Security). On the one hand we in GM were asking union workers to partner with management and streamline work processes; on the other hand, the reward for such partnering was to lose jobs, sending workers into the JOBS Bank. This means that they had virtually lost their jobs, and, yes they were paid for a period of time, but they were not generally redeployed to meaningful work.

The Synchronous Controversy

One area where conflicting understanding and efforts converged was in the precepts of synchronous manufacturing. The Quality Network has a leadership initiative, "Synchronize the Organization" and several action strategies to support this undertaking; redeployment to meaningful work is a integral part of this initiative. The corporation established a separate synchronous task team with no union representation and seemingly no redeployment focus. Since most synchronous activities were aimed at the plant floor, formation of this separate task team seemed to be a violation of the belief that all people should be partners in the business and all stakeholders should be involved in policies that affect them. Suspicion, distrust, and fear resulted. *Synchronous* became a bad word, and resistance from union members grew.

Tom Weekley on Synchronous Techniques

July 12, 1990, I sent a confidential letter to the UAW–GM Department staff to clarify for union leadership the advantages and friction that were centering on synchronous techniques. In my opinion at the time the tremendous confusion among our local union leadership was a direct consequence of improper implementation on the part of management at several locations. While I understood the benefits derived from synchronous efforts, I also understood the rancor that mismanagement caused, forcing us once more into an adversarial role fighting for our jobs. I did see that the way out was the use of Quality Network synchronous tools and techniques, which had been jointly developed, and created a manufacturing process to illustrate my point (Fig. 5-2). I offered the simple definition of *synchronous* as a means to ensure that all processes used in producing a product are designed to operate at the speed of the final output of the product.

> Every major corporation in the world today uses synchronous concepts in order to compete. If we are going to be successful in getting management to insource work and increase UAW content while at the same time paying better wages and benefits and increasing employment, General Motors must utilize synchronous concepts. If implemented properly, synchronous need not be a threat and can be used to obtain our goals as a union.[2]

The point this fictitious process illustrates is that although many subsystems are capable of producing more than is needed in a given period of time (here an hour), a synchronous process produces only what it needs. The consequence of a nonsynchronous operation can be seen in piles of unused inventory prone to damage and rust. Manufacturing floor space serves as storage areas rather than being better used in a productive manner. The controversy is over how you use the time of the people freed up due to less scheduled work. It is easy to see how workers could view synchronous operations as a means to eliminate jobs. However, if a redeployment plan is in place, workers are free to pursue activities such as training, improve processes, and solve problems.

The Conflict Continues

Union workers did get involved in synchronous activities primarily through the Quality Network. However, there were still two paths to follow, and at some locations the situation was extremely volatile.

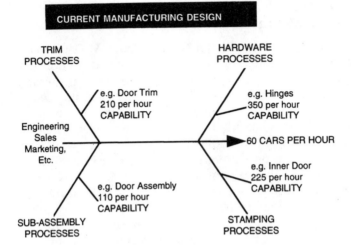

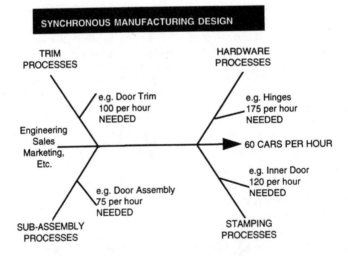

All numbers are for illustrative purposes only.

Figure 5-2

Management did not seem to understand the mixed messages it was sending. This matter was hotly debated in quality council meetings. In an effort to calm the situation, management agreed not to automatically place any worker in the JOBS Bank because of utilization of Quality Network action strategies. Efficiencies could be gained through the Quality Network, and workers were not in jeopardy. There was still conflict and misunderstanding. Tom Weekley wrote a second letter, September 24, 1992, in which he again addressed the problem:

> Our future jobs depend upon processes that produce high quality and are designed to fit machines to people, rather than people to machines. Our involvement in the Quality Network synchronous action strategies provides our members and leaders a way of doing this. If we refuse to be active, then we fall prey to the same mistakes that management has made in the past that will cost our members thousands and thousands of jobs. By being involved in the synchronous strategies, local unions are not agreeing to job reductions but are having a voice in the future of the members that they represent.[3]

A union representative was put on the management synchronous team and both sides agreed to find a way to work together to consolidate efforts. However, there had been a breech of trust at many locations. The damage had to be repaired. The upshot was clear language in the 1993 National Agreement that put the issue to bed: "The Union leadership felt they could not be party to asking their members to assist in 'working themselves out of a job' by supporting these efforts. In any joint effort, job security and 'people issues' have to be considered so that people would be redeployed to meaningful work."[4] The issue had been discussed at the January 13, 1992, GM quality council meeting and resulted in specific commitments to integrate synchronous efforts into the joint Quality Network process and explore ways to employ people more effectively with meaningful work to help improve the business. Both Steve Yokich, UAW Vice President and Director of the GM Department, and Lloyd Reuss, President of General Motors, were actively involved in the resolution of this matter. We still have pockets of resistance but, as locations reap the benefits of a synchronous organization, the resistance is lessening. The point is that major issues concerning the union-management relationship are discussed openly and fully in these quality council meetings. These are not grievance issues, and the council does not circumvent contractual language or intent. However, these forums quite often influence contract negotiations.

Implementation at All Levels

Quality councils composed of management and union leadership at all levels would function and meet regularly to discuss process and quali-

ty issues. All councils were to complete communication of the purpose, the structure, and the meaning of a Quality Network and the
Beliefs & Values to General Motors employees and labor union members. All councils were to implement training on workplace environmental strategies, develop and implement a plan for implementation
at their location, and demonstrate significant progress in 1991.

In order to truly implement the Quality Network, all business plans
were to include specific initiatives for Quality Network training and
full implementation. Integration of all ongoing quality initiatives with
the Quality Network process was a major goal.

One significant factor in the General Motors system is that in the
business planners are directed to look at the basic beliefs and values of
the corporation and develop action plans to be certain people are treated properly as part of their major objective of producing cars, trucks,
components, and services. This seems to be a sincere desire of the leadership, though it might lose some in the translation as it goes down
through the system. As we move further and further away from the
vision, traditional metrics muddy the water. A middle manager hears
what leadership is saying, but he or she can still pick up a paper and
read that General Motors has the highest hours per car. This is a sim-
plistic and often misleading figure that has been used to label productivity status. What is that manager to believe? We are in a transformation, and old values and tenets do not give up easily. However, there is
a fundamental commitment in this corporation to want to recognize
people for their efforts.

A Joint Steering Committee

A joint steering committee handled the day-to-day implementation of
quality council directives through interaction with various groups and
divisions in General Motors. Each major group within General Motors
[e.g., at the time, Truck and Bus, Chevrolet-Pontiac-Canada (C-P-C),
Automotive Components Group (ACG), Buick-Oldsmobile-Cadillac
(B-O-C), technical staffs, and corporate support staffs] had established
a jointly cochaired quality council to translate the corporate quality
council and steering committee directives into action within their
groups. The various divisions within each group also established quality councils to implement directives in their divisions (e.g., Lansing
Automotive, Saginaw, and Delco Remy). Finally, each plant established a joint quality council to affect plant-level integration.

These plant or staff quality councils are led by the *Key Four* leadership: Plant Manager, Chairperson of the Union Shop Committee,
Personnel Director, and local union President. Quality councils usually

include members of the plant-staff and other selected union leadership. In addition, a joint team of Quality Network Representatives— one management person and one union person—is appointed for each plant to help carry out plant-level objectives. These Quality Network Representatives are the navigators, supporting their quality councils with implementation efforts. For example, they will be actively involved in seeing to it that their locations continue "to provide the necessary organizational support for employees to be trained and use Quality Network problem-solving techniques to improve product quality, reduce costs, and become best-in-class in all products and services." Such organizational support is an example of their role in facilitating the implementation of a 1994 NAO UAW–GM Quality Network objective. In general, this interlocking structure of quality councils effectively communicates information across, as well as up and down, the corporate body.

The QNIST

The Quality Network Implementation Support Team (QNIST) was created, which we are responsible for as codirectors of the Quality Network. The work of this team encompasses action strategy development, interfacing with the action strategy teams, course development, implementation facilitation, management of knowledge transfer and lessons learned, and communications concerning the Quality Network. Team members were and are borrowed resources, both hourly and salaried from all the divisions and groups, as well as communication and quality consultants. Some have been with the QNIST for a couple of years and rotate from assignment to assignment. Some have become permanent staff members. Still others come for a specific project and go back to their home locations when their job is done. We have consciously elected to be flexible to take advantage of the expertise and experience resident in the plants and staffs throughout General Motors.

First NAO UAW–GM Quality Council Meeting, October 13, 1992

From 1988 through October 1992, the Quality Network concentrated its work on the development of both the tools and techniques and the training and educational materials required to support them. The direction of the Quality Network was redirected at the first NAO UAW–GM Quality Council cochaired by Steve Yokich, Vice President and Director UAW General Motors Department, and Jack Smith, Chief Executive Officer and President of General Motors Corporation. The council reconfigured to include an equal number of union and management representation. Management is represented by the NAO Strategy Board and the President of Delphi, General Motors component systems group. The union is represented by top UAW leadership responsible for the GM Department. At this council meeting on October 13, 1992, the council acknowledged the development work of the previous years and then turned its efforts toward implementation.

In order to accelerate implementation efforts on the plant floor, in response to intensifying efforts for product quality improvement, a layer of the Quality Network structure and the steering committee were eliminated (see Fig. 5-3). This restructuring better reflects the change within the General Motors corporate structure. The steering committee and group-staff level mirrored the group structure that was eliminated by the creation of the vehicle platform organization within NAO.

The divisional and platform quality councils are a direct link

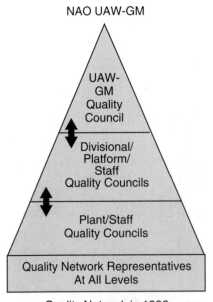

NAO UAW-GM

- UAW-GM Quality Council
- Divisional/ Platform/ Staff Quality Councils
- Plant/Staff Quality Councils
- Quality Network Representatives At All Levels

Quality Network in 1996

Figure 5-3

between the NAO UAW–GM Quality Council and the plant-staff councils. Eliminating a layer of bureaucracy sped up and simplified the communications process from top leadership directly to the plant floor. In addition, a full-time joint support staff took over the duties of supporting the implementation process formerly held by the steering committee. Staff members interface directly with Quality Network Representatives at all levels and work on specific assignments at the divisional, platform, and plant floor levels. For example, members of the support team who are experts in the new Quality Network suggestion plan are responsible for facilitating its implementation throughout the corporation. This fulfills a contractual obligation and one of the 1994 Quality Network objectives: "Each UAW–GM location is to fully implement the Quality Network suggestion plan by May 1, 1994."

Emphasis on Product Quality

Also at the October 1992 meeting, the leadership agreed that the primary focus for UAW–GM Quality Network efforts should be excellence in product quality, moving from the developmental stage to the actual implementation stage at the plant floor level. In a global effort, the Quality Network would continue to cultivate the larger scope of process management systems and philosophy. At the NAO, the focus on product quality improvement was responding to a sense of urgency and the knowledge that NAO was the prime profit center for the corporation. Cochairs Jack Smith and Steve Yokich announced the structural changes and the new product quality focus in a letter, dated November 5, 1992, to the leadership of both organizations. They closed the letter by saying: "Our shared objectives are to satisfy our customers and competitively grow the business. We are committed to working in a spirit of cooperation consistent with the Quality Network *Beliefs & Values*." As codirectors of the Quality Network, the authors were empowered to take the responsibility to assist the organization in implementing the Quality Network process for immediate, specific focus on product quality improvements.

Larger Picture

The Quality Network is worldwide; formal council structures are in place in Canada and Europe. There are quality councils in South America and our Asian Pacific Operations as well. Delphi Automotive

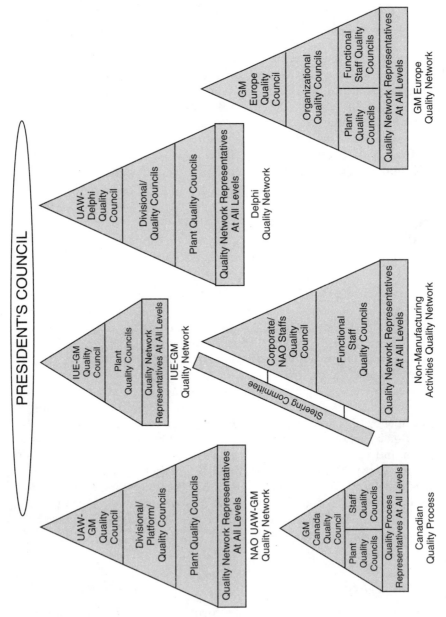

PRESIDENT'S COUNCIL

UAW-GM Quality Council
Divisional/Platform/Quality Councils
Plant Quality Councils
Quality Network Representatives At All Levels

NAO UAW-GM Quality Network

IUE-GM Quality Council
Plant Quality Councils
Quality Network Representatives At All Levels

IUE-GM Quality Network

UAW-Delphi Quality Council
Divisional/Quality Councils
Plant Quality Councils
Quality Network Representatives At All Levels

Delphi Quality Network

GM Canada Quality Council
Plant Quality Councils
Staff Quality Councils
Quality Process Representatives At All Levels

Canadian Quality Process

Corporate/NAO Staffs Quality Council
Functional Staff Quality Councils
Quality Network Representatives At All Levels

Non-Manufacturing Activities Quality Network

Steering Committee

GM Europe Quality Council
Plant Quality Councils
Functional Staff Quality Councils
Organizational Quality Councils
Quality Network Representatives At All Levels

GM Europe Quality Network

Figure 5-4

Systems, formerly the Automotive Components Group Worldwide, is global in its operation and has a formal quality council structure. The NAO UAW–GM Quality Council represents operations that include the Luxury and Mid-Size Car Group, the Small Car Group, North American Truck Platform, and the Powertrain Group. The IUE–GM Quality Council represents not only the International Electrical Workers membership but also the United Rubber Workers Union (URW). The Nonmanufacturing Activities Quality Council represents all those staff functions that support our operational groups but are not specifically linked to them in reporting structure (see Fig. 5-4).

A Note about Nonmanufacturing

Our implementation efforts in the past have concentrated on the NAO and Delphi organizations with particular emphasis on our manufacturing operations. While not lessening our commitment to manufacturing productivity improvements and product quality, we have turned to the nonmanufacturing activities to target aggressive implementation support. A total quality organization is just that, total in scope and influence. As the organization itself has moved to a structure that recognizes a systems approach to management, the application of Quality Network tools and techniques becomes more natural and the benefits more apparent. In some staff areas the Quality Network is still seen as that "union thing."

There are those who actually think the Quality Network was created to appease the union so that the rest of the corporation could get about its business. This belief is held by some union detractors as well. It will take time and patience to bring some of our staff areas along. Many have never been in a plant and are completely disassociated with the manufacture of cars and trucks. Their only contact with the union is to read about strikes or, in some locations, deal with the building support staff when something has gone wrong in their office. This situation has to be rectified, and the Quality Network is the vehicle to do it. As total quality practices are put in place, work will become more efficient and effective. Workers will be more involved with their own destiny. The benefits will become apparent. Additionally, since the nonmanufacturing activities leadership as well as the operational leadership all sit on the NAO Strategy Board, a natural communication mechanism is in place to further understanding and shared knowledge.

Production As a System

A system needs a plan. This concept, as simple as it sounds, was revolutionary in 1950 when Dr. Deming introduced a flow diagram of a production line that viewed production as a system. Previously, organizations viewed themselves in a hierarchical configuration. This belief fostered the notion that you were in business to please the person or staff or function above you on the chart. Your manager was your customer, and his or her job was to control what happened under his or her jurisdiction. Accountability transferred down the organization, which, when things went wrong, transformed into blame. The question was, "Who was delinquent in his or her duty?"

Dr. Deming viewed an organization as a system whose aim is to focus on satisfying the customer of the system. The question in this new archetype is, "What is deficient in the system?" He wrote, "The flow diagram was the spark that in 1950 and onward turned Japan around. It displayed to top management and to engineers a system of production. The Japanese had knowledge, great knowledge, but it was in bits and pieces, uncoordinated. This flow diagram directed their knowledge and efforts into a system of production, geared to the market—namely, prediction of needs of customers. The whole world knows about the results."[5]

Our Process Flowchart

The third element of the Quality Network is a process focus which has two elements: a flow diagram illustrating General Motors' production process as a system and a process model. The Quality Network provides a road map for the corporation (see Fig. 5-5). The GM Product Program Management Process (Four-Phase Vehicle Development Process, or Four-Phase VDP) depicts a uniform process for bringing GM products to market. The four-phase model lays out the structure and order to ensure that quality and conformance to the voice of the customer are defined and built into the products. The UAW was involved in the early stages of the four-phase action strategy development. Union and management Key Lead Persons (KLPs) were assigned to chair the activity. Currently, the strategy is being revised by a joint team; a member of the Quality Network Support Staff serves as a consultant.

In essence, the four-phase model is a flow diagram of the production system encompassing management and engineering. Each process step is clearly defined, roles and responsibilities are described: Work enters one stage, is changed in some way, and exits to the next step. Each step

Production Viewed As A System
W. Edwards Deming
The New Economics for Industry, Education, Government

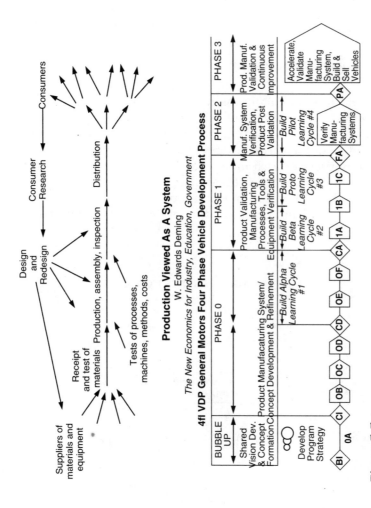

4fl VDP General Motors Four Phase Vehicle Development Process

Figure 5-5

in the chain has a customer and is a customer. Various measurements and feedback mechanisms along the chain keep the process in check. By laying out the entire process, people see where they fit in the system and how their actions and work influence the whole, how they relate to that GM car driving down the street. It provides a means to predict what will happen when any step in the process is changed. When a process is in control and relationships are understood, a change in the process can be managed. The desired results can be predicted and achieved.

Process Focus: The Quality Network Process Model

The General Motors Quality Network process model (Fig. 5-6) is a familiar model that utilizes the fishbone diagram and gives an excellent example of how a visual model can be used to help analyze and understand all of the various stages of a particular process. The model shows the purpose of each individual stage and portrays the interaction of the various resources at that stage.

Use of this type of process model compels one to examine all aspects of the process for a full understanding of the effect of any change. All

QUALITY NETWORK PROCESS MODEL

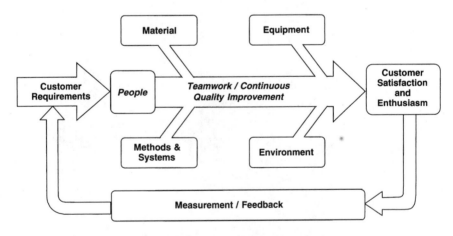

How work is accomplished within the process flow.

Figure 5-6

the resources must be considered as you look at the entire system. Such a visual picture helps us to see the effect that a seemingly small change may have on the entire system.

The Quality Network process is a standard way to approach analyzing and understanding a single stage in the Four-Phase Vehicle Development Process, as well as any other subprocesses; it defines the purpose of a particular stage and depicts the interaction of the various resources in that stage. If a work team should contemplate making an improvement in a process, use of the process model compels the team to examine all aspects of the process for full understanding of the effect of any change. All of the resources must be managed or blended to produce the correct output of the process. Additionally, the contemplated change can be tested against the production system process flow to predict its impact on the system as a whole. It is important to note that the heart of the process model is the *Beliefs & Values: Customer Satisfaction through: People, Teamwork, and Continuous Quality Improvement.* Each process, no matter how small, engages people working together in the spirit of teamwork to continually improve their part of the whole.

If the process under study was to install a new material flow system, then customer requirements would have to include input from the operators involved as well as skilled trades, engineering, setup personnel, and others. Their requirements might include timeliness, correct parts, ergonomic considerations, and accessibility. The people involved would include, in addition to those mentioned above, purchasing, health and safety representatives, material handlers, and others. Under methods and systems, implementation of a small-lot strategy would be examined as well as workplace organization and visual controls. When considering materials, pull system and containerization strategies might be considered. The pull system would ensure that the correct material is replenished in the correct quantity in a timely fashion. Containerization would allow the optimum choice of packaging to work within the new material flow system. A planned maintenance process, an equipment strategy, will ensure that the new system will operate at maximum uptime. The proper machine layout must be considered so that the new system will be synchronized with affected operations. Health and safety and ergonomic issues would be dealt with when studying the impact the new system will have on the work environment. They are integral to supporting the operator. As the new system is being designed, the voice of the customer will provide information that will be used to continuously update and refine the customer requirements. Without a measurement and feedback system in place, it would not be possible to know if customer requirements have been met. When all areas of a process are considered and balanced, customers should be satisfied.

Tools and Techniques of Implementation

Once a structure is established for overseeing quality improvement efforts that portray the values of the corporation, then it is necessary to specifically identify broad tools and techniques that will be used for operating the system within the general goals, beliefs, and structures established. Every aspect of the system must be considered, and specific strategies must be established that address all of the components within the overall system.

Some well-known examples of such planning include material pull systems, containerization, supplier development, small lot, quick setup, level scheduling, and transportation strategies. Such strategies address the technical side of the system by improving business processes. However, other strategies that aim at problem solving, statistical methodology, change methodology, the customer, and so on must be developed as well to support standard systems throughout the corporation. Additionally, a side of the total quality management picture that is often forgotten is the development of strategies that address leadership, cooperative (union and management) relations, support for employees, recognition for employees, and other personnel issues. These strategies must be developed and implemented as well.

Move to Standardization in General Motors

One of the first actions taken by the Quality Network was to establish standard methods and systems throughout General Motors. The strengths of the past had today become the weaknesses of General Motors. No longer could internal competition, division against division or brand against brand, be the driving force in improvement efforts. External competition had to be the focus of benchmarking and improvement efforts. Teamwork and cooperation had to replace internal competition. Best practices, whether from external or internal sources, had to be implemented. No longer could Chevrolet target Pontiac owners; both nameplates had to focus on their direct external competition. This is a major cultural change that has yet to be fully realized.

Initially 36 basic strategies were identified as critical to ensure General Motors' competitiveness in the workplace—for example, pull system, containerization, cooperative union-management relations, support for the employee, plant machine and office layout, and statistical methodologies. Joint teams examined the best practices being used within the corporation, by the competition, and in other industries. These cross-functional action strategy teams represented all the stakeholders, union and management alike, affected by the strategy. The teams conducted investigations, defined what is best for General Motors, and wrote guidelines for the strategies. These guidelines, 10-page Process Reference Guides (PRGs), were then developed to outline the basics of the strategies. They defined the strategy, its customers, its objectives, and implementation guidelines. Training materials, including videotapes, workshop guides, and training manuals, were then designed and produced by joint course development teams to supplement on-the-job training.

Jay Wilber on a Conversation with Dr. Juran

On April 11, 1994, Dr. Joseph N. Juran presented a seminar titled "The Last Word: Lessons of a Lifetime in Managing for Quality," sponsored by the American Society for Quality Control. During lunch, I had the opportunity to sit beside Dr. Juran and discuss General Motors' quality improvement efforts. Dr. Juran asked me how GM was spreading lessons learned. I explained our Quality Network action strategy development process and our quality best practices approach to continuous quality improvement. He applauded the approach and indicated that where most companies have difficulty is in the area of effectively sharing lessons learned.

Leadership Initiatives

We established four leadership initiatives to help focus our action strategy implementation efforts:

- Build a supportive environment.
- Create an organization-wide customer focus.
- Synchronize the organization.
- Detect, solve, and prevent product quality problems.

How does an organization like GM, working with its major partner, the UAW, focus the joint team and its leadership? Specific action strategies and related training had to be developed and provided to understand the necessity for a supportive environment, one that allows input from people producing the company's products and services. Top leadership commitment had to be evident to get everyone involved and focused. Cooperative union-management relations had to be explored and worked at continuously. A new method for proper communication had to be established across the organization—not strictly down through the organization but across the organization as well. A crucial element of the process had to be an organizationwide customer focus and a realization that the next person in line was one's customer, as well as the ultimate customer who purchased products and services.

Assurance of Continuity

Establishing basic uniform processes (such as the 36 action strategies) for decision making, problem solving, manufacturing methods, and so on throughout the organization ensures continuity, increased efficiency, and if done jointly, addresses everyone's concerns. These processes then govern the basic behavior of the organization. An additional benefit is that personnel moves throughout the corporation become much less of a concern since the employees are already familiar with the standard basic systems and processes throughout the company.

The Role of a Steering Committee

In order to begin this standardization process, it is necessary that all the major stakeholders be represented in the original formulation of "best" processes and be able to provide necessary resources for developing basic outlines followed by detailed training materials. We found that an effective way to do this is to establish a *steering* or *advisory* committee made up of representatives of all the stakeholders. Our Quality Network steering committee members' charge was to represent the views of their superiors and constituents. A committee such as this could be jointly chaired by a top management official and a labor union representative, if applicable, or a knowledgeable hourly employee. All parties must understand from the beginning the tenuous nature of their position. In the case of the Quality Network, the charge for the steering committee was to design and develop General Motors total quality system. Although a sunset date was not specified, the committee always knew its work would end when the focus shifted to implementation. The steering committee for the NAO UAW–GM Quality Network was disbanded after the October 1992 quality council meeting. Both Jack Smith and Steve Yokich believed the organization was better served with the steering committee members back in their home organizations accelerating implementation efforts since much of the work of the development stage had been completed.

The steering committee operated with the sanction of those who actually ran their respective organizations; the committee did not by itself have the decision-making authority to carry out day-to-day operating decisions. The committee's work represented consensus decision making, but implementation rested with the traditional organizational structure. Therefore, it was crucial for successful implementation that all parties commit to the standardized processes developed. Success, in our case, was dependent on our leadership pledging support to the ultimate goal of having standardized processes throughout the corporation. Even though there were several leadership changes throughout these formative years, the leadership allowed us the freedom to explore new ideas and develop and execute new strategies. We have had leadership support from GM Presidents James McDonald, Robert Stempel, Lloyd Reuss, and Jack Smith and UAW Vice Presidents and Directors of the GM Department Donald Ephlin and Stephen Yokich.

The steering committee's first task was to identify best business practices from both inside and outside the company. Strict observation and preliminary work required listing, in their entirety, those processes determined vital to General Motors' future success. Once the overall list was compiled, joint teams of experts from within the corporation were assigned for each strategy. These teams examined the various approaches currently in place within the organization. Following this initial examination, similar processes in other organizations were examined to determine their best business practices.

Action Strategies

Our teams, called action strategy teams (ASTs) found most corporations used strategies that address the actual work environment, such as communication, education and training, reward and recognition, suggestion plans, top leadership support and commitment, and in the case of the involvement of labor unions, union and management relations.

Strategies that address the importance of the customer throughout the organization include design of experiments, loss function, validation of criteria, quality function deployment, key characteristics, customer concerns, and various decision-making processes.

Another category of strategies designed to address the manufacturing system of any organization included a pull system, small-lot strategy, lead-time reduction, workplace organization, visual controls, plant, office, and machine layout, quick setup, error proofing, planned maintenance, level scheduling, machine process capability, supplier relations, containerization, transportation, reduction of variation, quality assurance, and people-focused work practices.

The final category deals with those types of strategies designed to detect, solve, and prevent quality problems throughout the organization, such as change methodology, problem solving, statistical methodologies, and costs arising from poor quality. Anyone questioning the value of examining external organizations for comparison or implementation need only think back to many of the Japanese delegations who have toured American factories. It was not unusual to see individuals rapidly writing down ideas throughout the tour or drawing pictures of what they saw.

Benchmarking—Purpose and Definition

Additionally, it is well known that benchmarking competitors and other organizations tends to provide data for strengthening one's own efficiencies. Once our action strategy teams had a broad overview of the best methods being utilized within their organization and by other organizations for a particular process, they then drafted an initial overview of the best process they envision for use throughout General Motors. This initial overview was restricted to 10 to 15 pages or less, and merely provided a snapshot of the process and its scope.

The original process draft was then distributed to all the key stakeholders in the organization for comment. When steering committee members kept their sponsors up to date, very little controversy and word changes were necessary. Most of the disconnectedness between the different groups represented on the steering committee were settled in committee meetings prior to going out into the organization. A united front is an important issue and sometimes not easy to come by, particularly with a corporation as large and diverse as GM. There were several cultures represented in one room, and they each had their own way of doing things. Car people are different from "truckers." Buick people are different from Chevy people. Component people are different from vehicle assemblers. Just ask them. The key was to get to the heart of each strategy and show how a standardized approach would benefit all.

A Design for Training

When all comments had been considered, adopted, and/or adapted, the working overview became the basis for development of actual training to ensure uniform implementation throughout the corporation. A team of training developers from within General Motors was then assigned to supplement the overview with practical training materials (videotapes, manuals, models, etc.).

All team members were not experts in course development; the team also needed people who were experienced in actual operations, who could give practical insight into what training was really needed to ensure effective implementation. We found excellent content experts throughout our organization who were excited and eager to contribute their experience and expertise. It is startling to discover the kinds of pitfalls that can be avoided when practical experience and cultural knowledge are added to the design process. The training development teams were supplemented with course developers from within the organization, as well as outside consultants, who directed the team's efforts in actual course design. Off-the-shelf courses designed by outside consultants may be of value if sufficient resources do not exist within an organization; however, this approach is clearly less desirable. They lack an understanding of the culture and, most evident in General Motors, the language of the business and of the company. We have our own way of saying things and our own way of doing things, and education and training efforts need to allow for both.

If the decision is made to utilize outside consultants and training materials rather than develop materials in-house, it is critical that in-house teams work with the consultant to "personalize" materials for the organization's use. Terminology and methods can be modified to apply directly to the organization that will use them.

What's the Cost?

Clearly both methods of course and training development are costly; however, the long-term gains far outweigh the initial investment. Once a total systems approach to management is developed and implemented within an organization, simple, small improvements can be made on a regular basis to improve the overall system and keep it at the cutting edge of efficiency. Once we had developed and piloted the training, each group or division used the approved processes, where applicable.

We learned early on that such jointly developed processes become "our development" and are a source of pride and teamwork that energizes the organization. Each individual and the divisions and groups he or she represents feel a part of the success. We began to move away from "kingdom building" as we began to view it as counterproductive. This was a major shift in thinking. We began to move to the GM way, rather than the Pontiac way or the GMC Truck way. This is not to say we are there yet, but we are moving in the right direction. As we advance in our systems orientation, we will uniformly recognize individuals for their efforts to assist others and the overall organization rather than for lone-ranger efforts that bring them personal glory at the expense of other team members, usually causing team suboptimization.

Quality Network Leadership Initiatives

Outstanding gains in joint participative leadership have been made at various GM locations, while some locations have shown no real effects from the Quality Network process. Only a sustained effort will show the sincerity of this attempt at corporate cultural change. As of July 1994, 38 action strategies had been identified that address corporatewide standardization of processes to promote efficiency, quality, and long-term job security, as market share stabilizes and grows. Education and training packages to be used in ongoing training of workers at all levels of General Motors Corporation gave a central focus based on the *Beliefs & Values*. The first five strategies and training packages to be completed deal with the work environment necessary to truly treat people properly. The balance deals with establishing "the one GM way" of doing things—in effect, outlining a jointly developed process management approach to product and process quality.

The strategies are grouped under our four leadership initiatives, which are actionable concepts that help focus their energies and illustrate the interdependency of the strategies.

- Build a supportive environment.
- Create an organization-wide customer focus.

- Synchronize the organization.
- Detect, solve, and prevent quality problems.

Keeping track of 38 action strategies and understanding how they come together to form the system was difficult for many to grasp. We developed the four initiatives to help with this undertaking. The initiatives also made it easier to explain the Quality Network process and its focus on our nonmanufacturing activities. After a heavy data dump of strategies, the initiatives answer the question, "But, what am I supposed to do? Where do I start?" These initiatives tell us what we should be working on to keep us moving to higher levels of customer satisfaction, even as our customers' requirements grow. The initiatives direct our actions toward closing the gap between where we currently are and where we want to be. The leadership initiatives galvanize our efforts and embrace the five elements of total quality discussed earlier: systems thinking, customer focus, Big Q, people involvement, and continuous improvement through a process focus.

Building a Supportive Environment

- *Definition:* Leaders and the organization focus on meeting the needs of our front-line people through demonstrated values, structures and systems, physical environment, rewards and measurements, job security, and leadership style.

- *Quality Network action strategies: Support for the Employee, Top Leadership Commitment and Involvement, Cooperative Union-Management Relations, Communication, People Recognition, Employee Excellence Development Education and Training*

Where to Begin? How do you build a supportive environment? Especially when the traditional relationship between General Motors and the UAW could best be described as adversarial. Our history gives us many examples of how people were pitted against each other. Standoff after standoff had a declared winner and therefore a declared loser. That was the way it was. Winning at all costs was what was important. The same was true for corporate entities. Each group and division in General Motors was a separate profit center that had to prove itself at the cost of another group or division; GM nameplate was pitted against GM nameplate. If Chevrolet won, Pontiac lost. Buick strove to take marketshare from Oldsmobile. Clearly we did not see ourselves as members of the same system.

Would our beginning days with General Motors have been different had a supportive environment been in place, or even a consideration? Would employee involvement then have placed GM in a better position to compete today? We are confident of the answers to these questions, but we cannot change history. We can learn from it, however, and we are certain that we can work together to direct our futures.

Overlapping Circles.   When the two of us former Labor Relations guys took over as leaders of the Quality Network, we had to learn to work together as individuals and then transfer that relationship to the two groups we represented. Remember, we first met in heated bargaining sessions across the negotiation table. We recognized that we had to set the tone and live the behavior profiled in our *Cooperative Union-Management Relations* action strategy. We began by doing a current state analysis of joint activities and areas where we felt we had common interests. Figure 5-7 conveys a representative list of activities we studied. We were both comfortable with the areas of mutual concern. Since we both had come from the Labor Relations arena, we were familiar with the contract, our first and oldest joint agreement. We were also comfortable with the Quality Network leadership initiatives that had also been jointly developed and were supported by the Quality Network action strategies.

What about Our Differences?   We recognized that each organization had legal, business, and ethical responsibilities that were unique to the organization. We envisioned a future state in which both organizations considered the impact of their decisions on the other. The exercise of drawing up our current state model helped us determine a baseline to describe where we agreed we currently were in our joint understanding and development.

Grow the Green.   Our current-state chart (Fig. 5-7) portrays, on the far left, those areas that are the union's responsibility. This is pictured in yellow. GM blue is the color used to illustrate GM management responsibilities, to the far left. Those areas of mutual concern and responsibility are depicted in green in the center of our chart. Our goal is to make the green areas grow. As we continue to grow the areas in which we work together, we will grow our business. Success will be reflected in both the bottom line and job security.

The Quality Network identifies the union as a valuable partner and includes union involvement at all levels in almost every area of process management. At the insistence of the union, the process does not envision a move to codetermination, although union concerns are considered in all aspects of decision making regarding quality council

(yellow) UAW RESPONSIBILITIES	(green) JOINTLY DEVELOPED AND IMPLEMENTED ACTIVITIES		(blue) GM MANAGEMENT RESPONSIBILITIES
UAW Responsibilities	Negotiated Contractual Provisions	Quality Network Initiatives	GM Management Responsibilities
• Executive Board Selection Process • Dues Determination • Companies and/or Staff Activities Targeted for Organization • Political and Lobbying Activities • Executive Board/Staff Compensation including Office of the President • Promotion, Recognition, Reward for UAW Staff • Political Strategies • Increasing Union Membership (Growing the Business) • Networking with other Union and Political Organizations (AFL-CIO) • Etc.	• Wages and Benefits • Job Security • Health and Safety Programs • Attachment "C" • Work Rules and Conditions of Empoyment • Grievance Procedures • Union Recognition • Sourcing Provisions • Human Resource Center Activities • Etc.	• Build a Supportive Environment • Create an Organization-wide Customer Focus • Synchronize the Organization • Detect, Solve and Prevent Product Quality Problems	• Progression and Succession Planning • Business Planning Process • Vehicle Pricing Policy • Facility Utilization • Integration of new initiatives • Executive Compensation • Reward and Recognition • MTC/GTC Strategies • Synchronous Organization • Process Capability Management • Supplier Rationalization • Natural Ownership of Action Strategies • Increasing Market Share (Growing the Business) • Etc.

The Beliefs & Values

Figure 5-7

activities. We then agreed to define and work toward a future state. Not surprisingly, initially the *Beliefs & Values* defined that future state for us.

A current-state analysis such as the one we conducted is an excellent way to begin a working relationship, especially if there is tension between the two parties. It should build on respect for each other's responsibilities and an agreement to operate in an atmosphere of trust. Both parties should recognize an obligation to perform as promised. This integrity ensures that trust given will be returned. Finally, open and honest communication becomes the basis for the relationship, as it did between us. Soon we were comfortable carrying forward to both our leadership and our subordinates a united approach to working together. The key is respect—respect for the job the other side has to perform.

A Maturing Relationship. As leaders of the Quality Network, we agreed to discuss the previously undiscussable to break down barriers that might make it impossible to work together. With the support of our top leadership, the word got out that we were truly committed to treating all the men and women of General Motors as true partners in the business. We meant what we said, and we acted accordingly. We were supported by our leadership, specifically by Jack Smith and Steve Yokich.

An example of how leadership can break the ice and really move an issue along came at a very dark time for GM. Rumors about the company were flying fast and furiously. Some papers had us declaring bankruptcy. In the past, financial data were not shared; the union in particular was left out of the loop, learning of the financial state of the company through the annual report. However, in February 1993, at the invitation of UAW Vice President Steve Yokich, GM CEO and President Jack Smith held a series of meetings with the top union leadership of several unions representing GM employees from across the country to discuss in great detail and frankness the financial state of the company. These meetings were private between the top GM executive and union leaders who had flown in from all our GM locations. It is a tribute to the respect union leadership held for this effort and the integrity they displayed that the content of these meetings was not leaked to the media. General Motors was headline news then, but this information remained within the company.

It's Sometimes a Matter of Law. The relationship between the union and the company is governed by many factors. Each organization has separate responsibilities, many required by law. For example, the

National Labor Relations Act specifically defines management's responsibilities. These are restated in Paragraph 8 of the GM–UAW National Agreement: "The right to hire; promote; discharge or discipline for cause; and to maintain discipline and efficiency of employees, is the sole responsibility of the Corporation except that Union members shall not be discriminated against as such. In addition, the products to be manufactured, the location of the plants, the schedules of production, the methods, processes and means of manufacturing are solely and exclusively the responsibility of the Corporation."[6] Unquestionably, it is management's job to run the business. However, empowering workers and encouraging their assistance and input into these decisions ensures a more successful organization.

Nontraditional Involvement. Today, represented employees participate in activities as far-reaching and nontraditional as marketing and supplier development. These are areas that technically "belong" to management and can be found listed on the far right of our current-state chart. Even though marketing and supplier development is management's responsibility, it behooves us to tap the talents of our represented work force. Only a few years ago it would have been unthinkable to have UAW members jointly administer new assessor training to Supplier Quality Engineers to assess supplier locations. When we began this program, there were many surprised looks in the classroom as the trainers introduced themselves and Dan Grant stated he was from UAW Local 22, the B-O-C Hamtramck Plant. We now have a UAW-represented QNIST member working with Worldwide Purchasing to create the Quality Network Supplier Quality Systems Process Reference Guide under the aegis of Supplier Quality Purchasing Directors.

The UAW's involvement in General Motors advertising was a topic at the 1993 national contract negotiations. When union-represented workers saw ads depicting plant jobs, they wanted to be involved in the ads. Management agreed to use actual workers and portray UAW emblems, jackets, hats, and so on prominently in its advertising. Document 41 on Product Quality of the 1993 National Agreement (October 24, 1993) formalizes the union's involvement in our national advertising campaigns:

> During the term of the 1990 GM–UAW National Agreement, UAW–GM Department representatives were provided the opportunity to input into Corporate marketing campaigns. It is the Corporation's intent to continue to provide similar opportunities in the future.
> Further, the parties discussed at length the importance of NAO domestic vehicle advertising campaigns involving or depicting

UAW-represented GM employees, the positive impact the message of such campaigns can have on our employees and customers. The Corporation informed the Union that a mutually agreed to process would be developed to preview for input purposes such future NAO domestic vehicle advertising campaigns involving or depicting UAW-represented GM employees.[7]

The 1995 national advertising campaign is an example of how this provision of the national agreement played out in the national press. An example is a two-page spread featuring Cornell Cherry, UAW Assistant Team Coordinator at GM Powertrain, talking about quality, standing in front of GM Headquarters. Cherry is quoted: "A quality automobile doesn't happen by chance. It's a hard-working thing. The managers understand I'm not just a warm body. I'm a thinking individual who has a mind how to run the business."[8]

Additionally, the UAW and GM established a joint motorsports program to further communicate the joint quality efforts between the two entities. Together, we cosponsor a series of NASCAR races. There is also a UAW–GM teamwork award based on the team that exhibits precision, speed, accuracy, and safety during the course of a race.

The Union's Role. The same provisions of the law define the union's roles and responsibilities, which do not require or encourage the union to consider problems the company may face. Clearly, self-preservation and common sense make such involvement necessary for a responsible organization concerned about its membership. There are many areas where interests overlap. These are depicted in the center of the current-state analysis chart (Fig. 5-7). Specifically, they are the many common concerns found in national and local agreements, as well as the development and implementation of the Quality Network. These overlapping areas can be grown and shared. It is also incumbent on both parties to be mindful of the other party's responsibilities. Decisions made by one part of a total system cannot help but affect the total system. As each party's understanding of the other matures, decisions made by either side will reflect this knowledge.

The Environment Action Strategies. For initial development purposes, all our action strategies were grouped in appropriate resource boxes of the Quality Network process model (Fig. 5-6). Each box had a union and management champion, an International Representative and Group Vice president, who provided resources and direction for the development of the strategy and subsequent education and training support materials. Early on the strategies were classified as either foundation strategies or technique strategies. *Foundation strategies* are those that support GM people and the *Beliefs & Values* and have a strong impact on the environment. There was a strong belief on the part of many early Quality Network leaders on the steering committee that environmental issues had to be addressed before any of the other strategies could be optimally implemented; therefore much is dependent upon a cooperative, open and honest environment. Four of the *Build a Supportive Environment* action strategies fell in the environment resource portion of the process: top leadership commitment and involvement, support for the employee, communication, and cooperative union-management relations.

Foundation for Customer Satisfaction. These foundation strategies were among the first Process Reference Guides (PRGs) to be written, followed by an environment action strategies *Foundation for Customer Satisfaction* workshop, which was rolled out throughout the corporation. This was not designed as a training program but rather as the first step for a quality council to take to initiate change in its organization. The Quality Network Implementation Support Team, with resources from B-O-C, C-P-C, and Truck and Bus, created and led this workshop designed specifically for joint quality councils, administered in five modules separated by periods of "soak time." Soak time permitted participants to digest the module content and to relate the content to their own work areas. It was also a time to gather data required for the next module, since workshop exercises revolved around real-world examples submitted by the participants. In the workshop, participants explored the four environment action strategies, compelling quality council members to come to consensus on their understanding of the following:

- The relationship between leadership, the environment, and the Quality Network
- How the *Beliefs & Values* impact their organization
- Their role as leaders in creating the environment
- Elements that support and do not support employees' efforts to do a good job
- Their existing communication process (often informal at best) and elements of a good communication process
- The roles of union and management and the impact that the relationship between the two has on their environment
- The current state of their environment and where the quality council wanted to take it

This sounds like a lot to ask and it was. For some locations, this was the very first time their quality council had met, and quite often it was reluctantly. We had some locations—in fact, one of the first pilots—walk out. In spite of skillful facilitation, the first module often became a gripe session, with tempers flaring and accusations flying. Many did not want to do that "warm-fuzzy environment stuff." What was happening, however, was that we were getting people together who previously only met to discuss grievances and argue contractual issues. This discussion, albeit antagonistic in several cases, was outside the grievance process, and this was a major breakthrough. Some of our locations had to go back and start the workshop a number of times. Often the consensus at the end was a straightforward understanding that there was virtually no cooperation and the environment was not conducive to supporting the employee. But, it was a start. In 1990, when Quality Network Implementation Support Team (QNIST) members began to facilitate these workshops, more councils than not identified environments that could best be described as having a we-they attitude, with councils literally sitting according to affiliation on opposite sides of a table. This makes a startling picture since the workshop specifically calls for round tables that seat 8 to 10 people; but, somehow they managed it.

Today. We are not going to say that all our quality councils sit in bliss, arriving at a consensus for every decision. However, the vast majority of our quality councils do meet regularly and tend to the business at hand. The maturation of the relationship spans a wide range, but all groups have progressed relative to where they started. The environmental workshop was a good start for most and is still being used today. Some of our locations, both at the plant and divisional level, regularly revisit the workshop for renewal purposes or when there has been a change in personnel. We have come a long way in recognizing the employee as the internal customer of both the system and leadership.

Health and safety and ergonomic issues are foremost considerations when any process or program is being created or improved. Formerly a process was designed, machinery and systems put in place, and people were fit in. Today we start with the people and try to include them in the design phase.

Trust—A Two-Way Street. We talk about trust a lot. It is a key factor in a total quality organization and should be the primary goal of activities designed to build a supportive environment. Some managers feel they can't trust employees. Mistrust can be a two-way street. Many employees feel they can't trust managers. Both have probable cause for their attitudes. Union and management leadership certainly can recite litanies detailing reasons to be suspicious and wary of the other party. Some people feel that trust has to be earned. We disagree. We believe that someone has to take the first step. You have to be willing to give trust if you are going to get it in return. As leaders, we must take the first steps toward building a supportive environment. Management must take this first step.

Creating an Organization-wide Customer Focus

- *Definition:* Focus the organization on meeting and exceeding the needs of our internal and external customers—the people impacted by our processes, products, and services.

- *Quality Network action strategies: Four-Phase Vehicle Development Process* (4φVDP), *Validation, Voice of the Customer* (VOC), *Quality Function Deployment* (QFD), *Key Characteristics Designation System* (KCDS), *Design of Experiments* (DOE), *Loss Function*

Start with Basics. Earlier in this chapter we discussed some of the major General Motors customer groups and our relationship to them. Our corporate vision and vision for NAO both hinge on customer satisfaction and enthusiasm. Our vision in essence becomes our quality policy. In all that we do we must develop the mindset that continually asks these questions:

- Who are our customers?
- Are we satisfying them?
- How do we know?

If we don't know who our customers are, we have no source of feedback and therefore no source to define requirements for continuous improvement. Without this input, we would stagnate or regress and eventually lose market share and business to our competition who would be right there ready to pick up where we left off. We must collect and use the data we derive from regular and constant communication with our customers to drive our improvement and innovation processes.

Implicit in asking these questions is that there is a plan for using this information to further customer satisfaction. The action strategies that support the customer focus initiative each provide a piece of our approach to satisfy and delight our customers. *Voice of the Customer* assists us in identifying our customers, our customer relationships, and customer wants and needs that drive our continuous quality improvement efforts. *Quality Function Deployment* translates identified customer wants and needs into requirements and deploys them throughout all aspects of our business including product and service design and manufacturing and assembly processes. When deployed within vehicle systems engineering, QFD is a powerful means to deploy the *Voice of the Customer* through vehicle, subsystem, and component product-process requirements down to the plant floor. This method focuses on the definition of the performance level of all functions necessary for customer satisfaction. The objective of QFD is to create effective product and process planning, for both vehicle and nonvehicle products and services, integrating cross-functional activities and driving *Voice of the Customer* throughout the product, process, and service cycle. *Four-Phase Vehicle Development Process,* as discussed earlier, is our uniform process for bringing an outstanding product to market. It is the road map that incorporates QFD data and technical requirements into the production system. *Key Characteristics Designation System* is a common process used to identify, document, and communicate key product characteristics (KPCs) and their related key control characteristics (KCCs) to internal allied and affiliated manufacturing and assembly operations and outside suppliers. In other words, once the *Voice of the Customer* specifies customer wants and needs, QFD translates these into technical requirements that will have ranked characteristics (KPCs). Process control characteristics (KCCs) are determined in order to ensure that these characteristics are met each and every time based on customer-based targets. *Design of Experiments* deals with different methods to improve the quality of the processes and products by investigating several sources of variation simultaneously. *Loss Function* estimates the loss of values that occurs when products and services vary from the customer-based targets. *Validation* assesses the degree to which the output of a process meets the *Voice of the Customer.*

Just the Beginning.   The products of General Motors' core business, personal transportation, and their related services have a life of their own. When a car or truck leaves a dealership, our job is not over in the eyes of our customers. Their ongoing relationship, what we call the *Customer Ownership Experience,* lasts on average over six years. During this time customers experience continual contact with General Motors through their perception of our quality, reliability, dependability, durability, and service. General Motors is not just selling cars and trucks. It is selling a total ownership experience.

Keith Crain, publisher of *Automotive News* and other industry and business publications, talked about this issue in a column he wrote for *Crain's Detroit Business* upon his return from the 1995 National Auto Dealers Association convention. The editorial is titled "A Good Product Alone Won't Be Enough in Future."

> I recently spent a few days with all the automobile manufacturers and their dealers and was struck at how differently the business has changed over the past decade or two.
>
> Make no mistake, the product is still king. Always was, and probably always will be. But for many products, the real difference in the next decade is not going to be the product itself but the process. Having a great product with great quality and the right price will be just the beginning. We will expect that up-front. No ifs and no buts.
>
> We now make our decisions on the entire process of shopping and buying. For manufacturers, that is going to be scary because they rely on retailers to sell their products and, in may cases, to service them as well.
>
> That's going to change the equation for us when we start to shop around for a television set or a major appliance or, certainly, a car. We will really care about how we are treated when we walk into the store. And if our product ever needs service, then we are going to pay particular attention to just how good the service was. Our neighbors are going to know what we think.[9]

Customer Ownership Experience. GM Vice President of Quality and Reliability, Ron Haas, and members of the quality and reliability team developed the model below (Fig. 5-8) to capture our understanding

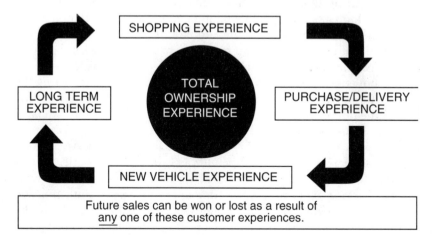

Figure 5-8

of our customers' experience with our products and services. Every owner or user of a General Motors car, truck, or service is somewhere in this cycle. It does not matter where in the cycle we begin. As Keith Crain wrote, the *shopping experience* depends on the way we are treated "when we walk into the store." Saturn is changing the way we in General Motors look at the sales experience, providing many examples of how this can be managed in a positive manner. Many other GM divisions are following suit. The *purchase and delivery experience* will be positive if it is based on a hassle-free pricing policy and loan approval process. The vehicle must be delivered in a timely manner, perfectly prepped and ready to go—in contrast to the experience of an associate of ours who tells of picking up her brand-new, $18,000 station wagon only to run out of gas less than a mile from the dealership. Crain's right, all the neighbors heard that story. The *new-vehicle experience* includes exciting customers with new features and styling, comfort, and performance. And then there's the *long-term experience,* not specifically addressed in Crain's column. Averaging over six years, the long-term ownership experience gives our customers literally tens of thousands of opportunities to be satisfied or dissatisfied. What is their service experience like: bumper-to-bumper warranty, cost, and treatment during servicing? Were parts available, loaners offered? What about roadside service promises—were they met? Future sales can be won or lost as the result of any of these customer experiences.

A Race for Customer Enthusiasm. We use the analogy of an oval racetrack as another way to look at the many parameters of customer satisfaction. This racetrack looks at the six-year ownership experience of our customers. During this time we have the opportunity to build customer enthusiasm: high gas mileage, low maintenance costs, a car that is toasty warm in the winter and cool in the summer, that starts right up every time, a new feature that was not a requirement at purchase but becomes a "gotta have" in subsequent purchases. How does the vehicle look after six years, how does it perform, and what is its trade-in value? During the course of the race, our customers pass through many experiences that afford us the opportunity to keep loyal customers or lose them. We have several mechanisms.

For early customer feedback we use J.D. Power and CAMIP data which measure new vehicle quality and operation. Further out, the CSI (Customer Satisfaction Index) and yearly Dialog Surveys look at warranty and service expectations, lifetime operating costs, high mileage durability and, toward the end of the ownership experience, how the customer feels about his or her out-of-warranty service experience. Over time, opinions will change and experiences will alter perceptions. GM is studying its customers' opinions throughout their ownership experience—"from the starting gate to the finish line and winner's circle."

The Renewal Cycle. We struggled to capture the dynamic relationship between the GM vehicle development process and our customers' ownership experiences. The interplay between the two defies a simple linear explanation. John Roach first verbalized the model that Jim Byrnes of the QNIST conceptualized in Fig. 5-9. It combines the *Customer Ownership Experience* with the 4ϕVDP model and presents us with a snapshot of General Motors as a total system. The *renewal model* was so named by Jamal El-Hout, a Director of Quality and Reliability, who caught the spirit and energy depicted in the model. As customers travel through the ownership experience (this is just the depiction of one experience), many things shape their vehicle requirements for the future. Those ABS brakes that came with the car, but were not required at the time of purchase, have become a requirement. The next-door neighbor's new car has a head-up display; maybe that's a new requirement. As customers are formulating tastes and requirements for their next purchase, vehicle development teams are traveling through their process, influenced by these changing customer requirements as well as changing government regulations, market fluctuations, innovations, and so on. General Motors' goal is to match the output of our process with the requirements of our customers.

All GM people, suppliers, and dealers are somewhere on this model. All have a relationship with the ultimate customer because the output of each person inputs the process that produces the product or service. This is why it is critical for everyone associated with the product or service to be knowledgeable of not only his or her own process and customer but how it fits into the greater scheme of things.

The Personal Link. Sharing the results of customer quality surveys and perceptions is one meaningful way to help all people in an organization realize the link between quality and the customer and therefore between quality and better wages, benefits, working conditions, and job security. Each person's job is critical in the process chain to the real outcome of quality and customer satisfaction. Also, consistent adherence to quality standards must be evident for all to see. In some instances, workers have seen parts rejected one day and then used another day in order to get quantity out. Now we are asking workers to judge their own quality and be the judges of what is passed on to the customer. Establishing a personal link between supplier (worker) and customer (worker next in the value chain) ensures the integrity of the product passed on and thus the final quality to the ultimate customer. We all want to be proud of the

General Motors Renewal Model
General Motors As A System

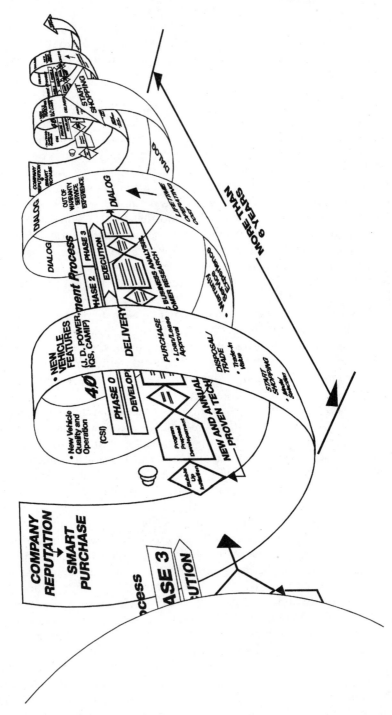

Figure 5-9

work we do. Figure 5-10 graphically depicts an individual's relationship to the ultimate customer and the success of the corporation.

Synchronizing the Organization

- *Definition:* Utilize a systematic approach to identify and eliminate waste and/or non-value-added activities through continuous quality improvement of our products and services.

- *Quality Network action strategies: Lead Time Reduction* (LTR); *Pull System; Workplace Organization and Visual Controls; Small Lot Strategy; Quality Verification; People Focused Practices; Planned Maintenance; Plant, Machine, and Office Layout; Reduction of Variation* (ROV); *Machine or Process Capability; Transportation, Containerization; Error Proofing; Supplier Development; Quick Setup; Level Scheduling*

Getting in Sync.   We synchronize the organization by balancing all our resources—people, equipment, materials, methods and systems, environment, and measurement and feedback mechanisms—to:

- Eliminate every form of waste (time, effort, talents, and materials)
- Reduce non-value-added activities and lower the cost of value-added activities
- Add value in everything we do

Seven Types of Waste.   Our synchronous action strategies help us work smarter, not harder, while we attack the seven types of waste in our systems:

- *Inventory:* Any supply in excess of process requirements necessary to produce goods or services just in time (JIT)
- *Overproduction:* Producing more or sooner than is needed
- *Correction:* Inspection and repair of a product or service to fulfill customer requirements
- *Processing:* Efforts, enhancements, or work that add no value to a product or service
- *Waiting:* Idle time that is produced when two dependent variables are not fully synchronized
- *Motion:* Any movement or action of people or machines that does not contribute added value to the product or service

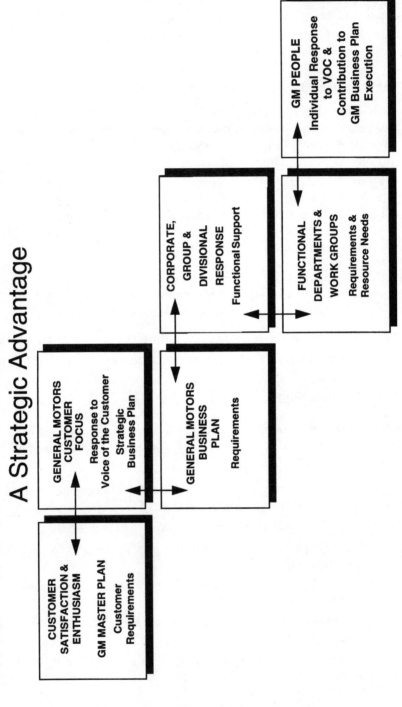

INDIVIDUAL LINK TO THE ULTIMATE CUSTOMER
A Strategic Advantage

CUSTOMER SATISFACTION & ENTHUSIASM

GM MASTER PLAN
Customer Requirements

GENERAL MOTORS CUSTOMER FOCUS

Response to Voice of the Customer
Strategic Business Plan

GENERAL MOTORS BUSINESS PLAN

Requirements

CORPORATE, GROUP & DIVISIONAL RESPONSE

Functional Support

FUNCTIONAL DEPARTMENTS & WORK GROUPS

Requirements & Resource Needs

GM PEOPLE
Individual Response to VOC & Contribution to GM Business Plan Execution

Figure 5-10

- *Material movement:* Any movement or material that does not support a synchronous system.

Working examples of waste fit into one or more of the categories listed above: customer dissatisfaction; warranties and litigation; lost sales; waivers and deviations; defective products and services; overhauling procedures; unsafe output; unnecessary inspection and checking; poor systems design; operational systems waste; unused talents, inputs, and innovation of our people; poor or no planning; unnecessary testing; procedure swamps; watching and waiting; high inventories; improper and inadequate training; and ineffective practices and procedures.

What the Synchronous Leadership Initiative Does. There are 17 action strategies that specifically support the synchronous leadership initiative. Each strategy is highly dependent upon the others; for example, pull system effectiveness and efficiency relies on good visual controls, an orderly containerization plan coordinated with a solid transportation scheme. Containerization is affected by a small lot strategy and health, safety, and ergonomic considerations. For example, workers must be able to move and handle parts containers without a strain to their back. Therefore, containers can weigh only 40 pounds or less.

Basically, a synchronous organization is coordinated for maximum efficiency, effectiveness, and flexibility, all to satisfy the customer. Small lots enable a quicker response time to customer demand and help to reduce in-process inventory. Visual controls help clear and accurate communication and serve as an excellent error-proofing device. Workplace organization and a proper workplace layout, be it an office, plant, or machine system, eliminate waste and decrease the chance for error. People focused practices support the operator by determining and communicating optimum sequencing and organization of processes and practices for common use.

When you consider that in many of our locations we run a three-shift operation, the use of common systems helps us reduce variation within the same work task from shift to shift. It ensures that when workers take over on a new shift, work areas will be ready to go and set up for them to do their best. They will not have to spend the first part of their shift reorganizing and setting up the operation and thus inadvertently introduce variation into the process. A quality verification component of any process encourages workers to exercise personal control, "stopping the line," using established standards and measurements, to be certain that quality is correct before passing their work on to the next station. Consider the fact that a rough rule of thumb is a cost of over $3000 per minute from lost production when a line is down. It is a formidable responsibility on the part of the operator to stop the line and an example of empowerment on the part of management to permit him or her to do so. Both the operator and the supervisor exercise their commitment to quality decision making, and both understand that the cost of poor quality far exceeds the cost of lost production. The customer will never know of the line that goes down, but the customer will know if the quality is not what it should be.

Lead-Time Reduction helps to build a full *Just-in-Time* manufacturing, service, and/or delivery system that ensures we produce and deliver what is needed when it is needed in the quantities needed and with the quality needed. JIT also enables a rapid response to changes in customer requirements, especially when coupled with a quick setup strategy that reduces changeover time, and therefore response time. The old way of keeping the line moving was just in case: We produced products that may or may not have been needed, in advance of being needed, producing more than was needed just in case. Just in case produces high inventory stores, covering up for such problems as breakdowns, long setup times, late supplier delivery, and absenteeism. *Just-in-Time* production surfaces these problems so that they can be solved. A capable planned maintenance strategy uses predictive, preventive, and planned maintenance to prevent line breakdowns, improve uptime and throughput, and help avert potential accidents.

A synchronous organization is dependent on skillful, knowledgeable employees who all work together in a coordinated effort. In order to synchronize work, the environment must be such that people are empowered to make decisions about their jobs and have the resources to back them up. But this improvement must be undertaken with the total system in mind. If you go back to the synchronous example earlier in this chapter, what good would increasing the production of hinges twofold to 700 per hour do for the overall system that can produce only 60 cars per hour and needs only 175 hinges per hour? The hinge line could brag that it had doubled its productivity, but to what avail? They would soon find they had no more space to store all those hinges the system could not absorb.

Detecting, Solving, and Preventing Product Quality Problems

- *Definition:* Encourage people to surface variation between the voice of the customer and the voice of the process (problems or opportunities), analyze and eliminate the root cause, and implement controls to prohibit recurrence. Constantly repeat this process as the catalyst for continuous quality improvement.[10]

■ *Quality Network action strategies: Change Methodology, Problem Solving, Assessment of the Quality Network Process, Statistical Methodology, Cost of Quality*

Too often we look only for the quick fixes. There is a tendency to put a Band-Aid on a problem that requires a tourniquet, and perhaps eventually surgery. It is then expected that the Band-Aid will hold out, produce, and bring about quality in some way. As leaders, we must not rely on quick fixes. It is critical that the root cause be addressed so that long-term, permanent process changes are made. Anyone who has had a leaky roof understands that the leak seldom if ever originates at the spot where the water is dripping. A bucket will contain the water, but do little else. You have to find the source or sources of the leak and correct it. Taking the analogy further, the root cause of the leak may be a faulty design in roof pitches and may take renovation to prevent further leaks. Additionally, the incorrect pitch should not be repeated in new buildings.

Leaders who are customer focused and advocate process management also cultivate a problem-solving environment. A problem-solving mindset is the heart of continuous improvement in an organization that puts its human and material resources to work to problem-solve through containment measures to irreversible corrective action that will prevent recurrence. This is not as easy as it sounds. We all want to jump to the solution, or perceived solution, and get on to the next issue.

This is where staying the course and walking the talk is evidenced. Employees know quickly if the system is going to back their efforts to ferret out the root cause. Physical material and equipment resources are one kind of support, but the primary support is time, time in the form of people resources to do a thorough and complete job. This presupposes that the problem is finite, which many are. The other opportunities are of a continuous improvement nature where the involvement is ongoing. Leadership's commitment to this attitude and activity should be the same.

Problem Solvers. A problem-solving mindset promotes the belief that we are all problem solvers and that problems are in fact opportunities for quality improvements, both in the product itself and the processes that create the product. The intention is to surface the variation between the voice of the customer and the voice of the process. This discrepancy is an opportunity for improvement.

The Voice of the Customer asks:

- Quality

  Functionality: Does it do what it should do?
  Performance: Does it meet customer expectations for durability, reliability, and repeatability?

- Cost

  Does it meet the customer's expectation for cost and values for the money?

- Responsiveness

  Is the product and service at the right place at the right time in the right amount?

The Voice of the Process asks:

- Customer satisfaction

  Quality? Cost? Responsiveness?

- People and teamwork

  How involved are people?
  How well are we doing our jobs?

- Business needs

  Does it return enough revenue for the money spent?

- Technology

  Is technology doing all it can?

We recognize that the employees on the job are best able to identify variation and remove waste in their processes. There are tremendous advantages to using their experience and skills: They are available to consult; they have knowledge of the problem; they already have the problems prioritized; they cover, in their experience, the entire range of products, services, and processes; they will assist in preventing recurrence of problems, they are rapid and efficient; there is little or no learning curve; they are in-house so there is no consulting fee.

Problem-Solving Action Strategies. In solving problems, the gap between the current output of the process and what it should be must be determined and reduced to meet customer-based requirements. This can be achieved by systematically applying appropriate action strategies. The *Problem-Solving Process* action strategy, and its related *Change Methodology*

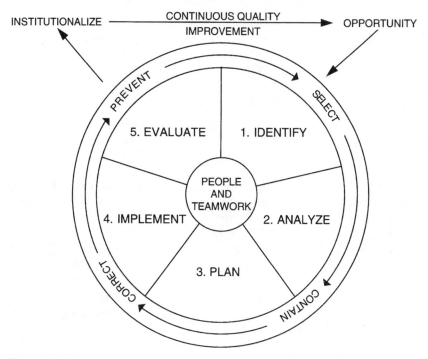

Figure 5-11

action strategy, are the heart of this initiative. The Problem-Solving Wheel (Fig. 5-11) illustrates the process we follow to ensure that the problem will not recur.

The use of this process provides a consistent, proven approach to solving problems and provides a way to track our process to be certain problems are truly resolved. Customers of the problem-solving process are all those impacted by the process. Problems that are passed along the value chain can compromise internal customers, be masked by the process, and, like the roof leak, surface later downstream. By this point the problems may have been compounded several times. The four tasks in the problem-solving process are simple and logical; they tell us what we should be doing:

- *Select:* Define the problem that is being worked on and the benefit to be gained. This ensures that we are working on the right things with the highest overall benefit.

- *Contain:* Describe the *immediate fix* to ensure that the discrepancy does not reach the customer. It is temporary in nature and must always be recognized as such. The Band-Aid approach would stop here.

- *Correct:* What is the *root cause* of the selected problem, and what *irreversible corrective action* will be taken to permanently remove the root cause? This task permanently removes the root cause in the most effective manner.

- *Prevent:* What actions and/or error proofing are in place to eliminate the selected problem from recurring? This task eliminates the possibility that a specific problem can reappear or eliminates sensitivity to its recurrence.

A data-driven process of "hows" within each task helps keep the process on track: Identify, analyze, plan, implement, and evaluate. The problem-solving process is supported by statistical methodologies that help develop a systematic thought process and the use of statistical methods for application in continuous improvement efforts. Our *Cost of Quality* action strategy helps us determine the cost of doing things wrong, the cost of doing the wrong things, and the cost of preventing mistakes. We use our *Assessment* action strategy to compare a unit's or location's performance to the ideal model as represented by the Quality Network. This strategy enables quality councils to track their progress in becoming a total quality organization.

Institutionalizing Problem Solving.   Problem solving supports an environment of continuous improvement, especially when problems are no longer looked upon as obstacles but rather as opportunities for improvement, innovation, and learning. Union and management leadership recognized the importance of such an attitude. Years of traditional thinking had driven a wedge in between workers and supervisors, resulting in the supervisory function becoming that of inspection. We realized we had to help the problem-solving process along and help reconcile these traditional differences.

Document 40 of the National Agreement.   Today there exists a joint action process, epitomized in the design of the Quality Network, in which both parties resolve to approach mutual and common problems in a coequal environment. Document 40 of the National Agreement is an operational example of this belief. It spells out a process for "employees to raise product quality concerns in the course of carrying out their required work assignments." What is significant about this provision is that it specifies that this process is outside the grievance procedure. A concern may be settled immediately on the plant floor, or it could go as far as the NAO UAW–GM Quality Council should the resolution require resources or policy changes that go beyond plant or divisional jurisdiction.

> The Plant/Staff Quality Council will implement an expeditious process flow for employes[11] to voice their product quality concern(s), independent of the grievance procedure, for timely resolution of such concerns, based on the following:
>
> - Employe/supervisor [sic] discussion to attempt to resolve concern, consulting as required with plant quality resources.
> - If unresolved, the District Committeeperson, if requested, will assist in the resolution of the employe's concern.
> - The supervisor and/or District Committeeperson may request the assistance of the Quality Network Representatives to participate in the resolution of the concern.
> - Thereafter, if unresolved, the concern will be discussed with the Plant/Staff Quality Council at the next meeting. If unresolved, either Plant/Staff Quality Council Co-chair will request the issue to be referred to the Co-chairs of the next higher level Quality Council. Thereafter, such concerns, if unresolved, will be referred to the NAO UAW–GM Quality Council for discussion.
> - The Quality Network Representatives will advise the Plant/Staff Quality Council on the status of quality concerns referred to them. Feedback regarding the status of the employee concern will be provided to the originating supervisor and the employee on a regular basis by the plant Quality Network Representatives until the concern is resolved.[12]

Figure 5-12 depicts the process resolution flowchart specified in Document 40. Figure 5-13 is a copy of the Quality Improvement Opportunity Communication (QIOC) called for when a Quality Network Representative becomes involved in the process. It is based on the Quality Network Problem Solving Process and is common to all locations. This is particularly important when a problem surfaces that may be cross-departmental or even cross-divisional. The common reporting process cuts down on miscommunications and helps to eliminate misinterpretation. Even more important, the process reduces the element of blame and focuses on a favorable outcome for all.

A Texas Document 40. Recently an operator in an Arlington, Texas, assembly plant raised a concern about the fabric fit on the bucket seats he was installing. He had complained about the problem in the past to no avail. It just seemed to come back again and again. He personally experimented by sewing an extra piece of material to the area that had been

DOCUMENT 40 FLOWCHART

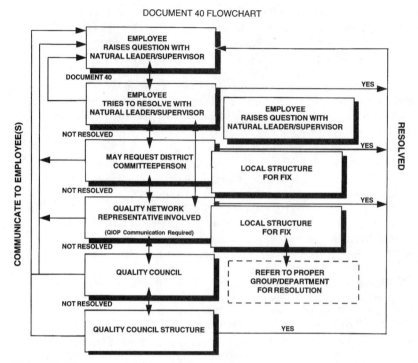

Figure 5-12

pulling out farther up the assembly line. Using the Document 40 process, he notified his supervisor, and together they brought the problem, and in this case the solution, forward. Ultimately the supplier, a GM component plant, changed the specifications and eliminated a quality problem. This may sound simple and logical, but the size and complexity of the GM structure greatly compounds simple remedies. The concern went from the plant floor of one plant, up the division and group levels, across group lines to the components group (now Delphi-AS), down those divisional lines and ultimately to the plant floor. No one was blamed, and the problem got solved.

The Three-Legged Stool. People use the analogy of the three-legged stool to illustrate the equal importance of parts to the whole. Without any one of the legs, the stool would not stand. If one of the legs were shorter or longer, the stool would stand but would not be properly balanced. This is true of the Quality Network Leadership Initiatives. There must be a balanced approach to their implementation in order to realize the maximum benefits of each. Document 40 is an operational application of the four ini-

DATE: _____   NUMBER: _____

QUALITY IMPROVEMENT OPPORTUNITY COMMUNICATION

Employee's Name: Badge: Shift:
Supervisor: Group: Team:
Committeeperson:
District:
Department:

1. SELECT (define the problem that is being worked on and the benefit to be gained):

2. CONTAIN (describe the immediate fix that ensures the discrepancy does not reach the customer):

3. CORRECT (what is the root cause of the selected problem and what irreversible corrective action will be taken to permanently remove the root cause):

4. PREVENT (what actions and/or error proofing are in place to eliminate the selected problem from recurring):

_____   _____
Quality Network Representative (UAW)   Quality Network Representative (Mgmt.)
Date:

	Problem Received
	Referred to Plant/Staff Quality Control
	Supervisor/Employee Notified

CC: Local determination

Figure 5-13

tiatives. It supports the operator, the supervisor, and all those affected in the problem resolution process. There is no blame, no finger pointing. It focuses on the customer. We do not want the customer to receive a defect when he or she takes delivery of one of our products. In this case, we do not want the seat fabric to pull out after use. We use synchronous techniques to look for solutions and analyze the problem for its root cause. And finally, the problem is solved. The four initiatives working together solve problems, engender trust, improve quality and satisfy customers, and positively impact the bottom line. Implementation of all four initiatives must be balanced to achieve the greatest synergistic benefit.

What's Synergy?   A preacher in an old country church best explained this principle when in a sermon on working together, he defined *synergism* as a fancy word that could best be described as he had witnessed it. While at a country fair he saw single horses able to pull a 6000-pound load individually, yet when teamed with another horse, they could pull a 22,000-pound load. The interaction of the four initiatives and their various strategies build on each other's strengths and produce more than could be accomplished individually.

Notes

1. *Quality Network Leadership Guide,* January 30, 1989, p. 11.
2. Tom Weekley, confidential interoffice communication to UAW–GM Department staff, July 12, 1990.
3. Tom Weekley, interoffice communication to L. E. Bunch, UAW Assistant Director, GM Department, September 24, 1992.
4. GM–UAW 1993 National Agreement.
5. Dr. W. Edwards Deming, "Introduction to a System," *The New Economics for Industry, Education and Government,* seminar, July 14–17, 1992, module 3, pp. 48 and 49. Dr. Deming has since published a book under the same title and based on a notebook he used. MIT Center for Advanced Engineering Study, Cambridge, Mass., 1993.
6. *GM–UAW 1993 National Agreement.*
7. Document 41 on Product Quality, *GM–UAW 1993 National Agreement,* pp. 405, 406.
8. Example of GM advertisement from March 6, 1995, *Time* magazine, pp. 74 and 75.
9. Keith Crain, "A Good Product Alone Won't Be Enough in Future," *Crain's Detroit Business,* February 20, 1995, p. 6.
10. These four definitions can be found in *Quality Network Action Strategy Summary* (QN No. 1435), published by Quality Network Publishing, January 1993, pp. 11, 23, 31, and 41.
11. For a time both General Motors and the GM Department of the UAW spelled employee with one *e* (employe). Therefore, documents prior to 1993 appear with this spelling. As the National Agreement is amended, *employee* will appear with two *e*'s.
12. Document 40, Quality Network, *1993 GM–UAW National Agreement,* pp. 402 and 403.

6

The People Component

Total quality management is an amalgam of many excellent business philosophies and principles shaped by years of cultural and historical influences. It looks at the big picture, the total system, and the vital relationships that direct and guide the system's decisions and actions. Total quality expands each of the contributing viewpoints by centering on the involvement of people. The role human resources play in total quality is that of leadership and teamwork at all levels and in dynamic, living relationships. Leadership's role at every level has evolved over the years, and today in successful enterprises progressive leaders must recognize the critical role that workers and others within their sphere of influence must play in the overall process. Teamwork is the underlying operational attitude. That does not mean we all line up in a row, step out on the same foot, and hum the same tune. Teamwork is about how we work together—contributing, collaborative, and collegial.

The Evolving Role of Leadership

It is no longer desirable to operate in a top-down, authoritarian style of management. Many decisions and actions that were rewarded in the past are not only nonproductive but are also detrimental to the "new way of doing business." Today's leaders must cast off many of the traditional behaviors that brought them personal success and recognition in the past. Just as the various subsystems of General Motors—nameplates individually managed in the past (such as Cadillac, Buick, Olds, Pontiac, Chevrolet)—have to come together and work in concert as North American Operations (NAO), so too leaders must work together for the good of the entire organization, trusting in each other to do the right thing. In the case of General Motors, leadership includes suppliers, dealer organizations, and unions. It is naive to believe that internal politics can be eliminated, but certainly there has been a shift toward a reward system that recognizes teamwork and the necessity of good people skills.

Peter Senge of the MIT Sloan School of Management writes about three new roles for leaders to help define new leadership: designer, teacher, and steward. As a designer, leaders must be willing to establish a strong foundation for the sections of the organization influenced by their leadership. They must be able to create a long-term vision for what can be rather than clinging to what has been. The leader as designer must provide direction and a road map and live the values consistently. And the leader must also be willing to maintain a constancy of purpose.

Jay Wilber on Looking at the Big Picture

I was asked by the President of North American Operations, Rick Wagoner, to meet with each of the leaders of the NAO Strategy Board and discuss the Quality Network and both its position and status in their respective organizations. These top leaders of NAO are each responsible for one of the "basketweave" operations that together design, build, and deliver our products and services to market. The areas where each of these operations overlap each other is where we work together to support the vision of total customer enthusiasm. These relationships are so critical and so forceful that the model should really be three dimensional. We're working on it! When I reported back to Rick about my findings, we literally put the basketweave structure on the floor and looked down on the total picture as we discussed the relationships between the various entities represented on the NAO chart. The responsibility of the leaders of NAO is to be certain we all back up far enough to see the entire organization—the NAO system—and not focus on just our piece of that system at the expense of others. GM leadership realizes that, as members of a team, if we are to reach our goals, we must construct, improve, and manage the whole system.

We Are Teachers

The leader as teacher has to be knowledgeable and understand the organization's vision and the gap between where the corporation is and where it would like to be. Additionally, the leader as a teacher must have knowledge of the strategies that can be used to close that gap. Then he or she must motivate and inspire people, much the same as a coach does in athletics. A leader has to be willing to teach and educate others in a better way of doing business. GM leaders are embarking on extensive employee development programs that include components of diversity, mentoring, career pathing, education and training, and communication to nurture and develop today's young talent to be the leaders of tomorrow.

Keeper of the Faith

Finally, the leader as steward is responsible for the people he or she leads and must show care for each person, realizing that the people are his or her greatest resource and provide the real edge for competitive success. The leader as steward is also responsible for preserving and guarding the mission of the enterprise, balancing the individual needs of the components for the good of the whole. Leaders must be willing to change the system to better serve the overall goals of the system. This is done with long-term planning.

Ultimately, it is the leader's responsibility to transform the organization, to take it from where it is or what it was to where it can and will be in the future. Like all the other areas of total quality, the leadership profile cannot be taken apart and cherry picked. As designers-teachers-stewards, leaders must see the total system, understand the role of its people, plan the learning of the organization, stay on course with the vision of the organization, see that all stakeholders understand and support the vision of the organization, and continually improve the long-range plan to achieve the vision. Leaders cannot pull out one piece of responsibility and delegate the others. However, top leadership can work together as a team to fulfill the leadership role, contributing individual strengths to heighten the effectiveness and excellence of leadership performance.

If leadership of any organization desires to be proactive rather than reactive and truly wants to establish a culture that encourages continuous improvement, continuous change must be acceptable and encouraged. Phrases and attitudes like "teamwork," "continuous improvement," "joint input," and "trust and relationship" must begin to be institutionalized to replace past restrictive cultural norms.

Leadership Philosophy in Action

Implementation of a cohesive leadership philosophy begins with an organization's top leadership (e.g., CEO, President, Board of Directors, top corporate officers). If change is desired or required, top leaders must not only be willing to provide necessary resources (people, finances, etc.) but they must also be willing to modify their behavior to model the behavior expected from all who are part of the organization. The establishment of the NAO Strategy Board sent a clear signal throughout General Motors that a NAO team was running the show. Employees under the NAO umbrella now feel connected to the entire organization, and not isolated in their own group. It will take many years for old allegiances to soften, and it might be beneficial that they not disappear altogether. However, leadership's actions are displaying a harmony between group pride and a sense of belonging to a larger totality. It is not unlike balancing regional and national loyalties. As a nation, we had to band together to create a more perfect union, only to then begin rebuilding that union after a devastating war between the states. We haven't completed the job, and state and regional belonging will always be a strong emotion, but we have built a nation of "parts" that truly see their place in the whole.

Marketing is a perfect example of how this philosophy is driving business decisions. As we have mentioned often, competition among GM nameplates was fierce and a successful strategy in the past. Today, it is counterproductive. The marketing functions of each nameplate worked as rivals for good media buys, position, and marketplace recognition. When Phil Guarascio took over General Motors Marketing and Advertising, one of his first moves was to consolidate media buying across the board to leverage General Motors' size and scope to obtain favorable placement and rates. Taking this strategy a step further, Guarascio, as GM Vice President of Marketing and Advertising, has contracted for GM to be the exclusive domestic car and truck sponsor for the 1996 U.S. Olympic Team and the Summer Olympic Games in Atlanta. Special editions of Buicks, Chevrolets, Pontiacs, Cadillacs, and Oldsmobiles will feature the Olympics' symbolic interlocking rings. Yes, the individual brands will be featured, but in a plan designed not to reduce or detract or vie with each other. Guarascio's intentions are clear:

> We will orchestrate each division's promotions in a way to maximize the outreach....For example, if Buick has a special edition Park Avenue, we won't overlap that with another vehicle in the same segment.[1]

Delphi Automotive Systems

This leadership philosophy also manifests itself in the recent reorganization and name change of the Automotive Components Group Worldwide to Delphi Automotive Systems. The men and women who make radiators, batteries, instrument panels, steering columns, ABS brakes, and so on are now recognized as providers of integrated component systems to a worldwide automotive industry. Each division's products and services are actually highly developed subsystems that deliver specific capabilities to larger systems, that is, cars and trucks delivered to our customers. The new name seeks to define the systems nature of the divisions' products and the integration of their systems for their customers. The President of Delphi Automotive Systems, J. T. Battenberg III, revealed the motivation behind the change:

> This announcement is the next logical step on the course we have been charting since 1992....We are moving to unify the divisional names to strengthen and clarify our visibility in the market, as well as to reinforce the systems capabilities of the overall organization....The rapidly changing automotive industry increasingly demands integrated component system solutions, and we have achieved great success in winning new customers when we've had close integration between our organizations. We need to accentuate that advantage.[2]

Charting the Course

Leadership must be involved in establishing the long-term vision for which the organization must strive. This vision must encompass the needs of all of the people in the organization, the internal customers, as well as anticipate the long-term requirements of the customers whom the organization serves, the ultimate customers.

Once the vision is established, leadership must take an active part in the design of the overall system or process to be used by the organization to accomplish the long-term vision. This may not mean day-to-day development, but it does mean empowerment of trusted, capable representatives who solicit and synthesize feedback to verify that the process that is evolving accurately reflects the leadership's vision or permits modification of the leadership's vision, if necessary. A leader must also be actively involved in foundational process planning, not simply endorsing a presented plan.

Once the leadership has actively been involved in the process development and has a real understanding of its design, the natural evolution to teacher begins. An organization is influenced most when the introduction of change is taught by the top leadership. When the top leadership actively participates in the design of any new process and then portrays its obvious knowledge by actually presenting the new process, impact throughout the organization is immediate and fruitful. Involvement as a teacher also improves the communication process in an organization as information is given by top leadership strengthening understanding, solidifying commitment, leading to united action. At the 1995 Key Four Leadership Conference, a new training program was introduced that will be implemented at all UAW-represented sites; *Faces of Cooperation: Reflecting and Valuing Our Differences* tackles the difficult and uncomfortable issues around sexual and racial harassment and hostile environments. UAW Vice President Steve Yokich and GM Vice President Personnel Jerry Knechtel introduce the program and state both organizations' policies in a training curriculum videotape that, module by module, lays out the UAW and General Motors position on behavior not tolerated in the workplace. In essence, the training starts from the top consistently, for every employee. Plant Key Four leadership and joint training teams will carry the message forward. As a statement jointly published by the UAW and GM states, "The goal is to help our people reach their full potential through developed systems, cultural change, and full utilization—without regard to race, gender, family status, military service, ethnicity, religious beliefs, sexual orientation, education, age, and physical abilities."

Teaching by Cascading

Cascading from one leadership group to the next on the organization's flowchart has been used by organizations to assure leadership's involvement as a teacher. General Motors used this approach in the early stages of the implementation of its Quality Network process. If top leadership is truly committed to a cascading process, it can be a very effective way of securing understanding, commitment, and united action. The drawback with this method of securing organization-wide support and action is that it is very time-consuming for top leadership and their involvement tends to trail off due to other responsibilities. Subordinates interpret this as lack of interest and begin to "guess" what the next "program of the month" will be. If top leadership is not committed as an active designer and teacher and not willing or able to be involved as a long-term commitment, then cascading may not be the way to roll out the process. In such a case it is more effective to appoint other top leaders (ideally at the vice presidential level) to act as champions or sponsors of specific sections of the process with the Chief Executive Officer or President as the de facto leader of each section. In the case of a unionized location such as GM plants represented by the UAW, the Vice President and Director of the GM Department authorizes staff members and International Union Representatives to lead various parts of the process, reporting back to the Vice President for feedback and assistance. The presence of these representatives of top leadership provides a mechanism to update top leadership on a continual and timely basis and allows leadership to monitor the process, albeit once removed. What results is that top leadership can be involved in the process without being there on a day-to-day basis. This method for implementation spreads the leadership role as designer and teacher to the top leaders of an organization without giving the impression that interest is waning.

The top leadership then becomes the guardian or steward of the process, monitoring implementation and guiding the process to keep it in line with the overall vision of the organization. The leader as steward recognizes the fact that people will not strive to accomplish long-term goals unless they see top leadership committed to staying the course. Many improvement processes fail because leadership changes directions based on immediate seemingly overwhelming obstacles (e.g., lost market share, unexpected financial liabilities). As stewards, it is critical that original planning take into account possible unforeseen crises and assure that "...for richer or for poorer..." the long-term implementation of the new process will continue. This may mean that original implementation plans may not be as ambitious as one would like. Being a steward requires the ability to plan and pursue actions that are practical and possible to carry out through any type of circumstances.

The Quality Network Leadership Seminars

General Motors began its process with the adoption of a set of beliefs and values, as outlined earlier in Chapter 4. The company's top leadership, along with union hierarchy, then presented their total quality management process, the Quality Network, to its divisional and plant leadership, as well as corporate and technical staffs. The design of the rollout was based on top leadership's teaching divisional and plant leadership who would, in turn, teach their subordinates. The Quality Network Steering Committee made up of top union leadership and General Motors Divisional Representatives directed this ambitious undertaking. Members of the Education and Training Action Strategy Team, composed of union and management people with needed expertise, designed the training that was written and produced by General Motors in-house communications group, GM Photographic. There were ten seminars in the first quarter of 1989, one each for Service Parts Operations (SPO), Chevrolet-Pontiac-Canada (C-P-C), Truck & Bus, Buick-Oldsmobile-Cadillac (B-O-C), Power Products and Defense Products (PPDP), corporate support staff, GM technical staffs, Delco Electronics, and two for the Automotive Components Group. Most of the seminars lasted two days and ranged in attendance from 350 to 750, with most having around 500 participants. Participants were seated in their own quality council groups at round tables seating 10 people, which included the Plant Manager, Union President, Personnel Director, Shop Chairperson, joint Quality Network Representatives, and other plant leaders. Each table was assigned a facilitator. The seminars were held off-site in Florida and are often referred to as the "Florida Seminars." There were complaints on the part of some that going to Florida in the winter sent the wrong signal. Others, once at the seminar, complained that they had no time to enjoy being in Florida, they were being kept so busy in the seminar. The truth of the matter is that the best financial and logistical deal that could be cut was with the Florida facilities. For the most part, the source of the criticism was individuals and organizations, both union and management, that wanted little or nothing to do with jointness. Of course, the criticism was most often couched in terms of how much money this effort was costing. When then GM President Bob Stempel was asked about the cost of these seminars during the Q&A portion of an ACG seminar, his answer was short and to the point. He told the crowd that we simply could not afford not to do this.

A Facilitator-Driven Design

The design for conducting the seminars required hundreds of individuals in specific facilitation, production, instruction, and administration functions. Approximately 50 *core facilitators* were recruited from the operational and support groups. This meant that these people had to be freed up from their official positions across the organization. For the most part, these were highly skilled facilitators from both union and salaried ranks that served in this capacity at the group or divisional level in their respective organizations. There were also members from the organizational development community. Getting leadership to commit the services of their valuable support resources was no easy feat. In early December 1988, after an initial pilot for the steering committee, the core facilitators came to Detroit and participated in a pilot training program along with selected quality councils from a few plants. Even at the pilot program tension surrounding the jointness issue was evident as one quality council got up and left when the word *teamwork* was first mentioned. Members of the Education and Training Action Strategy Team conducted the training. The Key Lead Persons (KLPs) of the Education and Training Action Strategy Team, Cheri Alexander and Bob Farley, were master facilitators for every seminar. After the pilot program, feedback was offered, the core facilitators were trained, and they were sent back to their home locations to identify facilitators who would run their organization's seminar tables. The two-day seminars had extensive table exercises that required hands-on facilitation. For example, Joe McAdams, UAW Local 1005, and his counterpart, Pat Camarati, from the Parma, Ohio, Plant in the C-P-C organization, were master facilitators who presided over several of the Florida Seminars. Both men were active Quality Network Representatives at their plant. They helped to identify the 75 facilitators who would run the C-P-C seminar, which was the largest with over 750 participants.

Teaching the Teachers

While the facilitators were being selected and revisions were being made, the natural leaders of the groups were being trained. Two sessions were held at the GM Management Training Center during which top GM and UAW leaders were led through the seminar and given the modules they would teach. There was opportunity for their input and customization of the material for their particular group. During the two days the sessions took place, every major Vice President and General Manager of General Motors and the top officials of the UAW were trained to teach principles of total quality, the *Beliefs & Values,* and structure, processes, and strategies of the Quality Network.

Production Design

There were two distinct production aspects to the seminars. Course work was produced in three-ringed binders, since each seminar would take on a slightly, or in some case drastically, different look. Pages were designed to be customized for each group. We produced leadership manuals, participant workbooks, facilitator guidelines, "tool kits" for an action strategy exercise, preprinted flipcharts for many exercises, plastic pocket cards, pamphlets on the *Beliefs & Values* and the *Roles and Responsibilities of the Quality Network Representatives*. All speakers (usually at least 20 per seminar) were supported by three-screen slide material. Videotapes were produced and presented as program support as well. In some cases, a group produced a tape on its products or services. Power Products and Defense Products wanted each of its divisions to understand what the other manufactured, and a lively videotape featuring trains, planes, and tanks fulfilled the requirement. An animated program module, requiring original music, was designed to get everyone in the mood. All this was trucked to Florida and warehoused at a production facility contracted in Detroit and Florida to support the seminars. And, since the top leaders of both organizations were all going to be in place in Florida for a few days, we had to set up full offices so that GM and UAW business could go on as usual.

The second facet of production was the event itself. It was a widescreen, rear-screen projected show. We had video enhancement for the speakers, which required three video cameras and a sports truck to switch and record every seminar. We had wireless microphones and follow spots to cover Bob Boruff, now Vice President of Saturn, and Dick Jones, UAW International Representative, currently the union administrator of joint education and training programs, as they wandered the audience for a three-hour session exploring the *Beliefs & Values*. Videotapes of each seminar were edited and used by each group or division as the core of their rollout activities back at their home plants or offices. This means that B-O-C employees were not only taught jointly by their immediate leadership (perhaps a department head and a district committeeperson or the plant manager and the shop chair) but they also saw their plant leadership being taught by top leadership, J. T. Battenberg III, B-O-C Group VP, and Mike Gracey, UAW Quality Network Representative, on the group level. As each seminar closed, production videotape was shipped to Detroit, and GM Photographic Executive Producer Bill Kidwell edited the material and created the training modules for group rollouts. Additionally, a separate ENG (electronic news gathering) production unit captured all aspects of each seminar, from the arrival of planes at the airport, to registration, seminar sessions (close up and informal), meals, and so on. This video was the closing module of the seminar, designed to be a thank-you to all the participants who had just put in two tough days of learning and work.

A Five-Day Cycle

Each seminar, excluding all up-front preparation, ran about a five-day cycle. Since we were moving an average of 500 people in and 500 people out on a rotating schedule, there were many times when the seminars could not be perfectly back to back and the hotel had booked other events. Therefore, day 1 was often the beginning of setup. Light trusses, cameras, speakers, microphones, TelePrompTers, screens, projectors— all had to be loaded in and balanced in one way or another. Days 2 and 3 the core facilitators and group facilitators arrived. Bob Farley and Cheri Alexander, along with the core facilitators, trained the group facilitators at this time. Leadership also arrived and were rehearsed during these two days. The afternoon of day 3 the participants arrived, registered, were hosted at a welcoming reception and were given their schedule for the next two days. It was a very full agenda.

The Quality Network Leadership Seminars put all leadership up front on the issue of quality and customer satisfaction through People, Teamwork, and Continuous Quality Improvement. Many at the seminars struggled with these new ideas; others embraced them. Some refused to sign on. The same plant that walked out of the pilot program got up and walked out again in Florida. Other quality councils enthusiastically endorsed the process in their closing report-outs. Quality council members from one plant wrote a song, which they performed for all a cappella. The reception of Quality Network ideas and principles at the seminars was a good representation of the reaction of the entire GM organization. Implementation efforts have had to deal with this wide range of emotion and readiness.

The Rollout

Each group had its own set of printed and videotaped material. The rollout plan was left to the discretion of each group. In some cases this was accomplished through full-day training sessions with every employee in the plant scheduled to attend on a planned schedule. In other locations, all employees were addressed at one time. Nonunion salaried employees were also invited, and staff leadership was informed of how the process worked in staff areas of General Motors. Quality councils at the corporate, group, division, plant, and staff levels were charged to carry top leadership directives throughout the organization. Councils were established where none had existed previously. The leadership directives were formulated by the corporate quality council, described earlier, consisting of the top UAW and GM leadership and chaired by the President of General Motors and the

Vice President of the UAW and Director of its General Motors Department.

Approval of action strategies and joint product quality efforts begin with the corporate quality council (today the NAO UAW–GM Quality Council) and are passed on as objectives to group quality councils chaired by the Group Vice President and an administrative staff person from the UAW–GM staff. UAW International Representatives and group staff attend these council meetings. Objectives from the NAO UAW–GM Quality Council are translated into actions within the groups. Objectives from the groups are then implemented through individual plant quality councils. Quality council objectives are adapted for staff (salaried) quality councils in nonrepresented areas. Nonrepresented, or nonmanufacturing, activities are currently the focus of an aggressive implementation effort. At the time of the leadership seminars, emphasis was placed on implementation of the Quality Network in the joint, manufacturing arena. The implementation task was great and resources seemed better served, at the time, to focus on our production processes and product quality. Many administrative and staff activities throughout the organization have recognized the benefits of total quality management and have applied tools and techniques first used in our manufacturing environments to their staff areas. While not lessening our commitment to manufacturing productivity improvements and product quality, the Quality Network has now turned to the nonmanufacturing activities. Our plan was submitted to the NAO Strategy Board in October 1994, and we have identified members of a steering committee to help lead implementation efforts in nonmanufacturing activities.

The Key Never Changes

The real key to successful implementation lies in strong, visible support from the very top of the organization, followed by expected participation by successive leadership all the way to the plant floor. As stated previously, it is critical that each successive level of leadership be given a good understanding of the process through honest information exchange. If the desired objectives are to improve efficiency, profits, market share, and so on, then it is necessary to make clear the benefits these changes will have for all employees, hourly and salaried, union represented and non-union represented. Increased sales mean additional jobs and facilities. Increased profits should also result in increased wages, benefits, and job security. Every communication must clearly address the issue of "what's in it for me," if personal commitment is to be gained. This is not merely an issue of money. It is an understanding that people want to be proud of the work they do. They want to be free from fear. To tap the best of an individual, that individual has to want to give his or her best. Dr. Deming and others have proven that dangling the proverbial carrot or threatening with a stick simply does not motivate people. When top leadership sets the example through open, caring communications and an obvious concern for employees, their actions will bring about organizational commitment and will lead to success.

If implementation of any new process is to be successful, it is essential that leaders walk the way they talk. If an organization is in financial straits and sacrifice is needed, then that sacrifice must be evident to all. Leadership must lead the way. Many perks of the past may have to be eliminated or modified to share in future goals. Elimination of the executive cafeteria and remodeling of the existing employee cafeteria to make it more pleasing for all has been undertaken by many companies. General Motors has removed its executive dining room at its Detroit headquarters. A more relaxed dress code has helped some organizations, for example, Saturn in Tennessee, bridge the communication gap and portray a more caring attitude.

The old way of doing business is changing. In some ways, simple, outward gestures such as dress styles and dining rooms may seem trivial. However, they are strong symbols of traditional attitudes that found comfort in authoritarian roles and hierarchical structure. Mutual respect and teamwork, rather than militaristic ranking and recognition, will maintain a proper discipline and order without putting down others. This was the key to the success Bill Malone realized at the Lordstown Metal Fabricating Plant. As cited earlier, the plant was plagued with labor unrest. As a leader new to the plant, Bill's first job was to earn the trust of local union leaders. After that, problems became issues to be resolved rather than obstacles to progress. The foundation for working together in a sustained, long-term relationship is and always will be trust—a simple statement that is sometimes extremely difficult to attain.

Shedding the Baggage of the Past

In the beginning of our association, when we were getting to know each other, we had to take a business trip to New York City. While there we decided to visit Ellis Island. There is a picture in the visitors' center on Ellis Island of a throng of people carrying an exorbitant amount of baggage as they waited to be processed. They were hoping that they could prove that they had a trade so they could get into the United States. They believed that their baggage helped define them and give them value. But having a trade didn't matter at all; all they needed was to pass the medical exam and $25. It is important to realize that what has gone on in the past is really excess baggage; it should not mold what happens in the future. It does not define us as individuals and does not limit our value. It certainly should not taint our ability to build new, trustful relationships. Managers can be the change agents to see the future as something different for all of the people of a company. Trust is really the bedrock of our relationship; it should intertwine in an organization's beliefs, values, and goals. And, it must be promoted and exhibited by top leadership.

Our Ellis Island experience formed the basis of our relationship as the two new leaders of the Quality Network. We shed the emotional baggage of our past and traditional confrontational roles we both had played in favor of an assumption of trust and integrity up front. We consciously decided how we would work together. Going to Ellis Island probably does not fit the stereotypical business trip to New York. But that trip and the resulting action symbolize not only our relationship but also the nature of the job our leaders asked us to do. Traditional foes, a corporate giant and a powerful union, with leaders on both sides who came up through their respective systems, assigned us the job of implementing a total quality system together. Everything about it was and is nontraditional. So we have had to leave traditional behavior behind. The past is now a bunch of old war stories. We find ourselves wincing when reminded of some past behavior. It's fun to reminisce. The good news is that we wince together.

Leadership Turnover

Changes in leadership are cited many times for failure to provide continuing, ongoing commitment to quality and process improvements. Systems must be so institutionalized that changes in leadership will not affect the overall process. This point was dramatically made on the same trip to Ellis Island. From Ellis Island, if you look across the horizon as you board the ferry, there is a large rock formation protruding from the water. When you view a film from the 1920s of the island, you will see the same rock formation. That unchanging bedrock foundation is what a company must establish in its efforts to treat people fairly. It is that foundation which leaders must strive to institutionalize in their organizations. The waves of time have not washed that bedrock away because its foundation is so deeply rooted. Total quality efforts must be like that bedrock. A consistent, long-term commitment must be established that provides methods for improvement but firmly embeds the basic, fundamental principles and values of a process management approach into the organization's foundation. Changes of leadership then may bring improvement but not a collapse and restructuring of the overall system. There may be momentary lapses as new leaders learn their roles; however, long-term commitment assures continuation and improvement of the current system. It's what we mean by "institutionalizing the process." It becomes part of General Motors' culture, and not dependent on an individual.

A long-term vision that can be adhered to through thick or thin will generate committed action by all parties involved. Too often a new program is introduced that is very ambitious and has all the right ingredients but is scuttled because of a change in leadership, lack of leadership commitment, finances, or some other cause. A case in point is the relationship we were developing with our suppliers. We had a program that was working. External economic forces and new leadership changed the direction of that relationship. In some cases, faith and trust were broken. We are now redesigning our supplier quality relationship.

Leaving the Course

We were using a supplier development and certification program, *Targets for Excellence* (*TFE*), with all GM suppliers. Arthur D. (Don) Wainwright, Chairperson and CEO of Wainwright Industries, a supplier to General Motors and 1994 Malcolm Baldrige Quality Award winner, mentioned TFE in his address at The Quest for Excellence VII, the official conference of the Malcolm Baldrige National Quality Awards:

> 'I'll tell you, Wainwright, really, we got religion with this *Targets for Excellence* from General Motors. That's a program that started in 1987. Very much like the Baldrige criteria. We ran in '89 for that, and they gave a site visit. We didn't make it the first year. In '90 we captured that award. We were the 125th supplier out of 50,000 to win that award, a very prestigious award.' Wainwright was told, based on becoming a General Motors *Targets for Excellence* company he should apply for the Baldrige, 'It's a lot easier than *Targets for Excellence*.'[3]

The supplier-customer relationship is rooted in the belief that each partner is expected to help the other to achieve quality. When General Motors adopted synchronous principles, we encouraged our suppliers to do the same. We even trained our suppliers in our synchronous methods and systems, knowing that we would be the beneficiary of their improvements.

> MIKE SIMMS, PLANT MANAGER, AT WAINWRIGHT INDUSTRIES: We use General Motors' terminology for the engineering process. We call it Synchronous Organization. It applies both in manufacturing and in the business support units. Our associates are trained in this process and use it as a guideline for their improvement process and improving their work.[4]

> CHARLES DONALDSON, DIVISION MANAGER, WAINWRIGHT INDUSTRIES: More than four years ago, our customer...said to us, "You must introduce Synchronous Organization into your operation if you expect to remain competitive in the future." And..., when our customer spoke, we listened. We found out that our customer was holding extensive, week-long training sessions in synchronous concepts. We signed up....We sent 10 percent of our work force to this outside training. Then, in typical Wainwright fashion, we stole shamelessly. We developed our own training process and today train all associates in Synchronous Organization. What we learned from our customer was the importance of having a structured process improvement plan in place.[5]

A Change in Leadership

Inaki Lopez came to the United States from GM Europe at a time when General Motors was in grave danger. Red ink was spilled across the balance sheet. Within two weeks of his arrival, he reorganized GM's massive purchasing activities into a single worldwide unit. Everything that had anything to do with purchasing was reported to him. He put pressure on suppliers to eliminate waste in their process and to lower their prices across the board. At supplier locations Lopez conducted a GM-developed quality and productivity improvement process named PICOS Workshops. These workshops focus on selected products or processes requiring improvement in cost, quality, and/or delivery. The workshop participants are composed of cross-functional teams including the workers involved in the process. These workshops are similar to the Synchronous Workshops that had been conducted internally at GM and opened up to suppliers prior to Lopez's arrival in North America. Lopez's approach had the bulldozers idling as the workshop concluded to implement the recommended changes. The measures were drastic, and several suppliers of long-standing went by the wayside. Other suppliers hung in there. The concept of partnership had been discarded.

Dr. Deming on Inaki Lopez

As Dr. Deming entered the room for our meeting, we could tell he was failing physically as he gave us a short greeting. After sitting down, and without conversation, he sorted through some papers he had brought with him.

He appeared to be looking for an item. Finally he found an article he had been keeping regarding Inaki Lopez's approach with long-standing General Motors suppliers. The article was highly critical of the approach and characterized Lopez as heavy-handed and not interested in the suppliers' viability. Dr. Deming turned the article toward us and said, "What are you going to do about this? Suppliers must be treated as long-term partners so you both can improve the process together." We told Dr. Deming that we had developed a process in the Quality Network to accomplish just that. Dr. Deming told us that without treating our suppliers as part of the GM system, we would fail.

Maryann Keller, in an article discussing GM's North American Operations' long way to go to reach their potential, commented on Inaki Lopez's lasting effect on supplier relations: "As much as Inaki Lopez helped GM stave off a financial crisis, his legacy still lingers on in the form of soured relations with suppliers. He also signed contracts with some suppliers which could not meet GM's needs."[6]

The leadership must be good stewards and stay the course. President of North American Operations, Rick Wagoner, presided over General Motors awards to companies selected as *Worldwide Suppliers of the Year 1993*. Wagoner was CFO and had succeeded Inaki Lopez as head of worldwide purchasing at the time of the ceremony. Wagoner stated that the winning companies

> understand that when GM enters into partnership with a supplier, that partnership is market driven and comes with very high mutual expectations. Our partnerships bring more to our products to generate customer enthusiasm.[7]

GM Evolutionary Leadership

In General Motors there have been many changes in both the UAW and GM leadership, yet the Quality Network process has become more firmly entrenched with each change. The ambitious goals and lofty ideals expressed at the awareness rollout in 1987 predictably bogged down, as a change in corporate and union leadership took place in 1989 and early 1990. A fiery trade unionist, Stephen P. Yokich, came to the helm of the UAW–GM Department and then GM President, Bob Stempel, known for his practical expertise and sensitivity to "people issues," was elected as the Chairperson of the Board of General Motors. Both were strong leaders who believed in high standards of quality and who cared about the members of the UAW and the people of General Motors.

Transition created a gap in directives in both organizations as secondary leadership changed, and doubt regarding the sincerity of both union and management commitment to the Quality Network surfaced. As leadership was stabilizing, external forces came into play. Corporate leaders looked for excuses to "backslide" on their commitment to people values or unwittingly fell back into old habits. Discontent within the GM–UAW membership that had been brewing long before the leadership transition asserted itself as opposition to the joint process because of the perceived hypocrisy seen in management actions. Decisions to close plants that were viewed as "cooperative" and to outsource work that the UAW felt could be done "in-house" inadvertently lent credibility to dissident charges.

UAW Leadership Transition: One Voice on Quality

UAW Vice President Stephen P. Yokich took the helm during these turbulent times with a determination to see GM "walk as they talked." If GM said people were GM's most valued asset, as they proclaimed, then he would insist that people be treated as such. If joint programs were to be utilized, then they would truly be "joint" and not a sham or façade, and would truly benefit people in a meaningful way. Yokich was known as a avid advocate of product quality at Ford where he held the same office as the one he assumed at GM in June 1989. In April 1987 while at Ford, he and Peter Pestillo, Vice President Employes[8] and External Affairs, established the UAW-Ford Joint Quality Steering Committee, which was an agenda item at the Ford–UAW 1987 bargaining sessions.

This was in this same time frame that Don Ephlin was cosponsoring the development of the Quality Network at GM. Ephlin, who held Yokich's position at Ford before moving to GM, felt strongly that management had to take the initiative. In a leadership briefing to B-O-C leaders in October 1987, Ephlin acknowledged that some plants had made great strides, improvements coming from the bottom up, but that this was not the ideal. He was frustrated because at Ford, management had taken the lead, and he was urging the leaders of B-O-C to do so as well. The union had just granted an 80 percent acceptance of the new contract, and this was the time to engage all the people of GM.

"Quality is the strategy and the solution to our competitiveness, job security, and customer satisfaction. Quality is our greatest opportunity."[9]

Both Ephlin and Yokich understood the importance of quality to the health and welfare of the men and women they represented. In a report to the Ford workers two years later, Yokich and Pestillo presented a united front on the issue of quality and jointness and the progress that had been made. Peter Pestillo stated that the customer dictated what was to be done, and that it was a single effort and "we're single-minded about it."[10] Steve Yokich made the UAW's position clear. His words foreshadowed the position he would take when coming to GM in June 1989:

> When we went to the bargaining table in 1987, that was one of the main issues we talked about, job security and quality. That was right up on the table. And we said, "Listen, quality is important enough to us as a union that you have to share these decisions with us. We have to work together." We understand that we have to put it in writing so people understand it here at the bargaining table. And, we have to understand that's not where you stop, not at the bargaining table. You go in and you go to the CEO of the company and the Vice Presidents of the company, and they stand up and say, "Yes, quality is important. We won't tolerate junk." And then you have the UAW standing next to them saying, "Yes, quality's important because it means job security to us as well as doing a good job." And when you have top people saying that, then you go into the second level, and they're saying the same thing. And then you go down to the workers, and they look up and say, "If they're sincere, we can be sincere once again too." And I think that's the success story of quality in the Ford system.[11]

GM Chairperson-to-be Robert Stempel strongly asserted that GM would live up to the high ideals set in the *Beliefs & Values* in the face of capacity underutilization, ingrained bureaucracy, established hard-line leadership, and increased competition:

> Whenever people ask us [Don Ephlin and Bob Stempel] to talk about quality, they expect us to concentrate on product quality. But our experience at General Motors (GM) has been evolutionary. We started out working on product quality, then realized that was only part of a bigger challenge. Now we are working to change our corporation to a total quality corporation based on quality people and guided by a consistent set of quality policies.[12]

Both Stempel and Yokich faced a tough set of negotiations in the fall of 1990, and both were well prepared and qualified for the challenge.

One resounding theme sliced through speeches given by both leaders: proper treatment of people and an emphasis on quality were necessary if General Motors Corporation was going to win back the hearts and trust of America.

The negotiations in 1990 produced an innovative contract with far-reaching implications. Job security provisions were strengthened, and innovative new approaches to assuring employees' income over the life of the agreement were established. Commitments to joint product quality improvement efforts were strengthened, and a specific process was established (Document 40) that permitted individuals, anywhere within the corporation, to register product quality concerns with their supervisor, which if unresolved, could be processed up through the corporation, ultimately reaching the top leadership of the corporate quality council.

Commitment to Quality

The agreement set the pattern for the auto industry and established, for the first time, a joint memorandum on quality between the auto companies and their major union, the UAW. Document 119, *UAW–GM Memorandum of Commitment to Product Quality* (Refer to Chapter 3) firmly established the basis for utilizing total quality management within the American auto industry. Many companies have adopted process management principles, but few have attempted to jointly develop the process with employees.

Recognizing the Value of People

Major corporations are using total quality systems because they recognize that the old methods of maintaining employee relations by coercion, force, and power are no longer valid in today's society. The person best qualified to make many of the decisions that affect a particular operation is the person who works on that operation on a day-to-day basis. Having a say in how an operation is to be set up or the type of material to be used or the type of equipment to be purchased is not only a desire of each individual employee but in most cases, is a practical way of assuring that parts can be turned out in the most efficient, safe, and quality manner.

Mistakes Made at Lordstown

In the 1970s the news media focused on the labor unrest and turmoil in the Lordstown, Ohio, complex. At this plant General Motors attempted to establish contiguous sheet metal and metal-fabricating operations to directly feed parts to a final assembly plant all in one location. Body parts and stampings were produced at the metal-fabricating plant attached to a car assembly plant by an overhead enclosed conveyor system that transferred panels directly from the stamping operation to the assembly line. Other component parts were shipped in, but many of the parts were made and assembled at the Lordstown site. During this period there was a tremendous amount of labor unrest as management began to implement new manufacturing methods and systems as well as deal with the bargaining representatives of the people in those locations. A combination of new automated processes as well as a complete change in management style brought about tremendous turmoil. The term *blue-collar blues* began to circulate in the news media as workers voiced their displeasure over being forced into new operating methods that they saw as inefficient and ineffective. Absenteeism, quality, morale—all suffered as management used more and more of an authoritative approach to implementing change, completely ignoring input from a young, highly motivated work force. Labor unrest mushroomed, manifesting itself in many local work stoppages and strikes and a failed launch of a new fuel-efficient car into an economy that was reeling from a gasoline crisis:

> From March 3 to March 24, 1972, approximately 8000 workers struck the Lordstown Plant. Agis Salpukas, a reporter for *The New York Times*, covered the strike and reported that it was over two of the oldest issues in American industrial relations—speedup of the assembly line and management's supposed evasion of work rules established by contract. But Salpukas also reported some other facts:
>
> 1. The workers at Lordstown were very young.
> 2. The workers had engaged in widespread sabotage.
> 3. The "dumb" workers on the line were saying some rather thoughtful and articulate things.
>
> Overnight, Lordstown had become the symbol of idealistic youth standing up to dehumanizing technology. Actually, these workers were mainly just tired of running their fannies off.

The T-Shirt Story

It is no secret that in the early 1990s General Motors was well into its commitment to high-tech production. State-of-the-art automation was considered the answer to quality, cost, and delivery performance excellence. A story is told that workers arrived at their plant one morning to find signs on all the new equipment stating, "Treat me well and I will do good work for you." The workers retaliated by appearing shortly thereafter with T-shirts bearing the same inscription. The message was clear to both sides. Management valued its new, shiny equipment, and the workers knew it. While we cannot pin down a source for this story, it is told often and, whether fact or fiction, makes the point.

A Change in the Climate

The Vega automobile lasted several years but was plagued with production problems, quality and engine problems, and fuel inefficiency and served to underscore that a management philosophy that ignored the worker could no longer successfully produce a quality product. Following one particular long work stoppage of six weeks at the fabricating plant, management in General Motors Fisher Body Division felt it was necessary to look at a new management decision-making approach. Following high-level meetings in this division of General Motors, plant managers, personnel directors, and labor relations supervisors were called into a brainstorming session to explore and outline ways to avoid the disastrous labor policies used in the Lordstown startup. Their efforts eventually resulted in a thirteen-point program for dealing with Fisher Body employees, which was one of the forerunners of the major quality of work life programs subsequently implemented throughout the auto industry.

Irv and Barry Bluestone note that since the time of Frederick Taylor's studies establishing methods for utilizing people in mass production processes, workers have been assigned and directed to perform operations with very little opportunity to provide helpful input. This has resulted in people being fitted into processes rather than processes being designed to fit people.[13]

Employee Relations and Employee Involvement in Decision Making

Total quality techniques and methods in various forms and structures have been utilized by corporations worldwide to improve operations, processes, and the physical and social environments. In recent times, such processes have received more emphasis due to comparison with the Japanese production systems. The Japanese concept of employee involvement has made it clear that workers can not only contribute with manual labor but can also be involved in the decision-making process. Such involvement results in enriching the worker's quality of work life by having the opportunity to contribute to the overall goals and objectives of the enterprise. Workers are more effective and are more dedicated to their jobs when they believe they are able to contribute to how the job is to be done.

A Brief Scenario: The Way It Was

Anyone who worked in a manufacturing operation 10 to 20 years ago will recognize the following scenario, which persists even today in some places. It has been played out thousands of times. A new line is being installed. There has been no conversation with any of the workers who are going to install the equipment, any of the people on the line who are going to use the equipment, or the production supervisor. Installation of the line takes place: Engineering blueprints are followed exactly, placing various pieces of equipment along with accompanying lighting and ventilation systems. The next step is to assign workers to prepare the line for the actual production run. Enter the Skilled Tradespersons who invariably discover many problems that necessitate changes before the line will run properly in a production cycle. Then production workers are placed on the line to operate the equipment. Another series of changes is now called for to accommodate the people who are to run the equipment. Work stations are too high or too low; lighting is inadequate or misplaced, especially since so many changes have taken place from the original installation. The same is true for the ventilation system. Locations of start and stop buttons are not in the proper position for effective operation; materials are too close or too far away. The list goes on.

Supervisors acknowledge and sympathize with the workers' concerns, but, to the surprise of no one on the plant floor, the corrections require large capital expenditures on an operation that is supposed to be up and running. The pressure to begin production supersedes the legitimate concerns of people on the line over issues of efficiency and increased production, health and safety, and the environment. The line gets off to a less than satisfactory start. Ergonomic problems begin to appear as well as delays in line operations because of not properly addressing all of the concerns before the process was installed and "locked in concrete."

Grievances are filed, and ultimately settlements are made that are less than satisfactory to both parties. The ventilation system probably looked good on paper; however, experienced Skilled Tradespersons know it will not be accepted as satisfactory by line operators. Early in the process changes could have been made that would adequately deal with operator concerns. Every plant has a large cache of fans that attest to this scenario.

Jay Wilber on Designing to Specifications, Not People

I recall working on a potential local strike situation at the new Wentzville, Missouri, Assembly Center in 1984. I was told by the local union leadership that management did not take into consideration the concentration of employees when the location of toilets was considered. I asked the management leadership of the plant if this was true, and they indicated that the first design had the bathrooms installed on the plant floor, but when the production equipment was laid out, there was not enough floor space so the toilets had to be raised up above the plant floor and stairs were installed. Management said that employee concentration was considered. However, when looking at a blueprint of the plant's final arrangement, the toilets were spaced exactly the same distance apart in six different areas of the plant, having nothing to do with proximity to employee concentration. To add insult to injury, a tour of one of these raised toilets revealed a stall designed for people with handicaps, in particular wheelchair users. When I asked how they got up the stairs, I was told they had no employees in wheelchairs. Besides, they also had no elevators.

It's Easy to Lose Sight

Toyota recently announced that it is changing its celebrated production system. The Toyota Production System (TPS) has been studied by most major manufacturing organizations worldwide. What could cause Toyota to announce this change? The change, in fact, is actually a return to Toyota's original premise of designing production systems around people. Hitoshi Yamada, General Manager of the PEC Kaizen Education Center, stated:

> While car makers around the world studied Toyota's production methods, Toyota itself forgot what it had learned. The key issue is not whether inventory exists or not. Rather, it is the problem of subordinating people to machines. Only people have the ability to respond to changing circumstances. People must be given mastery over machines. Toyota has simply taken the Toyota production method back to its origin.[14]

People Issues

Leadership must be vigilant. Even Toyota got away from one of its basic beliefs that the overall success of the process depends on a constant awareness of people issues, which must be considered in every decision. This basic concern for people is key to every aspect of the union-management relationship. When capital expenditures are contemplated, health and safety questions must be the first issues addressed. If processes are to be changed or new processes implemented, the first consideration is the effect these changes will have on the workers. Market fluctuations affecting volume have a direct impact on workers; therefore, there must be a long-term commitment to job security that can withstand the swings in the market. Employee involvement at every level of the decision-making process has become commonplace. Access to top management is widespread; common cafeterias and parking lots, casual dress, and so on have erased much of the class structure differences between salaried and hourly workers. A components plant in Flint, Michigan, made a ceremony out of taking down the wall between management's private dining room and the workers' cafeteria. It symbolized the changes that had occurred. Such changes affect most labor relations issues, traditionally resolved through the grievance procedure or left to fester due to the lack of an adequate process for employee input.

Through the proper use of Quality Network action strategies, such as *People Focused Practices, Workplace Organization and Visual Control, Plant, Machine, and Office Layout,* people who will eventually install and run the line are consulted first, before any plans are finalized. In many cases, mockups are made to test ideas and plan job assignments. At the Detroit Hamtramck Cadillac Plant, future models are assembled in a mini-production line by Hamtramck workers. Operators, job setters, supervisors, skilled trades, and plant engineers work with product and manufacturing engineering and suppliers to put together the optimum line. Costly mistakes are prevented, and innovation occurs at the most opportune time, before the machines are set and the track is laid. The entire operation is then planned to fit the line to the needs of people rather than the other way around. This eliminates many disputes over health and safety, environment, skilled trades, and other issues that, in the past, have caused problems for everyone. Benefits include a supportive environment and reduction of waste leading to lower costs, higher quality, and faster model changeover. This simple, commonsense approach creates opportunity for both management and labor to win and engender teamwork.

What about Redesign and Reconstruction?

Another paradigm concerning reconstruction and improvement has been redefined. Like the example of the installation of a new production operation, the redesign and reconstruction of existing production operations were often stuck in interminable planning stages. Some improvement ideas were informally touted but never accomplished. People on the plant floor were frustrated; they knew how to make their processes better, more efficient, more capable, but they were not often part of the redesign team. Today there are quality and productivity improvement teams that are composed of experts in all facets of the production operation, specifically including job setters and operators. Quality Network action strategies are their tools for effective change. An area is analyzed for improvement opportunities, and the team agrees on the changes to be made. When necessary, bulldozers that have been literally waiting in the aisles move in and the changes are made then and there.

A Collaborative Effort

At a speedometer cluster assembly and inspection area in a Delphi-EES plant in Flint, a team of engineers, operators, union representatives, and supervisors put their heads together and designed a better way to process the assembly and inspection of cluster assemblies. Their collaboration improved quality, reduced cost through improved productivity, and corrected an ergonomics problem at an employee work station. Changes to the new machine layout were literally performed by Skilled Trades workers sitting on idling bulldozers ready to start work as soon as the team completed its design.

If modifications or refinements to the changes are deemed necessary, they are made with as much dispatch. This activity could not happen without the cooperation of union and management leadership in the plant. A commitment to a redeployment plan for affected workers is fundamental. Cooperation and understanding is critical on the part of all affected functional groups: operators, job setters, the Skilled Trades, engineers, financial planners, schedulers, material handlers, health and safety representatives, and so on. In addition, production workers both upstream and downstream of the affected area must be informed and considered. The results of these efforts have been gratifying. Workers like it because they are listened to and their workplace is being improved; ergonomic and safety considerations are always a function of the changes made. Non-value-added wait time is minimized. Quick, if not immediate, response is gratifying to those involved and boosts morale. Better processes support the operators and lead to better products and better bottom lines.

The *Beliefs & Values* and Decision Making

General Motors' *Beliefs & Values* are used to guide the decision-making process at all levels of the organization. In the area of employee involvement, "Make GM people full partners in the business" ensures that all stakeholders are included when decisions are made that affect them. It is when a decision is first being contemplated that a true sense of teamwork can be engendered by considering issues such as those discussed previously. Joint teams should be empowered to consider the issue and realistic, effective solutions before any moneys are spent on brick and mortar.

Leadership's Role Is to Engage Its People

Total quality at GM is a business management philosophy, an involvement process that accepts the legitimacy of the joint efforts of labor and management. This philosophy comprehends that cooperative relationships between employers and employees are worth developing and believes that every employee has the ability and the right to offer intelligent and useful inputs into decisions affecting their roles and responsibilities within the organization. Management, unions, and employees learn how to work better together, determining for themselves what actions and improvements are desirable and workable and can be achieved. The foundational values should be used to weigh the effects of any decision. Consistent adherence to these values will help eliminate the hypocrisy associated with saying one thing and doing another. This is especially true if the value system is posted on all the walls for the world to see but are never evidenced "on the floor." If decisions align with the foundational values and input from those affected is sincerely considered, resolutions will be more widely accepted and provide the opportunity for cooperation that can build real teamwork, even in the face of overwhelming obstacles. A mindset that recognizes individual talent and opinions understands that the success of most organizations depends on how well people at all levels within that organization can work together for the ultimate good of all. Teamwork, both in the formal structured sense and the informal, cooperative sense is an integral part of a total quality system and typically includes activities focused on areas or specific processes.

Teamwork Means Communication

Honest and open communication about good or bad news can pave the way for joint decision making. For example, a plant closing can be an opportunity to build positive relationships. In the past, General Motors, out of concern for low morale and fear of imparting bad news, has waited until the very last second to notify collective bargaining representatives and workers that a plant was going to close. In a corporation such as GM, having many various locations, notification of closure as early in the process as possible enables collective bargaining representatives and workers to prepare to move to other locations or to undertake training to prepare them for a change in career or occupation. It readies the work force that is affected and exhibits respect for them. Additionally, the union is not caught off guard and can try to make plans to assist workers in this crisis.

Team Concept

The team concept is an integral part of any total quality system and plays a vital role of secondary leadership. The basic premise of team concept is that the more input that can be given on a particular issue and handled in an effective manner, the better the chances to produce a good, if not the best, decision. Additionally, overlaps in assignments, absenteeism, quality, and other areas of concern can be ironed out by the team in ways that not only bring about a better quality of work life for the team itself and individuals on the team but also accomplish the goals and objectives of the corporation.

The downside of this is that team concept strikes at the heart of traditional union-management behavior. Empowered teams have less use for the heavy hand of traditional supervision, which sought to inspect all work and catch all mistakes—mistakes as perceived by the supervisor. On the other hand, team concept starts to challenge strict lines of demarcation as delineated in national and local union agreements. The threat to this activity is the perception that a team is being pulled together to eliminate jobs. Obviously, team concept can really be effective only in progressive, trusting environments. It will not work in an atmosphere in which either party believes that it is selling out, getting in bed with the enemy. Because of the negative baggage that has been attached to the team concept, there are many locations in General Motors today, functioning and flourishing in teams, who will not use the words *team concept*. The words do not matter, but feelings must be considered. It is not important what label it wears, the spirit of teamwork and cooperation is pervading the corporation.

Japanese Teams

There are many examples of team principles being used today, not only in the United States but overseas as well. Japan is commonly thought of when the team concept is discussed. "There is a strong sense of 'groupishness' in Japan as distinguished from the American sense of individuality. The Japanese worker is committed not only to the norms and values of the work group, but to the larger group, his company, indeed to the nation. And the company is an extension of his close-knit family life. One might say that workers and managers alike are conditioned to group cooperation."[15]

Each person on the team is responsible for a specific job function on a given day as determined by the team. Work assignments are changed around, and supervisors basically become facilitators and advisers for the team rather than authoritative figures making all of the decisions. Each member of the team is free to interject his or her opinion and their feelings, and the team itself then works out a solution to the problem that confronts them. For team concepts to be successful, leaders must be willing to invest large portions of time and capital in establishing effective work methods and work stations that accommodate team concept principles.

General Motors, Toyota, and Teams

In General Motors' joint venture with Toyota, New United Motors Manufacturing, Inc. (NUMMI), there are various team meeting stations along the assembly lines, permitting team members to meet and discuss the problems—such as quality, absenteeism, and improper parts—that may face them during the course of a day. They are given the authority to make decisions in these meetings within specific parameters, which helps the team feel it is truly a part of the overall effort by New United Motors Manufacturing, Inc. Additionally, work stations are set so that various team members can assist each other, and all team members learn each other's jobs and rotate on these various jobs. Robert Hendry, Vice President of NAO Business Support, was at NUMMI when a new manufacturing organization was developed for a traditional GM plant and work force, using the basic precept of pushing authority down the chain of command. He explained it this way, "We take a plant and break it into four pieces, for example, the body, press and paint shops, and final assembly. We put four guys over those little areas, so you have a production unit manager with responsibility over that area, and he has engineering, materials resources, and production people available to him." This was in direct contrast to the prior GM approach of managing people in that plant.

Skilled Trades and Team Concept

In Skilled Trades areas, the team concept can be used effectively if management realizes that trying to train someone to be a jack-of-all-trades is not the best utilization of manpower and training. People who are specifically trained in each given trade can work together assisting each other in overlapping work assignments. Specialization will still need to be maintained in those critical areas for which long-term training is required.

For example, a team of skilled employees such as a millwright, an electrician, and a pipe fitter may be assigned to a given production area. When a problem arises, they will assist each other in removing guards, getting tools, and getting equipment. However, if the problem is electrical, the electrician will do the very technical aspect of the job. If the job involves simply pushing an electrical reset, any member of the team may be trained to perform that function.

Team-Building Requirements

Successful team building requires that goals be clearly stated and team members understand the purpose of the team and the parameters that they have in decision making. Teams have the ability to work out many people problems that plague most managers today. Team members may truly be able to assist one of their own who is having serious problems with personal issues and may begin to miss work. Team concepts tend to prove to be more efficient overall, based mainly on the flexibility that they provide. All the team members are trained in all the various jobs so that if someone is absent, a team leader or team member can perform the work. Or a person who is not a member of the team may come in and be assigned a job within the team that does not take a high degree of skill and the team can continue to operate effectively.

Team concepts also tend to reduce the cost of management in the long run because fewer supervisors are needed and those supervisors can concentrate most of their time on the real problem areas involved on the job rather than having to make every decision on every issue that arises.

A Case Study: Delphi-SSS Plant 6

Saginaw Plant 6, part of Delphi Saginaw Steering Systems, manufactures steering columns in Saginaw, Michigan. Plant leadership felt a compelling sense of urgency to change the way it manufactured its products for its ultimate customer, the production worker at the assembly plant who installs steering columns in the vehicles.

> MIKE HUSAR, PLANT MANAGER: It got obvious that some of our practices weren't world class in terms of quality and delivery and some of those issues. We were going to have to change our system if we were going to end up being able to compete and be a world-class system.[16]

> GARY SHEPHERD, ZONE COMMITTEEPERSON, BARGAINING COMMITTEE, UAW LOCAL 699: I knew that if we weren't going to change, we'd just be another plant that went by the wayside, one of those plants that shut down....The key word to all this is continuous improvement. If you're going to sit back on your heels, you're not going to change. The only things that don't change are dead things.[17]

Saginaw Establishes the Quality Network Manufacturing System. The plant has replaced its traditional way of doing business with their Quality Network Manufacturing System, which establishes joint team or production cells—smaller production teams empowered to make decisions on the plant floor and responsible and accountable to identify the most effective processes to get the job done. Joint leadership sent strong signals that it was serious about the direction it was proposing by including the Quality Network Manufacturing System as part of the local agreement between plant management and Local 699. Its inclusion in the agreement, according to Jim Raymar, Joint Activities Representatives, "makes it very difficult for us to get back to the old ways of doing things."[18]

Toyota Business. The plant has a litany of satisfied customers and counts Toyota and Chrysler among its new customers. This was not always the case. Toyota paid three visits to Plant 6 before awarding the plant its business. On the first visit Toyota laid out its expectations. On the second visit Toyota representatives focused on how well the plant was implementing processes to fulfill their requirements. On the third visit, with processes fully implemented, Toyota was impressed with the plant's execution and quality and awarded its business. Outside business is important to the bottom line and the work force since it accounts for about 15 percent of the production of the plant, which translates into 300 jobs. Plant 6 is leveraging what it has learned from its Toyota experience to provide world-class products and service to all its customers:

> MIKE HUSAR: I think initially our response to the *Voice of the Customer* was arrogance. We didn't listen to them. We didn't hear what they were saying. I don't think we did a good job of addressing their quality concerns. Hopefully, we have turned it around. For example, with Toyota, we have an engineer stationed in Japan that works right with the design engineers.[19]

Plant 6 team members work directly with their customers to ensure customer satisfaction. Dick Deitlein, an assembler from Department 61, has direct contact with his customers: "If they have any problems, they'll be able to call right down into the department and talk to us, or we'll be able to call them and see what kind of problems they have so we can take care of the problems."[20]

The Cost of a Culture Change. Plant Manager Mike Husar realized that if he and the rest of the leadership team wanted to create a culture change, there would be a price to pay up front. That price could have ranged from reallocation of human resources to capital expenditures. Things may not have moved as quickly as they wanted. Suggestions for improvement may have gone well beyond initial expectations. All ideas would have to be entertained. Additional training would have to be put in place. More people would have to be trained at a higher level. While costly and time consuming at first, this training would allow them to use the talents of their people at a fuller capacity. And there would be the issue of the traditional role of supervision:

> STAN MANSFIELD, UNIT COORDINATOR, LOCAL 699: I think the role of the advisor has changed immensely because they are no longer just the boss, they're part of the team. And as such, it's a changing role for them, and many are uncomfortable because they are really an integral part of the department rather than just the overseer.[21]

When executing a production cell design, major line changes often occur. For example, Department 57-1 moved its large Barnsworth multifunctional transfer operation with 24 stations across the plant to include it in its production cell. The result has been a more streamlined, smoother operation. Before the move, in order for a part to exit this segment of the process, it moved over 3 miles. Over 100 people in the line were part of the process. The new production cell approach contains the part and eliminates costly travel time. Fifteen people build the part from scratch, with everyone communicating as part of a team. The team experienced a 60 percent reduction in idle inventory. Before the redesign, the process needed from 10 to 20 gondolas of parts, 2000 parts per gondola, to support the process. With the redesign, with the part going right from the presses to the "Barns" (the Barnsworths), there is a maximum of 2000 parts total sitting in front of the machines. Less inventory, less travel, less handling, less opportunity for problems and errors.

Not Letting Fear Invade

As Dr. Deming reminded us often, management must drive fear from the workplace. This is particularly true when transforming an organization. Imagine trying to make these changes without the knowledge and cooperation of all involved. Certainly it would seem that jobs would be lost. The supervisor's sphere of influence appears to have been reduced drastically. The key to making it work is how you treat your people. Zone Committeeperson Gary Shepherd believes that the single most important first move is to inform everyone involved, in this case the entire plant, where you are trying to go and why. It is a question of taking the time to educate people so that they truly understand leadership's direction and motivation. The second step is to give the people the ability to have input in the changes. Clearly this is what happened at Saginaw, as evidenced by the changes being included and ratified in the local agreement. It was a partnership for change:

MIKE HUSAR: The bottom line is that if you don't have any credibility and the people really don't think your heart is in the right place or that you're doing the right thing for them and for the plant, it just doesn't happen....You don't take on the world, and you don't probably go after your worst situation first. What you try to do is have some successes that people can see and say, "Hey, this is a winner."[22]

What Do the People Think?

MARILYN GARLINGHOUSE, ASSEMBLER, LOCAL 699: We have more say because we're a team. We solve more problems together, working together as a team....I hope the next generation can learn to work together and real-ize that by reaching a goal of satisfying their customers, they're saving their jobs.[23]

RICHARD "DOC" SAVAGE, DEPARTMENT 76 COORDINATOR: With people and commu-nication, there shouldn't be anything we can't solve.[24]

WAYNE "SPANKY" SASSE, B-ZONE SHOP COMMITTEEPERSON, LOCAL 699: I have always believed that the people themselves are the ones that can make this work or not work....I believe if we don't go to this Quality Network System, that we will lose customers. Because all your customers all over the coun-try and all over the world are going to this system of running....And if we don't do the same thing, we'll be last place instead of first.[25]

Future Utilization

There are mixed reactions today in many locations as to whether team concept procedures will be utilized more and more in the future. However, the current working examples of the process in action tend to confirm that people are more content and that they are more willing to participate in company objectives where team concepts are utilized. It seems to be clear that individual members of any organized group consider their input important and, in fact, do have insights that can add to the overall effectiveness of the entire group.

Quality Network and Labor Relations

The evolution of the Quality Network Process has affected all areas of labor relations at General Motors. Advance discussion, total informa-tion sharing, mutual concern for problems, and so on, have improved the worker-management relationship. The relationship between union and management has changed. Trust is being built. Document 40 of the National Agreement, discussed in Chap. 5, epitomizes this change. Workers are now engaged in solving problems that affect their work.

This increased involvement requires additional time and resources. Administrative functions within the union have increased, requiring additional resources and advanced training. Overall, joint involvement in the decision-making process has secured the union's position as an effective instrument for worker advancement and has changed the role of total adversary to partner in areas that benefit workers.

Contract negotiations can be based on an attitude of mutual concern and address issues of competitiveness and quality as joint initiatives to the benefit of all parties involved. There are still basic philosophical differences that can be resolved only through collective bargaining efforts. Time spent on bargaining grievances can be better spent jointly resolving the issues that cause the grievances in the first place. It is more important to spend less time on disputes and more time on understanding people issues. For instance, determining ways to work together to improve the ergonomics of a work site can result, in the long run, on less absenteeism, less injury, and less stress. When employees do not have to strain to do their jobs, when they are not fighting the system, quality improves. Counterbalanced tools, platforms of appropriate heights, and stock delivery at a constant level have helped reduce back injuries.

At General Motors, collective bargaining proposals and resolutions have created a better working environment, one in which workers have input into their own destiny. The Quality Network is process focused, thereby surfacing differences and addressing issues in a way they can be handled. The Quality Network helps create a better climate for labor relations; a climate in which other contract provisions that support employee involvement may be dealt with such as outsourcing, subcontracting, job security, and health and safety.

Outsourcing

If a particular operation is not competitive and management is considering sourcing that particular job out to a supplier who could be more competitive, real communication and discussion may lead both parties to see that changes could be made to make the operation competitive and be kept at that location. Issues involving quality problems, if addressed jointly and in a spirit of teamwork and cooperation, will promote individual efforts that go far beyond the call of duty in resolving problems that may otherwise continue to affect quality.

Health and Safety

Issues involving health and safety and ergonomics affect workers every day on the job, and efforts by an organization to take care of such legitimate issues lend credence to foundational values that point out the importance of people in accomplishing the desired goals and objectives. A side benefit is decreased injury costs and a safer workplace. Health and safety is a primary focal point for both GM management and the union.

A Change in the Bargaining Environment

Viewing other contractual provisions on the basis of the *Beliefs & Values* helps promote a win-win attitude and changes the bargaining environment. These changes are widely supported by the UAW membership, tempered by a natural reluctance to change. As mentioned, previous experience with quality of work life (QWL) activities caused caution and, in some locations, distrust. Dissenting sentiments warned of the dangers of cooperating with management. They saw joint activities as a serious threat to union solidarity. The Quality Network attempts to balance the WIIFM (What's In It For Me?) consideration among the stakeholders:

- *Management:* Improved quality and productivity

- *Employees:* Improved work site ergonomics; health and safety and job security

- *Union:* Improved response and concern from management regarding areas of historically difficult negotiations, for example, employee workplace issues and training

The evolution of traditional union roles had been a hotly debated issue throughout the UAW. An active debate ensued at the Collective Bargaining Convention in Kansas City, Missouri, in preparation for 1990 negotiations. Union leadership understood that a significant change in emphasis of the union's role was necessary to protect workers. The UAW felt it could no longer allow companies to make decisions prior to UAW involvement and that workers' equity should be considered up front, along with the interests of stockholders and others. Delegates to the convention overwhelmingly accepted the premise that the union must be proactive in seeking further input into areas previously left up to managers in order to successfully represent workers in the future. The 1990 and 1993 collective bargaining proposals reflect this new attitude and collective bargaining will continue to do so in the future. Contract ratification in 1990 was very high, and support for the notion that job security was provided in exchange for working with the company on improved quality and productivity has remained high through the life of the agreement as shown by internal and external surveys.

Management's Role in Labor Relations

General Motors has changed in its view of traditional labor relations, recognizing the need for open information sharing and joint processes in every aspect of the business. This has required an extensive change in labor relations practices; the same changes faced within the union confronted General Motors Corporation. More resources had to be redeployed into problem solving and joint decision-making processes designed to avoid problems rather than react to them. This required a change in the working environment at every level of the corporation, and this remains an ongoing challenge. People skills are now important considerations in promotions. Trust can be developed only in an atmosphere of total honest and open communication requiring sharing of previously "confidential" materials. During the 1993 national negotiation, the company openly disclosed financial data and future product plans. Plant operations considered for closing as well as those requiring new tooling and modernization were also discussed. Only a few short years ago this would have been unheard of; information of this nature would not have been shared until the very last moments before implementation of the decision.

The management of an organization cannot expect the leadership of the union to support decisions that affect the people they represent unless information is forthcoming. The attitude concerning communication in general has changed. Employees have become used to seeing joint teleconferences and receiving jointly published letters. The Quality Network leadership hosts *Representative Conversations,* a video program that addresses topics of the day. One scheduled for January 19, 1994, explained all the new contract provisions affecting the Quality Network. These programs are typically taped before a live audience with a spontaneous and often lively question-and-answer period. Copies of these programs are distributed to all quality councils via their Quality Network Representatives with facilitation hints to promote discussion at quality council meetings. *Representative Conversations* is part of a communication strategy that seeks to keep everyone up to date and informed (see Chapter 11).

Leadership's Challenge

Total quality management systems can be effective only if workers and management personnel see progress in accomplishing overall company goals, while at the same time meeting individual needs by taking into account human factor approaches to managing people. It is leadership's responsibility to create and give life to a shared vision that links individuals to the organization and engages their hearts and minds as well as their strength.

Notes

1. "GM Looks for Gold As Olympics Sponsor," *The Detroit Free Press*, March 10, 1995.

2. Press release from Delphi Automotive Systems issued February 13, 1995, simultaneously from Delphi-AS Headquarters, Pontiac, Mich., Tokyo, Paris, and São Paulo.

3. Arthur D. Wainwright, Chairperson and CEO, Wainwright Industries, Inc. Excerpted from his remarks at *The Quest for Excellence VII*, the official conference of the Malcolm Baldrige National Quality Awards, Washington, D.C., February 6–8, 1995.

4. Mike Simms, Plant Manager, Wainwright Industries, Inc. Excerpted from his remarks at *The Quest for Excellence VII*, the official conference of the Malcolm Baldrige National Quality Awards, Washington, D.C., February 6–8, 1995.

5. Charles Donaldson, Division Manger, Wainwright Industries, Inc. Excerpted from his remarks at *The Quest for Excellence VII*, the official conference of the Malcolm Baldrige National Quality Awards, Washington, D.C., February 6–8, 1995.

6. Maryann Keller, "GM's Problems," *Automotive Industries*, December 1994.

7. John McCormick, "Interview with Richard Wagoner," *Automotive Sourcing*, February 1995.

8. Like GM, Ford Motor Company also spelled *employee* with one *e* for a time.

9. Remarks from a briefing by Donald Ephlin to the Buick-Oldsmobile-Cadillac leadership comparing Ford to GM, October 27, 1987.

10. Excerpt from *Reflections on Quality*, a videotape program featuring Stephen

P. Yokich and Peter J. Pestillo, sponsored by the UAW–Ford Quality Improvement Implementation Committee, 1989.

11. Ibid.

12. Excerpt from "GM's Quality Network: Quality and Customer Satisfaction," *Journal for Quality and Participation*, vol. 12-1, March 1989.

13. Irving Bluestone and Barry Bluestone, *Negotiating the Future*, Basic Books, New York, 1992, pp. 48–49.

14. K. Okine, "Toyota Changes Its Famous Production System," *Automotive Industries*, February 1995.

15. R. Guest, "Quality of Work Life: Japan and America Contrasted," *The Wheel Extended*, April 1983, p. 9.

16. Remarks excerpted from *Saginaw Plant 6*, a videotape produced by the Quality Network, 1995.

17. Ibid.

18. Ibid.

19. Ibid.

20. Ibid.

21. Ibid.

22. Ibid.

23. Ibid.

24. Ibid.

25. Ibid.

7

Customer Satisfaction through Continuous Improvement

There is a lot of discussion about learning organizations, reengineering efforts, reinventing the organization, total quality systems, continuous improvement, and other approaches for managing and growing the business, whatever that business may be. We hear much touted along these lines to improve government, higher education, secondary education, the health care system, and our own transportation system. Public- and private-sector institutions, for-profit and nonprofit organizations, manufacturing and service industries—all are embracing some sort of change in philosophy to plan, predict, and procure a place in the future. All these approaches, on a large or small scale, are about plotting and managing change. Change itself in inevitable, and it is up to us to direct the change to better serve our customers and, therefore, our organization. There are many different tools and techniques to use within a change process, many of which are action strategies of the Quality Network. The scope of the opportunity helps determine which methods to use and on what scale. The Quality Network has developed a change methodology that can be utilized to improve any situation, process, or organization. As always, the key to the process is people; where leadership stands, how people are treated, and what understanding is fostered—all will help determine if people are the catalyst for change or an obstacle to it.

Systemic Tension: People

Human beings are not comfortable with change. A newly married couple accepts change as part of an adjustment to a new lifestyle. Furniture can be arranged and rearranged with little strife or discussion. Tasks fall into a natural division and become routine. The same couple 5, 10, or 15 years later requires a third-party mediator to change tasks or rearrange the home. "His" job falls into well-defined categories as does "hers." "His" favorite chair *must* be in "his" favorite spot. The same mindset with the routine permeates every organization. Young new organizations start out with flexible plans and processes. Success then tends to institutionalize the process, methods, attitudes, etc. Long-term success builds invisible walls around an organization to "capture" all that has led to past successes. These same walls then insulate the organization from changes necessary to continue to be successful in a changing world environment.

"That's the way we've always done it, why change?" "We've tried that before." "It's not my job." What's the boss want?" "No, because I said so!" "If it ain't broke, don't fix it." Such sentences are heard more and more often as an organization slowly develops the fatal disease of hardening of attitudes. Continuous success in any environment requires breaching and breaking down walls, being open to new ideas, commitment by top leaders to ongoing improvement, an environment that encourages and rewards continuous improvement, and a willingness to invest in training. Most leaders feel they fulfill these requirements and are willing to change if necessary; however, in actuality, many necessary shifts in leadership's thinking normally result from external events, like lost market share, governmental regulations, legal entanglements, and natural disasters.

Organizational Change

Ultimately, it is leadership's responsibility to transform the organization, to take it from where it is or what it was to where it can and will be in the future. This is depicted, in part, by the *Organizational Transformation* chart discussed earlier (Fig. 7-1). This model is a power-

ORGANIZATIONAL TRANSFORMATION

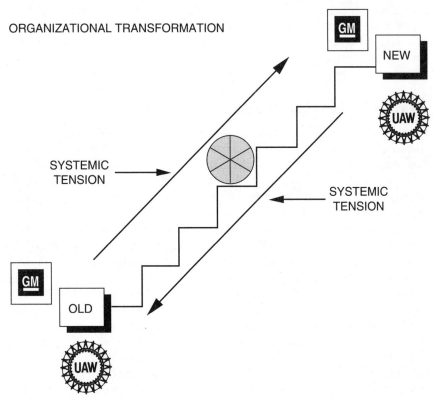

Figure 7-1.

ful way to show why organizational change is so traumatic for all concerned and certainly represents the importance of strong, dedicated
leadership to move against such resistance. In Chapter 3 we discussed
the transformation process in General Motors. There are the visionaries who readily see the necessity for moving from the old to the new.
They look at the world and General Motors' relation to it in a whole
new way and are able to visualize the corporation doing things never
done before. These may encompass small innovations or breakthrough
concepts. Certainly, onboard satellite communication systems and
smart vehicles that avoid collisions were not considered merely a few
years ago. However, there are also people who are satisfied and successful with the way things have worked in the past by utilizing old
systems and methods. Some want to change and others do not. In earlier chapters this chart is utilized to evaluate current and desired states
of an organization depicting the gap between the two.

Some want to change quickly, and others want to change cautiously and slowly to ensure that no mistakes are made. These different views create "systemic tension," or countering forces that slow progress toward the future state and can become formidable obstacles to change and growth. The tension, or passion, for change must be greater than the resistance to change in order to succeed. The rate of progress is in direct relationship to the strength of the resistance. The stronger the resistance, the slower the pace. Ultimately, for a corporation to be successful, systemic tension must be overcome. The strengths of the past establish the foundation for the changes that become the strengths for the future. In many cases it is necessary to philosophically disassociate with the past in order to accomplish the changes necessary to survive in an ever-changing world.

Recognizing the Need for Change

The implementation of any new process is fraught with new challenges and will face many obstacles. The concept of transforming General Motors into a total quality corporation is mammoth. Resistance comes in thousands of different guises. The scale of effort spans the entire corporation down to small staff and departmental changes that can be as obstinate as the larger effort. Resistance to change ultimately comes from people. People are afraid of failure, especially in an environment that does not encourage or value risk taking. People do not want to be reminded of past failures that were related to change efforts. Program-of-the-month dooms change efforts to failure due to lack of support, commitment, and trust that, this time, "we mean what we say." Change also takes us out of our comfort zone. The status quo may not be perfect, but it is familiar and, to a certain extent, controllable. Fear of leaving familiar ground can seem to have dire consequences. If you do not understand the proposed, new process, how can you be part of it? Why would you want to be part of it? Finally, change can alter existing turfs and thereby erode perceived power. New ideas may threaten the authority and control some individuals cherish. After all, they worked hard to get it.

Can People Change?

To make change happen, stakeholders must understand why change must occur, the nature of the change contemplated, and how it will impact them personally. Three defining statements of the *Beliefs & Values* place change in a personal perspective:

- Accept change as an opportunity.

- Make continuous improvement the goal of everything we do.
- Establish a learning environment at all levels.

The key is to take fear out of the equation. In process management, the people component is so well articulated that fear no longer has a function. The idea in process management is to manage processes that are so well designed and executed that they are in control and do not need controls. Inspection is an external (to the process) control that is necessary because the process itself is not in control. This philosophy carries over to change. Rather than the many kinds of change activities that occur as reaction to external or uncontrollable events or actions, typically referred to as *firefighting*, the preferred condition is an effective change methodology that is controlled, proactive, planned, and considered a priority. The key factor, again, is people. They do not want to be changed, they want to be part of the change process.

Quality Network Change Methodology

A cross-functional group of GM employees from several vehicle groups (both cars and trucks)—advanced engineering, the component organizations, corporate staff functions, represented and nonrepresented employees—surveyed GM locations to better understand how changes were being made. The group, the Quality Network Change Methodology Action Strategy Team, took the best practices from the processes studied and developed a single change methodology to be used by all GM people aimed at continuous improvement of any process to better satisfy our customers.

Two Types of Change

Everything we do is part of a process in a system. When we make a change, we do it in order to improve that system by improving the process. The flowchart in Fig. 7-2 depicts change methodology as part of an overall change theory. The process to be improved can be analyzed for understanding by using the Quality Network process model (see Chapter 5, Fig. 5-6).

Change methodology is used with two basic types of change. Each change has potential impact on the process involved. When something within a process suddenly changes (*uncontrolled*) and does not meet customer requirements, we become *reactive* in our response. We look inside the process and try to discover what caused the change to occur.

TWO PATHS FOR CHANGE

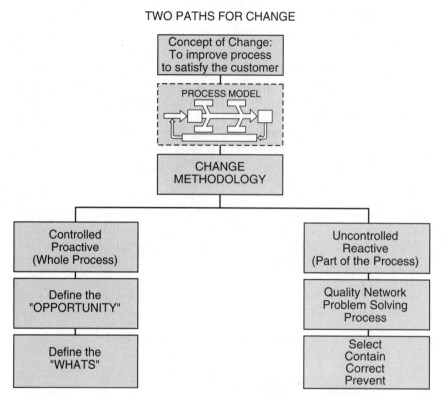

Figure 7-2.

We try to solve the problem. The Quality Network Problem Solving Process is an application of change methodology that focuses on the detection, solution, and prevention of problems. The emphasis is on *selecting, containing, correcting,* and *preventing* these problems, ensuring that they never reach the customer.

The other type of change deals with changes we want to have take place, such as continuous improvement activities and application of lessons learned. This is a *controlled* change that is usually *planned* and becomes *proactive* in our response and involvement. The emphasis is on the whole process and is intended to enhance our ability to satisfy our customers. Business plan initiatives or special projects are examples of controlled change.

Change As We See It

Change methodology is defined as a generic approach to developing opportunities and institutionalizing change throughout General Motors that leads to continuous improvement and customer satisfaction. *Change* is defined as any deviation from current state of methods and systems, environment, equipment, materials, or people. *Opportunity* is a chance to alter the current state in order to improve customer satisfaction to attain a desired future state. To *institutionalize* is to establish a change as the new way of doing thing through communication, updated reward and recognition criteria, and daily actions. This is where corporate learning takes place.

Change methodology includes the *change process model* (see Fig. 7-3) with process checkpoints and the focus model (see Fig. 7-3) used to assess each step of the change process model by keeping the focus on customer satisfaction and a balance between people and teamwork, business needs, and technology.

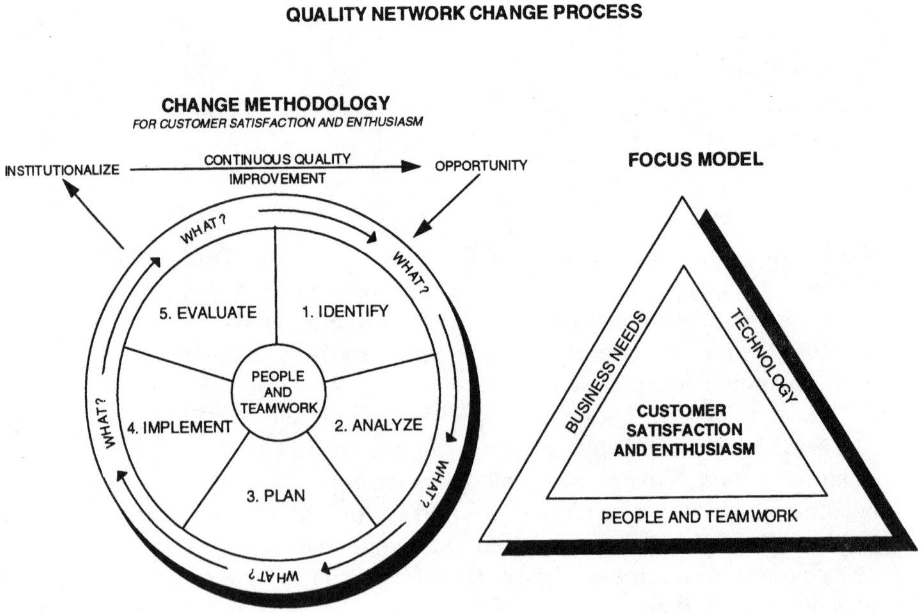

QUALITY NETWORK CHANGE PROCESS

CHANGE METHODOLOGY
FOR CUSTOMER SATISFACTION AND ENTHUSIASM

Figure 7-3.

The Quality Network Change Process

The process starts with an opportunity to define the "Whats?" that need to be changed: specific events, behaviors, attitudes, characteristics, procedures, and so on. The sequence in which the opportunities are attacked is based on the location's priorities. The "Whats?" are tackled using five steps of the change process: identify, analyze, plan, implement, and evaluate. These steps form the basic structure for a consistent methodology (see Fig. 7-4). They provide a logical sequence of thought that we use every day when we approach a project or want to create a change in our lives. Planning a vacation or redecorating a room would logically and easily lay out in the change process. The danger is to overcomplicate the process for the sake of the process and then get bogged down in so much minutia that the project for improvement never gets completed. A clear vision and the right people involved will go a long way to keeping the project on track.

When all the identified improvement opportunities have been made, the changes are institutionalized by making them part of the new process design, the new way of conducting business. This is the first step to continuous improvement and discovering new opportunities. For each of the five steps, process checkpoints have been developed to act as thought starters. Not all will apply all the time, and that is to be expected. The process checkpoints can and should be adapted for unique organizational needs.

Identify.   To *identify* is to collect and organize information for the purpose of determining the gap (variation) between where we are now and where we need to be in the future.

Process Checkpoints:

- Recognize opportunity(ies).
- Confirm champion(s) and sponsor(s) with primary interest and support.
- Identify customers and suppliers, both internal and ultimate.
- Identify key participants and team leaders.
- Assemble and train the team.
- Define scope—the boundaries of the opportunity.
- Define current state.

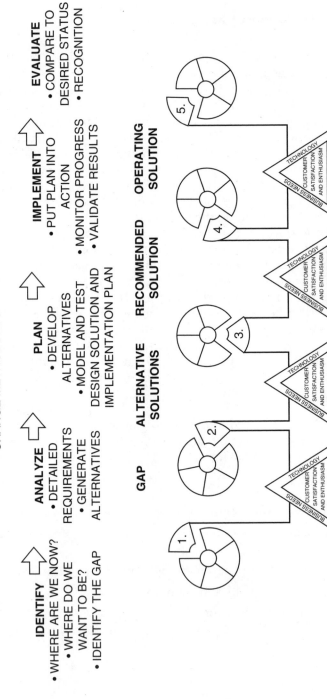

CHANGE METHODOLOGY FLOWCHART

IDENTIFY
• WHERE ARE WE NOW?
• WHERE DO WE WANT TO BE?
• IDENTIFY THE GAP

ANALYZE
• DETAILED REQUIREMENTS
• GENERATE ALTERNATIVES

PLAN
• DEVELOP ALTERNATIVES
• MODEL AND TEST DESIGN SOLUTION AND IMPLEMENTATION PLAN

IMPLEMENT
• PUT PLAN INTO ACTION
• MONITOR PROGRESS
• VALIDATE RESULTS

EVALUATE
• COMPARE TO DESIRED STATUS
• RECOGNITION

GAP   ALTERNATIVE SOLUTIONS   RECOMMENDED SOLUTION   OPERATING SOLUTION

TECHNOLOGY
CUSTOMER SATISFACTION AND ENTHUSIASM
BUSINESS NEEDS
PEOPLE AND TEAMWORK

Figure 7-4.

230

- Define desired state—customer expectations.
- Identify key measures for *Voice of the Customer* (*Customer Satisfaction*).
- Quantify the gap—apply key measures to current and desired state.
- Set measurable goals.

Focus assessment: Apply the focus model criteria. Based on this assessment, decide whether to proceed, stop the development, or return to the appropriate place on the change model.

Questions that might be explored in the identify step (Fig. 7-5):

- Is this a one-time occurrence or does it happen many times?
- What is the gap?
- What is the process delivering?
- What does the customer see?
- What might the customer really want?
- Describe the question in *Voice of the Customer* (VOC) and *Voice of the Process* (VOP) terms (Fig. 7-6).
- Is the situation a problem or an opportunity for improvement?

Analyze.   To *analyze* is to apply systematic and/or statistical methods to determine cause-effect relationships and generate solution alternatives.

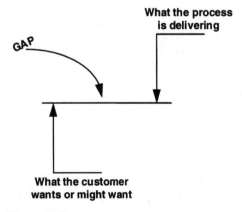

Figure 7-5.

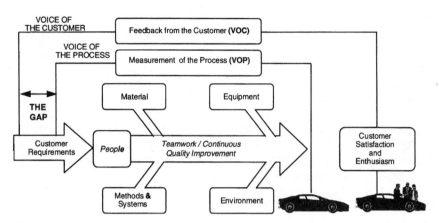

Figure 7-6.

Process Checkpoints:

- Define strategies—how to get to the desired state.
- Define appropriate tools (seven old tools, seven new tools, and so on).
- Define detailed requirements.
- Define implementation roadblocks (technical, political, and cultural).
- Evaluate against world leader.
- Define critical success factors—things that must be in place to allow success.

Focus assessment: Apply the focus model criteria. Based on this assessment, decide whether to proceed, stop the development, or return to the appropriate place on the change model.

During the analyze step, collect data, both historical and new data, from different perspectives. Understand that the only reason to collect data is to do something with it, take action. Ask how do upstream processes and conditions influence the process under analysis? Use the Quality Network process model to analyze the process and identify areas that are most influential in creating the gap.

Plan.   To *plan* is to develop and validate the most appropriate alternative by testing and/or comparison. Document timing, responsibilities, and resources required.

Process Checkpoints:

- Assemble and train team if new skills are required.
- Define roles and responsibilities.
- Develop the project plan.
- Test the plan.
- Evaluate and revise the plan based on test results.
- Develop an implementation plan.

Focus assessment: Apply the focus model criteria. Based on this assessment, decide whether to proceed, stop the development, or return to the appropriate place on the change model.

During the plan step there are several questions to address:

- What customers (of the process) and suppliers (of the process) will be involved in the improvement?
- By what method will you improve?
- How will you know when you have improved the process and by how much?
- What data will be collected and by whom?

Implement.   To *implement* is to carry out the elements of the plan, monitor progress against the plan, and validate the results. "Just do it!"

Process Checkpoints:

- Conduct training.
- Build and test elements of the solution.
- Combine elements, and test the solution.
- Put the plan into action.
- Complete appropriate training.
- Update documentation—maintenance and operational instructions.
- Obtain initial customer acceptance of solution.

Focus assessment: Apply the focus model criteria. Based on this assessment, decide whether to proceed, stop the development, or return to the appropriate place on the change model.

When in the implementation step, you must understand to what extent the plan is actually carried out as designed. Were shortcuts taken? Were parts of the plan thwarted? It is important to have this information to understand how these deviations from the plan may limit your actions. Or, in fact, improve upon them.

Evaluate. To *evaluate* is to compare results against the identified need, define new opportunities, and recognize accomplishments of participants.

Process Checkpoints:

- Compare results against the desired state.
- Recognize the contribution of participants.
- Define action to institutionalize the change.
- Define future opportunities based on knowledge gained.

In the evaluate step, the following questions should be answered:

- To what degree was the gap reduced?
- What other data are needed to be certain?
- What data should be continually monitored in future cycles of the five-step process?
- Have unforeseen problems resulted from the changes?
- What has been learned that can be applied to other opportunities or problems?

Balancing Systematic Change. In order to ensure customer satisfaction, there must be a balance between *business needs, technology,* and *people and teamwork.* A change in any one or more of these three areas will affect the entire system. Ramifications to the entire system must be examined. Often what is good for one part of a system may be detrimental to the system as a whole. The Quality Network has developed a strategy within the change methodology to keep all continuous improvement efforts focused on the aim of the system, satisfying the customer. The focus model balances our approach so that we design and manage change aligned to systems thinking. After each step in the change process model, an unwavering customer focus is ensured by testing actions and decisions made against the three areas of the focus model:

- *People and teamwork:* People's expectations and requirements
- *Business needs:* The organization's requirements for successful operation

- *Technology:* Knowledge applied to satisfy people and business needs

Focus model criteria are to be applied at the end of each of the five steps in the change process. The key question to be answered while progressing through the change process toward customer satisfaction is: "How well does the change step account for the interaction of people and teamwork, business needs, and technology?" The following criteria are thought starters only.

Focus Model Criteria

For People and Teamwork, Test Against:

- Quality Network *Beliefs & Values*
- Jointness
- Health and safety issues
- Contractual requirements
- Training needs
- Environment/workplace requirements
- Input opportunity for stakeholders
- Opportunity for achievement/satisfaction
- Opportunity for reward
- Communication plan
- Workload balance
- Plan for gaining acceptance for change
- Compatibility/synergy with current programs
- Empowerment to get the job done
- Impact on team members regarding time, travel, priorities
- User-friendliness
- Timing impact

For Business Needs, Test Against:

- Improved quality, cost, responsiveness
- Integration with business operating systems
- Information flow
- Internal versus external needs
- Process focus versus problem/results focus

- Objective and vision
- Flexibility
- Customer requirements
- Value added
- Simplicity
- Loss function value between the *Voice of the Customer* (VOC) and the *Voice of the Process* (VOP)
- Promotion of continuous improvement
- Compatibility with other Quality Network action strategies
- Protection of technical/competitive advantage

For Technology, Test Against:

- Appropriate level for task
- Value-added technology
- Available interim and alternate technology
- Process capability improvement
- Appropriate use of local technologies
- Improvement of local technologies
- Appropriate use of worldwide technologies
- Balance of proven and leading-edge technologies
- Implementation in controllable modules
- Internal maintenance capability
- Compatibility with existing technologies
- Supplier dependence
- Ergonomic requirements
- Transferability to multiple applications
- Compatibility with future technologies

Change at the Engineering Center

The NAO Vehicle Development and Technical Operation Group uses the Quality Network change process as the methodology for its Quality Network Implementation Process (QNIP), designed to enhance the knowledge and skills of functional work group leadership with respect to Quality Network tools and techniques to focus on process improvement. During the past five years over 375 people, 9 per functional work group, have gone through QNIP training and are actually engaged in implementation. To date, 32,736 improvements have been implemented resulting in savings to the Engineering Center and its customers of $110,435,252 and 1,538,242 hours. Dollars and labor hours saved were used to help meet shrinking budgets, redeploy workers to more meaningful, value-added work, and meet increased customer demands.

Change at Delphi Saginaw Steering Systems

The former Saginaw Division, now Delphi-SSS, undertook a large-scale reengineering of the salaried work force to lean the organization and restructure to meet the critical demands of the business (Fig. 7-7). They began the process in 1993 with timelines that projected to the year 2000. All reorganization decisions were tied to the goals and objectives of the business plan. Major focus of the restructuring was to eliminate redundancies: duplicated efforts in quality functions, engineering functions, and administrative functions. This was critical since they identified that they were lacking in new products and were short (at least 250) the highly technical personnel required to develop these new products. The restructuring plan became a massive redeployment plan as well. All goals (there were 34 targets for 1994) were in the areas of cost (9 goals), quality (10 goals), great (8 goals), and fast (7 goals). They were also challenged with growing their international business. The methodology used was Quality Network Implementation Workshops; for example, the Director of Finance held more than 30 workshops to get the waste out of the financial staff.

Change methodology served as the basis for restructuring activities. In general, Quality Network principles were embraced; there was an emphasis on common systems, use of benchmarking, and a customer focus at all times. Saginaw has restructured from a business unit structure into functional staffs: sales, marketing and planning; engineering; manufacturing operations; finance; quality; personnel; and purchasing. They adamantly identified and retained the benefits of the business unit structure in their redesign. Members of the executive staffs also serve as chairpersons of each product business team. Thus, the reorganization has also established an effective communication network.

They use several measurements to track their progress:

■ *Levels of communication:* The benchmark is four levels from top to bottom to be effective and eliminate "passing the buck." In the first year, each functional staff eliminated at least one level, reducing the communication process by 20 percent.

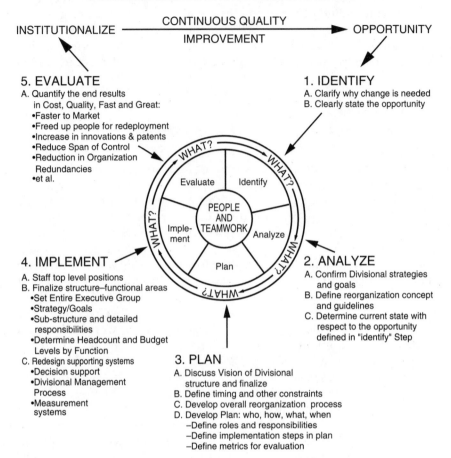

DELPHI-SSS REORGANIZATION PROCESS
FOR CUSTOMER SATISACTION AND ENTHUSIASM

INSTITUTIONALIZE ———— CONTINUOUS QUALITY IMPROVEMENT ————▶ OPPORTUNITY

5. EVALUATE
A. Quantify the end results
in Cost, Quality, Fast and Great:
•Faster to Market
•Freed up people for redeployment
•Increase in innovations & patents
•Reduce Span of Control
•Reduction in Organization
Redundancies
•et al.

1. IDENTIFY
A. Clarify why change is needed
B. Clearly state the opportunity

Evaluate   Identify

PEOPLE AND TEAMWORK

WHAT? WHAT? WHAT? WHAT? WHAT?

Imple-ment   Analyze

Plan

4. IMPLEMENT
A. Staff top level positions
B. Finalize structure–functional areas
•Set Entire Executive Group
•Strategy/Goals
•Sub-structure and detailed
responsibilities
•Determine Headcount and Budget
Levels by Function
C. Redesign supporting systems
•Decision support
•Divisional Management
Process
•Measurement
systems

2. ANALYZE
A. Confirm Divisional strategies
and goals
B. Define reorganization concept
and guidelines
C. Determine current state with
respect to the opportunity
defined in "identify" Step

3. PLAN
A. Discuss Vision of Divisional
structure and finalize
B. Define timing and other constraints
C. Develop overall reorganization process
D. Develop Plan: who, how, what, when
–Define roles and responsibilities
–Define implementation steps in plan
–Define metrics for evaluation

Figure 7-7.

- *Span of control:* More people, fewer bosses, pushing decision making down. There was an overall 18 percent improvement in this area, with an increase of 6.7 workers per supervisor from 5.9. Thirty-four supervisory positions were eliminated, and supervisors were redeployed into technical work where they were greatly needed.

- *Redeployment to meaningful work:* Saginaw needed to grow its human resources in the areas that supporte d new-product design and development. While they were able to meet their organizational headcount goals, they were also able to increase worker participation in the areas of product engineering and manufacturing. This is a major thrust of their business plan and supports growing the business both in this country and abroad.

It should be noted that Delphi-SSS announced recently that it had developed two new electric power steering systems, "offering dramatic benefits in fuel economy and design flexibility." These products are designed to be used in vehicles around the world.

Roles and Responsibilities

The Quality Network change methodology distinguishes the roles of two distinct groups, the leadership, along with suppliers and dealers, and all GM people. Leadership, in the form of the quality councils at each location, and suppliers and dealers must have a full understanding of change methodology: the change process model, the focus model, and the process checkpoint and focus criteria. Through this understanding, they can adapt the detail to specific local requirements, including terminology and additional checkpoint considerations, while maintaining the basic structure of the methodology to ensure consistency across the organization. Product, and therefore process, differences, cultural differences, and local agreement provisions must be folded into the methodology to make it work at a specific location. Leadership must provide the necessary encouragement and resources so that the organization practices the change methodology. All individuals must actively support continuous improvement by using change methodology in their work, particularly at their work stations and within their departments. This is where the "single hits," or small incremental improvements, accumulate to big quality gains. They must also identify opportunities, assist in the analysis of possible change, participate in the planning and implementation of change, and evaluate how well the *Voice of the Customer* is satisfied.

Benefits of a Common Change Methodology

Change methodology will result in improved quality, cost, and responsiveness and, therefore, increased customer satisfaction. This is accomplished by consistently applying the five-step change process model and maintaining a focus on customer satisfaction, people and teamwork, business needs, and technology. Some of the benefits that are realized from application of this methodology are:

- Establishing a common approach and language across the organization
- Recognizing change as an opportunity for improvement
- Improving confidence to proceed with a change
- Improving the rate of success
- Ensuring an appropriate fit between people and teamwork, business needs, and technology for achieving customer satisfaction

Interrelationship of All Strategies and Change Methodology

The Quality Network has many different strategies for product and process improvement. They are dependent on each other for implementation and success to lesser and greater degrees. Since they all involve change and continuous improvement, they are all dependent upon change methodology. Certain strategies—communication, top leadership commitment and involvement, cooperative union-management relations, support for the employee—should be in place to expedite the success of change methodology.

Measurement

Measurement is a prerequisite to effective change and should identify both the *Voice of the Process* and the *Voice of the Customer.* The overall objective is to minimize the gap between the two:

- *Voice of the process:* The progression of change methodology can be measured by following the change process checkpoints and reviewing the focus model assessment areas at the end of each process step: customer satisfaction, people and teamwork, business needs, and technology.

- *Voice of the customer:* The results from the application of change methodology are measured by the degree of customer satisfaction. The measurements should be in internal and external customer terms:

  - Quality

    Functionality: Does it do what it is supposed to do?
    Performance: Does it function according to all customer expectations: durability, reliability, and repeatability?

- Cost

  Cost: Total cost impact.

- Responsiveness

  Time: Schedule, right product and/or service at the right time.

Application of Change Methodology

We have found that change methodology is the basis for the implementation of many of the Quality Network action strategies as well as other endeavors such as General Motors Worldwide Benchmarking and Business Analysis Activity and the GM Business Process Modeling, Improvement, and Integration Activity. We employed the model to develop a redeployment plan for represented workers during the 1993 national negotiations that was modeled on one developed at C-P-C and championed by Group Vice President Mike Mutchler.

The Issue of Redeployment

When synchronizing an organization and applying the practices of process management, time is taken out of the system, unnecessary materials and equipment are identified and removed, and certain redundant tasks are eliminated. There is no way we can ask the men and women of General Motors to work to improve the system and eliminate their jobs without reassuring them that they will be redeployed to meaningful work. Certainly in any improvement process some tasks may be found to be obsolete. However, that is not to say that the people performing the jobs are obsolete. Indeed, for the most part they are the very people whose improvement suggestions exposed the wasted efforts in the first place. The expression "lean and mean" has connotations that trouble many of us, union and management alike. There is nothing wrong with a process that is without waste (lean) if it is the result of a careful and thoughtful improvement process that considers all aspects of the system. Just cutting heads and asking fewer people to do more work will not improve quality, cost, or timeliness for long-term gains. This thorny issue came to the table during the 1993 negotiations. The result was Document 57 of the National Agreement, *Quality Network Implementation Redeployment and Meaningful Work.*

During the term of the 1990 GM–UAW National Agreement, the Quality Network had moved from development to implementation.

Concurrently, NAO encountered operating losses that required immediate action in the areas of more efficient processes and product quality.

> Implementation of Synchronous Workshops, Accelerated Workshops (i.e., PICOS), Lean Manufacturing, and other quality improvement activities, such as best practices, resulted in health and safety, ergonomic, and operational improvements affecting quality and the cost of GM products and services. In many cases, these activities resulted in UAW-represented GM employees being placed in a JOBS Bank[1] under the terms of the 1990 GM–UAW National Agreement. The Union leadership felt they could not be a party to asking their members to assist in "working themselves out of a job" by supporting these efforts. In any joint effort, job security and "people issues" had to be considered so that people would be redeployed to meaningful work.[2]

At the January 13, 1992, GM Quality Council meeting, cochaired by Lloyd Reuss and Steve Yokich, a commitment was made to integrate all synchronous efforts into the Quality Network process and to develop a redeployment strategy for affected workers. By March 2, 1992, funding for the JOBS Bank was exhausted, and those workers who had been placed in the JOBS Bank were laid off. At this time an employment policy was established which retained employees at work and did not lay them off if their jobs had been lost due to "jointly initiated product quality and operational effectiveness improvement efforts."[3]

The 1993 negotiations discussed these events and examined examples of successful redeployment processes. Both parties agreed to jointly develop guidelines for redeployment processes modeled after the examples that had proven to work successfully at the divisional and plant level:

> Such guidelines are intended to assist the local parties with the development of plans that put first emphasis on redeployment of employees to meaningful assignments, which can include regular productive assignments and "nontraditional" work, as well as efforts to competitively retain or insource new work. It is the intent of the parties to not place employees in underutilized or unproductive assignments or only contemplate utilization of the job security provisions of the National Agreement."[4]

Accordingly, the Quality Network issued a document titled *Guidelines for Redeployment and Meaningful Work,* that utilized the change methodology to assist each quality council and local JOBS Bank committee in developing their redeployment plans (Fig. 7-8). The *opportunity* for change is "redeployment process for employees whose jobs are impacted by productivity and/or quality improvements."[5] *Institutionalize* the process by providing "impacted employees with

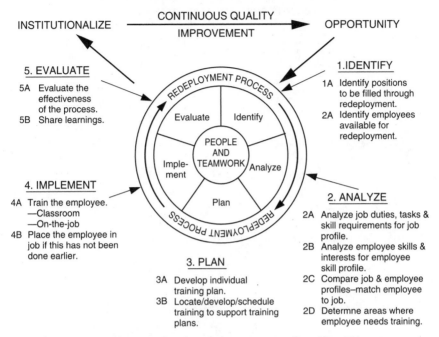

REDEPLOYMENT PROCESS
FOR CUSTOMER SATISFACTION AND ENTHUSIASM

INSTITUTIONALIZE —— CONTINUOUS QUALITY IMPROVEMENT ——▶ OPPORTUNITY

5. EVALUATE
5A Evaluate the effectiveness of the process.
5B Share learnings.

1.IDENTIFY
1A Identify positions to be filled through redeployment.
2A Identify employees available for redeployment.

REDEPLOYMENT PROCESS

Evaluate | Identify

PEOPLE AND TEAMWORK

Imple-ment | Analyze

Plan

REDEPLOYMENT PROCESS

4. IMPLEMENT
4A Train the employee.
   —Classroom
   —On-the-job
4B Place the employee in job if this has not been done earlier.

2. ANALYZE
2A Analyze job duties, tasks & skill requirements for job profile.
2B Analyze employee skills & interests for employee skill profile.
2C Compare job & employee profiles–match employee to job.
2D Determne areas where employee needs training.

3. PLAN
3A Develop individual training plan.
3B Locate/develop/schedule training to support training plans.

Note: To ensure a proactive approach to the redeployment process, Steps 1A and 2A should be addressed before redeployment of employees is necessary.

Figure 7-8.

meaningful job assignments to fully utilize their skills, knowledge, and experience to improve the business and encourage teamwork and an improved working environment."[6]

The guidelines are clear that redeployment does not supersede local contractual agreements or provisions in the National Agreement. They do not apply to results external to plant productivity and/or quality improvement activities such as design for manufacturability (DFM) or design for assembly (DFA). Use of change methodology established an approach of continuous improvement and opportunity to a situation that, in the past, had loomed as a large and seemingly unsolvable problem. The change process was known throughout General Motors, so plant quality councils did not have to learn another, separate process to develop their plans. This common approach focused quality councils on the whole business, so that decisions concerning redeployable workers were balanced against people and teamwork, business needs, and technology (Fig. 7-9).

There is still debate concerning the job security provisions of the 1990/1993 GM-UAW National Agreement. We were undertaking an

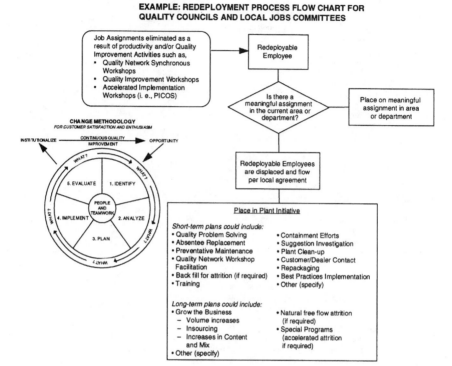

EXAMPLE: REDEPLOYMENT PROCESS FLOW CHART FOR QUALITY COUNCILS AND LOCAL JOBS COMMITTEES

Figure 7-9.

organizational transformation, and we were asking our people to be full partners in the undertaking. It seemed essential that we drive fear and distrust out if we were to make any progress at all. A failure on the part of the largest manufacturing company in the world to retain its people through very tough times would have violated our commitment to our value system. Change was happening all around us, and we had to be certain that we could control its effects.

Notes

1. Jobs Opportunity Bank Security (JOBS). The JOBS program provides employees active status when they would otherwise be laid off due to operational improvements or other related activities.
2. *1993 GM–UAW National Agreement*, Document 57, *Quality Network Implementation Redeployment and Meaningful Work*, p. 435.

3. Ibid.
4. Ibid.
5. *Quality Network Guidelines for Redeployment and Meaningful Work* (QN 2251), published by the Quality Network, October 28, 1993.
6. Ibid.

8
Technological Advance

The *Beliefs & Values* state that we must "Use technology as a tool," a seemingly simple statement that should not elicit any controversy. The focus model of our change methodology looks at technology as the application of knowledge to satisfy people and business needs for customer satisfaction and enthusiasm. Yet, technology has put fear in the hearts of many. Even Toyota admits that they lost sight of their famous Toyota Production System (TPS) in the wake of technology's lure. The current international business climate, coupled with the Japanese economic burst of growth in the 1980s, focused Toyota's attention: "Taking our destiny into our own hands. Manufacturers needn't be helpless in the face of economic developments."[1] Toyota leadership has decided to respond to the vagaries of economic turns by maximizing cost savings from continuous improvement efforts (*Kaizen*) in the workplace and by using new strategies to reduce its cost structure.[2] One such competitive cost strategy is to "modify production processes to make them more cost efficient."[3] "We got carried away with automation a few years ago. We were trying to cope with the trend toward shorter working hours."[4] The goal is to be flexible and to simplify the work. As described in Toyota's annual report, the redesign of a tire-mounting system is cited as a example of new production efficiencies. "The work is simple and takes an employee only a matter of seconds to perform. It's less impressive to watch than the fully automated feeders in some of our plants. But it's another way we are keeping our prices competitive."[5] The report further cites a plant on Japan's southern island of Kyushu, opened in 1992, that embodies a number of cost-savings advances. "Equally important, it accompanies those advances with numerous features for easing the burden on employees."[6] These advances were made in a plant that was originally touted for its state-of-the-art automation. Anticipated cost savings did not pan out. Toyota found that while the number of line workers required in this new plant was reduced, the need for maintenance workers increased dramatically. It was mainly the maintenance worker who understood the robots and, since the process was so highly automated, the opportunities for continuous improvement became very narrow in scope.[7]

The Toyota Production System, dubbed "the machine that changed the world" in an MIT study and subsequent book, is looking at technology in a different light. "Toyota is pushing ahead again. This time, it is toward a system which, rather than replacing workers with machines, tries more clearly than ever to restrict the machines to doing only those things that make life easier for the workers."[8] Again, the balance is between business needs (cost efficiencies and lower prices), people and teamwork (easing worker burden), and technology. In an article in *Automotive News*, Hitoshi Yamada, General Manager of the PEC Kaizen Education Center, discussed changes put into place in the Toyota Motomachi and Miyata plants that are being used in other Toyota locations. "While car makers around the world studied Toyota's production methods, Toyota itself forgot what it had learned. The key issue is not whether inventory exists or not. Rather, it is the problem of subordinating people to machines. Only people have the ability to respond flexibly to changing circumstances. People must be given mastery over machines. Toyota has simply taken the Toyota production method back to its origin."[9]

Fear of Technology

We need to look at the impact technological innovation has had on the workplace and the quality movement. Any quality improvement effort should take into account the effects of technological advances and the relationship those advances have to the overall process. Changes in manufacturing techniques or information systems, materials, methods, and so on can have a tremendous impact on the implementation and overall goals of any process management system. During the 1980s many predicted that technological advances in the form of automated equipment would cause a radical transformation of the workplace in America affecting every sector of the employment market. Most felt that to remain competitive on a world basis, automated systems had to be planned and installed to replace workers, thus lowering labor costs and increasing quality.

The increasing inroads made by foreign manufacturers into the American market proved that many American consumers would demand high-quality goods at competitive costs without regard to the national origin of the product.

Workers felt threatened by the advances in new technology and felt that as automated processes were integrated into the plants, their jobs were in jeopardy. Not only were job security concerns causing fear in the workplace but also new challenges came with technological advance for which many workers were not equipped. Employee skills had to be improved as new pieces of equipment and new processes began to replace familiar workplace processes and practices. Though many people moved into higher-paying jobs in semiskilled areas, fear of change permeated workplaces.

Technology Versus People

During the early 1980s consumer confidence waned as the economy faltered, causing widespread fear of job loss. In the later 1980s management in the industrial sector of America began to realize that automated processes and technological advance could not alone guarantee quality products or customer satisfaction. The realization that people were needed to make the difference in the pursuit of quality and productivity began to drive corporate America. It is this realization that has deemphasized the role that advancing technology plays in quality efforts and has placed a priority on the development of people-oriented processes that utilize advancing technological breakthroughs but are not driven by them. Enlightened management and labor organizations recognized the necessity of addressing technological advance and its effects on workers from its early beginnings. The United Auto Workers Union began in the 1930s and at their first convention held in 1935 talked about many of the issues that are still relevant today. Their resolutions agreed to by management addressed such things as standardized wages, economic security, and company profits, which are still issues of importance to workers and managers.

Technology and Collective Bargaining

Management's need for profits and the union's efforts to provide protection for working men and women, in the form of benefits and security on the job, converged and became centerpiece discussion items for negotiations. In the 1950s concern over the effects of technological advances began to be a focal point for workers' concerns.

In a speech before a joint session of Congress on October 17, 1955, Walter Reuther, President of the United Auto Workers International Union, provided congressional testimony that outlined the union's position on technological advance and included some predictions for the future that proved to be very accurate. Technology could not be counted on to replace people. Society must harness technology in a way that ensures the livelihood and security of workers. His predictions in the 1950s have since become the basis for many positions on technological advance by labor leaders and the unions they represent. During this time period a type of industrial revolution had begun, bringing about a massive change to automated equipment such as in-line transfer machines that are widely used in industrial plants today. Such pieces of equipment have been implemented in great numbers since the 1950s.

The many types of basic automation currently used in manufacturing processes today have evolved from the automated equipment of the 1950s. UAW President Walter Reuther was once asked what effect automated equipment would have on the UAW membership as time went on. He pointed out something that is still true today: "Robots cannot buy cars and neither can people who are not working." There is a certain built-in security in our society. If people are not working, they do not have money and cannot purchase cars and other goods; therefore, the companies cannot make a profit. For this reason companies must face the fact that they have a social commitment to provide jobs, if for no other reason than to maintain their own profits. Reuther went on to negotiate contract provisions that addressed those issues he predicted. The negotiated gains created jobs by allowing members time off while, at the same time, the plants could continue to be operated full-time. There would not be a drop in production but an actual increase, even though workers were spending less time in the plant.

Succeeding UAW presidents, Leonard Woodcock and Douglas Fraser, and other prominent leaders of major U.S. labor unions, with support from their management counterparts, continued this concept, coming up with new types of benefits and proposals to reduce work time and create jobs, while at the same time, providing security and increased productivity.

It is important to note the principles of a very strong and important provision that has been in the UAW-GM National Agreement since 1950:

(101) (b) **Performance Bonus Payments.** The Performance Bonus provided herein recognizes that a continuing improvement in the standard of living of employes [sic] depends on technological progress, better tools, methods, processes and equipment, and a cooperative attitude on the part of all parties in such progress. It further recognizes the principle that to produce more with the same amount of human effort is a sound economic and social objective. Accordingly, a Performance Bonus payment will be made to each eligible employe....[10]

It was recognized by labor and management alike in GM that increased productivity brought about by better processes was a desirable goal, embracing a principle later recognized by joint efforts within the Quality Network. Unlike the railroad and steel industries in the United States, the automotive industry provision recognized the importance and necessity for continuous technological improvements. It also recognized the necessity for cooperation between the two parties and the need to reward employees through improved wages and benefits in exchange for the unfettered right to improve productivity and quality. Simply put, management will have the right to introduce new technology as long as introduction of such technology results in employees being provided an opportunity to work smarter and not harder, wages will be protected, and the new technology will not result in employees having their wages cut due to changes in work.

Tack Spitters

An example of this extremely important provision is the "case of the tack spitters." At one time the headliner in a General Motors vehicle was installed completely by hand by employees who were referred to as "tack spitters." Tack spitters would install the material on the edges of the cloth headliners and would literally tack the place where the material and the supporting rib came together. It was a very highly skilled job, and such employees were paid a premium wage rate for performing this work. Mistakes resulted in torn headliners since headliners are clearly visible to the customer, defects in this area are immediate customer dissatisfiers. As composite materials such as foamed-back cloth were developed, the headliner could be installed as a single piece, eliminating the former tacking process. Although the skill and work involved in the prior assembly methodology changed dramatically with the one-piece headliner, the base job rates for the employees installing such headliners were not changed. Employees retained their premium rate. Unlike the steel and railroad industry, General Motors has had the right and the capability to introduce new technology, resulting in state-of-the-art equipment and processes.

The Feather-Bedding Issue

Thus the automotive industry avoided "feather-bedding" operations that retained workers even though those workers' jobs had been eliminated by the introduction of new technology. By comparison and in contrast, the "fireman" was retained through union insistence in the engine cabs of diesel engine locomotives even though fires used to heat water for steam were no longed needed. Similarly, steel industry unions demanded that the "tapman" position be retained even though new electric furnaces replacing Bessemer technology eliminated the "tap."

Both union and management leadership in General Motors recognized that increased productivity brought about by better processes was a desirable goal. This is certainly embodied in the Quality Network.

Technology As a Servant

In the 1970s automation took a leap forward, and new types of automation began to be used. Management approached the issue from a people perspective and used automation mainly for jobs that were tedious, repetitive, or had health and safety implications such as welding and spray painting. The healthy economy coupled with demand for more and more cars and trucks masked the effect of this increase in new technology. As a result of a constant increase in the demand for vehicles, displaced workers were redeployed into other work with minimum difficulty.

During this same period, there was a continuous increase in the construction of new facilities. People were hired or transferred from existing operations to those new facilities and, as a result, automation was generally accepted as it had been in the 1950s. It was viewed as a benefit not only to management but to the workers as well.

In the 1980s the United States faced another stage in the evolution of automated equipment, one that affected every area of the employment market requiring more advanced equipment, better processes, and advanced skills. During this period it was recognized that in order to create better-quality products, management had to design and engineer better products and processes. In order to optimize the process it was recognized that people on the shop floor could contribute and should be given opportunity to input into the process.

Displacement of Workers

Union and nonunion members alike felt threatened by the advance of new technology. The decrease in car demand in these years and the poor shape of the economy brought into focus the fact that as automation came into the plant, people would be displaced. People may not necessarily have been laid off as a direct result of new automation, for there is always attrition in the work force—people retire or leave for one reason or another—but some people were displaced or moved from their jobs. Displacement moved people into higher-paid jobs or jobs in semiskilled areas, but displacement also forced people to seek jobs in other industries or required new skills for which they were not prepared. Jobs were created because of automation, but at the same time workers faced displacement within manufacturing facilities with the potential of transfer to new industries. This required leaving the company or moving to other existing plants or newly opened facilities.

Use of automation continues, but workers must be permitted to share in the benefits it can bring. The process should not be one-sided; jobs will be lost to automated processes unless all concerned parties continue to focus on redeployment and new skills for the work force. There will be fewer production facilities in the future.

In General Motors these facts influenced the 1993 contract talks and a specific agreement was reached providing for redeployment of workers displaced by process changes in the workplace. Provisions have also been included in past contracts ensuring that the skilled work force would service and maintain new equipment and that all workers would receive necessary training on new processes and technologies to prepare them for the future.

Job Security

A major area of concern with technological advance is the issue of security. Security must be the basis on which workers can continue to accept advancing technologies. Employment guarantees assure that workers can contribute to growth and form a cornerstone of the Quality Network process. But, such guarantees are only possible if General Motors is a viable entity. Retraining for more highly skilled jobs, along with increased in-house production of parts and design work, establishes an environment that eliminates fear of change. Worker participation in the decision-making process is a necessity for long-term quality assurance and workplace harmony.

Deskilling

Not only will our society have to address the replacement or infiltration by automation of semiskilled or production-type operations but there is also going to be a tendency to break down further some classifications and job operations and, wherever possible, to assign these jobs to less skilled groups. In General Motors, a basic core group of skilled classifications is recognized as a necessity. However, many splinter groups have been brought back within the "basic" trades, eliminating some splinter classifications that have developed over the years. Nonskilled classifications have been reduced, broadening job duties and making assignments more flexible and interesting. The workplace environment is affected in other ways as well. Design of equipment takes into account safety and ergonomic issues for those who work on and operate the equipment. Automated equipment must be absolutely safe. Equipment is being designed to conform to the human operating the equipment, rather than forcing the human to conform to the equipment. Equipment and processes must be purchased with people in mind. More and more workers are included in the design and development process in order to assure compatibility. Strategies within the Quality Network such as workplace organization, quality verification, people-focused practices, and others address these critical concerns through joint input and decision making.

The *Employee Excellence Development* action strategy addresses the education and training needs of union-represented individuals whose jobs have changed and whose skills must be updated, as well as personal fulfillment and enrichment. Twenty-five years ago, close to the average seniority of many GM workers, high-level math computation and computer programming skills were not in the job description of a typical production worker on the line. In contrast, operators today must understand statistical process control and be able to read and interpret control charts in order to maintain process quality. Programming robots and working with highly sophisticated machinery is commonplace. It is therefore incumbent upon the corporation to maintain and grow the abilities of the work force to meet the demands of new job definitions and requirements. Joint training and education programs are now considered part of the job.

Reducing Fear

To reduce fear, the security of workers is a top priority, and health and safety must be assured. Common sense suggests that advanced discussion and communication is necessary before the introduction and implementation of any technological advance, and the Quality Network communication process assures that this is not overlooked. Introduction of technological advance is timed to benefit workers as well as the company. Natural attrition, rather than spur-of-the-moment layoffs, are used to reduce the work force. In order to win the trust and support of workers, GM and the UAW have agreed to terms that provide employment and job security for people during good times when the economy is strong and in bad times when it is weak.

The Quality Network process establishes the basis for advance discussions to be held with all parties involved, from those who are considering the purchase through those who will ultimately use the machine. Regular involvement from everyone who will be affected by any type of technological advance smoothes implementation and garners support from operators who have first-hand experience to those who install the new equipment, plan new processes, or work with new materials.

The UAW–GM Approach to Balancing the Focus

Leaders in their mid-forties today graduated from high school in the sixties. Many had a typing classes and utilized IBM electric typewriters to learn the skill and dexterity necessary to be able to take handwritten or dictated material, translate it, and create a typewritten document. Technology has certainly impacted how information is processed today. Mechanical typewriters to electric typewriters, electronic typewriters with erasing capability to electronic typewriters with screens to see what you are typing to today's sophisticated computer-based PC systems, systems that were used to write this book. E-mail, electronic bulletin boards, and the infamous Internet expose us daily to more than can be absorbed. Along the way, new skills had to be developed. As authors, we both know the ABCs, although we have struggled at times with appropriate grammar and use of words. But in writing this book, we wanted to be more efficient, and consequently we learned how to use a word processing software package and a computer.

What was required of us to create this book is similar to what the American automobile industry has faced. The average employee is in his or her mid-forties was hired at a time when technology was impacting the industry, although not as much as it is today. Systems were changing, machine tools and equipment were changing, and some reskilling was required. The jobs workers hired in for 25 years ago, for the most part, either no longer exist or do not exist in the form they do today. The requirements have changed, and workers had to change with them.

If the industry was going to survive, it had to use technology to assist employees and not threaten them through its introduction. The result, as stated earlier, is a series of provisions of the GM–UAW National Agreement. Those provisions require the parties to closely examine the introduction of new technology to be certain employees are properly trained, appropriate wage rates are established, and no "erosion of the bargaining unit" occurs, meaning no union-represented work is inappropriately transferred to nonrepresented employees.

Determining Who Does What When with New Technology

During the late seventies and early eighties, the two of us had the opportunity to work together on several new-technology–related issues. As participants in labor negotiations, we were faced with dealing with new-technology issues to determine the appropriate wage rate and classification for such work. For example, we can recall being assigned to investigate the introduction of a three-axis measuring machine, capable of measuring, from an on-line computer, all the specified points on a foundry-cast cylinder block. Prior to this time such blocks would have to be set and leveled on a perfectly flat marble plate and checked using precision height gauges and measurement instruments to determine whether or not the block met dimensional specifications.

With this new high-tech, multiaxis measuring machine, driven by a computer system, operators were able to place a digital description of the part in the memory of the computer. For the purpose of clarifying for the reader, think of a large cube the size of a food freezer and recognize that every point within the freezer can be defined in terms of its X axis, Y axis, and Z axis position. Within the memory of the computer of a multiaxis measuring machine, the size of the cube is defined based on the physical limits of the machine, for example, maximum height. It has the cube defined in terms of X-, Y-, and Z-axis points. When data that dimensionally describe an engine block casting is provided, the machine can check the casting against the specified data in terms of X-, Y-, and Z-axis points. When the casting is placed within a described area and starting points are determined, the computer, through a sensing pointer, can check each of the points. These multiaxis measuring machines of course are capable of measuring anything that can be digitally defined and can fit within the physical limits of the machine's cube, whether it be a connecting rod, a cylinder head, or a crankshaft. As long as a part can be described digitally, it can be checked by the machine.

The introduction of this technology had profound impact in this sense: Previously, employees in Skilled Trades classifications had been assigned to perform "first-part checks" of all parts coming out of a changed or new process. Thereafter, production employees or employees who were not Skilled Tradespeople would routinely check these parts to be certain the process continued to meet the specifications. Such employees utilized measuring fixtures, gauges, and so on that were mostly hand-held. In some cases fixtures were designed to place the part in a predetermined position, and with simple devices such as "flush pin" gauges or "step" gauges, the part was checked. When the new multiaxis machine was introduced, both skilled and production employees could use the equipment to perform their work. This, now, presented both management and union leadership with a challenge.

Historically in the examination of new-technology cases, the parties would determine the appropriate classification(s) based on the function performed with the piece of equipment. It was not typical to classify a machine; it was typical to classify the work performed by the machine. In the case described above, when the equipment was being utilized to check the first part coming out of a process or new piece of equipment, the work belonged to the Skilled Trades employee. When the equipment was being used to check the ongoing quality of the product that was coming out of the already certified process or equipment, the operation of equipment was assigned to the production employees. In both cases, employees required training to perform the task, and management had to decide whether or not this new technology was worth the investment versus performing the work with old methods and systems.

The Joint Process and Technology

Workers understand industry's need for technological advance to remain competitive, but this must not happen at the expense of their livelihood. Workers must share in the benefits of new technology. Society as a whole must face the fact that for America to continue to prosper, people have to work. That consideration in and of itself must guide American industries in facing the responsibility of providing job security for their employees. All of the concerns raised by technological advance can be addressed by joint management and employee processes designed to allow worker input and address management and worker concerns. Once core business requirements are satisfied, management and union leaders must jointly adopt the principle of a "boundaryless organization." If a worker is displaced by productivity improvements, he or she should be trained and redeployed on meaningful work elsewhere within the organization. New core business should be developed and pursued. If employees are truly a company's greatest asset, then old machines and businesses should be replaced by new exciting products and/or services.

Technology As a Win-Win Proposition

Technology should be viewed as an opportunity to enhance the quality, effectiveness, and efficiency of a process while at the same time enhancing the environment of the workers involved in that process. Helping workers work smarter, not harder, has become almost a cliché when talking about the benefits of introducing technology into the workplace. Ergonomic advancements and health and safety improvements are important components in technological innovations. A stable, capable process in control enables the worker to consistently produce a quality product in a timely and waste-free manner. Instead of viewing technology as a threat to jobs, it should be viewed as an improvement to jobs.

Planned Maintenance

The *Planned Maintenance* action strategy is a primary user of new technology on the plant floor and will serve as an example of how technology helps build a supportive environment, focuses on the customer (in this case the operator), supports a synchronous operation, and detects, solves, and prevents problems.

For General Motors, maintenance is a multibillion dollar business. GM's maintenance expenditures, treated as an independent business, would hold the 32nd largest American company position on the

Fortune 500 rankings. By *maintenance* we mean all activities and strategies that deal with the upkeep of machinery and equipment, reliability and maintainability, spare parts inventories, computer systems, and many other related areas. As a large part of GM's business, maintenance affords a golden opportunity for small and breakthrough improvements that directly impact the bottom line and worker satisfaction.

Quality Network Planned Maintenance (QNPM)

The Quality Network Planned Maintenance (QNPM) strategy is a total systems approach to maintenance involving all employees to increase throughput and uptime, improve the quality of process output, reduce repair maintenance costs, and improve safety by continuously improving equipment operation. A comprehensive planned maintenance system has three components that, when managed in a balanced systems approach, can significantly contribute to a plant's, and therefore the total system's, competitive position:

- *Predictive maintenance:* Compiling and analyzing machine condition data to warn of impending failure and identify defective parts
- *Preventive maintenance:* Scheduled routine inspection and improvements to intercept failure
- *Reactive emergency maintenance:* Unplanned or unscheduled maintenance due to breakdowns; firefighting

The goal is to drastically reduce instances of unscheduled maintenance through the implementation of predictive and preventive maintenance techniques and practices.

Planned maintenance as a concept has been part of the GM Technical Staffs for many years. In 1992 a joint planned maintenance training team was established to aid plant locations in implementation of this strategy. The team consisted of 35 UAW and 18 salaried GM employees led by QNPM cochampions Chris Manning (UAW International Representative) and Bruce Winkler (GM Planned Maintenance Coordinator). The entire effort is under the auspices of NAO Industrial Engineering Maintenance Operations directed by Klaus Blache, Group Head. Implementation has a two-pronged approach. One is to create the foundation of an ingrained maintenance process that will lead to a plant's success in the long term. The second is to meet the immediate need of cost savings through spare parts reduction, application of new technologies, and increased predictive and preventive maintenance.

> KLAUS BLACHE: Top plant union and management leadership's cooperation is the key to the success of Quality Network and, more specifically, planned maintenance....Plant leadership must set the example for implementation and provide resources to ensure success....The end result is for the plants to have autonomous problem-solving teams in maintenance capable of addressing opportunities in the maintenance process.[11]

The thought is that, as the cost savings and ancillary benefits are realized, the case for an overarching maintenance process is being built and reinforced. This is particularly meaningful in the area of spare parts. Chris Manning explains, "Lack of planned maintenance means frustration. In some plants where there is no spare parts control process in place, 50 percent of what GM buys is eventually thrown away due to excess and obsolete material. For every dollar in controlled inventory, there is approximately $4 in uncontrolled inventory."[12]

The Quality Network Planned Maintenance Team is a resource support to any location that jointly requests implementation assistance. The team provides technical assistance and tools, in-plant needs analysis, and training. It is up to the plant to design its implementation plan, assign leadership responsibilities, and provide the resources. Ultimately, it is up to each location to devise a master plan for long-term success.

Delphi Interior and Lighting Systems, Adrian, Michigan

Using technology as a tool for planned maintenance at GM's Adrian Delphi-ILS plant is part of leadership's plan to have a fully synchronous organization. In order for an operation to be synchronous, the machines have to be up and running properly all the times. As Bruce Holey, an electrician and member of UAW local 2031, puts it:

> As far as the customer goes, when we ship parts from one department to another inside the plant, which we have to do on many of the assembly operations, if the embossing department isn't turning out the pads, then the edge folders can't work, and then the edge folders can't send the parts over to the door assembly. And if the

edge folder and the embossing department are working, but the injection molding machine isn't working, then they can't assemble the doors. We can't put them on the truck to be sent out the back door.[13]

The significance of keeping the operation running smoothly has been compounded by what the Japanese call *Kanban,* or just-in-time delivery (JIT). Just-in-time replenishes parts, materials, and products from the preceding process, or supplier, on an as-needed basis as part of an even and level production flow. The philosophy of just-in-time reduces the accumulation of expensive inventories and helps ensure highly efficient operations. In the case of Adrian, "out the back door" means the plant is shipping its door panels to its customer, the assembly plant.

> JACK KIRBY, SUPERINTENDENT OF PLANT ENGINEERING AND MAINTENANCE: We have products here that we actually ship within a four-hour window to an assembly plant where their paint shop gives us a broadcast, and from that broadcast we have four hours to ship them the doors in sequence, the color....Quality is very important here because a single hiccup could cause them a line stoppage at the assembly plant. Our uptime is critical in that area because when you only have a four-hour window, you have to make sure your processes are up so you don't impact the assembly plant customer.[14]

As a rule of thumb, assembly plants produce 60 cars per hour, so the cost of losing production time is great. Planned maintenance increases the amount of maintenance done on a planned basis versus an unplanned basis, which has a direct impact on the bottom line. Technologies such as vibration analysis, laser alignment, tribology (the study of oil and its properties), infrared, ultrasound, and fiber optics can and are used on the plant floor on a proactive maintenance program.

Tie Rods

Injection molding machines have massive tie rods that are monitored over time for cracks that may develop. Often these cracks are not on the surface of the tie rod and cannot be seen by the operator or Skilled Tradesperson. Ultrasound equipment is used to identify which tie rods need changing. If a rod is changed prior to an actual fracture, it can be repaired. If the rod is allowed to fracture, the cost for replacement versus repair virtually quadruples.

TERRY PITT, MACHINE REPAIR, UAW LOCAL 2031 (about monitoring tie rods as part of a predictive maintenance strategy) We try to track a flaw, and, under normal circumstances, you can actually watch a slow grow. Sometimes they grow a lot faster than you anticipate. We had a catastrophic failure on number 25, and we lost eight days on that piece of equipment. Versus one day if you can predict that you're about to have a failure.[15]

A different technology is used in the preventive maintenance mode to forestall the development of cracks in the tie rods in the first place. These cracks are typically caused by a machine that is not level or is out of square. Laser alignment equipment is used to level and square off the machinery.

BRUCE HOLEY: It used to be that we would wait until something broke down before we went out and fixed it. That's like driving a car without changing the oil until the engine seizes up, then putting a new motor in it. That's what used to be our maintenance strategy. But now we're changing our oil on a regular basis.[16]

Technology is one leg of the focus model for customer satisfaction and enthusiasm. Application of technological innovations in a planned maintenance strategy should support both the organization's business needs and people and teamwork requirements. At Adrian, the decision to purchase each piece of new equipment is evaluated to make sure it makes economic sense.

JACK KIRBY: The benefit we've gotten out of our predictive equipment has far outweighed the cost of that equipment itself. And it even more outweighs the cost of purchasing a brand-new injection molding machine.[17]

The people benefits are best represented by remarks from Paul Brent, Adrian Plant Manager, and Tim Holt, Chairman of the Shop Committee, UAW Local 2031. Together, Paul and Tim chair the plant quality council.

PAUL BRENT: It has to be a joint team. We both agree and would have to fight for that because it will not happen if it's management driven, and it will not happen if it's union driven. It's got to be a joint team…people working together that are committed to achieving results.[18]

TIM HOLT: Years ago we had an adversarial relationship, and we were going nowhere fast. We were losing work. Absenteeism was up, had a lot of problems, a lot of grievances. About five years ago we started really working together jointly. The grievance load is way down.

Absenteeism is way down. The morale in the plant is up. We've grown the business. I don't think we could have ever done that if we had an adversarial relationship because it just doesn't work....You sit down and try to work out problems....Not only Paul and I do it, but the people out on the floor with the supervisors, hourly people. It's a combination of everybody working together and that will make you world class.[19]

Mutual Benefits

Process management systems that provide for joint input from management and workers will establish a foundation of trust and mutual concern that fosters the use of technological advances as new tools to accomplish mutual goals. Profits will increase, but so will pay and benefits, assuring a higher standard of living, a safer work environment, and secure meaningful jobs. A work force free of fear who can trust its management to make decisions based on input from employees and with their best interests in mind will assist in utilizing technological advances to enhance corporate goals. Such a supportive environment is a necessity when establishing the foundation for a process management system.

Notes

1. *Toyota 1994 Annual Report,* October 1994, p. 1.
2. Ibid.
3. Ibid., p. 4.
4. Ibid.
5. Ibid.
6. Ibid., p. 17.
7. "Toyota's New Approach Is with Fewer Machines," *The Detroit Free Press,* March 14, 1995.
8. Ibid.
9. Keijiro Okino, "Toyota Changes Its Famous Production System," *Automotive Industries,* February 1995.
10. Agreement between UAW and the General Motors Corporation, September 17, 1990.
11. "Quality Corner: Quality Network's Planned Maintenance," *Center Exchange,* January/February 1995, p. 8.

12. Ibid.

13. Bruce Holey, Electrician, UAW Local 2031, excerpted remarks from the *Quality Network Planned Maintenance Videotape*, QN #2094, January 1993.

14. Jack Kirby, Superintendent of Plant Engineering and Maintenance, excerpted remarks from the *Quality Network Planned Maintenance Videotape*, QN #2094, January 1993.

15. Terry Pitt, Machine Repair, UAW Local 2031, excerpted remarks from the *Quality Network Planned Maintenance Videotape*, QN #2094, January 1993.

16. Bruce Holey, Electrician, UAW Local 2031, excerpted remarks from the *Quality Network Planned Maintenance Videotape*, QN #2094, January 1993.

17. Jack Kirby, Superintendent of Plant Engineering and Maintenance, excerpted remarks from the *Quality Network Planned Maintenance Videotape*, QN #2094, January 1993.

18. Paul Brent, Plant Manager of Delphi-ILS Adrian, Mich., plant, excerpted remarks from the *Quality Network Planned Maintenance Videotape*, QN #2094, January 1993.

19. Tim Holt, UAW Shop Chairman, Local 2031, Delphi-ILS Adrian, Mich., plant, excerpted remarks from the *Quality Network Planned Maintenance Videotape*, QN #2094, January 1993.

9
Implementing the Process

Making It Work, 10 Steps

Why Change?

In order to implement process management in an organization, some change is necessary regardless of how progressive the organization may consider itself to be. Therein lies the major concern and obstacle to successful implementation of any new process. As we stated earlier, human beings are not comfortable with change. Often the impediments to change are not apparent to both those who champion change and those who resist it.

Get to the Root Cause

The strength of a company's existing culture is not in what you see but in what you don't see. That culture is defined by the company's roots. The older the company, the more difficult it is to alter the culture. New people with new ideas can influence the thinking of an organization. However, change will result only when the highest authority in the organization values the truth about its culture and is willing to examine and question root beliefs and practices. Leadership must create a vision of where it wants to take the company and then unwaveringly lead the charge. Leadership cannot stop until the vision is accomplished. The analogy of the tree and its roots holds true. It is only by understanding the roots that organizational transformation can take place. Often we tend to try to shape the tree not realizing that this is, at best, a temporary fix. The roots determine how the tree will grow. Restructuring the tree by pruning branches and guiding the direction of some boughs may alter the appearance of the tree but will not have lasting results.

A crucial factor stressed by Dr. Deming is that the new process has everyone working on the right things. The most meticulous implementation plans may be followed, but if the process is directed at something other than what the customer wants, an organization may still fail. That is why it is so critical that joint management and employee involvement start at the very earliest stages of the process. Assuring customer satisfaction is part of the leader's role as designer, teacher, and steward.

Successful attempts at process management implementation have several things in common:

- Top leadership is committed to long-term plans, creating a positive work environment that emphasizes people issues (health and safety, ergonomics, job security, and so on).

- Employees at every level of the corporation are aware of the need to please the customer. This awareness is brought about by excellent communication.

- Management leads by example.

- Training is viewed as an investment rather than a necessary evil.

- Processes are designed to fit people.

- There is a shared sense of teamwork and trust.

- There is an unwavering commitment to not knowingly ship a defective part or product.

All of these traits flow from top leadership's design, teaching, and good stewardship. Rollout or implementation plans vary, but the above common ingredients must be long-term goals. Once implementation begins, there is no turning back.

The Quality Network Implementation Process

The Quality Network developed an implementation process that attempted to address key characteristics of successful total quality organizations. By design, we created an approach to implementation that adheres to the core values and tenets of total quality, while leaving room for flexible interpretation for the many different cultures that make up General Motors. The matrix displayed in Fig. 9-1 helps define the process of accelerating the implementation of Quality Network principles and practices. The matrix consists of five related parts:

- *Steps:* The 10 steps of the corporate implementation process to be completed.
- *Beliefs & Values:* Support for the step is derived from the *Beliefs & Values.*
- *Objectives:* A specific objective is defined for each implementation step.
- *Level indicators:* The level indicators provide a road map for accomplishing each step of the process.
- *Goals:* The goal for each step describes the condition that exists when the step is fully institutionalized within the organization.

The matrix provides General Motors quality councils and their joint union-management leadership with both an assessment tool and a planning tool. Quality councils can use the matrix definitions to assess their current state and the progress since their most recent assessment. The matrix can also be helpful when used to define the specific goals to be attained within a given planning period. The same can apply to nonrepresented environments if top leadership addresses these issues in regular meetings.

In general terms, quality councils should progress through the steps (listed across the top of the matrix) in the order listed (from left to right). Within each step, the level indicators progress downward from top to bottom. Bulleted detail accompanies the matrix and provides questions and thought starters for quality council discussions and actions.

In theory, achieving all of the level indicators for a given step will make the following steps easier to achieve. In a practical sense, each organization is probably in the middle of several of the implementation steps at the present time. There is no intent to redo completed tasks or to discontinue current activities. Quality councils should use the matrix to assess their current state and move forward aggressively from their current positions. The urgency of our current situation and the maturity of each organization will determine when and how it is appropriate to apply resources to subsequent steps.

Figure 9-1. Quality Network 10-Step Implementation Matrix.

Create a Sense of Urgency	Develop Awareness of Quality Network as GM's Total Quality Process	Educate Top Leadership	Develop Vision	Educate and Involve All Employees	Develop Process Measurements	Develop Master Plans	Implement	Assess and Recognize	Continuous Improvement
	Beliefs & Values								
	Customer Satisfaction and Enthusiasm through People, Teamwork and Continuous Quality Improvement.	Take responsibility for leadership.	Demonstrate our commitment for people.	Establish a learning environment at all levels. Make communications work.	Put quality in everything we do.	Invite the people of GM to be full partners in the business.	Recognize people as our greatest resource. Build through teamwork and joint action.	Demand consistency in the application of this value system.	Make continuous improvement the goal of every individual.
	OBJECTIVES								
To lay the groundwork for change	*To define the Quality Network as the process enabling the effective operation of General Motors.*	*To define and communicate leaderships' evolving role in a continuously improving (learning) organization.*	*To create a shared vision of what GM will be like when Quality Network is fully implemented*	*To empower the people of General Motors by providing them with the skills and knowledge to fulfil the vision.*	*To develop and define indicators that will demonstrate implementation progress.*	*To develop detailed plans, integrated into business plans at every level of the organization, which achieve the vision.*	*To execute the plan(s) and thereby achieve the vision– Just Do It!*	*To evaluate the plan itself and how well it was followed. To recognize efforts and celebrate accomplishments.*	*To strive for perfection by continuously improving the process.*
					INDICATORS				
0. No recognition of the need for change	0. No awareness of Total Quality Process	0. No understanding of leaderships' changed role in the new organization	0. No vision or many visions	0. Knowledge and empowerment vary greatly throughout the organization	0. No Quality Network Implementation Process measures in place	0. No evidence of master plan(s)	0. Implementation efforts inconsistent	0. No formal evaluation and recognition policy exists	0. No process for continuous improvement in the organizational culture
1. Assess current and future state	1. Understand Total Quality Process	1. Understand role(s) in the new organization	1. Understand the need for a single, shared vision	1. Conduct assessment of current state level of understanding	1. Establish measurement requirements	1. Recognize and support need for master plan(s)	1. Communicate master plan(s) to all stakeholders	1. Acknowledge need for assessment and recognition	1. Identify and analyze need for continuous improvement
2. Test current vision against vision required to succeed	2. Understand Quality Network as a Total Quality Process	2. Develop needed skills and knowledge	2. Examine existing visions	2. Develop communication plan based on assessment	2. Define indicators of requirements	2. Assess current state/future state and the gap	2. Demonstrate leadership commitment and involvement	2. Define and establish informal and formal recognition process	2. Continuously improve implementation plan
3. Examine nature of change	3. Understand linkage between Quality Network and Business Plan	3. Align behavior with value system	3. Develop a single, shared vision	3. Implement communication plan	3. Define data, collection methods	3. Create plan	3. Implement plans	3. Conduct assessment	3. Communicate improvements as the process unfolds
4. Leadership committed to leading change in the organization	4. Leadership embraces Quality Network as GM's Total Quality Process	4. Leaderships' responsibility assumed and enthusiastically communicated	4. Leadership supports and communicates THE shared vision	4. People of General Motors feel fully empowered	4. Leadership uses process measures	4. Leadership committed to leading implementation of plan	4. Master Plan fully integrated into the "way we do business"	4. Assessment outcomes form basis (information) for continuous improvement	4. Implement continuous improvement efforts with all employees committed to action
					GOALS				
Everyone understands the urgency of the current situation and is committed to action.	*Quality Network is the one process for continuous improvement of customer satisfaction and enthusiasm*	*All top leadership is part of the fabric of the learning organization*	*One shared vision that excites all*	*A learning environment exists at all levels of the organization*	*Stakeholders empowered to self-assess and continuously improve processes*	*Implementation of Master Plans enable continuous improvement throughout the organization*	*All GM people fully involved in planning, implementation and continuous improvement of customer satisfaction*	*People recognition is a top organizational priority*	*Continuous improvement is viewed as an opportunity for ongoing renewal*

While the Quality Network itself is General Motors' overriding total quality philosophy, full implementation of its methods and practices within General Motors requires that each quality council take responsibility for completing the entire implementation matrix. It may be possible to work on several of the implementation steps concurrently, although the goals of implementation must build one upon another. These goals as a unit will work to:

- Build a supportive environment.
- Create an organization-wide customer focus.
- Synchronize the organization.
- Detect, solve, and prevent product quality problems.

The following is the explanation of the step-by-step approach recommended to the various quality councils to implement the Quality Network at their staff or plant location:

Step 1: Create a Sense of Urgency

Objective. To lay the groundwork for change.

Beliefs & Values. Recognize change as an opportunity.

It probably goes without saying, but if change is going to occur, there are some fundamental steps that have to be taken. Words alone won't make it happen. Management working alone will not make it happen. Together, with everyone involved in the cultural transformation, is the only way it will work. Resistance is part of change. Energy wasted resisting change, properly redirected, can become energy for change.

In order for change to come about in an organization, the groundwork must be laid. One of the key components and drivers for change to occur is creating a sense of urgency in an organization. Urgency in this sense is meant to convey to employees the necessity for change to occur. Unfortunately it's generally associated with some significant emotional event such as the threat of a plant closing or the loss of a product line or a financial difficulty or any one of a number of other issues—all driving the necessity for the company to focus itself and understand that if it continues on the same course that it is on with no sense of urgency, more than likely it is destined to go out of business. In order to alleviate this problem in an organization, a clearly understood and communicated sense of urgency is essential. *Recognize change as an opportunity* is a Quality Network *Belief & Value* that would apply in this situation.

Level 0: No Recognition for the Need to Change

This is the first step in the process when evaluating the current state. Generally level 0 is associated with a mindset in the company where there is no recognition for change or the necessity for change. It's where an organization believes that everything has always been okay and will continue to be that way, and therefore there is no reason to change. In addition, management and union leadership maintain their traditional roles as opposed to seeking improved ways of working together. Real-world information is not communicated in an open and honest forum. Management maintains its own records and does not provide union leadership or employees in the company with access to that information. Product quality is not the highest priority, and generally in companies in this situation only profit is deemed the right focus. There is no drive to achieve best-in-class status in quality, reliability, and durability in both products and services provided, and there is no concern nor common vision for the long-term viability for the company or for the employees of that company.

Level 1: Assess Current and Future States

At this level of performance organizations begin to evaluate their competitive position. They seek out companies that are in the same business that they are in or companies that have similar methods of operations. Generally, they analyze their situation both globally and domestically. At this level organizations identify opportunities for growth. They evaluate their current capability and understand better what their systems are doing and whether or not their systems are capable of taking on additional requirements. Further, they begin looking downstream toward future capability as to whether or not they will be able to meet future demands.

Examining organizations at this level will begin to study their current organizational structure. How does the system really work within the company? What are the relationships between the processes, if any? Is there good teamwork, are people communicating with each other, and are they working to try to improve their parts of the system as well as those that have a supplier-customer relationship with them? How are the systems and resources integrated, if at all? These items are analyzed in depth. At this level of performance the company also begins to examine its relationships. It asks itself, how do men and women in this company really behave? What is okay to do and not okay to do? They develop a sense of their beliefs and values.

How do they work together? How to work together becomes a key issue to be examined between the parties. Whether this is in a unionized environment or not, employees and management begin to examine how they must work together and where they can focus to make improvement.

What are the employees' attitudes about the organization and its leadership? These issues are explored, and the picture begins to emerge of what the company really represents and the way its employees feel about it. What is the morale like in the organization? How do the men and women in the company really feel about coming to work each day? Do they feel that they want to contribute, or are they only looking to put in their time each day without making a contribution?

Product quality, if the company is a manufacturing organization, or service quality, if a company is providing a service, is analyzed. How well is the company doing? Is it satisfying its customers? Does it understand its customers' requirements, and what systems are in place to understand those issues? Further, the organization carefully examines its competition. In-depth product quality analysis is conducted.

Level 2: Test Current Vision against Vision Required to Succeed

At this level of performance an organization begins to study closely what it takes to succeed to be a world-class company, one that is focused on the customer and one that is interested in success. The company begins to understand the importance of vision and evaluates what it is in business for. Management leadership of the company begins to carefully analyze whether or not its current products or services are in fact what the company's focus should be and should continue to be.

Leadership realistically looks at its organization's current vision and asks itself, is this where we need to be heading? Does it make sense with the resources we have and the level of competition that exists? They analyze the vision to determine if the vision will inspire the men and women in the organization to strive to make continuous improvement their goal. Further, companies during this analysis period look very closely at where they are and where they want to be and begin to understand the size of the gap and what is required to close the gap. It is critical at this point that there is an understanding of the importance of quality, reliability, and durability when speaking of manufactured goods. Without QRD or a focus on quality, reliability, and durability companies will more than likely be driven out of business by competition that is focused on QRD.

Leadership in the company understands what is needed to become best-in-class in all of its product lines and services. It knows its competition, and it knows the gap between where they are now and where they need to be as a company. It understands all of its products and services, its processes and its relationships.

Level 3: Examine Nature of Change

At this level of execution there is an understanding of how change happens in an organization. The company has identified its obstacles and roadblocks to change and is in the process of developing action plans necessary to overcome those obstacles and roadblocks. It recognizes that systemic tension exists within the system. It's focusing on the men and women in the organization who are trying to make change come about. It is working with those men and women who resist change to help them better understand why change is a necessity. Understanding how processes can be changed with predictable outcomes becomes a focal point for joint partnering—*partnering* in the sense of developing and understanding what's in it for all the stakeholders in the company. In the case of General Motors, the Quality Network change methodology is utilized as a way to look at subsequent steps in the implementation process. The Quality Network change methodology process requires that the organization:

- Identify its current state and its desired state
- Determine the gap between the two
- Develop a plan to close the gap
- Implement the plan
- Evaluate the plan

Level 4: Leadership Committed to Leading Change in the Organization

At this level of execution within a company, the leaders agree to create and/or support a worldwide quality policy in the case of a global company. The companies of a smaller scale are focused on one common understanding in their definition of *quality*, that is, to be the best at what they do. All decisions and actions are aligned with the company's beliefs and values, or the company is walking the talk and is treating employees consistently regardless of their status in the organization.

Leadership understands that it is necessary to accept risks and to take risks in order to provide for continuous improvement in the organization. Resource issues are resolved quickly with appropriate focus placed on key areas of the organization so that high-quality performance becomes the result. The leadership of the company communicates its personal and ongoing commitment to change as a team by actions as well as words. Constancy of purpose is understood in the company and becomes a focal point for the organization. Long-term planning becomes a way of life.

The organization is focused on best-in-class requirements for quality of products and/or products and services. It concentrates on its processes and relationships as well as on quality, reliability, and durability. The leaders of the company are committed to excellence.

Step 1 goal: The goal or the highest level of attainment in the area under *Creating a Sense of Urgency* is that everyone understands the urgency of the current situation and is committed to action. All employees are provided with the information needed for understanding, which will result in a commitment to action.

Step 2: Develop Awareness of Quality Network As General Motors' Total Quality Process

Objective. To define *Quality Network* as the process enabling the effective operation of the organization.

Beliefs & Values. Customer Satisfaction and Enthusiasm through People, Teamwork, and Continuous Quality Improvement.

Common sense suggests that your chances of succeeding are much better if people in the organization understand what the process is, what it is going to focus on, and what's in it for the stakeholders. We still have more than 30 percent of GM people who are not aware of the Quality Network. We are working on that.

The above objective clearly defines the purpose for this step. Every organization, once committing itself to total quality, must make sure that all employees throughout the organization have an understanding that such a commitment has been made. The Quality Network four-step communication process, discussed in Chapter 10, has been an effective way for General Motors to communicate its focus on the Quality Network, the company's total quality process. This objective is supported by the *Beliefs & Values*, and it comprehends the full scope of those *Beliefs & Values*: customer satisfaction through people, team-work, and continuous quality improvement.

Level 0: No Awareness of Total Quality Process

At this level of execution there would basically be no awareness of the total quality process on the part of employees within the organization. The leadership of the organization is unaware of total quality as a way of doing business. The Quality Network and the associated tools and techniques are basically unknown, and the product quality is stagnant, is leveled out, or lacks a continuous improvement focus.

Level 1: Understand Total Quality Process

At this level of understanding, the organization recognizes the total quality process exists; furthermore, they gain understanding in essence of the total quality process and its departure from traditional management thinking to a new level of recognition that the total quali-ty process links to product quality, process quality, the quality of rela-tionships, and the success of the business. It also recognizes the obliga-tion to stakeholders, the ultimate customers, employees and families, stockholders, suppliers and their employees and families, dealers and their employees and families as well as the communities in which this particular organization does work. There is a commitment to change, and it is apparent, and it begins to drive plans for future action.

Level 2: Understand Quality Network as a Total Quality Process

At this level of execution the organization understands that the Quality Network is in fact General Motors' total quality process. It can demonstrate the Quality Network as General Motors' total quality process by examining its elements. Employees are familiar with its history; they know that it was created by GM people for GM people. It has beliefs and values as its foundation, there is a structure in place for communications, and it has a process model as well as the four quality leadership initiatives. In addition, there is an understanding that action strategies exist, and they represent the best-of-the-best tools and techniques both internally and externally observed.

It is understood that the Quality Network is a total system designed for organizational attainment of a master plan, customer satisfaction.

Level 3: Understand the Linkage between the Quality Network and the Business Plan

At this level of execution the organization understands linkage between the Quality Network and the business plan. They adopt the Quality Network as the process to achieve the vision and mission of the organization. It is understood that the vision and the mission drive the business plan. They also understand and analyze the linkage of the four Quality Network Leadership Initiatives to accomplish the business plan. They understand how the Quality Network enables the other NAO and Delphi-AS strategies to succeed. The Quality Network is the "how" to accomplish the "whats" of the business plan. It is also recognized that the quality plan and the business plan are one and the same. If the business plan does not focus on continuous quality improvement, whether it's in service or product quality, the organization will not survive. It understands and supports the one process for the organization and that one process is the Quality Network.

Level 4: Leadership Embraces the Quality Network As General Motors' Total Quality Process

At this level of execution, leadership fully embraces the Quality Network as General Motors' total quality process. Leadership is actively and visibly involved and demonstrates its commitment to the Quality Network. The leaders provide the time and resources, they commit personally to lead the process, and they communicate it on an ongoing basis. The Quality Network process is the framework for all planning activities of all levels of the organization. No project is undertaken unless it is within the framework of the Quality Network and supported and/or directed by the quality council. Quality Network initiatives become the top priority for action because the Quality Network leaders has developed an appropriate understanding of the importance of the process and they also understand that through their actions and leadership they will get the appropriate results to accomplish the business plan. It is clear that the goal at this point is that the Quality Network be the one process for continuous improvement of customer satisfaction. Furthermore, that goal is clear to the leadership of the staff or location.

Step 2 goal: The Quality Network is the one process for continuous improvement of customer satisfaction and enthusiasm.

Step 3: Educate Top Leadership

Objective. To define and communicate leadership's evolving role in a continuously improving (learning) organization. The particular supporting statements of the *Beliefs & Values* that have a strong relationship to educating top leadership are "taking responsibility for leadership" as well as "establishing a learning environment at all levels" in the organization.

Beliefs & Values. Take responsibility for leadership.

This is where the fun begins. The struggle is between leaders who think training is a waste of time and money and those enlightened leaders who know that knowledge is more important to the organization than capital. Good minds, inspired by good leaders, will overcome any obstacles. Education is an investment, not a liability. Top leaders cannot take themselves out of the learning equation. In fact, top leadership sets the learning style for the organization. If top leaders are to be teachers, then they will have to be learners as well.

Level 0: No Understanding of Leadership's Changed Role in the New Organization

At level 0 there is no understanding of leadership's changed role in the new organization. There is a lack of focus and obviously a lack of support.

Level 1: Understand Role(s) in the New Organization

An organization that has executed at this level has defined characteristics of a continuously improving or learning environment. There will be a flexible mindset, always expanding and evolving, looking for new and better ways to accomplish tasks as well as looking for new and better ways to improve relationships. The organization will also have internalized leadership's roles. Leaders will recognize the importance of being the designer of the process and of having to establish the vision and the mission for the organization for which they lead. They will realize that they are the architects of the master plan for customer satisfaction. They understand and support the notion of teacher/coach and facilitator as a key role for the leadership. They understand that they are stewards of the people and the design—the master plan of the process—and make sure that the organization is consistently aligning its behavior with the *Beliefs & Values*.

Level 2: Develop Needed Skill and Knowledge

At this level of execution, the leadership understands the need for developing its skills and knowledge. Leaders attend classes with other employees in the organization. They visit other locations, both those that are successful in implementing the Quality Network process as well as those that are struggling. They know what the right questions are, and they ask those questions. They do not accept the pat answers. Through their dialogue with others in the organization, they are causing people to stretch their minds and reach beyond where they have reached before. They are capable of actively teaching the principles of the Quality Network, and they also understand that self-learning occurs when one is teaching.

Level 3: Align Behavior with
Value System

At this level individual leadership behavior begins to align with the value system. Leadership is demonstrating a commitment to the *Beliefs & Values* through its visible behavior. Leaders expect and demand behavior from others to consistently align with the value system, and they will stop proceedings if they are inconsistent with the principles of the *Beliefs & Values*. Leadership also at this point recognizes and will reward behavior that is consistent with the *Beliefs & Values*. When people are behaving correctly, leadership recognizes it and takes the opportunity to reward that behavior. At this level of execution the leadership demands consistency in the application of the value system; that is, it demands that the values are applied equally to all people within the organization. Furthermore, leaders do not allow behavior that is inconsistent with the *Beliefs & Values* to go unchecked.

Level 4: Leadership's
Responsibility Assumed and
Enthusiastically Communicated

At this level of execution, leadership's responsibility is assumed and enthusiastically communicated to the organization. Leadership commits to playing a vital role in the definition and articulation of the new organization. Leaders actively participate in its design implementation. They personally are involved in teaching those that are unaware, they coach those that need direction, they teach those that need encouragement to overcome obstacles, and facilitate the process by providing the resources and knocking down the roadblocks. There are constant reviews to assess progress, to ensure constancy of purpose. There is a clear understanding at this level of execution by leadership that it must accept the role of steward of the vision and of the people who share the vision. Leaders protect the vision while stretching its boundaries, mindful of values and the mission of the organization. They are constantly monitoring the vision to be certain that the direction they are going in will maintain a viable organization into the future.

> *Step 3 goal:* All top leadership is part of the fabric of the learning organization.

Step 4: Develop Vision

Objective. To create a shared vision of what General Motors will be like when the Quality Network is fully implemented. When we talk about *one vision*, we are referring to one vision that is shared by leadership communicated with a single voice. The vision is General Motors. Goals attached to the vision should inspire the desire for perfection. The vision and goals should not fall short of the attainable. The vision should be the one that integrates all functional processes into a single process. The quality plan, the business plan, and the other plans come together here to become one: the vision of perfection and an attitude of excellence. The *Beliefs & Values* associated with this particular step put quality in everything we do and demonstrate our commitment to people.

Beliefs & Values. Demonstrate our commitment to people.

Without vision, men/women will perish. Proverbs 29:18. Enough said.

Level 0: No Vision or Many Visions
Leadership of the organization, and thus the organization itself, does not understand its purpose or focus, either because one shared vision has not been defined or, more commonly, leaders have individual visions that are applied to their sphere of influence and are often in conflict with one another. In either case, the organization flounders without direction.

Level 1: Understand the Need for a Single, Shared Vision

At this level the organization understands the need for a single and shared vision. Leaders are in the process of examining the nature of visions. They are imagining where they want to be—the future they wish to create—and they seek agreement that a vision cannot be imposed. All must want to attain the vision and aspire to get there. Leadership understands how a single vision provides a common identity, who we are in a common destiny, where we want to get to.

Level 2: Examine Existing Visions

At this level of execution, the organization is examining existing visions. It is in the process of identifying the many stakeholders and their respected visions. It is like looking at all the different facets of a gem, each seeming to be the one true picture of the whole. At this point we are trying to draw on all of the pieces that make up visions and from them glean the one vision that will direct the full energy of the organization. Members of the organization are examining the commonalties, they are looking for opportunities for efforts to overlap so that they can have a common focus and can execute action plans around that common focus. The organization also will identify and discuss the differences that do exist. It will have a clear understanding of why those differences exist and what plans are necessary to overcome the differences.

Level 3: Develop a Single, Shared Vision

At this level of execution, leadership has developed a single shared vision, which is tested against the value system. The vision is required to define a future that everyone aspires to attain, it is based on trust and respect for all the parties and their concerns, and it supports organizational goals and objectives.

Level 4: Leadership Supports and Communicates the Shared Vision

At this level of execution, leadership supports and communicates the shared vision with the organization. The vision is deeply held and articulated by leadership on an ongoing basis. It is constantly kept in front of all who are asked to become a part of successfully attaining the vision. All efforts and energies are directed toward attainment of that vision. There is an ongoing commitment to create a communication plan to share the vision with the entire organization. Visions for individual units are in concert and advance the single vision for the corporation.

Step 4 goal: One shared vision that excites all.

Step 5: Educate and Involve All Employees

Objective. To empower the people of General Motors by providing them with the skills and knowledge to fulfill the vision.

Beliefs & Values. Establish a learning environment at all levels. Make communications work.

> Synergy—it will occur when people in an organization are provided with an opportunity to learn and apply what they have learned. When you are using common information to educate the organization—same tools, techniques, terms, and values—synergy will occur at all levels, and employee involvement will be aggressively pursued.

Level 0: Knowledge and Empowerment Vary Greatly throughout the Organization

At this step knowledge and empowerment vary greatly throughout the organization. Information is not consistently shared throughout the organization, and the level of understanding varies greatly.

Level 1: Conduct Assessment of Current-State Level of Understanding

At this level of execution, leadership has agreed to conduct an assessment of the current state of the level of understanding. Leaders use the communication assessment instrument developed by the Quality Network process to provide information that will become the foundation for their communication plan. They identify the skills and knowledge required to fully execute the plan.

Level 2: Develop Communication Plan Based on Assessment

At this level of execution, the organization has developed a communication plan based on the assessment. The plan includes disseminating information throughout all levels of the organization, ultimately reaching the employees who are responsible for the day-to-day maintenance of product or service quality. The communication plan focuses on educating and involving all the employees by articulating the vision and providing the empowerment and excitement to accomplish the vision.

There is a common foundation for understanding that includes knowledge of the current state to facilitate moving more quickly to the vision, usually driven by urgency. There is a clear understanding of the nature of the total quality process and of the Quality Network as General Motors' total quality process. There is also an understanding of the four Quality Network initiatives as the way to reach the vision by harnessing the power of the Quality Network tools and techniques. Appropriate resources are identified, and training is provided on an ongoing basis as required and as available.

Level 3: Implement Communication Plan

At this level of execution, the communication plan has been fully implemented, resources have been provided, leaders at each level of the organization teach the principles of the process, leaders listen openly and invite feedback for continuous improvement, and leaders actively facilitate solutions to obstacles.

Level 4: People of General Motors Feel Fully Empowered

At this level of execution, the people of GM feel fully empowered. Leaders at all levels teach, coach, and facilitate the process. All levels of the organization understand the shared vision and incorporate it into all planning. There is recognition that implementation of the four Quality Network initiatives means that the vision will be achieved and the business will be successful. The Quality Network action strategies are the tools and techniques used to implement—to focus the organization on implementation of the four Quality Network initiatives.

Step 5 goal: A learning environment exists at all levels of the organization.

Step 6: Develop Process Measures

Objective.   To develop and define indicators that will demonstrate implementation progress.

Beliefs & Values.   Put quality in everything we do.

> If you can't measure it, don't do it. If you can measure it, constantly improve the process, which will improve the results that are being measured. Beware of spurious causality. Be certain you have your finger on the right button when you think a process is going awry.

Level 0: No Quality Network Implementation Process Measures in Place

At this level of execution, no Quality Network implementation process measures are in place, and there is no understanding of the necessity for those measurements.

Level 1: Establish Measurement Requirements

At this level of execution, the organization has established measurement requirements. It understands the current state, and it is aware that a baseline is necessary to measure progress. The organization also uses implementation progress of the four Quality Network initiatives as its measurement to build a supportive environment, create an organization-wide customer focus, synchronize the organization, and detect, solve, and prevent product quality problems. It also has incorporated the *Beliefs & Values* into all measurement requirements.

Level 2: Define Indicators of Requirements

At this level of execution, the organization has defined the indicators that are required. For each Quality Network initiative, the leadership asks, how do we know we are doing these things? Are we doing them well? What are the results showing us, and what evidence is there of small incremental improvements? In addition, the organization has determined if its indicators reflect progress toward accomplishment of the business-sector objectives.

Level 3: Define Data Collection Methods

At this level of execution, the organization has defined data collection methods. It uses the Quality Network tools and techniques when appropriate and fully understands the necessity for a measurement process and being data driven.

Level 4: Leadership Uses Process Measures

At this level of execution, leadership uses process measures. The measures are understood by all, and measurement requirements are followed by all persons in the organization. The measurements are posted so that everyone understands what is required. The measurements are properly used to direct the implementation process. They are not used to rank order, people, or processes. No tampering or adjustments of the process are based solely on the output. Process thinking prevails in the organization. No changes are made without involvement and consensus.

Step 6 goal: Stakeholders are empowered to self-assess and continuously improve processes.

Step 7: Develop Master Plan

Objective.   To develop detailed plans, integrated in business plans at every level of the organization, which achieve the vision.

Beliefs & Values.   Invite the people of GM to be full partners in the business.

If you allow people to plan for the organization who are not familiar with the tools, techniques, terminology, and values, the plan will not be accepted and supported. Education of the company planners in the principles of TQM must precede development of the master plan for TQM in the company. Then the planners will understand the importance of stakeholder involvement and knowledge to the overall design and success of the plans.

The Quality Network belief and value associated with this step is that the people of GM must be invited to be full partners in the business. Partners have a stake in the outcome of the business and benefit from its success.

Level 0: No Evidence of Master Plan(s)

At level 0 of execution in an organization, there is no evidence of master plans. There is no linkage of the Quality Network to the business plans, no resources have been identified, there is no stakeholder involvement, and there is no understanding of how the organization is going to attain the vision.

Level 1: Recognize and Support the Need for Master Plan(s)

At this level of execution, there is recognition and support for the need of a master plan or plans. We seek the involvement of all stakeholders to use the Quality Network process as the basis for planning. The organization is evolving to one process with one language with one common vision. There is one plan; the quality plan and the business plan are inextricably linked and become a common plan. The organization examines and understands the interrelationship of all stakeholders and the process elements. It understands the customer chain from the internal customers to the ultimate customers.

Level 2: Assess Current State and Future State and the Gap

At this level of execution, the organization has assessed its current state and future state and understands the gap. The Quality Network change methodology process is used to determine the gap between where the organization is and where it wants to be. Information from the communication assessment is applied to determine the gap for the total organization.

Level 3: Create Plan

At this level of execution, a plan is created. The stakeholders' planning group creates an implementation plan. The implementation plan uses a Quality Network process to execute the business plan. Roles and responsibilities are defined and well understood by all participants.

They identify the appropriate Quality Network action strategies to be used within the organization in conjunction with the master plan for implementation. The plan also includes process measures.

Level 4: Leadership Committed to Leading the Implementation of the Plan

At this level of execution, leadership is committed to leading the implementation plan. Each level of the organization understands and is committed to leading the implementation of the plan as it relates to their part of the organization. There is a definite linkage between the business and other operating plans, which is fully supported by the leadership. The leadership is also linked to support other parts of the organization as necessary in order to accomplish the overall master plan. There are linkages with the total organization so that the company does not suboptimize.

Step 7 goal: Implementation of master plans enable continuous improvement throughout the organization.

Step 8: Implement

Objective.   To execute the plan(s) and thereby achieve the vision. Just do it!

Beliefs & Values.   Recognize people as our greatest resource. Build through teamwork and joint action.

There is not much else for us to say here except, just do it! In some ways this is easier said than done. Often we plan and plan and plan. Sooner or later we may get promoted or transferred, the plan never having been executed. Dr. Deming often said that it didn't matter where you started in the transformation, just start.

The Quality Network belief and value associated with this step is that people are recognized as our greatest resource, and as such the organization uses joint action and teamwork to maximize their contribution.

Level 0: Implementation Efforts
Are Inconsistent

Implementation efforts are inconsistent. There is no communication or awareness plan that is evident. A process structure is not in place.

Level 1: Communicate Master
Plan(s) to All Stakeholders

At this level of execution, master plans have been communicated to all stakeholders. Roles and responsibilities have been defined. All GM people know where they fit into the master plan and what is expected of them. They can illustrate the corporate vision and supporting visions intellectually, logically, and emotionally. All GM people understand how the vision for their unit supports and advances the vision for General Motors.

Level 2: Demonstrate Leadership
Commitment and Involvement

At this level of execution, leadership demonstrates its commitment and involvement. Leaders are teachers, and they are involved in implementing the plan. Leadership provides the time and resources to empower employees with knowledge and skills to implement the plan. Leadership supports an environment that encourages problem-solving innovation and risk taking and provides for continuous quality improvement. Support is evident among all stakeholders, union management, cross-functional organizations, and cross-functional teams as well as cross-organizational teams. Department-to-department staff and staff-to-staff communication channels are in place.

Level 3: Implement Plan(s)

At this level of execution, the organization has implemented its plans. Then it reviews its progress and provides recognition for the efforts of the stakeholders.

Level 4: Master Plan Fully
Integrated into the "Way We Do
Business"

At this level of execution, the master plan is fully integrated into the way we do our business, quality goals are exceeded, and the *Beliefs & Values* are part of the very fabric of the organization.

> *Step 8 goal:* All General Motors people are fully involved in planning, implementation, and continuous improvement of customer satisfaction and enthusiasm.

Step 9: Assess and Recognize

Objective. To evaluate the plan itself and how well it was followed. To recognize efforts and celebrate accomplishment.

Beliefs & Values. Demand consistency in the application of this value system.

> Everyone likes a little pat on the back. We are not talking about a big celebration with marching bands; we are talking about leadership saying thanks and encouraging continued improvement. And, we are talking about people being recognized for behavior exemplifying the *Beliefs & Values.*

The Quality Network belief and value for this step is that leadership demands consistency in the application of this value system. It is essential that leadership remain true to the *Beliefs & Values* and thereby its treatment of those who do the same.

Level 0: No Formal Evaluation and Recognition Policy Exists

Throughout the organization there may be locations in which enlightened leadership has established an informal, perhaps unwritten, code of evaluation and recognition. However, the organization itself has no common evaluation and/or recognition system consistent across divisions and platforms.

Level 1: Acknowledge Need for Assessment and Recognition

At this level of execution, the organization acknowledges the need for assessment and recognition. It builds awareness on the power of employee involvement through recognition, and it develops an understanding that the assessment policy should be fair and consistent and should focus on behavior aligned with the *Beliefs & Values*.

Level 2: Define and Establish Informal and Formal Recognition Process

At this level of execution, a recognition process is defined and established both formally and informally. The recognition process reflects the *Beliefs & Values*, and the people recognition action strategy is used to drive the process.

Level 3: Conduct Assessment

At this level of execution, the organization conducts an assessment to evaluate the plan and to evaluate the implementation of the process. It also applies the fifth step of the change methodology action strategy—evaluate.

Level 4: Assessment Outcomes Form Basis for Continuous Improvement

At this level of execution, the assessment process outcomes form the basis for the information for continuous improvement. The organization is improving its plan, it's focused on further refinement of its implementation efforts, and it constantly enforces the behaviors of the organization consistent with the beliefs and values.

Step 9 goal: People recognition is a top organizational priority.

Step 10: Continuous Improvement

Objective.   To strive for excellence by continuously improving the process.

Beliefs & Values.   Make continuous improvement the goal of every individual.

> Once you have implemented the master plan, the process starts over again based on a thorough and honest evaluation of the progress made. A determination of the organization's effectiveness in disseminating information and developing understanding to engender personal commitment to action drives the direction and content of continuous improvement efforts. The idea of continuous improvement is to maintain leadership in customer satisfaction and enthusiasm.

Level 0: No Process for Continuous Improvement in the Organizational Culture

Continuous improvement is a mindset that flies directly in the face of the prevalent cliché "if it ain't broke, don't fix it." "It" can always be "fixed." Organizations typically look for startling innovations, not aware that continuous, incremental improvements lead to innovative outcomes. There is not an understanding of continuous improvement as an operational characteristic necessary for growth and customer satisfaction.

Level 1: Identify and Analyze Need for Continuous Improvement

Assessment data should be used as the basis for continuous improvement plans. As an organization identifies the quality gap in a process, product, or service between itself and the industry benchmark, it exposes opportunities for improvement. If, in fact, the process, product, or service in question is the best-in-class standard, analysis will also provide improvement opportunities in order to maintain and sustain its leadership.

Level 2: Continuously Improve Implementation Plan

As the Quality Network is being implemented throughout the organization, opportunities for improvement will arise. All involved stakeholders are included as their input is valuable in these implementation efforts. Small teams with functionally related representation are an excellent resource for these efforts. The point is to continually examine the process. Renew the sense of urgency, recognizing that the competition is not sitting still. The master plan should be reviewed for its strengths and weaknesses—what worked and what did not work. When was the plan circumvented in order to "get things done?" What shortcuts helped, and when were they a mistake? All these activities are natural in the execution of a long-term plan. It is important to honestly document the plan's execution. If a supportive environment is in place, there are no repercussions for honest reporting. Employees free from fear are encouraged to try new ideas. Problem-solving techniques are used to overcome persistent obstacles.

Level 3: Communicate Improvements as the Process Unfolds

As the master plan is revisited for continuous improvement, leadership facilitates the open and honest exchange of information throughout the organization. The outcome of all tested theories and ideas are studied in order to improve the plan and share the mistakes as well as the successes. Although the master plan has long-term goals, the route to these goals changes along the way due to the learning that takes place.

Level 4: Implement Continuous Improvement Efforts with All Employees Committed to Action

The master plan is capable of accommodating system improvements, which are communicated as they occur. This supports organizational learning and growth. Continued education and training at all levels support these new ideas and prepare the path for innovation and breakthrough. The mindset of continuous improvement pushes the quality system cycle to higher levels as learning takes place.

> *Step 10 goal:* Continuous improvement is viewed as an opportunity for ongoing renewal.

The above implementation process was developed from the input of a number of people within the Quality Network community, and we appreciate their contribution. We hope this implementation process will help other organizations implement a process for change.

Management's Role in Implementation

Management's role is to identify people who have the ability to motivate and lead people. In most organizations some areas just seem to get things done all the time. Closer examination will show a real respect for the leader in that area because of his or her care for people and his or her business goals. Rewards and recognition can no longer be based on "numbers out the door" but must be based on a person's ability to stimulate teamwork as well as personal skills.

Leadership can inspire its work force by providing the proper environment in which to work. As we have discussed, this supportive environment is made up of many different aspects that all contribute to a feeling of mutual trust and respect between the workers and their leadership. Inclusion in the business planning process, designing a master plan, the use of technology as a tool to enhance workers' abilities to do their jobs safer and smarter, and an atmosphere free from fear and intimidation are all characteristics of such a supportive environment. So too is the open and honest exchange of information that leads to actions that further the vision.

The following chapter deals with the Quality Network communication strategy, which links the development of personal commitment to the achievement of the vision. Keep in mind the evolving levels of each step in the implementation matrix. Although not an exact numeric fit, there are four phases of an effective communication process, and our matrix features five (0 through 4) levels of growth, and the philosophy is alive and well in the implementation flow. Each step in the matrix represents a learning process, as does a good communication process.

10
Communicating the Process

Traditional Views

Traditional management in many instances has inadvertently limited the success of environmental initiatives and productivity efforts by not spending the time to develop understanding and commitment prior to implementation or action. Orders are given, and it is expected that an immediate heartfelt response will follow. Communication is reduced to decree rather than a swelling consensus of opinion leading to united action. In most organizations, information is provided, and it is expected that everyone throughout the organization will conform to the desired changes and bring about successful implementation.

Today, communication cannot be entirely successful if it is delivered vertically, from the top down, as if from on high. To be truly successful, communication must extend up, down, and across an organization; it must derive from a conscious attempt to secure trust, understanding, and commitment. In the past, two-step, or top-down, communication was accepted as effective. Information was guarded as a protected asset, unshared unless it was personally expedient to do so. The kind of information that can lead to understanding was hoarded to control situations and individuals; trust was not part of the equation. But this was the standard way of doing business—no questions asked. There is no way to measure what opportunities have been missed and what levels of attainment have fallen short due to this attitude on the part of both parties. The current economic problems faced by many organizations raise the question, "Could better communication of desired actions have avoided the economic and environmental crisis confronting leadership today?" Profitable industries may have had even more successful histories if all actions had been implemented enthusiastically by everyone in the organization. Many half-hearted attempts at success fall upon the rocky shoals of misunderstanding and lack of long-term commitment. Agreement with a new process or change is not as critical as the understanding of its purpose and a commitment to implement it as originally planned and conceived.

Organizational Communication

At General Motors we have a primary communication action strategy of the Quality Network. Its definition from the Quality Network Process Reference Guide is:

> Organizational communication is a structured process for the honest exchange of information. When combined with consistent behavior of leadership, it empowers all employees to:
> - Do a quality job
> - Contribute to the success of their organization
> - Achieve customer satisfaction
> - Enhance job security

Organizational communication focuses on communication geared to objectives of the organization. It cannot be left to chance; it must be planned and tied to individual and organizational responsibility and authority. The ultimate measure of the effectiveness of a communication process is the attainment of organizational goals.

Leadership Sets the Tone

Leadership must recognize its role as the key communication catalyst. Additionally, all members of an organization have communication responsibility. However, it is leadership's communication style that is usually emulated throughout an organization. We believe that all leaders must articulate their belief that communication is a fundamental component of the business. Leaders must sustain the communication process and ensure that it is planned and clearly identifies and explains business issues in a consistent and reliable manner. Leaders must learn to be good listeners, willing to modify their plans if communication efforts are to produce ideas that improve overall goals and objectives. Leaders who are open to, and actually encourage, challenges to their beliefs make their accessibility known to all: the "open-door" policy. It is part of their leadership style, and, this is critical, it cannot be thwarted by those around them who may not agree with this management technique.

Leaders must be steadfast and not succumb to well-meaning "filters" in their organization. Yes, leaders are busy—but we can never be too busy to listen. This is very threatening to individuals who traditionally have surrounded the leadership and have always "had the inside track." When openness and accessibility become the prevailing attitude, ideas are generated freely, and trust can result.

Jay Wilber on Representative Conversations

Tom and I had been on the job for a couple of months. We had inherited a network of Quality Network Representatives, about 400 strong, most of whom did not know who we were. Basically, there is at least one represented and one salaried Quality Network Representative (QN Rep) at each location. Some of the larger plants have more than two. We decided that a videotape was the best way to reach them, both from a convenience and cost consideration. We called the program *Representative Conversations* and scheduled this live-on-tape session for May 14, 1990. We brought in 12 teams of representatives from across the corporation. This was to be our great experiment with communicating directly, face to face with a team of management and union Quality Network Representatives in a live question-and-answer format. There were no scripts, notes, or prescreened questions. The format was a dramatic departure from traditional TelePrompTer speeches. The approach proved very successful and resulted in the identification of several issues that were used as our agenda going forward from that session. I'll never forget the looks of concern on the faces of the UAW and management leadership from the Quality Network steering committee as we stepped up to two stools in front of 24 experts with microphones in front of them, most of whom had been on the job with the Quality Network for two or more years. We were the neophytes. As we fielded questions and discussed the status of the Quality Network for three hours, steering committee members gathered in a screening room watching us and listening to every answer. They, too, had been on the job longer than we had, and I'm not sure we had instilled great confidence in them at this point. When the taping was over, we had our marching orders in hand. The representatives provided us with the issues we had to address. Who would know them better than the men and women who have to do the work in the field? There was a sigh of relief and spark of excitement as we set off to tackle the issues. This session was completely extemporaneous, not the traditional "GM way." If we didn't have an answer, we promised one in the near future. If we strayed off the point, the Reps brought us back at once. It was lively and fun. Tom and I agreed that all future sessions would be approached in the same spontaneous manner.

Four-Step Communication

General Motors has developed a four-step communications model that is easy to understand and provides a simple four-step process from which all communication efforts can be planned and evaluated.

Step 1: Providing Information

As you can see by the model shown in Fig. 10-1, effective communication begins with information that is gathered in a three-way exchange

ACTION ORIENTED COMMUNICATION

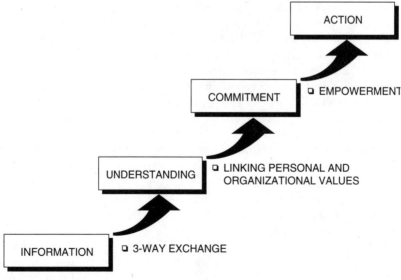

Figure 10-1

from everyone affected up, down, and across the organization or department: up to the leaders, down to those in subordinate processes, and across functional and/or divisional boundaries. If an organization is serious about viewing itself as a total system, then all stakeholders—direct and indirect—need to be involved. This ensures that input from all levels of the organization is permitted, which begins the communication process.

Tom Weekley on Traditional, One-Way Communication

While working as a young tool and die maker, I was assigned to try out and put into operation a number of draw dies that were very complicated because of their intricate detail and the depth that metal had to be stretched in order to obtain the desired form. The general foreman responsible for the operation came out to the floor and told me and another employee assigned to the job that he wanted the die modified so that a part could be made with as little metal flow restriction as possible and without any type of lubricant.

Immediately we objected and outlined that in our experience such a deep draw, or forming of metal, to such a depth could not be accomplished without severe restriction on the metal to allow it to stretch over the male portion of the die. This would produce such great friction that it was absolutely essential that some type of lubricant be used to assist the metal flow. Without these essential requirements the metal would wrinkle and split.

The general foreman rejected our input and gave us orders that required some extreme modifications of the die itself. Ken Laubert, the additional journeyperson on the line, and I conformed with the required directions. However, we knew that it wouldn't work and the general foreman wouldn't get the results he expected. Now, both Ken and I were hired at this location because of our past experience and expertise in working on this type of die, but we were still not listened to.

As the weeks stretched on, the die became more and more mutilated, based upon the general foreman's orders and his complete disregard of the input from the people working on this operation. Eventually Ken and I lost all incentive for suggesting to management what was obviously needed to obtain a final panel.

Finally, the general foreman made a decree that brought an end to the mutilated die's misery. He instructed us to grind a deep cavity in the lower corner of the die in a long, flat drawing area that metal must flow over before it actually enters the die cavity. On top, a long, thick strip of metal was added, called a *sausage*, that would match the cavity in the draw area on the bottom and would solidly grab the metal, preventing it from stretching. In this area the metal was required to flow and stretch to a depth of about 10 inches. The addition of the sausage meant that the metal could not flow and would be held stationary. The metal was approximately thirty-thousandths of an inch thick (0.030 inch)—the thickness of an auto body panel—which obviously would not stretch into a 10-inch-deep die cavity.

The die metal was made of air-hardened tool steel, and I attacked it with enthusiasm and vigor, knowing full well that the general foreman's orders would require complete rehabilitation due to the mutilation of the die.

At the shift change the tool and die superintendent arrived just in time to see the first panel made from the now decimated die. As predicted by the two experts on the job, the employees, the metal split and tore in several areas of the panel. The superintendent looked at the die and then turned his wrath on us, who had worked so hard to follow the misguided orders of the general foreman.

After his tirade and accusations of incompetence ceased, I detailed the orders that had been given. The superintendent spent some serious time in consultation with the general foreman. He then came back and asked if the die could be salvaged and a panel made. We shared our feelings on what had to be done to revive the mutilated die and, if such changes were made, that a panel could easily be produced in one shift. The superintendent looked skeptical but agreed to follow the suggested course of action.

The next day, the die had been welded, machined, and restored to its original condition with some visible scars and imperfections. Ken and I worked through the shift, and by the end we were able to produce a panel of exceptional quality that passed vigorous inspection on the first try.

Examples like this, ignoring the parties involved in the initial implementation of any process, are widespread and, in most cases, doom implementation plans to failure, or at best limited success. In this example it is easy to see that initial plans, though well meaning, did not take into account all of the information available from all of the people involved in the job. The general foreman appears to be the villain: "Why didn't he listen?" But he was no different from hundreds of foremen whose supervisors don't listen to them. An order is given that has an admirable outcome in mind. The environment will not tolerate questioning the order. The order is passed along the chain of command, with disconnects occurring all along the way. Again, leaders need to listen and be open and forthright with their information.

Step 2: Developing Understanding

Moving from the initial *information-gathering process* to an *understanding* of not only what is expected but also of what is possible is necessary if people are going to link their personal goals with those of the organization. In the example above, if everyone had come to a real understanding of all the information available and then had used that understanding to establish an atmosphere of mutual respect and trust, the outcome would have been much different.

In any organization, if information is provided to all parties so that they understand why something is to be done and have an opportunity to have input and link their goals and values with that of the organization, then the next step of being committed to a successful outcome begins the actual launch of the desired action. If information is disseminated and input is received so that all understand why a particular action is expected, then it is inevitable that commitment to such action becomes a firm foundation for teamwork and ultimate success. The link between information and understanding is critical. Information here must be so inclusive of all relevant data, and the policies and practices that drive that data, that its transfer causes a state of knowing, or understanding, in the recipients. It is actually an educational process that establishes a teacher-student relationship between the person with the information and the person requiring the information. This is not just a top-down relationship, as is evident in the *Representative Conversations* example where the new leadership learned from the field representatives. The general foreman initially did not learn from the tradesmen on the plant floor.

We have changed the way we look at information at General Motors. For example, in the past, quality data were held close to the chest. Only top executives knew the full quality story. Today, this information is shared with all employees. In a live teleconference to quality councils, Ron Haas, Vice President of Quality and Reliability, broke with tradition. He gave a report on the current state of GM quality relative to the competition and internal, ongoing measurements. The teleconference presented product quality information heretofore kept guarded and limited to a small group of top management leaders. GM workers were used to using quality data retrieved on-the-job and therefore very job specific. The teleconference presented the quality picture in the macrosense, looking at the whole system and sharing competitive data. Audience feedback was immediate and positive, indicating a strong interest in knowing and understanding corporate product quality data and its relevance to an individual and his or her job. Audience reaction was consistent with employee surveys, confirming that there is a strong desire on the part of the work force to be the best at quality. This information had not been shared openly throughout the corporation previously. Due to the overwhelming response, data for regular quality updates of this nature are now provided to Quality Network Representatives quarterly. It is their responsibility to share this information with their quality councils. When you consider that the quality of our products and services is determined in every stage and in every process in the customer ownership experience, it makes sense to share quality data with the people who can make a difference.

Step 3: Commitment Secured

It is critical at this point to understand that the people who are committed to the final success of any action must be empowered to do their best in making sure that the action results in success. In the case of the mutilated die, having two experienced, enthusiastic, and idealistic young persons available to accomplish the desired action of obtaining a quality panel became liabilities rather than assets. The circumstances established prevented their commitment and the necessary empowerment to ultimately produce a good panel.

There is another aspect of commitment, alluded to earlier in this chapter, and that is leadership commitment. How many times has the phrase "But what does the boss think?" been uttered. Silence can be powerful. No voice from the top is most often perceived as a sign of lack of support. If the leadership ignores it, it will go away. On the other hand, visible and vocal leadership support is a powerful catalyst for action. It reinforces the direction you are heading in and assures you that support will be there if you need it. Late 1992, the NAO UAW–GM Quality Council decided that Quality Network implementation efforts should concentrate on product quality improvement. This was not a complete change of direction for the Quality Network, but it did require a refocus of some initiatives and programs to hone in on product quality issues. It was extremely important that everyone in the organization understand and support this direction. And so, we broadcast the first Quality Network telecast live to quality councils at 528 locations across the United States on January 15, 1993. We had to "stop the bleeding" and substantially improve product quality.

Leadership Communicates Commitment. The format echoed the style of *Representative Conversations* in that it featured an open question-and-answer session with Jack Smith, Chief Executive Officer and President of General Motors, and Stephen P. Yokich, Vice President and Director of the GM Department of the UAW. We facilitated the session in our roles as Codirectors of the Quality Network. There were no prepared statements or teleprompted scripts. The session was open and lively. The major thrust of the conversation was the importance of product quality and top leadership's joint support for the Quality Network process. This message was produced live-on-tape and was the cornerstone of the teleconference. Other major union and management leaders participated, stressing the importance of management and the union working together to close the product quality gap and to become and surpass the best-in-class in all GM products and services. It was during this teleconference that Ron Haas first presented his quality data report. The theme of the teleconference was *Quality, Our Futures Depend On It.*

Jack Smith was asked about the importance of trust and the role of the *Beliefs & Values* in the decision-making process. "If we don't build mutual trust for one another, we won't be successful. And we've had a history that hasn't been great. And yet, we know today that if we don't work together, we're not going to have the quality we need or a really satisfied customer. So, we're all in it together, and when we're in it together, we can win."

Steve Yokich continued, "And I'd like to add to that because we just had a National UAW–GM Council meeting, and…I said, we're all faced with our sins of the past—a large corporation that used to make decisions and…just announce them, and then argue about what we're going to do.…And we were a large union doing the same thing. 'Well, let them make their decision, and we'll just take them on.' In today's world, it's a different world. A union that can't change in a fast-changing society will not survive.…I've seen a change in attitude; we are in this together. I think it's important that people understand that."

Later in the telecast Yokich went on to state, "Quality is everybody's business—every individual that works for this corporation, UAW or non-UAW, it's still their business."

Jack Smith followed, "It's a total team effort. I certainly echo what Steve is saying. Clearly, the focus has to be on the best-in-class as our vision.…The GM Mark of Excellence should be the symbol of quality on a world basis.…We're going to push very hard to be best-in-class in everything we do. Then we have a catalyst for change, and with that catalyst everyone is going to win. The company is going to win, and everybody on the team is going to win." After this teleconference there was no doubt, in anyone's mind, where we were heading and that we were going there together. Leadership commitment was out in front for everyone to see.

Step 4: Action Assuring Success

Finally, if information is shared in a three-way exchange and all understand the reason for a particular action and are given the opportunity to commit to the success of that action, then the action itself will have a much greater opportunity to succeed. Commitment is converted into action by empowering individuals through supportive behavior and deeds, providing the resources necessary to support the plan and achieve the desired results. This means the right equipment, materials, people, methods, and systems (including training) in an entrusting environment that encourages risk taking and looks at mistakes as opportunities from which to learn. "Just do it" may be the spirit behind the action phase of the communication process, but only after the proper preparation.

Think about It.   If you take a moment to examine some of the most frustrating experiences in your working life, and by contrast some of the most successful, the value of proper communication becomes very clear. In instances where superiors or leadership listened to your input and then allowed you the flexibility to move forward toward your desired objectives, there was a sense of fulfillment and partnership in the final outcome, even if the final actions did not accomplish all that you had envisioned. On the other hand, if you would think of those occasions when you were given direct orders that contradicted your own understanding of a given situation and were ignored when you tried to interject your expertise and were not given the empowerment to carry things out to the best of your ability, you felt a sense of powerlessness, frustration, and ultimate resignation to what may well have turned out to be a lost cause.

A structured communication process is absolutely critical to an organization, it is the means to link all the various systems and subsystems within the larger business system. The communication process helps define the internal and external customer-supplier relationship that drives the organization's business system. In order for process management to succeed, leaders must freely communicate their expectations and empower people to carry on discussion and planning, which will result in effective plans for successfully obtaining organizational objectives.

Applications

Leaders need not be charismatic speakers or excellent presenters to effectively communicate their desires and objectives to the entire organization. In fact, spit-shined and polished presenters usually come across as insincere. They turn their audience off before they can deliver their message. Passion for a subject, delivered from the heart, moves listeners and engages them. Being a good and involved listener and displaying sincerity and a willingness to keep people informed of all details affecting the organization can propel the least experienced speaker to great levels of respect in the eyes of employees and fellow workers. In keeping with the *Beliefs & Values,* leaders "must make communication work." Use of employee newsletters, departmental meetings, and organizationwide communication sessions can effectively communicate a message throughout an organization.

"Diagonal slice" meetings that cut across organizational boundaries and invite representatives from all groups within the organization to short, informational meetings with give-and-take can be used to help spread the word and monitor the tone of an organization. Such meetings, held on a regular basis with different employees from each group, provide leadership with an opportunity to reveal personal commitment and to build relationships throughout an organization.

What a Suggestion Plan Can Do

Suggestion programs can assist in the product, process, and/or service improvement areas of communication if rewards and recognition are granted in a timely manner portraying a genuine and sincere gratitude for suggestions that assist the organization in improving. Such programs must provide quick feedback and recognition if they are to be successful and open; honest communication must permeate the entire structure to assure a sense of justice among participants. General Motors and the United Auto Workers Union established a joint suggestion program that includes hourly workers participation in determining awards and processing suggestions, further enhancing trust of the process. It was a major step for the corporation since the suggestion program had for many years been a corporate program with a corporate staff. Initially, management leadership resisted approving a suggestion process that allowed represented employees to determine the monetary award for fellow employee suggesters. Our experience since we implemented the new suggestion plan has demonstrated that the new plan and its rules are adhered to without exception. Joint resource teams or joint facility teams have shown a disciplined and thorough commitment to serve both the suggester's and the company's needs. Jeff Palicki, Suggestion Plan Coordinator, UAW Local 14 with Powertrain in Toledo, Ohio, puts it this way:

> We want to be sure that every suggestion is handled basically in a nameless fashion, almost, so that we process the idea and we present the idea to the organization, and whatever the finding is, we are consistent in how we process that suggestion from beginning to end.[1]

Again, the effectiveness of such a program can be assessed by applying the four-step communication model presented earlier. If a person feels that he or she can freely turn in a suggestion that will be honestly considered and the process is well understood by all, then commitment to further participation is decided, and ultimately an employee will begin to look for improvements that can help the organization:

> GARY SOVA, SUGGESTION COORDINATOR, DELTA ENGINE PLANT, LANSING, MICHIGAN: If you're talking with the suggesters, and if you're listening to them, then you're going to decrease the amount of problems that may surface later on....It's a matter of we're all working together. It isn't me against them, or you against us. We're all employees working for General Motors, and so we need to work together as a team.[2]

Development of the Communication Process at General Motors

In order to provide support to the organization for implementing the Quality Network *Communication* action strategy, the joint UAW–GM Communication Resource Team (CRT) was formed in fall 1991. The team was created in response to the stated need for cultivating a total systems approach to communication improvement within General Motors.

The team's charge was to provide hands-on consulting services to organizations implementing the Quality Network *Communication* action strategy. The design of the contract between the CRT and the organization it was consulting with can best be described as people-to-people. Initially the CRT guided its customers. However, soon after the

relationship was formed, the exchange became two-way. As the customer group got further along in the process, the CRT consultants
backed off. Clearly, the CRT acted as a catalyst for its customer groups,
coming from outside the group while still being part of General
Motors. A reference manual was developed by the Quality Network
Implementation Support Team, *Communication Action Strategy
Assessment Manual.* Its primary purpose was to keep participants of the
process on track and prevent backsliding after the fact.

The team was chartered by group-level GM Public Affairs Directors
(under the former GM structure) and was initially staffed by salaried
communication specialists. It was not long before the relationship
between the team's efforts and other Quality Network initiatives was
realized. Consequently, the Quality Network formally sanctioned the
team, and UAW members were added in February 1991. At its peak,
the communication resource team was a staff of 16 team members
drawn from a cross-section of the organization.

Communication Resource Team's Mission

The communication resource team defined its mission as follows:

- Provide assessment process consulting on a demand-pull basis in
  support of Quality Network action strategy implementation at the
  operating unit level.

- Help units help themselves by teaching them how to conduct communication environment assessments and supporting their planning efforts in response to learning.

- Counsel client organizations on how to create a learning environment that enables the organization to make the most of assessment
  learning.

- Provide hands-on support in the gathering and analyzing of data for
  client organizations when possible and as appropriate.

In General Motors we have made use of the assessment process
purely optional; it is not required to begin implementation of the
Communication action strategy. Nevertheless, it is suggested that plants
and staffs consider its use in helping joint leadership adopt a structured approach to building a supportive environment, a key initiative
of the Quality Network and essential to a solid communication plan.

Tackling the Communication Environment

The *Communication Environment*, for UAW–GM purposes, is defined as the environment within which action-oriented communication is attempted. Typically when communication is assessed in an organization, emphasis is placed on what and how information flows. In contrast, the scope of assessment activities supported by communication resource team members gauges the extent to which understanding is created and whether that understanding translates into commitment and ultimately action. In the process, client organizations learn what in their organizations helps or hinders effective communication, defined as the transformation of information into action.

By engaging in an assessment of this nature, leadership develops an understanding of the organization's dynamics: how it works, how things get done, and why they sometimes don't. Such an understanding enables leaders to better determine what systemic changes are necessary to ensure that desired actions˙ or organizational objectives are achieved. Actions required may include structural, procedural, and policy changes or clarification of roles and responsibilities, apart from clearly articulated communication process and content strategies. Therein lies the value of such an assessment to leadership. The assessment can serve as the basis for planning cultural changes that are necessary for successful implementation of the Quality Network, plain and simple. Provided, that is, that Leadership is ready and willing to make such changes. And this is the key. This works best in an environment where union and management leaders are both ready. The communication assessment, in essence, is an assessment of the environment. By providing a snapshot of the current state of an organization's culture, the *Communication* action strategy plays a primary role in the leadership initiative to build a supportive environment.

Communication Resource Team's Assessment Methodology

The CRT's methodology is simple and straightforward. The first step is a call from someone in the organization. It could be a Quality Network Representative, a Key Four member (one of the four top leaders at a plant location: Plant Manager, Union Local President, Personnel Director, or Chairperson of the Local Bargaining Committee), a plant- or division-level communication specialist, organization development or training professional, or simply an interested party. Regardless of functional alignment or placement in the organizational hierarchy, the communication resource team reacts to the "pull" signal. In response, the team generally arranges a discovery meeting in which team members provide an overview of what the team does, explore the organization's needs, and determine if there's a good fit.

A couple of preparatory meetings might precede a formal presentation to a unit's quality council or other appropriate leadership body. The purpose of these prep meetings is to involve the appropriate stakeholders in discussion and determine how an assessment might fit into other change activities under way at a unit. Stakeholders might include Quality Network Representatives, Organization Development/Human Resource Development specialists, joint activities coordinators, communication coordinators, plant floor (operations) representatives, and/or measurement coordinators.

Ultimately, a member of the organization arranges a presentation to joint leadership to create awareness about the assessment process and determine leadership's level of interest in proceeding. The following is a portion of the team's assessment overview package.

Areas covered include:

- Assessment as an element of change
- Assessment process focus and objectives
- Assessment methodology
- Process benefits

Assessment As an Element of Change. The *Change Methodology* action strategy is used to determine how best an organization moves from a traditional mode of communication (information to action) to an action-oriented mode, defined as the four-step communication process shown in Fig. 10-2.

The desired state of organizational communication in General Motors is defined as the successful application of the action-oriented communication model. The first two steps of the change process, *identify* and *analyze,* constitute what we refer to as "assessment."

Assessment Process Focus and Objectives. The desired outcome of the assessment process (the identify and analyze steps) is leadership and employee understanding of key factors that influence action-oriented communication in the organization and the commitment to address obstacles that prevent its occurrence.

The desired outcome of the total change effort (through planning,

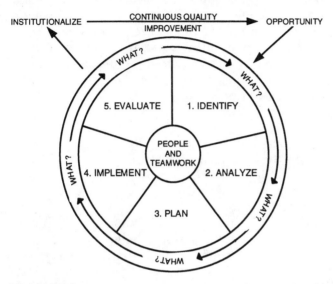

Figure 10-2

implementation, and evaluation) is planned and sustained actions that improve the environment in which communication occurs by building on organizational strengths and overcoming systemic weaknesses—those standard operating procedures and behaviors that get in the way.

With a clear understanding of the current state and cause-and-effect relationships, leadership is in a better position to plan and implement changes that increase the likelihood of focused and predictable action. The question is, how do the UAW and GM conduct an assessment?

Assessment Methodology. As with any successful change effort, the assessment methodology used is research based, encourages employee participation, and requires top leadership involvement. We emphasize the importance of timely action in response to learnings as a visible demonstration that leadership has heard the organization, understands what needs to be done, and has responded.

The research-based methods we use include interviews, focus groups, and surveys. These data collection activities are intended to build on each other to provide a balanced set of qualitative and quantitative data. Some organizations have opted not to conduct focus groups or have deferred their use until the "planning" step in the change process, choosing instead to limit assessment activities to interviews and a written survey. Generally, a survey alone is not recommended since it does not allow the opportunity to explore respondents' answers. The mere act of writing survey questions without interaction with the customer assumes you know all the right questions to ask. It is an example of information direct to action. Question development is critical. Without some customer input, you may easily miss a key unique cultural concern. In any event, each location determines the approach based on that organization's needs, expectations, and constraints.

Once the approach is determined, representatives of the communication resource team work with designated point people at a location to conduct an assessment designed to that organization's specifications. Typically, these process coordinators are union and management counterparts and become the communication resource team representative's key contacts throughout the assessment process. CRT consultants help coordinators become resident experts in the change effort by teaching them assessment techniques, counseling them on process strategy, and helping them evaluate options and alternatives. This was challenging for GM since the process coordinators' skill base and experience varied greatly from location to location.

The consultants and coordinators, in turn, lead the charge. They work cooperatively with a cross-sectional or interdepartmental task team (usually 8 to 12 people) that plans data collection and analysis activities, carries them out, and makes recommendations to leadership. The CRT developed its own software to handle the data and organize the results. The ultimate output of the assessment effort is a written report developed by the CRT consultants for leadership, summarizing learnings and recommending next steps.

Depending on the skills and interests of task team members, as well as leadership's expectations, the team may limit its recommendations to suggested approaches for communicating results and setting priorities for action, or they may actually develop improvement plans to be reviewed and implemented by leadership.

Ideally, once the results are shared, members of a unit's leadership team become "champions" of various initiatives and participate in planning and implementing changes. In reality, transfer of ownership at this point is difficult to achieve without a clear agreement with leadership up front that they will assume this role at the conclusion of "assessment" activities.

For this reason, ongoing dialogue between the process coordinators, the assessment team, and joint leadership is critical to a successful assessment and total change effort. Prior to forming the task team and at each important juncture in the process, the assessment team's charge is to keep leadership informed, build its understanding, and gain support for next steps. This requires access to top leadership, team member credibility, and, in some cases, a lot of determination.

Again, Leadership Is Key. Key success factors are leadership based (Fig. 10-3). As interested leaders progress through the assessment process, they begin to see their organization differently and take ownership for change. Disinterested leadership wants to hear only that everything is OK and does not want to face negative findings. Comparing characteristics of Quality Council X (disinterested) and Quality Council Y (interested), the reasons for success become evident.

A successful effort requires a well-defined plan of action or project timeline that is openly communicated and adhered to. A timeline that includes target dates and key interface points with leadership keeps the project on track and assures that nothing falls through the cracks.

This type of assessment is a lot of work but well worth it *if* leader-

Key Factors for a Successful Assessment	
Quality Council X	*Quality Council Y*
Going through the motions	Real interest and visible commitment
Little communication	Lots of communication
Key Four closed to candid communication	Key Four has open door policy
Criticism taken hard and often rejected	Criticism sought out and taken healthily
Many council meetings canceled or postponed	Council meetings with CRT always honored
Council members not in attendance	Majority of council in attendance
Mind is made up–knows what it wants at the onset–knows all the answers	Has an open mind–interested in learning–continuous improvement mindset
Keeps tight control–just wants a check mark in the box	Empowers the team and supports it by providing resources (time, people and material)
Results oriented	Process oriented
Does not want change	Embraces change
Assessment is the end of the process	Assessment is just the beginning. Becomes ongoing. Repeat in 18 months and tracks change

Figure 10-3

QUALITY NETWORK PROCESS MODEL

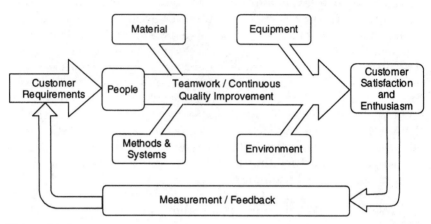

Figure 10-4

ship is serious about changing for the better and is able to create some energy within the organization to make change happen. But how do you know if an assessment will work to bring about change? When you look at assessment from a process model (Fig. 10-4) perspective, you can see that the end is also the beginning.

Use of the Process Model. By design, the leadership report or feedback is intended as the impetus for change in the organization (client satisfaction). Whether and to what extent that feedback is accepted determines the impact the assessment will ultimately have. Environmental factors such as leadership style, union-management relationships, business priorities and practices, and an organization's history will influence not only the impact of the effort but whether to begin an assessment at all (environment). Experiences with other change efforts, past and present, as well as how an organization in general is doing today will also affect the decision (measurement and feedback).

When an organization has sorted through all that, it determines whether or not it wishes to continue. Some choose to exit the process at this point with the final report. Others decide to continue the process. If asked, the communication resource team works with the organization to develop a plan for collecting data and using feedback (customer requirements) that would seem most effective at driving the kinds of changes being sought. The plan includes the kind of information to be collected (material), data collection methods to be used (methods and systems), and the tools that will be needed to pull it off (equipment).

Together with the communication resource team, the organization determines who should be involved in the process and in what way (people). At this point the task is begun. While there are no guarantees, an assessment that reflects the unique personality of an organization, addresses the needs that are important to that organization, and involves leadership has a high probability of success at driving change *if* it is coupled with a well-managed planning and implementation process.

Consider the model of change, shown in Fig. 10-5, developed by David A. Nadler, a behavioral scientist.[3] If energy is created by the feedback generated through assessment and that energy is positively directed, change will occur, provided structures and processes exist to turn energy into action. If any of these elements is missing, the result is likely to be failure.

Assessment Process Benefits. The following questions and their answers attempt to illustrate benefits for all stakeholders in this assessment process:

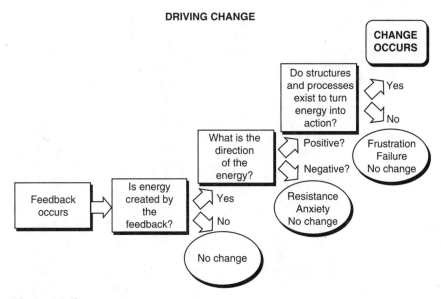

DRIVING CHANGE

Figure 10-5

What's in it for leadership?

- A structured way to "walk the talk"
- Upward, unfiltered communication
- A way to build a supportive environment
- An objective basis for discussing the "real" issues

What's in it for the assessment team?

- Learn how to collect and/or analyze data to plan change
- Serve as a change agent
- Become the "voice of the organization"
- Develop skills and credibility to sustain process
- Continuously improve the process

What's in it for an organization's employees?

- An opportunity to share their ideas and views
- The chance to influence leadership
- A way to get involved in making change happen
- A meaningful way to relate to the Quality Network

What's in it for the representatives of the workers, the UAW, and GM?

- A way to focus the quality council
- An opportunity to bring sparring parties together
- Help! Resources, techniques, direction, and so on
- Energy to sustain change in an organization
- A means of evaluating efforts on multiple fronts aimed at implementing Quality Network principles, practices, and strategies
- A way to begin cultural change
- A process to look at the facts of a situation and make rational decisions

Product Quality Link

Since optimizing a system (GM) requires that all subsystems and processes contribute to achieving the aim of the system, it is fair to ask, "What does an assessment have to do with product or service quality?" The answer is, *everything!*

If you interpret "action" in the four-step communication model to mean build quality products or provide quality services, an organization is on its way to understanding the value of a focused assessment. This process can help leadership understand why quality is and isn't being achieved.

When quality objectives and goals are not being met, leadership is sometimes quick to ask, "Aren't employees committed?" "Don't they understand why quality is so important?" Assessment helps leaders shift their focus away from *who* is the problem to *why* a problem exists and how best to fix it, or *what* needs to be done. Leadership will learn why employees, despite their understanding of the importance of quality and a commitment to achieve it, are unable to do so. They'll also gain insight as to why employees insist leadership is not as committed as they are. With this knowledge, leadership will begin to view the floor or staff organization differently. With the help of the UAW–GM Quality Network Representatives, they will start to see opportunities for practical application of assessment findings in their daily activities. Their knowledge will thus become profound, and their wisdom will be reflected in their behaviors.

Where to from Here?

That was the question asked of 650 UAW–GM Quality Network Representatives at a workshop in Atlanta, Georgia, April 30 to May 2, 1993. Communication resource team members Chris Brandt and Mike Warchuck stated: "First, ask yourself if this is something that could help your organization. If it is, give us a call or link up with one of the resource people listed in the support materials provided. In our team's brief history, we have served many different organizations. From assembly plants to engineering staffs. From office environments to component operations. Plant- and division-level quality councils. The list goes on."

Brandt and Warchuk continued: "Just as our customers have differed in nature, so have their needs. Not surprisingly then, the assessment process has been initiated for a lot of different reasons. Among them:

- To improve plantwide and divisionwide communication efforts
- To develop an understanding of the organization as a total system
- To provide input on developing a strategy for change in an engineering organization
- To evaluate implementation of Quality Network *Beliefs & Values* and action strategies
- To establish a common vision and build teamwork

Effective communication is essential if process management efforts are to succeed. The UAW–GM approach to broad-based support is driven by the belief that we could do a lot better job with communication assessment if we used a joint team of professionals. Atlanta conference attendees were instructed:

> A number of people out there have had a variety of experiences with this process of assessment, most of them good, some bad. We encourage you to link up with people close to home, either geographically or hierarchically speaking. Get their views, share your ideas. Likewise, Communication Resource Team members are present here in Atlanta to answer any questions you might have concerning the assessment process and how it might work for your organization.

Communicating the Quality Network Process

The Quality Network leadership designed a communication approach with several key elements. The first element was a monthly update letter that was sent from the Quality Network leadership to all of the Quality Network Representatives across the company. The newsletter focused on successes and challenges experienced at various locations, as well as general current quality information. The newsletter has since evolved into a publication titled *Knowledge Transfer,* and it combines lessons learned and success stories from the Quality Network, the Suggestion Plan Activity, the Planned Maintenance Leverage Team, and Environmental Activities Staff. It comes out quarterly and is distributed worldwide to Quality Network Representatives, quality councils, PR Directors, Environmental Engineers, the GM Knowledge Center, planned maintenance personnel, the NAO Quality Staff, Suggestion Administrators, and Communication Coordinators as well as top union and management leadership. The size and scope of issues reported on run the gamut. A few examples from the January 1995 issue give the flavor of the publication:

- Quality, Reliability, and Durability (QRD) System Integrity Improvement Teams Using Problem Solving at GM Powertrain Headquarters
- NAO Lansing Car Assembly Body Plant Using Planned Maintenance to Plan for the Future
- NAO Industrial Engineering Improving Paint Circulation Systems Using "POPS," Their Paint Operating and Planning System
- Columbus Inland Fisher Guide Plant Eliminating Use of Methylene Chloride by Developing Alternative Paint Stripping Method Using

Hot Water, Consistent with the Quality Network *Conserve Resources/Prevent Pollution* Action Strategy

Each story contained the process owner or subject matter expert and his or her phone number. Submission of an article signals a willingness on the part of the process owners to respond to inquires and share process and implementation details. The articles themselves are merely snapshots of the work that has been done.

Internal Survey Process

The second element involves surveys of top UAW and GM leadership to monitor implementation progress and to gather feedback on overall quality efforts. The level of trust that has developed within the overall organization is reflected by the candid responses received on the self-assessment surveys that have to be agreed to and signed by the top two management and union representatives (the Key Four) at each location. It is important that we, as leaders of the Quality Network, not use the information as a score card.

At GM we had to break from past behavior and be constant in our belief that internal competition does not serve the system well. Most of all, we had to communicate our position in such a way as to convince those who had been burned in the past that we meant what we said. Assurances of lack of reprisals for candid answers produced an accurate picture of the current environment, technical progress, and implementation efforts at all locations. It is the difference between being the best you can be rather than better than someone else. If you are just trying to be better than the next best, you are letting that person or organization determine the standard. It's how good you can be for yourself, your organization, that drives you to be the leaders.

Is It Really Backsliding?

An interesting phenomenon we have observed from the data is that in some circumstances plant and staffs actually regress in their self-assessment status. The reason we think is simple. It is not that they have fallen back on implementation but rather they have learned more about how far they must go. This learning causes a more realistic appraisal of their progress. Typically, these groups are more vocal and seek help. Assistance can be and is provided in specific, identified areas. Additionally, locations with marked progress and successes are asked to share these with the rest of the organization. Common traits within areas of difficulty identify opportunities for the Quality Network Support Staff to work on.

The fourth element, mentioned earlier in this chapter, was the creation of the *Representative Conversations* videotaped program series of live-on-tape, question-and-answer dialogs. We formulated this design concept at the urging of communication experts who wanted us to push the envelope. We realized we were the ones, ultimately, who would be out in front dependent solely on our faith that honesty is the best policy. If we had the answers, great—we'd share them. If we didn't have the answers, we'd promise to get them in a timely fashion. And, we had been empowered by our respective leadership to lead the Quality Network. The process works. We have had favorable reaction across the board. An interesting added feature is that, since we have made a number of these programs over the years, we meet people all over the corporation who feel that they know us personally. Because of this, we are often approached by strangers, to us, with issues that need to be addressed. The theme of the programs varies: In some cases, the programs are used as a platform for us to respond to current issues; or we might provide timely information relative to the implementation process; or we introduce new training opportunities or contractual changes. Almost always the programs spend a portion of time on current product quality measures. The tapes are designed for the Quality Network Representatives and their quality councils, linking us directly to top joint leadership throughout GM.

Topics from Representative Conversations

Piecing Together the Business Plan. After our initial session taped at the GM Technical Center in Warren, Michigan, we decided to move locations to involve participants from as many GM locations as possible. We traveled to Dayton, Ohio, where General Motors has several component plants as well as a truck assembly plant. We began the discussion with dialog around the significance of the *Beliefs & Values:* Customer Satisfaction through People, Teamwork, and Continuous Quality Improvement. The question "What does being 'full partners in the business' mean?" was a major point for discussion. We talked about the current state of the Quality Network, using our current-state chart to generate thoughts around organizational and cultural transformation. All this led up to a detailed presentation of the General Motors North American Operations business plan. The business plan model is complex, so we built it piece by piece, both figuratively and literally. We had the plan constructed in large, jigsawlike pieces, which we assembled as we explained each stage of the plan. We had fun with the visual concept but were serious in our dissemination of the plan, which had never before been shared with a joint audience in such detail. The fact that one of the presenters was a UAW International Representative as well as a Codirector of the Quality Network was even more amazing. It went well. What is normally a dull and onerous topic became alive. Since a major goal of management is to achieve the business plan objectives, it is essential to garner support and commitment from all participants in the system. Understanding the business plan helped move people to work toward accomplishing its goals.

Pre- and Post-Representatives' Workshops. We have used several *Representative Conversations* to discuss different issues concerning our Quality Network Representatives' workshops, eliciting preference for topics and reporting on feedback issues ranging from high praise to vehement suggestions for continuous improvement. We have had two workshops to date, with a third in the planning stages. The first workshop was held in May 1991; its theme was *Accelerate Implementation of Quality Network.* This first-ever workshop had been postponed from earlier in the year, and rumors were flying about the reason for the postponement. A *Representative Conversations* let us dispel them all; we had had a conflict in dates, plain and simple. The second workshop, *Quality: Our Futures Depend On It*, was held in Atlanta, Georgia, in April 1993. Both events were attended by over 650 union and management Quality Network Representatives. There is always a lot of energy at these events, which generates a lot of questions. *Representative Conversations* has been an excellent vehicle for this purpose. Many questions are submitted to us throughout the course of a workshop, and time does not permit all of them to be addressed on-site. *Representative Conversations* allows leadership to fulfill its obligation and commitment to answer all questions. In some cases, additional information is needed or consultation with interested parties is solicited to provide in-depth answers. As always, inquiries are encouraged, and phone numbers and addresses are provided at the end of each program. These questions are answered on a one-on-one phone call or letter, depending on the nature of the question.

Q&A. It should be surprising to no one that the question-and-answer segments of any presentation or response to any publication elicit the most intriguing and often insightful issues. In the tradition of any American political body, union members are not shy when it comes to pursuing a point. Just as our political leaders must face their public, so must corporate leaders be prepared to face their work force. Management counterparts in a joint arena, such as the Quality Network, have learned much from their union partners, to the betterment of all.

People ask questions because they care, and it is their spirit, after all, that we are trying to engage.

At our Atlanta workshop closing, we opened a Q&A session by listing the issues as they were being raised on a 20-ft screen. The process was simple. Linda Garrison, Administrative Assistant to the Quality Network Directors, was backstage at a computer. As we fielded the questions, we would call out to Linda, and she input them into a computer that was hooked up to a projector which broadcast them onto the screen. We had a lot of fun with the process while at the same time were able to dramatize the importance of this freewheeling discussion. When we had finished, we had our agenda of items to work on for the next several months. The QN Reps knew from past experience that when we told them we would deal with their concerns and ideas, we would.

Action Strategy Updates.   In the beginning of our implementation efforts, 12 "starter strategies" (out of the 38 action strategies in total) were singled out as a priority for action. *Representative Conversations* was used to highlight these strategies and convey the plan for their implementation. It was also important to explain the rationale for their selection.

Since that time various action strategies have come to the fore for attention. We use our video forum to introduce these strategies, have leadership express its support of implementation efforts, and ask subject matter experts to explain the strategies. These presentations often feature corporationwide implementation efforts such as those for the Quality Network Suggestion Plan and Planned Maintenance Implementation. Both of these strategies have great potential to reduce costs, improve safety, and improve quality at General Motors. We even featured one of General Motors' outstanding teachers and presenters, Julie Schell, demonstrating to the organization her approach to assisting nonunion staffs in understanding their role and responsibility in the Quality Network process.

Top Leadership Support.   We traveled to Rochester, New York, and talked about the importance of top leadership commitment to and involvement in the Quality Network with 26 plant leaders: Quality Network Representatives, Chairpersons, Personnel Directors, Local Presidents and Plant Managers. We worked to define *Support for the Employee* and *Top Leadership Commitment and Involvement*, both action strategies of the Quality Network. We also discussed how to more effectively utilize all local UAW–GM joint resources for the implementation of the Quality Network process and what we, as an organization, needed to do to help accelerate implementation of Quality Network to the plant floor.

A later *Representative Conversations* presented the *Ten-Step Implementation Process,* featured in Chapter 11, and its relationship with the four leadership initiatives. Quality council leadership was the targeted audience for this session since it dealt with a documented process to implement the Quality Network at their locations as well as the common focus on closing the product quality gap that pertains to all quality councils. *Representative Conversations* in this case was used as a vehicle to roll out a process for all locations to use to accelerate implementation. The value of using this venue is that everyone hears and sees the same message; it is consistently applied and yet, because it is disseminated at the council's location, leaves room for local discussion and application plans.

Beginning in 1993, for the first time in GM history, CEO and President John F. Smith and UAW Vice President Stephen P. Yokich held a Key Four conference with the top leaders from all the plant locations, divisional and group heads, and additional union and management leadership representing Solidarity House and NAO. As leaders of the Quality Network, we have attended these meetings and often have been presenters as well. We then use *Representative Conversations* as a forum to report out to the field what topics were covered and what decisions were made. This is consistent with our belief in openly sharing information to both transfer knowledge and maintain an atmosphere of trust.

We also use *Representative Conversations* as a communication link between the NAO UAW–GM Quality Council and the rest of the quality council structure on divisional and plant levels. This quality council sets direction and issues a yearly set of objectives that quality councils in the field are expected to accomplish. Progress on these objectives is assessed by the survey discussed earlier. These results, in a macropicture, are reported back to the quality council for review.

Communications Link

We both believe in and are committed to this communication approach, developed by the former Quality Network steering committee and the communication experts in General Motors; it has served to maintain constancy of purpose in both the process and the message. It is extremely important that, once process management is undertaken by an organization, communication regarding its status and direction are communicated immediately and effectively throughout the organization. In a company as large and diverse as General Motors, we feel that this approach has served us well, and we intend to continue in this direction in the future. We intend to move to live broadcast to all quality councils. It is our plan to share current quality data and provide for an unscripted Q&A on any issue raised by our audience.

Leadership Communicates the Vision

The January 15, 1993, telecast warrants further discussion as it put into vivid reality the joint commitment to quality first mentioned almost 6 3 years earlier in the first UAW–GM National Agreement. Jack Smith and Steve Yokich presented a united front in their discussions about the importance of product quality and the Quality Network as General Motors' Total Quality Process. Employees cannot get enough affirmation from their leadership. Again, the prevalent question is always, "What does leadership think? Where do the leaders stand on this issue? Where are we going?" This teleconference went a long way to satisfying these queries.

> JACK SMITH: To all leadership, I think it's important that we all understand the product quality gap. It's important to understand it, who's beating us, and how we improve on that....It's very important for the leadership to be working on the plan to close the gap. The interesting thing about the gap is it's not a steady state. It's a moving target, so it becomes quite difficult. As we start to improve, the other guy is improving at the same time so we have to recognize that in setting our plan to close the gap, it will be moving on us. It's important that we utilize the tools and techniques of the Quality Network; they're there. A lot of time has been spent to develop those techniques and processes, and we need to use them if we're going to win.
>
> STEVE YOKICH: You have to look at where we started and what we were trying to accomplish...by rolling out the strategies. Quite frankly, we've come a long way....I think the difference is that people understand and have the pride to do what has to be done, and so it's right the first time. That's what the Quality Network is about, and that's what quality of product is about....Everybody has got to be a part of the team: the suppliers, everybody with the General Motors' organization, the dealers—they're a major player in this—and the real major player, which is our customer. And so, when I look back to see where we've come from and how we have progressed, we've progressed fairly well. But that isn't good enough to continue, as Jack says, to shoot at that moving target because that target, those that have been doing a good job, they keep moving....And, we've got to keep moving; in fact, catch them and pass them.

Communication Provides the Linkage

Clearly, communication processes are a critical part of establishing an ongoing process management system that encourages teamwork, joint cooperation, and an overall commitment from all parties involved to product and process quality. The UAW–GM process may not be the complete answer; however, the principle of full disclosure and communication of all information in order to secure understanding, commitment, and ultimately action, addresses personal and group goals. The questions of *"Why?" "What must I do?" "What does this mean?"* and *"What's in it for me?"* must be answered to secure teamwork and loyalty. An effective communication process answers these questions and is an essential component in a process management system. Communication is the glue that holds a system together and binds all the parts to the whole while acting as the conduit for ideas, problem solving, support, and understanding.

Notes

1. Jeff Palicki, Suggestion Plan Coordinator, UAW Local 14, Powertrain, Toledo, Ohio, remarks excerpted from a videotaped interview, *Quality Network Suggestion Plan: Legal Issues,* produced for the Quality Network Suggestion Plan Consulting Activity, March 1995.

2. Gary Sova, Suggestion Plan Coordinator, Powertrain, Delta Engine Plant, Lansing, Mich., remarks excerpted from a videotaped interview, *Quality Network Suggestion Plan: Legal Issues,* produced for the Quality Network Suggestion Plan Consulting Activity, March 1995.

3. David A. Nadler, *Feedback & Organization Development: Using Data Based Methods,* Addison-Wesley, Reading, Mass., 1977.

11

Institutionalizing the Process

How do you put it all together? That's the final issue. It doesn't just happen, and no one method will work for everyone. And we recognize that the persistent nature of the quality journey and the continuous improvement mindset means that we will never "be there." At General Motors, we are in the midst of putting it together. On good days we feel we're pretty far along. On bad days we look at the mammoth job the corporation is facing and wonder. Our 1994 End-of-Year Report for UAW represented locations (102 responded by publishing date) on the 1994 Objectives tells us that our locations cover the gamut in terms of implementation progress.

One objective represents the overarching work of implementing GM's total quality process: *Each location to continue to demonstrate balanced and accelerated Quality Network strategy implementation to:*

> *Build a Supportive Environment*—Leaders and the organization focus on meeting the needs of our front-line people through demonstrated values, structures and systems, physical environment, rewards and measurements, job security, and leadership style.
>
> *Create an Organization-wide Customer Focus*—Focus the organization on meeting and exceeding the needs of our internal and external customers: the people impacted by our processes, products, and services.
>
> *Synchronize the Organization*—Utilize a systematic approach to identify and eliminate waste/non-valued-added activities through continuous quality improvement of our products and services.

Detect, Solve, and Prevent Product Quality Problems—Encourage people to surface variation between the voice of the customer and the voice of the process (problems/opportunities), analyze and eliminate the root cause, and implement controls to prohibit recurrence. Constantly repeat this process as the catalyst for continuous quality improvement.

Implementation progress of these leadership initiatives indicates how far along we are in terms of institutionalizing our total quality system and process management techniques and practices. This objective was also included in the 1993 objectives, and comparison of the two end-of-year reports tells us that we are moving in the right direction. Quality councils were asked to evaluate the current state of their location's implementation of the four initiatives on a scale of 0 to 10. Zero would indicate that nothing is happening, and 10 would indicate that the initiative is part of the standard operating system and subject to continuous improvement. Most responses fell slightly higher than the middle of the spectrum, with responses for 1994 generally further toward the 10. We still have those locations in which nothing is happening (0), albeit few, as well as those who feel they have incorporated the initiatives into their daily business life (10), also few. Some locations, judging their progress in *Build a Supportive Environment,* seemed to have lapsed from 10s and 9s to the middle of the spread. However, this regression is not alarming when verbatims are examined and it becomes obvious that some locations who thought "they were there" have become more critical and now realize there are more gains to be made.

Institutionalizing the Quality Network, in General Motors' case, or a total quality system in general seems to require two major thrusts that often come squarely in opposition to each other: facing and removing obstacles and identifying and putting key success factors in place. In many, if not all, cases this means unlearning old ways and trying on new and often uncomfortable approaches to leadership.

Barrier No. 1

Dr. Deming is quick to point out that many of the ills facing organizations today result from poor management. He is not saying that managers are incompetent or do not work hard but is rather pointing out that the lack of "systems thinking" in an organization leads to poor management.

Anyone who has ever made a presentation to "sell" a new idea knows the obstacle course you must go through to justify capital expenditures. Many good and necessary ideas fail to become reality because it may be difficult to meet predetermined return-on-investment (ROI) objectives. How do you put a price tag on having a good work environment conducive to necessary change?

Most every obstacle can be traced to the lack of a systems approach to managing the business or the lack of a process designed to address concerns. Problems with middle managers tend to inhibit many efforts because there is no process in place to truly analyze and address their concerns. An assessment process is necessary to measure communication efforts and perceptions. Leaders must understand the various strategies of their total quality process so they can ask the right questions and utilize the various strategies themselves. For the most part, it is a massive learning effort.

Developing New Habits

Have you ever tried to change a lifelong habit? It's very difficult to make the change and even more difficult to establish new habits that prevent us from going right back to our old way of doing things. Organizations have the same problem. Past ways of doing things tend to inject themselves into new efforts at every opportunity. Strengths can be built upon, but weaknesses must be "weeded" out if a change in the system is to be effective. Breaking from the past is imperative if meaningful change to a total quality system is to take place. Sustaining a new process or system becomes a critical and ongoing effort that requires much commitment by top leadership. Early implementation stages become ends in themselves if long-term commitment falters.

The Work Begins

The first critical period emerges after the initial excitement and hoopla begins to wear off. As efforts begin to prepare necessary training, based on the best practices available as benchmarked inside and outside the organization, those not involved in the development process tend to drift and waver.

Institutionalizing the process begins in earnest at this point. It is important for leadership to institute ongoing, continuous reports on development and directives concerning expectations during these initial efforts. Access to information being gathered by the development teams must be readily available and advice given as to how preparations can be made for ongoing implementation. For many organizations there is a time lag between initial announcements of the process and the ability to deliver promotional and training materials. If this lull in implementation is not anticipated and plans are not made for continuing communication and involvement, efforts will come to a standstill and interest will decline.

This happened in General Motors' implementation efforts. The initial meetings of 1987 generated a lot of excitement that evolved into frustration as the time lag between unveiling the new process and having training materials available for use dragged on.

In 1990 when we were appointed to lead the process, momentum was at a low point; skepticism replaced excitement. Anticipated leadership changes in both organizations had left many wondering what direction the Quality Network would take. One challenge that remains today is weathering leadership transition. Particularly in an organization such as ours, where balanced leadership depends on top leadership at the union and in management working together, the replacement of one leader can have a devastating effect. In some cases the joint program just disappears. In other instances, inertia sets in as each side tries to sort out the implications of the change. In the case of the Quality Network (emphatically not a program, but a management process), a sequence of leadership changes has ultimately brought an infusion of energy and a new way of looking at things. Yes, we had a period of uncertainty, but persevering through that time brought its own rewards.

Withstanding Leadership Changes

We have had many opportunities to gain character and sustain relationships as the UAW and General Motors Corporation both have experienced leadership transition. From April 1990:

- UAW Vice President and Director of the GM Department retired, Donald R. Ephlin. He was the UAW Codesigner of the UAW–GM Quality Network and Cochair of the corporate quality council. He was replaced by a more traditional Union Leader, Stephen P. Yokich. Steve Yokich faced reelection challenges in 1993.

- Lloyd Reuss, former President of GM, became Cochairperson of the corporate quality council following Robert Stempel. He later retired from General Motors.

- Former GM President and Chairperson of the Board Robert Stempel was the GM Codesigner of the Quality Network. He resigned as Chairperson and was replaced by John Smale, an outside board member.

- Jack Smith was named Chief Executive Officer and President of General Motors. He immediately formed the Strategy Board to oversee North American Operations (NAO) and became the Cochair of the NAO UAW–GM Quality Council with Steve Yokich.

- Plagued by heavy losses in NAO, "slow" progress by the UAW–GM Quality Network caused key management leaders to "hedge their bets" and develop a separate production system containing 17 of the same strategies as the Quality Network process, referred to as "synchronous manufacturing."

- Under the direction of Jack Smith and Steve Yokich, the UAW–GM Quality Network was refocused from development to actual implementation at the plant floor level. Constant monitoring and refocusing are necessary to continually improve the process and maintain support and commitment.

Both Sides Reacted in the Same Way

The value of having a total quality system overrode the differences new union and management leadership felt in 1990. Both organizations needed to fill the Quality Network leadership positions vacated by Bob Boruff, who left to head up manufacturing activities at Saturn, and Jim Wagner, who retired after almost three decades as a leader in the International Union. Leadership of both parties reacted in a similar fashion. Each identified new leaders for the Quality Network who had had extensive labor relations backgrounds. We shared a common language and operating procedures for working together. Indeed, we had worked together in the past in a different venue. Working together in the past meant that we were part of a team of opposing points of view that had to come together and fashion a mutually agreed upon labor agreement.

Renew the Process

As we took our new assignments, we both recognized the prevailing uncertainty and immediately set out to jump-start the Quality Network. We pressed for the resources to finish development of the training for the various action strategies with an announced time line for the release of each. Open communication lines were established, and our personal promotional efforts with top company and union leaders and their secondary leadership rejuvenated the process, renewing enthusiasm and support.

Mutual Understanding of Roles and Responsibilities

We, as leaders of a joint endeavor, had to be certain we were speaking the same language, that it meant the same thing, and that we were communicating the same message. This was also true for the base of understanding from which we were to operate. We had new jobs for new leadership in our organizations. Bob Stempel, Lloyd Reuss, and Steve Yokich had been in their respective positions less than a year. Shortly after we came onboard the Quality Network, our leadership clarified for us that a system based on "codetermination" would not work in General Motors, at least not in the near term. The original designers of the process had a vision of the Quality Network as General Motors' business system, and everything that GM did was to fall under the purview of that system. The leadership of General Motors is still sorting out the implications of this far-reaching approach with the unions as ultimate responsibility to run the company rests with management. Each day we are getting a little closer, but we are not there yet. Saturn's approach to codetermination has served them well and may be a model for the rest of the company. Saturn had the luxury of starting a new company with a "clean sheet of paper." They had a new product, new tools and equipment, new processes benchmarked against the best in the world and "new" employees, willing to give up historical rights to go to this new company. The people were right, the product was right, and most importantly the attitude was right. Saturn will be successful, and the rest of GM and the UAW will learn from that success.

In order to resolve the issue of codetermination, we worked together with the Quality Network steering committee to design our current-state model (see Fig. 5-7) to help the organizations, GM and the UAW, better understand where we currently stood on that subject. This model has served us well. It allows both parties to be comfortable with the areas of jointness and the areas that are under their respective purview. In a partnership of any kind, especially a new one, it is important that each partner not feel threatened, that his or her sphere of authority not be perceived as usurped. General Motors and the

UAW are no exceptions. We fall back on this exercise often when we are creating a new team or are bringing together disparate entities and ask them to work together.

Communication Begins
Day 1

The moment direction has been set for a new strategy or process, its basic premises must be made available to all the organization so that everyone begins to understand the changes this will bring in their area. Consider our new relationship as described above. We had to build understanding so that we could work together (commitment to action). The communcation model served as a way to organize information to create that understanding.

If a problem-solving strategy is to be implemented organization-wide, as we have stressed in both our 1993 and 1994 objectives, then the minute the decision is finalized, it must be communicated throughout the organization. Those with no established problem-solving process or those utilizing some other process are being asked to prepare for full implementation of the one agreed-upon process throughout the organization. Within General Motors we had over 66 problem-solving processes operable and successful to a greater or lesser degree. There was a lot of ownership. There was also a lot of confusion as cross-functional groups tried to work together. We needed a common system. Communicating this to the organization was critical to our problem-solving goals.

In instances like this, some will argue that their process is better, and it may be for their particular unit. However, looking at the organization as a system, top leadership's job is to determine what is right for the whole and then assure compliance throughout the organization. As leaders see a long-term commitment to standardized best practices throughout the organization, implementation efforts will continue to gain momentum. One key factor is the strategy or best-practice team that helped design the common system. This points out the need to place the organization's best resources on the strategy development teams. The people resources should reflect the ultimate users of the strategy in order to be cognizant of that group's requirements and, conversely, be able to assure that group that their requirements have been considered in the final design. If respected among colleagues and permitted to seek out the best practices of other organizations, the development team's efforts will be supported.

Make Communications Work

Open and honest communications convey an attitude. The information that is passed along almost becomes secondary. The manner used to communicate the information is critical. And, in communicating to a large and diverse population, timing truly is everything. In the case of developing best practices, if people know up front that their requirements are being considered, they will give the new design a chance. If they feel something is being shoved down their throats, the new design hasn't a chance of succeeding, even if it is the best idea in the world.

Grasping this simple concept is particularly important in a joint environment. Put yourself in a union leader's place. If you were told of a crisis as it began to unfold and asked to help look for a solution to keep the plant from closing or the company from going out of business, would you refuse to get involved, or try to make matters worse? How much better a solution it is to invite the unions to be a partner, keeping them abreast of financial conditions and why certain decisions are made, seeking their input and help during difficult times. Disagreements may still result, but they will not be as antagonistic and will result in opportunities that can be win-win for both sides. The "secret" information withheld from the union in traditional organizations is almost always revealed anyway. "Secret" memos turn up, conversations are overheard, umpire hearings require revealing of "secret" facts, legal challenges require revelation.

The Program-of-the-Month Syndrome

Good intentions, great ideas, come and go in organizations like General Motors. A new leader comes into a department and has to make his or her position clear. This may mean doing away with one process in favor of a process the new leader introduces. There are business management styles, fads, and gurus that are hot today and gone tomorrow. They are embraced with enthusiasm until the next silver bullet comes along that will do the job better, faster, and cheaper. Against this comes an idea whose time has truly come. Leaders with long-term vision understand its worth and begin integration efforts. How do these efforts differ from previous programs in the minds of the work force? They don't. If this new order is to be successful, leadership must be steadfast in its support and constant in its actions. If not, the new order will struggle under the burden of past failures and unforgotten broken promises. By its previous behavior, leadership creates this enormous obstacle, cynicism.

Mixed Signals

As we have mentioned in earlier chapters, General Motors' efforts to adopt quality of work life principles lacked leadership and, for the most part, failed. Such efforts were viewed by many as nothing more than a mechanism that delivered fans to hot workers on the plant floor and stopped there. Many union people thought it was designed to keep them quiet and divert their real concerns. Leo VanHouten, who coordinates UAW members of the Quality Network Implementation Support Team, sums it up this way: "It was a good people process that had no meat, no tools to take it to the next step." Its downfall served a stunning blow to those who believed in cooperative team building and participative management. It was a good idea that was not supported or sustained. Hence, a major piece of history added to the roadblock to jointness that was being built.

Fiero

In 1983 Pontiac began producing a hot little two-passenger sports car, the Fiero. Fieros were assembled in an old plant (built in 1927) in Pontiac, Michigan, that had formerly housed Fisher Body. Both the style and the design specifications—it was made of fiberglass—required new technology and an experienced work force. The Fiero was innovative in other ways. The plant was a model of union-management cooperation and the spirit of teamwork. The Fiero production system incorporated total quality techniques and systems. The Fiero was a new product, and there were problems, but they were addressed jointly.

Innovation spilled over into the labor relations arena as well. The UAW local agreement at Fiero was a "living agreement," open-ended and unique to Pontiac, different from the other "mainstream contracts" of Local 653. The UAW leadership had to stretch; many were skeptical of this nontraditional working arrangement. GM management met the union equally when it came to rewriting work procedures. The Plant Manager abandoned his traditional staff meetings and formed a joint group administrative team which was the forerunner to today's joint quality councils headed by the Key Four. The difference at Fiero was that, unlike most locations today that still have management staff meetings, all business was conducted in the joint meetings. The administrative plan had three levels: the Superintendent level which included the Shop Committeepersons, the Floor Supervisor level that included the District Committeepersons, and plant floor teams with elected leaders. These three levels had overlapping representation that served as the communication mechanism that drove information from the plant floor to the top joint leadership. Management believed so strongly in teamwork that it shut the plant down once a week for 30-minute team meetings, running only $7\frac{1}{2}$ hours of production. The work force policed quality. There were never more than 40 cars, one hour's production, in repair. Should more need attention, the line was shut down to prevent further defects from being produced. The skepticism of the International Union was met with equal suspicion from GM corporate management. Leo VanHouten was at Fiero and was instrumental in implementing the Fiero process. He believes that, for both entities, "Fiero was like trying to fit a round peg in a traditional square hole."

The plan worked. The Fiero operating philosophy prevailed in spite of changing plant managers five times in three years with numerous personnel directors. What happened? There is heated debate about why the car did not sell. Some say the public voted with their pocketbooks. Some say the car was never marketed properly. The argument is not important here. When the plant lost the product, the plant was shut down. New products were assigned to other plants, and the cooperative, participative Fiero production team was scattered into other GM organizations or were laid off. Once again, a clear message was sent. The Fiero work force was not rewarded for its innovation and joint groundbreaking working style. Why would any other organization go out on a limb to pursue a cooperative work environment? Is it any wonder that when the Quality Network appeared on the scene, many throughout the organization believed it was just another program-of-the-month, and a risky one at that? Surely history seems to support this point of view.

Happily, the baggage from incidents such as these was not carried by most ex-Fiero workers. Instead, they are to be found in many Quality Network activities and leadership positions throughout the union. The spirit of the Fiero experience has found a home at the Quality Network. As former Director of the Quality Network (currently with Worldwide Purchasing Production, Control and Business Process Management) Derryl Barringer put it, "Once you get into this stuff, you can never get out; you can never go back."

What Goes Around

On April 14, 1995, the UAW and GM unveiled an innovative labor contract that will give new life to the Wilmington, Delaware, Corsica plant
that was scheduled to close in 1996. A UAW official who asked not be
cited complained that in the past the company had closed many factories that had implemented innovative agreements: "The agreement
shows...that the two sides can cooperate in innovative ways to save
2,500 high-paying U.S. jobs....The agreement resembles local contracts
the UAW signed with GM in the 1980s at the Fiero plant in Pontiac and
the S-10 truck plant Shreveport, Louisiana."[1]

Trust One Another

Labor unions are only an obstacle if an organization is unwilling to
trust that union leaders and workers will make rational decisions or
there is a hidden agenda that is less than honorable. Undoubtedly,
some will think they know a case where unions struck and a company
went out of business. In such instances the union was probably not
kept abreast of the deepening financial crisis and certainly was not
invited to assist in looking for a solution early in the crisis.

Establishing the trust necessary to allow union leaders to become
part of the decision-making process can revitalize an organization.
Most labor leaders rise in the labor union ranks in much the same way
as managers rise within corporations. They work hard, are recognized
as leaders by their peers, and must be able to manage a large group of
workers with diverse views. If they and the workers they represent are
invited to become part of the business process, unity and teamwork
can flourish. The organization gains the expertise and resources available to a large labor organization and the labor union can better represent its members by having input into decisions that affect their members. Communication is a critical ingredient to making this happen.

The Importance of One
Process Management
System

It is absolutely critical that an organization establish one overarching
process management system, with its related specific strategies, subsystems and subprocesses, as the single, consistent management process to
be used throughout the organization. Here we can argue semantics and

will never satisfy everyone. However, we offer our understanding as the basis from which we operate. Processes receive inputs, add value, and produce an output that is designed to satisfy predetermined customer requirements. A system is the relationship of processes, how they are tied together. A system must have an aim or purpose. When that is determined, the processes that go into the system can be identified. A system cannot be divided. If this is attempted, the system will be destroyed and the aim diminished or unfulfilled. A vehicle, as a system, has the aim of moving or transporting someone from one place to another. The powertrain system within the vehicle is made up of a number of processes working in harmony so that the engine runs efficiently, effectively, and in a timely manner. If this system is taken out of the vehicle and fired up, it will run. The vehicle will not. The vehicle needs all of its subsystems to meet its aim. They must work together as one for they are, in fact, part of one system. Therefore, it is vital that everyone within the system understand the system and management's process for directing the system, running the business. Once committed to one process for running the business, management begins the process of institutionalizing change throughout the organization. Again, in our case, we have partners along the way: the unions, dealer organization, suppliers, the board, and the like.

The immediate advantages of this commitment are many. Training is standardized and results in lowering material and resource costs. Movement of people within the organization requires much less break-in and training time. If benchmarked properly, immediate human environment, efficiency, and productivity improvements result from using the best of the best processes. Continuous improvement procedures must be built into the overall process to allow for small incremental improvements suggested by any group or individual which increase ownership and commitment. Common processes link the entire organization as one team and permit rapid communication using terms and models that all are familiar with. Innovation and breakthroughs at the divisional and group level become constructive input for use by the entire system as common processes link various groups at all stages of the process. Communication within the organization takes a giant leap forward as the successes of common systems and processes are shared. Obstacles become opportunities for improvement, and an optimism permeates all that is done. A sense of long-term purpose, trust, and faith in the system builds cohesiveness and boosts morale. Changes and modifications are made in the initial planning process rather than through costly engineering changes and warranty.

"Full Partners" Includes Nonrepresented Salaried Workers

Staffs of designers, engineers, and financial specialists are sometimes left out of process management efforts, resulting in the process being viewed as a "blue-collar" program. This suboptimizes improvement efforts and is a major factor in dividing an organization's work force. When staff people have little or no understanding of union people, and union people have no understanding of staff people, the system cannot work cohesively to attain its vision, customer satisfaction and enthusiasm in our case. Process management must address traditional white-collar areas as well. Interaction between departments and groups must be managed to reduce redundancies and non-value-added competitive efforts. Complex design processes with critical exit criteria between phases require decision processes to ensure that design improvements are made early in the process, on paper, rather than as costly engineering changes on final products. Standard processes, such as design of experiments, facilitate identification of major flaws and systematic resolution.

The environment in staff and technical areas is as important as it is on the plant floor. Adequate tools, lighting, materials, and so on, are resources that enable staffs to accomplish their tasks in an efficient and healthful way. Trusting and empowering people to fulfill their responsibilities is critical. These so-called soft issues are as important as the technical processes in motivating and empowering people but are often overlooked.

We hear a lot about bureaucratic bloat and usually blame those associated with seemingly senseless and wasteful paperwork that swells delivery time. If you examine each process in the context of the system it is a part of, it is easy to see how the situation got so out of control. First of all, control is usually an issue. How many signatures does it really take to OK an expense report? If there is trust in an organization, and a simple process to follow, do you really need 20 people to check up to see that all is in place and no one is cheating the company? The number is hypothetical but, unfortunately, not improbable. When the check is late and the employee, the customer in this instance, is late in paying a Master Card bill, who benefits? Not the company, not the individuals in the payment chain who are probably the recipients of complaining phone calls, and certainly not the employee. And, who hears about this? The point is that the service-support systems of an organization are critical to the organization and need the same consideration and management attention. The opportunity for improvements on many levels is endless.

Continuous Improvement Mindset

An obstacle that seems to crop up overnight is competitors' improvements that tend to make other systems or processes obsolete. This is why total quality embraces the continual improvement mindset as an ongoing, evolving renewal process. An integral part of this philosophy is a continuous improvement loop that takes seriously every suggestion. It encourages a process that permits anyone in the organization to submit ideas for continuous improvement in a prescribed way. Once submitted, review, approval, and implementation procedures should produce rapid injection into the system and into all training materials. Notification procedures in place ensure that all personnel are familiar with updates. In General Motors this process is our Quality Network Suggestion Plan, which has recently been expanded to include some employees who previously were not allowed to participate. Since the changes, we have had significant gains in the number of suggestions, the number of adoptions, and the benefits to the corporation. Leadership stressed the importance of the program by including its implementation as one of the five Quality Network Objectives for 1993. In the *End-of-Year Report* response to the new plan was favorable. All parties benefit. As one report indicated, "Successfully and totally implemented in July 1993. Our GM savings of $12.9 million in 1994 resulted in awards to employees of $831,000."[2] Or another, "Fully implemented as of June 13, 1994. Program is running very well. There has been a huge increase in employee involvement."[3]

Maintaining a Customer Focus

Many quality improvement efforts fail because the entire process is focused on cost savings or production increases rather than customer satisfaction. Initial efforts must truly focus everyone in the organization on customer satisfaction. In today's consumer environment, quality, reliability, and durability are more important than reasonable differences in cost considerations. Though of critical importance, costing criteria must be examined in light of quality, reliability, and durability considerations. Process management will bring cost savings, and it is important to understand that such savings should not just be salted away as profits. Savings should bring about investment in new products, machinery, equipment, and people. If employees perceive that their efforts do not result in a better working environment, increased wages, better benefits, better products, more training, and input into the decision-making process, their contributions will wane.

Likewise, if customers do not benefit by receiving better products with fewer flaws, they will take their business elsewhere. It is important that each person in the organization understands that he or she has a personal customer and an ultimate customer that he or she must please. The personal customer is the next person, department, and so on that benefits from an individual's efforts. The extended or ultimate customer is the recipient of the final product or service. This focus on the customer, internal and ultimate, must be central to all efforts.

Voice of the Customer

Establishing "one process" that is developed by all the stakeholders in an organization breeds teamwork, continuous improvement, efficiency, and people-oriented processes that assure overall success. Dr. Deming would point out that, even if the right processes are in place, an organization must be working on the "right things" in order to be successful. Systems theory must extend beyond processes and methods into product or service determination and development at their earliest conception. Meeting customer requirements obligates management to have a clear picture of the customer in context of his or her environment. Data on the total picture allow us to predict where the customer will want to be down the road. No one asked for air bags per se before they were conceived. Customers have always wanted to drive a safer automobile. Chrysler was able to predict that customers would buy a vehicle with a safety device, once they knew about it. And timing, communication, and even serendipity have a lot to do with it. General Motors was putting its efforts into the antilock braking system, which has proven to be a "must have" in automobiles today. But the air bags got the glory because they came out first, and Chrysler understood its public and announced to the world that their vehicles would have them. Serendipity entered in when a fateful accident took place that totaled two cars whose drivers were protected by the actions of their vehicles' air bags. The issue is not between air bags and ABS.

The issue is that one company understood its customers and anticipated their needs.

Wants, Needs, Requirements, and Expectations

Ian Bradbury, a resident General Motors statistician and follower of Deming's teachings, cautioned us recently at a meeting concerning customers and their needs. He reminded us of the difference between an addicted person's perceived needs and actual needs. Not always is it prudent to give the customer what he or she asks for. It's a delicate balancing act. Often people in authority think they know what you need and put things into motion, totally missing the mark and, even worse, tampering. The expression, "I'm from central office and I'm here to help" elicits groans every time it is uttered. Decisions concerning the customer, both internal and ultimate, must be data-driven and made in context with the big picture fully in view. The most meticulous implementation plans may be followed, but if the process is not directed at working on the right things, an organization may still fail.

Active, Involved Leadership

Institutionalizing a total quality system is dependent upon and finds its greatest champions and roadblocks in its key success factor, leadership. Leadership must be out front: Establish the vision, understand and manage the total system, support and empower the work force. One voice, consistent behavior, unwavering commitment. Yet, in spite of the fact that the benefits of common systems theory are innumerable, many organizations at the slightest provocation retreat to old routes of successes, usually driven by the desire for personal success at the expense of the team. This retreat or reliance on past, outdated processes is stemmed by the leader who shows an active part in designing, teaching, and being a steward of the system as we have explained. Institutionalizing the process requires top leadership to become familiar with every aspect of the new process and to communicate future plans through the new language and models. Every decision affords the opportunity to show a steadfast commitment to process management. News releases and other public events can bring about an awareness to the general public of the benefit this new process is to them. At GM, training employees at every level involves them in the new process and familiarizes them with its language and models. This requires a substantial early investment of resources, but one that will reap long-term dividends.

Leadership can use seasonal slow periods or times of downturn to offer training to large groups of employees at a time. It is important that all employees be exposed to the process. Initial exposure may be through overview workshops offered to employees over an extended period of time. This overview should establish the organization's commitment to people, its foundational values, overall objectives, and the total commitment of top leadership to total quality management. Subsequent training can dwell on the strategies of the process and, in the case of General Motors, on those strategies that meet an immediate need such as those directly linked to product quality or service improvement. As people are trained in the new process and strategies, implementation resources come into play to carry application to the plant floor level. Charts, worksheets, posters, announcements, meeting agendas, and every written document or oral presentation should reflect the verbiage and models of the new strategies. When problems occur, the single, organization-wide problem-solving process kicks into action to ultimately eliminate the problem while containing it in the near term. When a new line or operation is planned, those in charge should make it very apparent that all the applicable strategies from the new process are being utilized to assure safety, quality, efficiency, and so on. The opportunity to provide input resulting in improvements in all areas of the operation and the use of common tools and techniques begin to assure everyone that the new process is here to stay. Start-up efforts should be delayed until everyone is certain that the process will produce the desired quality and service expected. If it is not right, it should not be approved.

Sharing As Part of a System

Institutionalizing the process requires a sharing of successes and missed opportunities throughout the organization for organizational learning. Barriers built to protect a department's, shift's, plant's, division's, or staff's successes from being copied or emulated must be broken down so that they can, indeed, be available to others to learn from. The same is true of protecting any group from the revelation of mistakes that have taken place and their ramifications. Fear in an organization leads to this kind of thinking. Rather, the rest of the organization needs to benefit from both positive and negative experiences. Plant visits, shared train-the-trainer sessions, written success stories in the organizational newsletters, and every other means available effectively spread the successes achieved in any given location. Problem-solving experiences offer lessons learned and, in many cases, solutions found. When leadership expects and rewards this open information sharing, "kingdom building" will no longer be tolerated.

Supervisors likewise must be encouraged to relinquish the tight reigns of control traditionally used to manage people and to promote a decision-sharing attitude for which they should be rewarded. Middle management must be assured that the joint decision-making process is preferred and is not a threat to their existence. If an employee's decision does not meet expectations, the situation should be reviewed to avoid recurrence. There is seldom a valid reason to assign blame and inflict reprisals.

Removing Fear

Fear has to be driven out of the workplace if employees and middle managers are going to truly accept a participative approach to total quality management. No one functions to the best of his or her ability when constantly second-guessing decisions due to fear of being criticized. Kathleen D. Ryan, author of *Driving Fear Out of the Organization*, was featured at our 1991 Quality Network Representatives' Workshop in Detroit, Michigan. Her presentation helped us all understand why changing an organization is so difficult. She defined fear as "feeling threatened by possible repercussions due to speaking up about work-related concerns."[4] And then she added that the "undiscussable" results from fear, that is, "an issue or problem not talked about with those necessary to its solution."[5] In our efforts to accelerate implementation of our total quality process we felt compelled to build an understanding of the power and immobilizing effects fear can have. Fear of repercussion inhibits a person's willingness to take risks, make decisions, make suggestions for improvement, and acknowledge or face problems. Fear creates an environment of "them versus us," feeds the rumor mill, inspires turf battles, and stifles open communication. In essence, fear is probably the root of all the roadblocks and barriers we encounter both on a grand scale and in small, daily activities. Fear constrains healthy relationships.

Fear acts out as a threat to individual and organizational behavior. Probably the most obvious for a work environment is the threat to job security. How is fear passed on from one person to another, one group or team to another? Through personal experience or the experiences of others, events that have occurred, assumptions and individual interpretations, and finally traditional stereotypes and associated behaviors. The primary goal of creating a supportive environment is to elevate fear in all its manifestations.

Kathleen Ryan has developed a "cycle of mistrust" that simply and powerfully depicts the relationship between a supervisor and employee that helps to foster fear in the workplace. This same depiction holds true for top management and their subordinates and union and management leadership. Figure 11-1 is an adaptation of Ms. Ryan's cycle, as adjusted for a union-management relationship.

Leadership is responsible for breaking the cycle of mistrust. Trust has to begin somewhere, sometime. Building a Supportive Environment is supported by a strategy, Cooperative Union-Management Relations, which strives to address this destructive condition. It seeks to break down stereotypes. By focusing on improving processes, and not on finding fault, the organization is mobilized to attack this distrust problem. Behaviors that seek to blame, make excuses, undermine others in order to enhance oneself, control the information flow, exclude certain individuals from decision making, and constantly voice cynical, suspicious opinions have no validity and hence no value

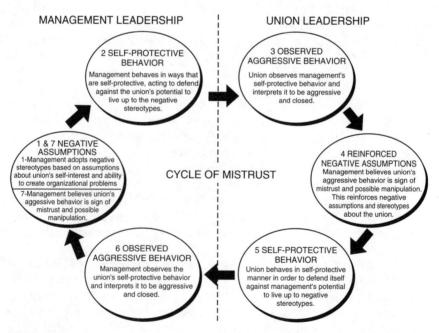

Figure 11-1

when a process is evaluated and not a person. Leadership must spearhead the transition toward process management by first and foremost being a role model for the organization. It's nontraditional, but it must be done.

Empowering people to pursue the right thing does not free them from responsibility, but it does allow them to feel they can make rational decisions in circumstances when their expertise can make a difference. In many traditional companies, if a worker notices a hole missing in a part, he or she may continue to run the defective piece if he or she fears being criticized for loss of production over such an item. One day a supervisor may stop the job, but the next, would keep it running. If the employee knows he or she is not expected, under any circumstances, to knowingly continue to run a bad part, and the supervisor supports this, the fear is gone. The employee stops the machine and gets a repairperson, or the supervisor, when this occurs.

It is important for top leadership to encourage middle managers and employees. Plant visits, letters of encouragement, quality awards, teamwork awards, and so on are some excellent means to let people know how you feel about the job they are doing. Video messages to middle managers and employees from top leadership are an inexpensive but effective way to communicate in a large organization. Telling people what is expected of them drives fear out and empowers people to make decisions that align with top leadership's directives.

Union Considerations

In labor union–represented shops, total quality management efforts can be implemented without labor union support, but they will fall far short of expected goals and potential. Labor union leaders need not be an obstacle if sincere efforts are made to include them as partners in the business. Labor law grants them leadership rights with their members; therefore, they do have a say in how the business is run. This is a large pill for many traditional management leaders to swallow, but it is a simple fact that in today's environment labor strife decreases if a company respects the labor union organization as an equal. Many times stockholders, suppliers, and the general public are kept abreast of company efforts while labor leaders are ignored.

Unions are reactive organizations by their very nature. They cannot, in most circumstances, lead the company in the direction it chooses to go. Traditional companies decide the direction they are going to go and, with little or no opportunity given to the union for input, act on their decisions. Unions react with grievances if the action violates existing contract provisions. Other than that, traditional union behavior dictates a "noninvolvement" attitude. Traditional behavior on the part of both parties plays itself out during contract negotiations, at which time unions will demand more restrictive contract provisions with stiffer penalties. In the most serious instances, unions will ask their members to withhold their labor. Final settlement of the issues rarely pleases both sides.

With the Union Onboard

Where labor unions represent employees, a key to success in institutionalizing the process lies in inviting labor union leaders to be real partners in the day-to-day operations of the organization. International officers at the union's national headquarters must be kept abreast of company plans. This means financial data as well as operations plans. Whether all information can be "on the record" or not depends upon the political atmosphere within the union and the information to be shared. According to former Ford CEO Donald Petersen, step 1 of the power of employee involvement is to "open up the books."[6] Necessary information on "where you stand, what customers think of the products, and why you are asking for help. You have got to give your employees a taste of what your company is up against."[7] Union leaders need this type of information in order to assist in implementing new processes. During a wave of plant closings at General Motors, Vice President of the United Auto Workers Union and Director of its General Motors Department Steve Yokich stated to leaders that "we want to be part of the solution....A union that cannot change will not survive." International Union of Electrical Workers (IUE) Secretary/Treasurer Ed Fire has supported joint efforts permitting members' input into business practices affecting their lives. At the 1989 and 1992 United Auto Workers Union International Convention, opposition to participation in joint processes was soundly defeated. Efforts to restrict further joint participation with employers is not supported by union membership. These progressive attitudes by union leadership are based on having information available supporting the need for changes in business practices so that job security, safety, and future participation in decisions affecting its membership is assured. Joint participation must not only be designed to keep union leaders involved but must provide benefits for union members if change is to be successfully implemented and supported. To say to union leaders that they should encourage their members to be actively involved in total quality management efforts that eliminate jobs and do not improve environmental conditions like safety and participative efforts is ridiculous. Common sense says that support for long-term total quality management efforts must address issues such as growing the business to provide jobs, efforts to assure long-term job security, health, safety, and ergonomic improvements, additional benefits, and better wages. The fundamental issue of job security is key to successful implementation of a total quality system:

> UAW President Owen Bieber, in a speech given in 1988, identified job security as "the most important thing workers want from workplace participation....They don't want to contribute their ideas about how to produce more efficiently only to see their co-workers thrown out onto the street. And they don't want to be told they are part of one big, happy family or one big team only to discover that daddy is moving their work out from under them because he can get it done cheaper somewhere else."[8]

Negotiations of contracts can be held on a win-win basis, improving quality and efficiency while benefiting employees and the union organizations involved. Costly labor battles can be avoided if companies realize they must respect labor organizations the same as they want to be respected by their workers. Mutual respect and mutual gain can forge a partnership without either side giving up their roles and responsibilities. Union officials can and must maintain their strong role as workers' representatives. Management leadership can remain strong and effective and not compromise their roles as company representatives. However, both can work together on issues that help everyone involved. Some of the oldest negotiated joint programs such as apprenticeship, health and safety, and employee assistance programs have proven this point. Quality improvement efforts can benefit all parties involved as can joint participative management efforts.

Build through Teamwork and Joint Action

Forging partnerships with unlikely parties seems to be a characteristic of total quality management. Adversarial relationships often evolve to allegiances over time. A relationship that has long been lacking in cooperation to the detriment of both parties is that between the Skilled Trades and production workers. Skilled Tradespersons and production workers must be encouraged to work together in ways that support each other. Skilled Tradespersons should be encouraged and empowered in assisting production workers in better job design and minute changes that fine-tune an operation. Likewise, production workers should be encouraged and empowered to assist Skilled Tradespersons in finding flaws and quality problems and their solutions. This relationship can be a big obstacle if each is not encouraged to work together as partners and permitted to implement changes they feel are necessary for the operation to produce quality parts. One of the reasons that planned maintenance programs have failed in the past is that such programs were considered just for maintenance and just for the trades within maintenance. At Adrian Delphi-ILS they tried implementation a couple of times, and it did not succeed. It was when they realized that it was a "whole-plant strategy" and engaged all the stakeholders that the strategy took hold.

Sourcing

Sourcing of parts and subcontracting services can be a concern if management is shrinking its work force while at the same time sourcing or subcontracting work to outside firms. Job security heads the list among workers' concerns. Layoffs create a very difficult atmosphere for implementation of quality efforts that are perceived as the reason for the layoffs or downsizing. If outside suppliers can do the job at a lower price with higher quality, the opportunity presents itself to ask employees' assistance to reduce this advantage and keep the work. Utilization of vacant floor space, unused equipment, or any unused capacity is an opportunity to grow the business and use idle assets while providing job security to the existing work force. It is a fact that job security is the foundation for the relationship between the organization and workers and their labor unions. How the job security issue is handled determines the quality of the relationship and resulting behaviors. If a worker believes he or she is being used by the company to get rid of jobs, cooperation and teamwork haven't a chance. Growing the business opportunities provides key areas for establishing cooperative relations and challenging both parties to creative and effective use of valued resources. Leadership at the Delphi Energy and Engine Systems facility, located in Flint, Michigan, and referred to as "Flint West," empowered a joint team to improve productivity and quality on a fuel tank manufacturing process. Their efforts resulted in the insourcing of a substantial portion of General Motors' gas tank business. The point is, they were in trouble competitively and tried to save the business they had but ended up actually increasing their business—a win-win situation.

Resolution of Disputes

Differences can be resolved within the grievance procedures and before umpires, but many other issues that benefit both sides can be resolved by addressing the issue together. Former UAW Vice President Irving Bluestone and his son Barry, Professor of Political Economy at the University of Massachusetts, address this issue in their book *Negotiating the Future*.[9] Modern labor agreements must utilize joint processes as part of a two-edged sword. Traditional methods of resolving differences form one edge of the sword while joint, participative management efforts form the other. Traditional grievance procedures provide after-the-fact ways to resolve disputes, whereas joint processes can be used to eliminate the need for the dispute. Both edges of the sword are necessary but can be brandished as a weapon of war or a method of determining the future in a way that benefits all involved. Labor union and management relationships can be likened to a marriage. There will be disputes, but mutual respect, trust, and striving for mutual gain can make the relationship one that will assure the lasting health of both parties.

Trade Laws

American trade laws represent another obstacle to many U.S. firms' success. Other countries are permitted free access to American markets but do not permit U.S. companies to compete on equal ground. Process management systems can eliminate many of the ills of American industry but cannot erase the advantage of foreign competitors who operate from protected markets that are government subsidized. This obstacle can be addressed only by joint collaborative efforts among company leaders, labor unions, and workers in changing the outdated "free-trade" mentality to one of fair trade, designed to assure that all firms operating in the U.S. market compete on level ground. A long-term industrial policy must be called for that addresses America's competitive future on a global scale.

Long-Term Commitment

A major obstacle that must be addressed is short-term planning and fixes. Most American organizations are viewed as being interested only in short-term results and fixes. However, long-term planning should be cultivated in our companies to address every area of the organization. A minimum of 10 years should be the time span over which the consequences of a new process or goal are evaluated. Some foreign competitors utilize 40 years and more in their long-term assignments. It is no longer enough to simply "fix" the problem for today. Plans must be in place on means and methods to prevent the problem from ever occurring again. Common sense says there is no need to go back and fight the same battle over and over.

In Vietnam there was a famous battle over a small hill later named "Hamburger Hill" because of the carnage of human bodies spread over the hill during a prolonged battle. Once the hill was taken at drastic loss of life, it was abandoned only to have to be taken again in a smaller skirmish. The frustration and despair of the men who fought this battle was later portrayed in a Hollywood film.

Workers and managers alike feel frustration when the battle they fought on one model run is resolved only to be renewed with the introduction of a new model or product. Methods must be established to monitor problems and long-term processes instituted to keep them from happening again. Corporate learning feeds the long-term planning process with tested improvements and innovative techniques, but it does not constantly seek and replace. Lean today, agile tomorrow, virtual someday only dilutes human effort and dissolves the spirit. What in lean can we build on to keep on track? How do agile key characteristics enhance all the good methods we are practicing from our lean implementation experiences? What will the virtual workplace add to our system? Being open and receptive to new ideas does not take you off track—it enriches and improves the trip.

Warranty Concerns

An example of the value of sharing learnings and feedback is the organization's internal linkage with warranty. Ideally, reporting warranty problems is centralized and the information passed on to designers to prevent recurrence. Often fixes are instituted in the field, but the data are not collected, analyzed, and made part of a long-term product or service quality system affecting future design. On the plant floor monitoring recurring die or fixture problems provides a wealth of information to be passed to engineers and designers to prevent recurrence.

Unfortunately, the information flow is often short-circuited or delayed. Loss of this data can be costly both in recurring problems and the associated costs and the frustration on the part of workers who seem to solve the same problems over and over. Soon these problems are thought of as part of the norm. Customers used to tolerate the same cycle. Taking a new car back to the dealership to clean up the few little bothersome items didn't upset most buyers. That was in the past. Today, this situation is not tolerated. Strong competition based on quality challenges demands that recurrence of problems be prevented.

Obstacles can be overcome by establishing effective reporting systems covering all aspects of the business and by establishing relationships that encourage win-win resolutions. Record keeping and statistical processes can monitor the systems, but long-term planning must prevent their recurrence. Obstacles can be addressed as opportunities from which continuous improvement flows and need not be considered as impenetrable fortresses. When systems theory is operational, obstacles become opportunities for growth and long-term planning.

Suppliers' Roles

Improving and redefining relationships with outside suppliers plays an important part in institutionalizing a total quality process. Sharing the new process with suppliers and explaining their role are critical to the success of any system as suppliers are part of that system. As participants in the system, suppliers must become familiar with the long-term objectives of the organization. Process management practices incorporate suppliers in their production design and plans. Often it is a good idea to establish a specific strategy and training development team to prepare detailed plans for defining future, long-term relationships with suppliers. This relationship must also engender trust and assure quality and delivery of goods and services. Dr. W. Edwards Deming encourages companies to rely on single suppliers capable of meeting an organization's needs and working with that supplier in establishing a long-term, mutually beneficial relationship. Training may be made available to suppliers to assist them in process improvements that will reduce or stabilize their costs while increasing their profits. As supplier improvement results become improvements to our products and services, they are integrated into the total system.

> DON WAINWRIGHT, WAINWRIGHT INDUSTRIES: We're a contract manufacturer. So, in other words, we really have to partner with our customers....We really concentrate on doing a lot of things for one particular person. So,...with the cost of developing those new customers, we try to con-

centrate on the ones we have. And have good select customers that we develop a great long-term relationship with. And then, make ourselves flexible enough to grow with them, For instance, General Motors. When our customer is in trouble, that's an opportunity for us to help our customer. And help ourselves at the same time. That's a good supplier. That's what you look for. And those are the guys that last.[10]

Companies that operate on a global basis face the same challenges in their world operations. Cultural differences may require some modifications; however, the basic principles outlined thus far remain the same and assure organizationwide benefits.

Ongoing Challenge

These efforts at institutionalizing the process require an obsession by top leaders to show their leadership in every area. Initial rollout, ongoing communication, continuous improvement, standard processes, long-term commitment, leadership example, investment in training, eliminating fear in the workplace, support for middle managers, improved union-management relations, improving trust, establishing respect and improved relationships with outside suppliers—all must be addressed as long-term, unwavering commitments. Leadership's long-term commitment in these areas will ensure institutionalization of the process and an aligning of all the factions within the organization.

The Cadillac Quality Turnaround: A Case Study

The Quality Network has become one of the first attempts at a jointly developed total quality management process. The Cadillac division of General Motors was awarded the prestigious Malcolm Baldrige Award for quality in 1990, and this division used the total quality management principles of the Quality Network to achieve this recognition. This award was created in 1987 to honor the nation's highest-quality businesses. On August 20, 1987, Congress established the Malcolm Baldrige National Quality Award to recognize "U.S. companies that excel in quality management and quality achievement."[11] The *1992 Award Criteria* state that the award promotes:

Awareness of quality as an increasingly important element in competitiveness

Understanding of the requirements for quality excellence

Sharing of information on successful quality strategies and the benefits derived from implementation of these strategies.[12]

The criteria list 10 core values and concepts that are embodied in 7 examination categories. The values listed are customer-driven quality, leadership, continuous improvement, full participation, fast response, design quality and prevention of errors, long-range outlook, management by fact, partnership development, and public responsibility. Candidates for the award are judged in the following categories: leadership, information and analysis, strategic quality planning, human resource development and management, management of process quality, quality and operational results, and customer focus and satisfaction.

In 1990, the Cadillac Motor Car Company became the first automobile company to earn the prestigious Malcolm Baldrige National Quality Award in the Manufacturing category. In a publication written to capture Cadillac's quality journey culminating with the Baldrige Award titled *Cadillac: The Quality Story,* the company revealed that the early 1980s brought the first real challenge to Cadillac's quality leadership since its founding in 1902. Response to this challenge did not "completely meet customer expectations. By the mid-1980s, Cadillac's prestigious image was in jeopardy."[13] It was Cadillac's answer to this challenge and the company's ultimate transformation that garnered the Baldrige Award. Three strategies were behind this transformation: a cultural change, a constant customer focus, and a disciplined approach to planning. The Quality Network played a major role in the execution of these strategies and is particularly credited for its effects on teamwork and employee involvement, the heart of Cadillac's cultural change.

Cadillac quality councils oversee quality improvement activities and are involved in the business plan implementation. The *Beliefs & Values,* General Motors' guiding principles, focus the entire organization on the customer. Cadillac's business plan is its quality plan, directed toward continuous improvement of products, processes, and services. The four-phase process is the disciplined road map Cadillac followed to execute each product program. The implementation of the Quality Network principles strongly supported Cadillac in meeting the Baldrige criteria. The chart in Fig. 11-2 illustrates the relationships of some of the Quality Network action strategies with the Baldrige Examination Categories. The Quality Network is summarized by a participative management style, customer focus, and continuous quality improvement.

Application of the Quality Network philosophy and principles is the foundation for an organization to meet the Baldrige criteria. Cadillac's success at fulfilling the Baldrige criteria was the result of a total quality process that was Quality Network principle-driven. Upon winning the Malcolm Baldrige National Quality Award, the Cochairs of the

**Quality Network Linkage with the
Malcolm Baldrige National Quality Award**
*Summary Correlation of Malcolm Baldrige
Examination Criteria to Quality Network*

Baldrige Examination Category	Quality Network Primary Correlation
Leadership	Environment Action Strategies: Top Leadership Commitment and Involvement, Support for the Employee, Cooperative Union/Management Relations, Communication.
Information Analysis	Technique Strategies that provide data systems: Design of Experiments, Statistical Methodology, Machine/Process Capability, Validation, Reduction of Variation.
Quality Planning	Technique Strategies that provide customer requirements and planning skills: Quality Function Deployment (QFD), Voice of the Customer (VOC).
Human Resource Utilization	People Action Strategies: People Recognition, Suggestion Plan, Employee Excellence Development.
Quality Assurance of Products and Services	Technique Strategies that provide the "How to" tools to assist our people in assuring quality: Work Place Organization and Visual Controls, Quality Verification, Pull System, Lead Time Reduction, Error Proofing.
Quality Results	The results from implementing Techniques Strategies (Measurement and Feedback).
Customer Satisfaction	Customer Satisfaction Action Strategies: Voice of the Customer, Quality Function Deployment, Four Phase.

Figure 11-2

Cadillac quality council, Bill Capshaw, UAW International Representative, and John Grettenberger, Vice President, General Motors Corporation and General Manager, Cadillac Motor Car Division, issued a joint statement:

The Malcolm Baldrige National Quality Award process has helped us to review, as a company, our total quality system. What we learned has been invaluable—giving us the assurance that we have the right processes in place and strengthening our commitment to stay the course....Winning the Baldrige Award is a great thrill for Cadillac, the United Auto Workers, our partners in General Motors, our dealers nationwide, and our suppliers....But we know that the Baldrige Award is just a stepping stone on our path of continuous improvement.[14]

Notes

1. John Lippert, "In Wilmington, UAW and GM Cooperate, Innovate to Save Jobs," *The Detroit Free Press*, Friday, April 14, 1995.

2. Remarks taken from *The Quality Network 1994 Objectives End-of-Year Report, 1995*, p. 14.

3. Ibid.

4. Kathleen D. Ryan, excerpted from remarks made at the Quality Network Representatives' Workshop, May 1, 1991. Material taken from her book, coauthored with Daniel K. Oestreich, *Driving Fear Out of the Workplace: How to Overcome the Invisible Barriers to Quality, Productivity and Innovation,* Jossey-Bass Publishers, San Francisco, 1991.

5. Ibid.

6. Donald E. Petersen, and John Hillkirk, *A Better Idea—Redefining the Way Americans Work,* Houghton Mifflin Company, Boston, 1991, p. 28.

7. Ibid.

8. Owen Bieber, "Total Involvement Requires Total Commitment: Success and Common Goal," *Journal for Quality and Participation,* vol. 11-2, June 1988, pp. A6–A8.

9. Irving Bluestone and Barry Bluestone, *Negotiating the Future,* Basic Books, New York, 1992.

10. Donald Wainwright, Chairperson and CEO, Wainwright Industries, Inc. Excerpted from his remarks at *The Quest for Excellence VII*, the official conference of the Malcolm Baldrige National Quality Awards, Washington, D.C., February 6–8, 1995.

11. *1992 Award Criteria, Malcolm Baldrige National Quality Award,* U.S. Department of Commerce, Technology Administration, National Institute of Standards and Technology, Gaithersburg, Md., p. 1.

12. Ibid.

13. *Cadillac, The Quality Story,* Cadillac Motor Car Division, Detroit, Mich., p. 1.

14. Ibid.

12

Continuous Pursuit to Answer the Right Questions

The Right Questions

The evolving relationship between the UAW and General Motors in the quality arena over the past seven years has generated several questions that remain as valid today as they were in 1987. The answers to these questions have a life of their own. They are not constant, not carved in stone. Many forces, internal and external, controllable and noncontrollable, knowable and unknown, impact their composition. What are constant are the principles, methods, and systems used to pursue their answers. The pursuit of the answers is part of the ongoing quality journey.

- Every organization should ask itself, "Who is our customer? Are we satisfying our customer's requirements? How do we know?" This is the heart of why an organization is in business. The *Voice of the Customer* tells us how we are doing and helps us predict what we will have to do in the future. There are many voices of many customers, and it is crucial that they are all recognized and understood.

- "What's in it for me?" The WIIFM factor. All stakeholders must understand how they fit into the total plan and how they will benefit from its success.

- "What's going to happen to me?" Job security for all workers, represented and nonrepresented, is a key issue. As Dr. Deming points out, *secure* means "without fear." Bargaining issues must be kept separate from quality management issues with the exception of the bridging issue of job security. Plans must be developed that provide redeployment of people to meaningful work. If downsizing of an organization is necessary, then it should be accomplished to the extent possible through the principle of attrition.

- "What are the key success factors in a quality system?"

  Management and union leadership support: Constant, consistent, visible, and sustained leadership is evident to everyone.

  Involvement of all stakeholders from the inception: Like the design of the production operation described earlier, all affected functions should be represented.

  Operationally defined leadership involvement that will endure changes in leaders, on both sides: For example, since 1987 General Motors has had three new Presidents and two new Chairpersons. The UAW has had one new Vice President and four new Administrative Assistants.

  A shared value system that is fundamental and profound with enduring impact that can withstand outside forces.

- How can there be a win-win situation?" Balance and harmony must exist, and they are based on trust and respect. Turf battles can no longer be tolerated. Balance means:

  A systems approach that balances considerations for people and teamwork, business needs, and technological innovation

  A process that is generic enough to be accepted as a common process, yet flexible enough to allow for local cultural and systemic differences

  An understanding and respect for each party's responsibilities and obligations, with the agreement to work together on commonalities

- "How is this different from all the other programs-of-the-month?" The answer to this question must be lived. This is not a program. This is the ongoing transformation of a business system with its partners, customer-driven and continuously improved.

For the UAW and General Motors, the Quality Network *Beliefs & Values* captures it all: *Customer Satisfaction through People, Teamwork, and Continuous Quality Improvement.* General Motors and the UAW know that they must work together to secure their futures by satisfying all their customers. Corporate and union leadership have agreed that the way to satisfy their customers is through joint involvement and action focusing on quality improvements and innovation.

Observations

There is no doubt in our minds that implementation of process management and the pursuit of total quality are vital to the long-term health and success of a company. Top leadership, both management and the union, along with the employees of a company must be guided by a common set of beliefs and values, and behave consistent with those beliefs and values.

While a lingering economic downturn punishes American industry, it also punishes our foreign competitors. As the economy improves for all of us, it will also improve for our foreign competitors. To maintain a leadership position (much less to improve it), companies must recognize that they have to move to full implementation of a total quality process or process management system of some type. The need is even more urgent because we know our foreign competitors use this time to plan further penetration of our key markets.

Key issues that must be addressed if an organization is to attain and/or maintain world leadership are:

- Defining a management process for total quality.
- Creating a vision of what it will be like when full implementation of this management process is achieved.
- Institutionalizing quality into the role of leadership.
- Linking business plans (what we are going to do) with process management (how we are going to do it) to satisfy our customers.

These are inseparable issues. They cannot be resolved independently of one another. They are like walls of a room. An organization can focus on them individually while recognizing that only when viewed together does one understand the room itself. Major revision or loss of any wall changes the structure of the entire room and will result in suboptimization and limited success.

Defining the Process

Total quality is the goal management should strive for. Process management is the means to achieve that goal. Typically, when people think of process management or total quality management, many think of the tools and techniques. Others relate to the structure or the Beliefs and Values. Only a few think the process management should be defined as *a* single quality process to be used in all parts of an organization. Perhaps it's similar to the Big Q versus Little Q concept. We can look at process management and see the values, the structure, and the strategies just as we can look at the quality and see product quality. But to really understand and gain full value of quality as a concept, we have to step back and see the Big Q, quality, in everything we do.

If we examine the Big Q aspects of process management, we see that the focus is on customer satisfaction. Product quality is an important part of it but not the only part. Once committed to pursuit of customer satisfaction, we realize that attainment is through people, teamwork, and continuous improvement. Process management's outcome is customer satisfaction. Total quality is a philosophy that envisions the business as a total system, which leadership guides and directs using process management practices. It's *how* they run the business, and it's management's responsibility to actively lead the process.

An Ever-Changing Goal

The vision for a total quality organization is customer satisfaction and enthusiasm. As a vision, it is a constant that everyone in the organization can strive to attain. However, its makeup is ever changing. Therefore, it is a valuable goal that encourages continuous improvement because customer requirements and the things that excite customers are constantly changing. We must be mindful not to focus too tightly on process for process sake, measuring progress by counting the number of "focused visits" made by leaders or how many units have implemented which action strategies. We run the risk of losing sight of the goal. Focused visits are important to help us understand the potential of what we can do. The number of locations that have implemented a given action strategy is perhaps one measure of implementation. Gathering data is important because it provides information that helps an organization understand where it currently stands. But full implementation of process management is not when all leadership has participated in a workshop or when all action strategies have been fully implemented in every part of a company. *Full implementation of a process management system will be achieved when everyone is focused on customer satisfaction and when decisions are made because they will achieve customer satisfaction and provide a healthier, safer work environment.* We are convinced that leadership must support this principle.

Quality Leadership Leading Quality

Many articles have been written on the differences between leadership and management. They all come to similar conclusions. People don't like to be managed; they want to be led. Managers work to sustain the status quo. Change requires leaders. One leads from the front of the line; one manages from the rear. Many companies in America are in danger of being managed to death. To be sure, there is a need for good management. Managers are the staff side of the organization. They serve many necessary and important functions. However, management is but one aspect of leadership. The management role will never supplant the role of leadership. Conversely, all managers must be leaders.

The leader's behavior must be visible and must reflect the goals and desired behaviors of the organization. A company desiring problem-solving risk takers must find a leader who solves problems and takes risks. If we want people to carry a heavy load, we had best be out in front with our own load on our backs. Leaders cannot lead from behind closed doors or based on the information supplied by others. Leaders need to be seen so they can be followed. They need to personally listen so they will be heard when they speak. While there is risk in being too visible and burden in receiving too much information, there is greater risk in being overly protected with the only source of information being what they are allowed to know. If an organization is to become a total quality organization, the leadership must be obsessed with quality. Quality should be the source of inspiration for all decisions, second to none.

No "Vice President for Quality"

Quality decisions cannot be separated from business decisions. Ed Czapor, retired GM Vice President of Corporate Quality and Reliability, understood this idea well. It was under Czapor's leadership that the Quality Network was launched at the leadership seminars in 1989, and he attended most of the them. Trained as an engineer,

Czapor became a leader in the Delco Electronics organization. He was known throughout his career as a people person, in spite of the fact that he had to make some difficult decisions that laid off workers and shut down plants. At the 1989 leadership seminars, UAW International Representative Dick Jones, who with his management counterpart Bob Boruff taught the sessions on the *Beliefs & Values,* never failed to tell his story of "being Zaporized." It was at these seminars that Czapor made his personal vision clear to all. "You see," he would say, "my job is to get rid of my job. I've got to put myself out of work " Ed understood that quality is everyone's job and not one person's job.

Linking the Business Plan with Process Management

There is no mystery to the need for linkage between the business plan and process management. The business plan sets the direction for the organization. It tells us where we are going and what we have to accomplish. Process management is the way to get it all done. The business plan and process management are two views of accomplishing a vision. Their perspective is different, but they are inseparable. Neither can effectively exist without the other. The question is, "How do we establish this linkage in the minds of our people?"

First, we need to establish a common language, which is what the Quality Network has set out to do. We need one vision shared between the business plan and process management. In the same way, there should be no difference between the business plan and process management regarding the mission, the values, or the objectives. Most of the differences that still exist in our organization are differences in words rather than basic meaning. The problem goes away when we make the words the same so there can be no misunderstanding of intent.

Linkage through Involvement

Second, an organization needs to be sure that everyone has an opportunity to participate in both processes. Participation is both providing input and taking action. Seeking out input is a leadership responsibility to each process. People also have to know where a company is going and how it intends to get there. They have to feel that it's possible to do, and they have to agree that they want to do it. It is important that workers understand their roles in achieving the vision. Increasingly management is inviting union leadership to participate in the business planning process. For example, at the Delphi Interior and Lighting Systems plant in Adrian, Michigan, this has had a profound effect on the entire work force. Joint leadership develops the business plan and then rolls it out to all employees. Tim Holt, Chairman of the Bargaining Committee and member of UAW Local 2031: "For the past five years, the local union and management have sat down and jointly put the business plan together. And I think that's probably one of the best things we've gotten involved with. It helps us understand the business and not only that, we've become a lot more advanced in the last five years putting the plan together. And once the plan is together, we usually do it at an off site so there's no interruptions, we...bring it back to the plant and we'll roll it out to all employees. They need to know where you're going. If they don't know where you're going, they can't get you there."[1] Workers also need feedback on their accomplishments. Recognition of efforts and reward for accomplishments are vital to removing the paralyzing fear of failure.

The Right Thing for Management

Too often, "doing the right thing" for management is seen as a sign of weakness or poor management. An honest, "caring for others" manager is often seen as being "soft" and not a real asset. Being the boss and in charge contains a certain pride that can lead to a false sense of accomplishment and success. The workplaces of today require managers who honestly care about people and mix a fierce dedication to their responsibilities with individual attention and concern for those they lead. These managers are charged with keeping the vision of the company at the forefront. They must be ever mindful of their customers and key stakeholders and be certain that each employee understands how his or her role contributes to customer satisfaction.

The Right Thing for Labor Leaders

A labor union leader's strength comes from being recognized by the membership as caring about people and representing workers' rights in the face of company bureaucracy that traditionally has excluded the input of the workers on the plant floor. But traditional management is changing, and so too is the role of labor leaders. As evidenced in the Adrian plant and many others, UAW leadership is getting involved in business decisions. They are combining their desire to be workers' champions, advocating basic rights and adherence to the contract, with active participation with management in modifying business practices to eliminate the problems threatening workers and the company's survival.

The Right Thing for Workers

Things are changing for workers as well. They face a world full of technologies that they are unfamiliar with. The work environment is constantly evolving, which can cause some workers to feel helpless and afraid of the future. Though workers and first-line supervisors are the day-to-day experts on the job, they often feel disenfranchised and alone in their desire to do their best and contribute to meaningful change. People thrive and blossom when called upon to contribute their expertise in a winning cause. It is the responsibility of workers and supervisors alike to participate in determining their own destiny by contributing to workplace change with a spirit of teamwork.

The Right Thing for Everyone

Management leadership, union leadership, supervisors, and workers all must forge strong alliances that transcend the traditional roles of the past. This means doing what is right rather than doing what is expedient or easy or safe. Business concerns are labor unions' and the work force's concerns. Concern for people is a top priority for management. This does not mean managers have to surrender their rights to manage; but it does mean they must temper those rights with a caring, compassionate respect for the workers they lead. Learning about their workers' families, hobbies, troubles, and triumphs is just as important as being aware of how the production process is meeting its requirements.

Labor union leaders still must pursue, with all the dedication and energy they can muster, the rights of the workers they represent. They should not fear an erosion of their political power as worker involvement in the decision-making process increases. In fact, worker participation tends to elevate the dignity of work and provides meaningful input into a person's destiny.

Workers have the right to expect these traits of management and labor leaders, respectively, but they must assume their role as the most valuable asset an organization can have. The future of America's industrial might depends upon workers who care about their jobs and can look up with dignity from their labors.

Management, labor unions, and workers alike share a common responsibility to preserve our way of life for future generations. To do this, a lasting coalition must be formed based on trust, respect, and integrity. A shared value system that communicates a common set of principles for "doing what is right" is the foundation for just such a relationship. Workers feel respected and important. Leaders can rally workers in mutual causes that benefit everyone involved. Differences become opportunities for the improvement of the environment, the relationship, the organization, and the return for stockholders.

The Final Say—The Customer

Customers play the final part in this workplace drama. Working together, management and labor can plan, design, produce, and sell the best product in the world or provide the best service. The customer is the final judge. Workplace disharmony, discontent, and turmoil lead to a losing verdict when the customer rules. Working together on constantly improving product quality, reliability, and service, and looking for ways to please the customer will lead to prosperity for all parties concerned.

The Quality Journey

Dr. Deming speaks of the "Quality Journey," which is ongoing and continual. Both the International Union, UAW, and the corporation, General Motors, have been on this journey since their respective inception. The first joint relationship between General Motors and the UAW began in 1937 with the first labor agreement between the two organizations. Both parties brought quality to the table. Today the Quality Network is recognized as the process for quality that has resulted from the progression of the quality journey and the maturation of the relationship between union and management.

President Franklin D. Roosevelt foreshadowed this cooperative spirit in an address following the creation of the Automobile Labor Board organized to support the implementation of obligations decreed by the National Industrial Recovery Act. He is quoted in the General Motors Twenty-Sixth Annual Report, for the year ending December 31, 1934:

> I would like you to know that in the settlement just reached in the automobile industry we have charted a new course in social engineering in the United States. It is my hope that out of this will come a new realization of the opportunities of capital and labor not only

to compose their differences at the conference table and to recognize their respective rights and responsibilities but also to establish a foundation on which they can cooperate in bettering the human relationships involved in any large industrial enterprise.[2]

A lot has happened since 1934. Both organizations have come a long way as they set standards and created benchmarks for the labor movement and industrial America. Now the world is the playing field, and both the international union and General Motors must transform themselves and transcend their differences to meet the global challenge. It is clear that the jointly developed Quality Network has changed the relationship between General Motors Corporation and the UAW and permits and encourages joint decision making without forfeiting responsibilities required of each organization. The success of General Motors and the future of workers represented by the United Auto Workers Union depend upon a mutual concern for each other's welfare and interests. Mutual respect and trust must be the foundation for the success of each organization. The destiny of both organizations is inextricably linked. Neither organization can make decisions detrimental to the other without hurting itself. Joint decision making does not compromise either organization's effectiveness but is a way of looking after each other's interests, while assuring one's own success. We have a choice. We can either shape tomorrow by what we do today, or we will be forced to react tomorrow by what *others* are accomplishing today. Each of us must fulfill our new roles, dictated by world competition, and say to the world, "Get a grip, we're coming, because *United We Stand.*"

Notes

1. Tim Holt, UAW Shop Chairperson, Local 2031, Delphi-ILS, Adrian, Mich., plant, excerpted remarks from the *Quality Network Planned Maintenance Videotape*, QN #2094, January 1993.

2. Twenty-Sixth Annual Report of General Motors Corporation, year ended December 31, 1934, as prepared for presentation to stockholders at the Annual Meeting held in Wilmington, Del., Tuesday, April 30, 1935, p. 11.

Epilogue

Lessons Learned: Process Management in a Unionized Environment

In addition to Dr. Deming's teachings, based on our experience over the past five years, we would like to offer some additional guidelines for process management and total quality integration.

Process Management Must Be a Joint Effort of Management and the Workers within a Corporation

It is stated in the last of Dr. Deming's Fourteen Points for Management that an organization must involve everyone in the transformation. This is particularly important in companies that have a relationship with unions and union leadership. It is extremely important that the process start with the involvement of all top leadership, both union and management. In multiunion organizations, it would be important that the top leaders of all unions potentially impacted by the introduction of process management be involved in the discussions.

Participation May Be Voluntary

Companies will find that there are employees within their organization that resist change and resist change to the point that they do not want to be involved in any process. If that is the case, those employees should be allowed not to participate. However, such employees should be made aware that their inability to adapt to the changing environment within the company will ultimately result in their having to do work differently from the way they are currently doing it or in their having to work an entirely new job. In some cases, hourly employees who are high in seniority and have advanced near retirement age may not want to try to take on new and different things at that juncture in their career. The system should be flexible enough to allow for those employees to perform their work at a pace at which they can effectively produce a product or service that is acceptable to the management of the organization.

There Should Be No Layoffs Directly Resulting from Process Management Activities

Employees should be operating within the company in an environment that is free of fear. Fear is driven frequently by the lack of job security. Employees who feel secure in their work would be more than willing to participate in productivity improvements that may result in elimination of their own job, knowing full well that the management of the organization will find other work for them to do. Failure to have such security will certainly cause the organization to suboptimize and not reach its full potential. It is extremely important that fear and, in this case, the absence of job security be dealt with up front, when process management techniques are initiated. The commitment needs to be communicated that any employee freed up as a direct result of process management activities will not be laid off, nor will any employee lose his or her opportunity to work for the company.

Process Management Must Not Be a Production Gimmick

Process management must include the "production system." It is important that the operations and manufacturing people within an organization realize that process management is not just a process designed to eliminate waste and improve productivity. It is a process that improves both the physical and social environment in which employees are expected to work, to grow, and to innovate. It is extremely important that process management systems be viewed and understood by all as encompassing the production system, but it is not intended to be a system only focused on improving productivity with-

out improving such things as health and safety, job ergonomics, and
"joy of work."

Process Management Must Be Separate from Collective Bargaining

It is very important in organizations that bargain collectively with
employee representatives that the question of whether or not the management of the company is going to pursue total quality and process
management not be the subject for negotiations. Management has the
right under the National Labor Relations Act, as well as the responsibility to maintain the viability of operations, to determine the methods
and the means of manufacturing products and delivering services.
Process management is the introduction of a process to improve productivity, quality, and the social and physical working environment for
employees. Whether or not total quality is going to be pursued by a
company is the unilateral right of management.

Total Quality Must Not Be Used to Circumvent the Grievance Procedure

Just as articulated in the above point, management has the unilateral
right to implement total quality practices and process management
activities in particular. These cannot be used to circumvent the grievance procedure, which provides opportunity for employees to have
voice and influence in their wages, benefits, and conditions of employment and have the right for a person or labor organization to represent
them in such discussions with the management of the company.
Therefore, process management activities should not replace the formal grievance procedure established for unionized work forces.
Process management should not eliminate the open-door policy or
other formal complaint procedures established for nonrepresented
employees. Such complaint procedures, whether negotiated with the
union or provided for employees, should be maintained independent
of process management.

Process Management Must Not Be Used As a "Bargaining Chip"

Management of a company should not introduce process management in formal contract negotiations with the intent of utilizing it to in some way offset traditional bargaining issues such as wages, benefits, and conditions of employment, nor should the union use its support or lack of support for working with management to implement process management in bargaining issues. This can be a very difficult area to deal with, but if you truly are going to have process management in an organization and provide for an environment that supports continuous quality improvement for both product and service, it has to be independent of the vagaries and emotion of the negotiation's process and the grievance procedure.

Some Additional Observations

Successful process management systems need to recognize some additional items over and above those articulated above. In addition to Dr. Deming's philosophy and the points the authors have raised, there are some general observations that we would like to make that we believe are extremely important, based on the experience to date that we have had in working with General Motors and UAW and our attempts to implement the Quality Network.

All Practices Should Be Eliminated That Stratify People within a Team

Every employee in the organization should be viewed as part of the total team. Within the organization there are subteams, groups of employees who are engaged in common work or in natural work units. Those employees should be encouraged to work together as a team. There should not be levels of stratification within those teams driven by different methods of paying wages. A system for paying union-represented employees as "hourly workers" and all nonunion employees as "salaried workers" creates a divisive and nonproductive discrimination. Those types of approaches to payment or wage issues should be eliminated, and all employees should be paid through the same method of payment. That does not mean that everyone in the organization should make the same wages. Wages should still be determined based on the level of responsibility within a company.

Recognize the Rights of Workers to Participate in the Decisions That Affect Their Working Lives

Employees who are impacted by the implementation of process management should be given an opportunity to input into the process, in particular as it relates to their own job or the group of jobs within their natural work unit. If we expect employees to support our new approach to managing the business, we certainly should be providing them an opportunity to participate in the design of such a process. Process management is based on the belief that people are a company's greatest asset. You certainly would not want to ignore your greatest asset when you are trying to bring about change and transformation within your company.

Acknowledge the Work of All Individuals and Their Right To Be Treated with Dignity and Respect

Process management has in its basis—Beliefs and Values. As previously stated, General Motors' *Beliefs & Values* are the foundation for the Quality Network. Every employee who works for the company should have the right to expect that he or she will be treated with dignity and respect regardless of what work he or she does. Their job has been defined based on a need determined by the management of the company, whether they are assigned to clean toilets, sweep floors, or manage a department of people or to manage a plant or to work on sophisticated Skilled Trades machines and equipment. They have the right to be treated with dignity and respect. True transformation will not occur within a company unless it is footed in the belief that every man and woman who works for the company is in fact its greatest asset and those assets must, at all times, be treated with dignity and respect. We must within our organization be willing to provide such dignity and respect before we can expect to receive it in return.

Recognize That Workers Are a Viable Resource in Mind as well as Body

Frederick Taylor's method of organization is outdated. Today we have to rely on the intellectual curiosity and creativity potential of all our employees in order to succeed. Failure to recognize the potential for every employee to make a contribution through their skills, talents, and innovations will mean failure for a company. The companies that tap this resource are the companies that will succeed. The Japanese have raised this ability to an art form. That is the reason they have been so successful and will continue to succeed. Until companies within the United States recognize that they are only as good as their ability to tap their human resource, they will continue to fall short and suboptimize.

Establish an Atmosphere of Trust and Openness

If a company is to succeed today, it must be willing to share knowledge possessed by the leadership within the company: financial data, competitive information, long-term plans, business plans, goals, and expectations. If you expect your employees to be creative and innovative and fully support your goals and long-term expectations, they have to be aware of them. The company must develop a vision, share that vision with all of the employees, and provide the right supportive environment so that everyone can become the best that he or she can be. Failure to do that will result in suboptimization.

Encourage Individuals to Maximize Their Human Potential

Peter Senge, author of *The Fifth Discipline,* suggests that the companies that will win in the nineties and beyond are those that become "a learning organization." If there are employees within your company who do not have the proper skills to meet the anticipated demands for your company as it is going forward, then you must provide comprehensive training programs that will meet those needs. Employees must be freed up and allowed to participate in such training programs in order to improve their skills. Many companies have workers who have been employed for a number of years. These employees were hired to do a narrowly defined set of tasks, and as a result their formal education was not considered as strongly as their physical capability and dexterity. The competitive world is changing, and as a result, the type of employees needed as companies go forward are those with a much broader base of understanding and capability. That does not mean that you abandon your current work force and hire a new work force. It means companies today must determine what tomorrow's skills are going to be, what tomorrow's requirements are going to be, and provide current employees with opportunities to acquire those skills, through formal education and on-the-job training. Continuous improvement will result only from employees who are provided the necessary tools, methods, and training to continuously improve their own personal capability.

Provide for Individual Growth and Development

Not only is it important that employees be given appropriate training to perform their job-related tasks but it is as important that companies focus on personal skill development to be utilized outside of the employees' normal work. An employee who is able to deal with the changing environment in his or her personal life and the changing skills required for day-to-day living will be a much better employee when he or she is in the workplace. For example, you may have employees within your company that have a basic literacy problem. As a result, they may have difficulty reading and writing. Such problems can drive behaviors within the workplace that would not normally be observed if it were not for the fact that the employee is covering up a personal problem that he or she does not want exposed to their peers and supervisors. Generally speaking, 20 to 25 percent of the men and women in this country have difficulty reading and writing. There are few companies, unless their employees were hired through a closely monitored selection process, that are free from the problem of illiteracy.

Involve All Organizational Development, Education, and Training "Change Agents" in the Design of the Process and Its Implementation Plan

Without question if your organization has several people involved or several parts of the company involved in organizational development, education and training, and so on, all of those employees should be involved in the design of your process management system. They should be given an opportunity to input into its design and its implementation plans. Failure to do so will result in the long run in those employees resisting process management because it introduces a different approach to change than has been historically contemplated, and there will be fear that the new process will impact such employees' jobs and job security. The larger the company, the more potential there is for separate activities or separate efforts to occur that are counterproductive to the primary goal of process management.

A jointly developed process management process and related beliefs and values, if utilized as one process for establishing general methods of operations throughout an organization, creates a firm foundation of respect and trust. If an organization implements such a process, it will establish the needed support for attaining the quality, job security, and customer satisfaction necessary for long-term success.

Implementing a process management system throughout an organization must be the goal of the entire enterprise. Though separate "change agent" functions may exist for unions, workers, and management, a real commitment to attaining mutual goals in areas of common concern can greatly benefit all parties. None must give up its reason for existing, and all must realize that from time to time differences will arise. The collective bargaining agreements can be a method for resolution for those areas where differences arise in union-represented organizations. Collective bargaining issues must be kept separate from the process management process. Differences on issues cannot be permitted to stop activity contemplated in process management systems. With non-union-represented work forces, the same degree of employee participation must be sought in order to resolve real and perceived workplace problems and to assure joint cooperation in the process management system.

The organization must still operate its facilities in a manner that will maintain viability and grow the business. With represented work forces the union must at times represent workers' interest in areas where people issues appear to conflict with corporate goals; however, our experience brings us to the undeniable conclusion that worker involvement in corporate decision making benefits all parties and can lead to a better working environment, corporate culture, and a more viable, competitive company.

The validity of the principle that development and implementation of a process management system enhances an organization's effectiveness is currently widely accepted. Making employees part of the conception, development, and implementation further enhances changes for success and in some cases is the final link for an effective total systems approach to organizational change.

Bibliography

Adler, Mortimer J.: *How to Speak, How to Listen,* Macmillan, New York, 1985.

Albrecht, Karl: *Stress and the Manager: Making It Work for You,* Simon & Schuster, New York, 1979.

American Psychological Association, Inc.: *American Psychologist,* February 1990.

American Management Association: *Blueprints for Service Quality: The Federal Express Approach,* New York, 1991.

American Society for Quality Control and Automotive Industry Action Group: *Fundamental Statistical Process Control,* Reference Manual, Troy, Mich., 1991.

American Society for Training and Development: *Gaining the Competitive Edge,* Alexandria, Va., 1988.

Argyris, Chris: "We Must Make Work Worthwhile," *Life Magazine,* 1967, pp. 56–58.

Armstrong, Frank A.: *Shut Down the Home Office,* D. I. Fine, Inc., New York, 1991.

Arthur D. Little, Inc.: "1991 First Quarter," *Prism,* 1991.

Atwood, Donald, Robert Stempel, and Lloyd Reuss: Letter of December 9, 1986, announcing a new GM production system.

Augustine, Norman R.: *Augustine's Laws,* AIAA 1984.

Badiru, Adodeji B.: "A Systems Approach to Total Quality Management," *Industrial Engineering,* March 1990, pp. 33–36.

Baillie, Allan S.: "The Deming Approach: Being Better Than the Best," *Advanced Management Journal* 29, 1986, pp. 15–23.

Ball, J., and L. Ozley: "Quality of Work Life: How to Do It and Not to Do It," *The Warton Annual,* 1983, p. 152.

Beer, M., B. Spector, P. R. Lawrence, D. Q. Mills, and R. E. Walton: *Managing Human Assets: The Ground Breaking Harvard Business School Program,* MacMillan, New York, 1984.

Bell, Robert: *Surviving the Ten Ordeals of the Takeover,* AMACON, New York, 1988.

Bennett, Mike: "A Conversation with Mike Bennett," *Labor Relations Today,* U.S. Dept. of Labor, Washington, D.C., 1991, pp. 4–5.

———: *Followers,* summarized by Robert E. Kelly and *The Harvard Business Review,* summary of article "In Praise of Followers," November–December 1988.

Bennis, Warren, and B. Nanus: *Leaders: The Strategies of Taking Charge*, Harper & Row, New York, 1985.

Bernstein, A., and W. Zellner: "Detroit vs. the UAW: At Odds over Teamwork," *Business Week*, August 24, 1987, pp. 54–55.

Bertrand, D., I. Deters, G. Griffith, Mary Matthews, Barry Michels, P. Rudolph, and P. Schmidt: *Ford Motor Company Communication Systems* (GM Restricted), April 24, 1991.

Bieber, Owen: Remarks at Canadian Auto Industry Conference, February 14, 1989.

————: "Total Involvement Requires Total Commitment: Success and Common Goal," *Journal for Quality and Participation*, vol. 11-2, June 1988.

Blache, Klaus M., Ph.D. (ed.): *Success Factors For Implementing Change: A Manufacturing Viewpoint*, Society of Manufacturing Engineers Publications Development Department, Dearborn, Mich.

———— and Renee M. Landgraff: "North American Maintenance Benchmarks," *Maintenance Technology*, November 1991, pp. 28–32.

Bluestone, Barry, and Irving Bluestone: *Negotiating the Future: A Labor Perspective on American Business*, Basic Books, New York, 1992.

Boghossian, Fikru H.: "Build Quality In: Don't Inspect It," *Advanced Management Journal*, 53 (4), Autumn 1988, pp. 44–47.

Braunstein, Janet: "GM Tight-Lipped on Manager's Sudden Retirement from Plant," *Detroit Free Press*, Section E, May 2, 1990, p. 1.

Brocka, Bruce, and Suzanne M. Brocka: *Quality Management: Implementing the Best Ideas of the Masters*, Business One Irwin, Homewood, Ill., 1992.

Brown, Peter: "Import-Big 3 Quality Battle Involves More Than Good Cars," *Automotive News*, June 4, 1990.

Byham, William C., and Jeff Cox: *Zapp! The Lightning of Empowerment*, Harmony, New York, 1988.

Cadillac, the Quality Story, Cadillac Motor Car Division Publication, Detroit, Mich., 1991.

Camp, Robert C.: *Benchmarking: The Search for Industry Best Practices That Lead to Superior Performance*, ASQC, Milwaukee, 1989.

Carnevale, Ellen S.: "Total Quality through SPC," *Technical & Skills Training*, July 1991.

Caropreso, Frank (ed.): *Making Total Quality Happen* (Report No. 37), Conference Board, New York, 1990.

Castor, Edward L.: "Reading, Writing, and Cover-Ups," *Across the Board*, September 1991.

Center Exchange: "Quality Corner: Quality Network's Planned Maintenance," January/February 1995.

Chaudron, David: "How OD Can Help Implement TQM: Opportunities for OD Professionals," *OD Practitioner*, March 1992, pp. 14–18.

Clausing, Don: "Taguchi Methods to Improve the Development Processes," *IEEE International Conference on Communications*, June 12–15, 1988.

Clinton, President William J.: Speech from "Drive American Quality," Washington, D.C., May 25, 1994.

Cocheu, Ted: "Training for Quality Improvement," *Training & Development Journal* 43(1), January 1989, pp. 56–62.

Cohen, William A.: *The Art of the Leader,* Prentice-Hall, Englewood Cliffs, N.J., 1990.

Cohen-Rosenthal, Edward (ed.): *Unions, Management and Quality: Opportunities for Innovation and Excellence,* copublished with the Association for Quality and Participation, Irwin Professional Publishing, Burr Ridge, Ill., 1995.

Covey, Stephen R.: *The 7 Habits of Highly Effective People,* Simon & Schuster, New York, 1989.

Covey Stephen R.: *The Seven Habits of Highly Effective People,* Carol Publishing Group, New York, 1994.

Cowin Associates: *Beyond Crisis Management,* February 1986.

Crosby, Philip B.: *Let's Talk Quality,* McGraw-Hill, New York, 1989.

————: *Quality Is Free: The Art of Making Quality Certain,* New American Library, New York, 1979.

————: *The Eternally Successful Organization: The Art of Corporate Wellness,* McGraw-Hill, New York, 1988.

Crain, Keith: "A Good Product Alone Won't Be Enough in Future," *Crain's Detroit Business,* February 20, 1995, p. 6.

DeAngelo, J., and B. Reilly: "A Look at Job Redesign," *Personnel,* February 1988, p. 64.

Debbink, John: Videotaped remarks at GM Power Products and Defense Quality Network Leadership Seminar, March 1989.

Deming, W. Edwards: *Out of the Crisis,* Massachusetts Institute of Technology, Cambridge, Mass., 1986.

————: *Quality, Productivity and Competitive Position,* Massachusetts Institute of Technology, Center for Advanced Engineering Study, Cambridge, Mass., 1982.

————: *The New Economics for Industry Education, Government,* seminar, 1992. Dr. Deming has since published a book with the same title drawn from a notebook used by Deming, MIT Center for Advanced Engineering Study, Cambridge, Mass., 1993.

Dertourzos, Michael K., Richard K. Lester, Robert M. Solow, and MIT Commission on Industrial Productivity: *Made in America: Regaining the Productivity Edge,* Massachusetts Institute of Technology Press, Cambridge, Mass., 1989.

Desatnick, Robert L.: *Managing to Keep the Customer: How to Achieve & Maintain Superior Customer Service Throughout the Organization,* Jossey-Bass, San Francisco, 1993.

Dewar, Jeff: "American Leaders Competing for Quality," *Manage* 40(3), May/June 1988, pp. 63–73,

Dilenschneider, Robert L.: *A Briefing for Leaders,* Harper Business, New York, 1993.

Drucker, Peter F.: *Innovation & Entrepreneurship,* Harper Business, New York, 1993.

————: *Managing for Results,* Harper Business, New York, 1993.

————: *Managing for the Future: The 1990s and Beyond*, NAL-Dutton, New York, 1993.

Ealey, Lance A.: *Quality by Design: Taguchi Methods and U.S. Industry*, ASI Press, Dearborn, Mich., 1988.

Elsila, Dave (ed.): *We Make Our Own History: A Portrait of the UAW*, International Union, UAW, Detroit, Mich., 1986.

Ephlin, Donald, and Robert Stempel: Videotaped remarks from 4th Annual ASQC Quality Forum, November 11, 1988.

Ernst & Young and The University of Michigan: *The Car Company of the Future: A Study of People and Change*, 1991.

Evans, John P.: *A Report of the Total Quality Leadership Steering Committee and Working Councils*, published by The Proctor & Gamble Company, November 1992.

Fallows, James: *More Like Us: Making America Great Again*, Houghton Mifflin, Boston, 1990.

Faux, Marian: *The Executive Interview*, St. Martin, New York, 1985.

Feigenbaum, Armand V.: *Total Quality Control*, 3rd ed., McGraw-Hill, New York, 1983.

Ford, Henry: *Today and Tomorrow*, Productivity Press, Cambridge, Mass., 1988.

Ford Motor Company: "NAO's Strategic Imperatives," *Ford World*, April 1991, pp. 8–10.

Fromm, Bill: *The Ten Commandments of Business & How to Break Them*, Berkley Pub., New York, 1992.

Fundamental Statistical Process Control Reference Manual, Prepared by the quality and supplier assessment staffs at Chrysler, Ford, and General Motors, Automotive Industry Action Group in collaboration with the Automotive Division of the American Society for Quality Control Supplier Requirements Task Force, 1991.

Gabor, Andrea: *The Man Who Discovered Quality: How W. Edwards Deming Brought the Quality Revolution to America—The Stories of Ford, Xerox & GM*, Viking Penguin, New York, 1992.

Garvin, David A.: *Managing Quality: The Strategic and Competitive Edge*, Free Press, New York, 1987.

General Motors Corporation: *Highlights of Total Quality Management Philosophies and Applications*, QN #1813 General Motors NAO Quality & Reliability, 4th ed. rev., 1994.

————: *Public Interest Report 1988*, May 16, 1988.

————: *Quality and Reliability Cross-Industry Study Report*, General Motors Quality & Reliability, 1984.

————: *Twenty-Sixth Annual Report*, Detroit, Mich., April 30, 1935.

————: *Quality Network Leadership Guide*, Detroit: GM Restricted, 1988.

————: *General Motors Corporation Operating Manual: "OP-34 Quality Network,"* 1988.

General Motors Corporation and United Auto Workers: *GM–UAW National Agreement*, 1987.

————: *GM–UAW National Agreement*, 1990.

————: *GM–UAW National Agreement*, 1993.

————: *Process Reference Guide: Synchronous Organization*, GM Restricted, May 1991.

Gerber, Michael: *The E-Myth: Why Most Businesses Don't Work & What to Do about It*, Harper Business, New York, 1990.

Gilbreath, Robert D: *Save Yourself: Six Pathways to Achievement in the Age of Change*, McGraw-Hill, New York, 1991.

Gitlow, H. S., and S. J. Gitlow, *The Deming Guide to Achieving Quality & Competitive Position*, Prentice Hall, Englewood Cliffs, N.J., 1987.

"GM Looks for Gold as Olympics Sponsor," *The Detroit Free Press*, March 10, 1995.

"GM's Quality Network: Quality and Customer Satisfaction," *Journal for Quality and Participation*, vol. 12-1, March 1989.

Goldratt, Eliyahu M., and Jeff Cox: *The Goal, a Process for Ongoing Improvement*, rev. ed., North River Press, Croton-on-Hudson, N.Y., 1986.

Gordon, J.: "Who Killed Corporate Loyalty?," *Training Magazine*, March 1990, p. 25.

Graham, Benjamin: *The Intelligent Investor*, 4th rev. ed., HarperCollins, New York, 1986.

Grayson, C. Jackson, Jr., and Carla O'Dell: *American Business: A Two-Minute Warning: Ten Tough Issues Managers Must Face*, Free Press, New York, 1988.

Greenwood, Ramon: "Workers Must Deal with Constant Change," *Business News*, 1990.

Groocock, J. M.: *The Chain of Quality: Market Dominance through Product Superiority*, John Wiley & Sons, New York, 1986.

Guest, R.: "Quality of Work Life: Japan and America Contrasted," *The Wheel Extended*, April 1983, p. 9.

Handy, Charles: *The Age of Unreason*, McGraw-Hill, New York, 1991.

Hardesky, J. L.: *Productivity and Quality Improvement: A Practical Guide to Implementing Statistical Process Control*, McGraw-Hill, New York, 1988.

Harless, Joe: "Is There Quality in Quality?," *Viewpoint*, January 1991, p. 130.

Hayes, R. H., and S. C. Wheelwright: *Restoring Our Competitive Edge: Competing through Manufacturing*, Wiley, New York, 1984.

Hellriegel, Don, and John W. Slogum: *Organizational Behavior*, rev. ed., West Publishing, Minn., 1986.

Hoerr, John: "What Should Unions Do?" *Harvard Business Review*, May–June 1991, pp. 1–9.

Holpp, Lawrence: "Achievement Motivation and Kaizen," *Training & Development Journal* 43(10), October 1989, pp. 53–63.

Holusha, J.: "An Assembly-Line Revolution," *The New York Times*, September 3, 1985, p. 1.

————: "A New Spirit at U.S. Auto Plants," *The New York Times*, December 1987, pp. 25–26.

Houghton, James R.: "The Competitive Advantage," *Fortune Magazine*, September 1987.

Huge, Ernest C., and Alan D. Anderson: *The Spirit of Manufacturing Excellence: An Executive's Guide to the New Mind Set*, Dow Jones-Irwin, Homewood, Ill., 1988.

Husar, Michael: "Implementing the Synchronous Organization—Quality Network Strategies," *NUMMI White Paper,* December 2, 1990.

Imai, Masaaki: *Kaizen (Ky'Zen): The Key to Japan's Competitive Success,* Random House Business Division for the KAIZEN Institute, New York, 1986.

————: Remarks at the 19th Annual Quality and Productivity Seminar, Partners in Business, Utah State University College of Business, May 4–5, 1994.

Ishihara Shintaro: *The Japan That Can Say No,* Touchstone Books, Portland, Ore., 1992.

Ishikawa, Kaoru: *What Is Total Quality Control? The Japanese Way,* translated by David J. Lu, Prentice-Hall, Englewood Cliffs, N.J., 1985.

Japan Human Relations Association Staff (eds.): *The Idea Book: Improvement through TEI (Total Employee Involvement),* Productivity Press, Cambridge, Mass., 1988.

Johnson, R.: "NUMMI Payoff," *Automotive News,* June 20, 1988, p. 50.

Jones, Thomas E. and T. P. Elaesser: *Entrepreneurism,* D. I. Fine, New York, 1988.

Junkerman, J.: "Lordstown: Yesterday's Rebels Are Running Scared," *The Progressive,* August 1983, p. 21.

Juran, Joseph M.: *Juran on Planning for Quality,* MacMillan, New York, 1988.

————: *Managerial Breakthrough: A New Concept of the Manager's Job,* McGraw-Hill, New York, 1964.

————, F. M. Gryna, Jr., and R. S. Bingham, Jr. (eds.): *Quality Control Handbook,* 3rd ed., McGraw-Hill, New York, 1974.

————: "Product Quality—A Prescription for the West," *Management Review* 70(6&7), AMACOM, a division of American Management Association, July 1981, pp. 9–14, 57–61.

Just-in-Time Project Team: *Fiero Production System Implementation Plan,* December 1, 1985.

Kano, Noriaki: Remarks from lecture presented at GM Systems Engineering Center, "Quality Planning and Quality Creation: Quality in the Year 2000," October 18, 1994.

Kanter, Rosabeth Moss: *The Change Masters: Innovation for Productivity in the American Corporation,* Simon & Schuster, New York, 1985.

Keller, Maryann N.: "Decisive Actions Restore Our Confidence in GM's Future," *Auto Industry Observation 15: General Motors Corporation (NYSE: 38-GM),* April 13, 1992.

————: "GM's Problems," *Automotive Industries,* December 1994.

————: *Rude Awakening, The Rise, Fall, and Struggle for Recovery of General Motors,* William Morrow and Company, New York, 1989.

Kelly, Al: *How to Make Your Life Easier at Work,* 2nd ed., McGraw-Hill, New York, 1988.

Kepner, Charles H., Ph.D., and Wilson Learning Corporation: *Team Decision Making: Teams and People Working Together,* 1991.

Kertsey, L.: "Team Concept Makes Mazda Flat Rock a Different Plant," *Automotive News,* February 29, 1988, p. 15.

King, Bob: *Better Designs in Half the Time: Implementing QFD (Quality Function Deployment) in America,* 3rd ed., GOAL/QPC, Methuen, Mass., 1989.

King, Norman: *The First Five Minutes.*

Klatt, Murdick, Schuster: *Human Resource Management,* Merrill, Columbus, 1985.

Klein, J. A.: *The Human Costs of Manufacturing Reform,* Harvard Business Review, March–April 1989, pp. 60–66.

Kobayashi, Iwao: *20 Keys to Workplace Improvement,* Productivity Press, Cambridge, Mass., 1990.

Koestenbaum, Peter: *Leadership: The Inner Side of Greatness,* Jossey-Bass, San Francisco, Calif., 1991.

Kouze, James M., and Barry Z. Posner: *The Leadership Challenge: How to Get Extraordinary Things Done in Organizations,* Jossey-Bass, San Francisco, 1990.

Kowalick, James: "The 11th Hour for American Manufacturing: Total Quality and the Transformation of Manufacturing Organizations into Customer-Conscious, High-Quality, Low-Cost Profit Centers," *Engineering from Design to Production,* American Defense Preparedness Association, March 6, 1990.

———: "Taguchi Design on Quality," *Cutting Tool Engineering* 41(2), April 1989.

———: *Organizational Excellence beyond Total Quality Management: Building the Robust Organization,* seminar presented at General Motors, Renaissance Leadership Institute, Oregon House, Calif., October 26–28, 1994.

Labor-Management Cooperation: *U.S. Department of Labor Bureau of Labor-Management Relations and Cooperative Programs,* 1990 State-of-the-Art Symposium, 1991.

Lareau, William: *American Samurai,* Warner Books, New York, 1992.

Lefitt, Theodore: *Thinking about Management,* Free Press, New York, 1990.

Lippert, John: "In Wilmington, UAW and GM Cooperate, Innovate to Save Jobs," *The Detroit Free Press,* April 14, 1995.

———: "Retooling Attitudes," *The Detroit Free Press,* March 9, 1992.

———: "Union Plants More Productive, Study Says," *The Detroit Free Press,* date unknown.

Lundrigan, Robert F., and James R. Borchert: *The Challenge,* North River Press, Croton-on-Hudson, N.Y., 1988.

Marchland, Roland: "The Corporation Nobody Knew: Bruce Barton, Alfred Sloan, and the Founding of the General Motors' Family," Steven W. Tolliday, ed., *Business History Review,* published quarterly by the Harvard Business School, vol. 65, no. 4, winter 1991.

Mateja, Jim: "Buick Takes on Big, Rear-Wheel-Drive Boys," *Chicago Tribune,* September 23, 1990.

McCormick, John: "Interview with Richard Wagner," *Automotive Sourcing,* February 1995.

McDonald, F. James: "Creating a Quality Culture," *The Quality Circles Journal,* 1987, pp. 56–57.

Mackenzie, Alex: *The Time Trap: The New Version of the 20-Year Classic on Time Managment,* AMACOM, New York, 1990.

Melcher, Richard A.: "A New Era for Auto Quality: Just As Detroit Is Catching Up, the Very Concept Is Changing," *Business Week,* October 1990.

Mid-America Project, Inc.: *Keiretsu, USA: A Tale of Japanese Power,* July 1991.

Miller, Danny: *The Icarus Paradox,* Harper Business, New York, 1992.

Mizuno, S. (ed.): *Management for Quality Improvement: The 7 New QC Tools,* Productivity Press, Cambridge, Mass., 1988.

Moskal, B.: "Quality of Life in the Factory: How Far Have We Come?" *Industry Week,* January 16, 1989, p. 12.

Nadler, David A.: *Feedback and Organizational Development: Using Databased Methods,* Addison-Wesley, Reading, Mass., 1977.

Nadler, Gerald and Shozo Hibino: *Breakthrough Thinking,* Prima Publishing, Rocklin, Calif., 1989.

Naisbitt, John, and Patricia Aburdene: *Re-inventing the Corporation,* Warner, New York, 1985.

Nakajima, Seiichi (ed.): *TPM Development Program: Implementing Total Productive Maintenance* (English translation), Productivity Press, Cambridge, Mass., 1989.

National Center on Education and the Economy: *America's Choice: High Skills or Low Wages!* National Center on Education and the Economy, June 1990.

Nemoto, Masao: *Total Quality Control for Management: Strategies and Techniques from Toyota and Toyda Gosei,* Prentice-Hall, Englewood Cliffs, N.J., 1987.

Oberle, Joseph: "Quality Gurus: The Men and Their Message," *Training* 27(1), January 1990, pp. 47–52.

Ohno, Taiichi: *Workplace Management,* Productivity Press, Cambridge, Mass., 1988.

——— and Setsuo Mito: *Just-in-Time for Today and Tomorrow,* Productivity Press, Cambridge, Mass., 1988.

Okine, K.: "Toyota Changes Its Famous Production System," *Automotive Industries,* February 1995.

Oliver, Thomas: *The Real Coke, The Real Story,* Penguin Viking, New York, 1987.

O'Dell William F.: *Effective Business Decision Making,* NTC Publishing Group, Lincolnwood, Ill., 1993.

O'Toole, J.: "Lordstown: Three Years Later," *Business & Society Review,* spring 1975, p. 65.

Parker, Michael, and Jane Slaughter: "Behind the Scenes at NUMMI Motors," *The New York Times,* December 4, 1988, p. 1.

Peters, Tom: *Making It Happen: Coming to Grips with the Dismal Record of Quality Program Implementation,* The Tom Peters Group, Palo Alto, Calif., 1989.

Peterson, Donald E., and John Hillkirk: *A Better Idea: Redefining the Way Americans Work,* Houghton Mifflin, Boston, Mass., 1991.

Pfau, Loren D.: "Total Quality Management Gives Companies a Way to Enhance Position in the Global Marketplace," *Industrial Engineering* 21(4), April 1989, pp. 17–21.

Phadke, Madhav S.: *Quality Engineering Using Robust Design,* Prentice-Hall, Englewood Cliffs, N.J., 1989.

Poka-Yoke: Improving Product Quality by Preventing Defects (originally published as *Pokayoke Dai Zukan*): Productivity Press, Cambridge, Mass., 1988.

Porter, Howard E.: "Malcolm Baldrige National Quality Award: Just Applying Makes You a Winner," *Industry Forum,* AMA, February 1990, pp. 1–4.

Pryor, Lawrence S.: "Benchmarking: A Self-Improvement Strategy," *Journal of Business Strategy* 10(6), November/December 1989, pp. 28–32.

"Quality Management," *Industrial Engineering* 22(3), March 1990, pp. 33–36.

Quality Network Action Strategy Summary, QN #1435, published by Quality Network Publishing, January 1993.

Quality Network Beliefs & Values, QN #851, published February 1991.

Quality Network Guidelines for Redeployment and Meaningful Work, QN #2251, October 28, 1993.

Quality Network Planned Maintenance Videotape, QN #2094, January 1993.

Quality Network Process Reference Guide, "Reduction of Variation," QN #52, September 1990.

Quality Network Suggestion Plan: Legal Issues Videotape, March 1995.

The Quest for Excellence VII, Audiotaped remarks from the Malcolm Baldrige National Quality Awards, Washington, D.C., February 6–8, 1995.

Quinian, Jim, et al.: *Product Improvement by Application of Taguchi Methods.*

Rapp, Stan, and Tom Collins: *The Great Marketing Turnaround,* Prentice Hall, New York, 1990.

Risen, James: "Job-Quality Plans Abused," *The Detroit Free Press,* November 10, 1983.

Ritvo, Roger A., and Alice G. Sargent (eds.): *The NTL Manager's Handbook,* NTL Institute, 1983.

RoAne, Susan: *How to Work a Room,* Warner Books, New York, 1989.

Robson, Michael: *Quality Circles: A Practical Guide,* 2nd ed., Gower Publlishing Company, Ltd., UK, 1988.

Rossier, Paul E., and D. Scott Sink: "A Road Map to Productivity: What's Ahead for Productivity and Quality Improvement?," *Industrial Engineering* 22(3), March 1990, pp. 24–27, 31.

Rukeyser, Louis: *How to Make Money in Wall Street,* Doubleday, New York, 1976.

Ryan, Kathleen D.: *Driving Fear Out of the Workplace: How to Overcome the Invisible Barriers to Quality, Productivity and Innovation,* Jossey-Bass, San Francisco, Calif., 1991.

Sakamoto, Shigeyasu: "Process Design Concept: A New Approach to IE," *Industrial Engineering* 21(3), March 1989, pp. 31–34.

Schein, Lawrence: "The Road to Total Quality: Views of Industry Experts," *Conference Board Research Bulletin 239,* 1990.

Scherkenbach, William W.: *Deming's Road to Continual Improvement,* SPC Press, Knoxville, Tenn., 1991.

———: *The Deming Route to Quality and Productivity: Road Maps and Roadblocks,* Cee Press, Washington, D.C., 1988.

Schlefer, Jonathan: "Making Sense of Productivity Debate: A Reflection on the MIT Report," *Technology Review* 92(6), August/September 1989, pp. 18–21.

Scholtes, Peter R.: *The Team Handbook,* Straus, Madison, Wisc., 1988.

———: *The Environment of Teamwork,* Scholtes Seminars and Consulting: Creating Pride and Joy at Work, seminar at General Motors *Crowd Meeting,* Auburn Hill, Mich., February 7, 1995.

Scobel, D.: "Doing Away with the Factory Blues," *Harvard Business Review,* November–December 1975, p. 138.

Sculley, John, with John A. Byre: *Odyssey: Pepsi to Apple...A Journey of a Marketing Impressario,* Harper Collins, New York, 1988.

Seal, Gregory M.: "1990's—Years of Promise, Years of Peril for U.S. Manufacturers," *Industrial Engineering* 22(1), January 1990, pp. 18–21.

Senge, Peter M.: *The Fifth Discipline*, Doubleday Currency, New York, 1990.

———: Excerpts compiled by Nelson, Mark F., *The Leader's New Work: Building Learning Organizations*, MIT Sloan School of Management, fall 1990.

———, Charlotte Roberts, Richard B. Ross, Byran J. Smith, and Art Kleiner: *The Fifth Discipline Fieldbook, Strategies and Tools for Building a Learning Organization*, New York, Doubleday Currency, 1994.

Sheridan, John H.: "Lessons from the Gurus," *Industry Week* 239 (15), August 6, 1990, pp. 35–41.

Sherman, V. Clayton: From Losers to Winners: How to Manage Problem Employees...& What to Do If You Can't, AMACOM, New York, 1987.

Shetty, Y. K.: "The Human Side of Product Quality," *National Productivity Review* 8(2), spring 1989, pp. 175–182.

———: "Managing Product Quality for Profitability," *Advanced Management Journal* 53(4), autumn 1989, pp. 33–38.

——— and V. M. Buehler (eds.): *Productivity and Quality through Science and Technology*, Quorum Books, Westport, Conn., 1988.

Shirouzu, Norihiko: "Line Leaders Blamed for Ills at NUMMI Plant," *The Japan Economic Journal*, September 1990.

Shores, A. Richard: *Survival of the Fittest: The Total Quality Control and Management Evolution*, ASQC Quality Press, Milwaukee, Wisc., 1988.

Simmons, J.: "Workers Have Brains Too," *Workplace Democracy*, summer 1982, p. 6.

Singo, S.: *Zero Quality Control: Source Inspection and the Poka-Yoke System*, Productivity Press, Cambridge, Mass., 1986.

Sink, D. Scott, and Thomas C. Tuttle: *Planning and Measurement in Your Organization of the Future*, Industrial Engineering and Management Press, Norcross, Ga., 1989.

———: "Total Quality Management Is...," *QPM Quality & Productivity Management* 8(2), 1990, pp. 14–25.

Sloan, Alfred P., Jr.: "Letter to All Employees in General Motors Factories," October 15, 1934.

Sorcher, Melvin: *Predicting Executive Success: What It Takes to Make It into Senior Management*, John Wiley & Sons, 1985.

Stein, James D., Jr., Herbert L. Stone, and Charles V. Harlow: *How to Shoot from the Hip without Getting Shot in the Foot*, John Wiley & Sons, New York, 1990.

Stratton, A. Donald: "Kaizen and Variability," *Quality Progress*, April 1990, pp. 44–45.

Suglyama, Tomo: *The Improvement Book: Creating the Problem-Free Workplace*, Productivity Press, Cambridge, Mass., 1989.

"Summary Judgments of the 1990 Cars," *Consumer Reports*, April 1990, p. 235.

Swan, William S.: *How to Do a Performance Appraisal*, John Wiley & Sons, New York, 1991.

Taguchi, Genichi, and Don Clausing: "Robust Quality," *Harvard Business Review* 68(1), January/February 1990, pp. 65–75.

Tetsuichi, Asaka, and Ozeka Kazuo (eds.): *Handbook of Quality Tools: The Japanese Approach*, Productivity Press, Cambridge, Mass., 1990.

Tompkins, James A.: *Winning Manufacturing: The How-to Book of Successful Manufacturing,* Institute of Industrial Engineers, Norcross, Ga., 1989.

Townsend, Patrick L., and Joan E. Gebhardt: *Commit to Quality,* John Wiley & Sons, New York, 1986.

Toyota 1994 Annual Report, October 1994.

"Toyota's New Approach Is with Fewer Machines," *The Detroit Free Press,* March 14, 1995.

UAW Education Department: *Highlights of the History of Organized Labor and the UAW,* Solidarity House, Detroit, Mich., May, 1993.

UAW–GM Joint Quality Study Committee: *UAW–GM Joint Quality Study,* March 1986, pp. 2–4 and Appendix A, p. 1.

Ury, William: *Getting Past No,* Bantam, New York, 1993.

U.S. Department of Commerce: *1992 Award Criteria, Malcolm Baldrige National Quality Award,* National Institute of Standards and Technology, Gaithersburg, Md.

U.S. Department of Labor & Bureau of Labor-Management Relations and Cooperative Programs: *Labor-management Cooperation: 1990 State-of-the-Art Symposium,* 1991.

Van, Jon, "Old Manufacturing Ideas Crippling U.S.," *Chicago Tribune,* Section 1, November 3, 1991, pp. 12–14.

Vansina, Leopold S.: "Total Quality Control: An Overall Organizational Improvement Strategy," *National Productivity Review* 9(1), winter 1989/1990, pp. 59–73.

Wadsworth, H. M., K. S. Stephens, and A. B. Godfrey: *Modern Methods for Quality Control and Improvement,* Wiley, New York, 1986.

Wagner, James: Videotaped remarks from GM Power Products and Defense Quality Network Leadership Seminar, March 1989.

Walther, George R.: *Power Talking,* Berkley Publishing, New York, 1992.

Wareham, John: *The Anatomy of a Great Executive,* Harper Collins, New York, 1992.

Weekley, Thomas L., Ph.D.: *Total Quality Management from a Joint Management and Labor Perspective,* The Graduate School of the Union Institute, Cincinnati, Ohio, 1993.

Wellins, Richard S., William C. Byham, and Jeanne M. Wilson: *Empowered Teams Creating Self-Directed Work Groups That Improve Quality, Productivity, and Participation,* Jossey-Bass, San Francisco, Calif., 1991.

Wheaton, Warde F., and Arnold M. Weimerskirch: "The Journey to Total Quality: A Fundamental Strategic Renewal," *Business Forum* 14(2), spring 1989, pp. 4–7.

Winter, D.: "Leading the Way to a Self-Managed Work Force," *Ward's Auto World,* May 1988, p. 64.

Ziegler, Bart: "U.S. Engineer behind Japan's Rising Sun," *Chicago Tribune,* April 22, 1990.

Zuboff, Shoshana: "The Age of the Smart Machine," in *Managerial Authority,* edited by Mike Bennett, Basic Books, New York, 1989.

About the Authors

THOMAS L. WEEKLEY and JAY C. WILBER are co-directors of the UAW–General Motors Quality Network.

TOM WEEKLEY is assistant director of the UAW General Motors Department. He originally joined Chrysler-UAW Local 122 as a Tool and Die Apprentice in 1965, and then joined GM–UAW Local 1714 in 1970 where he served as a shop committeeman, district committeeman, bargaining committee chairman of the Local, chairman of GM subcouncil 3, and in a variety of other capacities. He has published numerous articles and technical papers, was an Ordained Minister with the Assemblies of God, and received his Ph.D. in Management and Labor Relations in May 1993.

JAY WILBER is executive director of the Quality Network. He began his career with General Motors Corporation in 1965, and rose to become supervisor of labor relations in 1975. Throughout the following two decades, he played an instrumental role in contract negotiations. In 1985, he was appointed director of labour relations for GM of Canada, and in 1988 was named director of human resources management for GM's worldwide automotive components group.

Index